D0448833

THE NEW POLITICS
OF POVERTY

THE
NEW POLITICS
OF
POVERTY

THE NONWORKING POOR
IN AMERICA

LAWRENCE M. MEAD

BasicBooks
A Division of HarperCollinsPublishers

Library of Congress Cataloging-in-Publication Data
Mead, Lawrence M.
   The new politics of poverty: the nonworking poor in America/
Lawrence M. Mead
      p.   cm.
   Includes bibliographical references and index.
   ISBN 0–465–05962–7 (cloth)
   ISBN 0–465–05069–7 (paper)
   1. Poor—United States.   2. United States—Economic
conditions—1981–   3. United States—Economic policy—1981–
I. Title.
HC110.P6M34   1992
362.5′0973—dc20   91–43079
                                                                              CIP

Designed by Ellen Levine

93 94 95 96 PS/CW 9 8 7 6 5 4 3 2 1

For
Herbert J. Spiro

CONTENTS

PREFACE

THIS book is about the momentous political change that has resulted from entrenched poverty in the United States. Since the mid-1960s, the competing claims of economic interests and classes have ceased to be the leading domestic issues in national politics. Instead, the preoccupation is with the decay of the inner city. Politicians used to divide over whether government should be larger or smaller. They still do, but the question of whether to enforce social values is more contentious. Dependency at the bottom of society, not economic equality, is the issue of the day.

I believe this shift has occurred not because the country has become more conservative, but because traditional approaches to social reform have been exhausted. Government has failed to overcome poverty simply by expanding opportunity, the traditional American solution to social problems. This is because most of the poor do not work, so they cannot take advantage of most of the benefits that government and the economy offer. Nor has it proven possible, on the whole, to trace the work problem to racial bias or other barriers that government could remove. In response, social policy has become paternalist, increasingly seeking not to reshape society, but to manage the lives of the dependent.

The New Politics of Poverty grew out of my earlier book, *Beyond Entitlement,* published in 1986. There I contended that the welfare state had failed to integrate the poor not because it did too much or too little for them—the usual diagnoses of the right and left—but because it was permissive. It did not set behavioral standards for the dependent. I argued that the best way to overcome poverty was to require employable welfare recipients to work.

My book had some influence; it helped provide a rationale for the last important welfare reform, in 1988, which expanded work programs tied to welfare. But critics, especially among liberals, said I had not proven that the poor *could* work. This book began as a reply. Several chapters are devoted to showing that the barriers commonly cited by both the left and the right generally fail to explain nonwork among the poor, especially as unskilled jobs of at least a low-paid kind appear to be widely available.

Gradually, I came to see a larger issue at stake. The critics were defending not only a need for jobs or child care but the entire tradition of promoting equality by reforming society. I believed that the age of social reform was over: Following civil rights, no further governmental benefits or protections had been discovered that could overcome nonworking poverty. Accordingly, I added material arguing that, due to a lack of evident barriers, the process of social reform in the United States had halted. Because of the crises of the inner city—Kevin Phillips notwithstanding—America is not likely to see a new "politics of rich and poor."

Nor is this merely a partisan statement. A nonworking poor population undercuts liberal proposals for enlarging government programs, because the beneficiaries appear "undeserving," but it also undermines support for a reduced government, because it is difficult to imagine the poor coping without aid. In their prescriptions, both left and right presume a *working* population, but today's poor are largely nonworking.

I came to see, however, that if the old, reformist era had died, a new politics had arisen. Left and right today argue most strenuously about whether social expectations such as the work ethic should be enforced among the poor. That issue hinges on whether the needy can be responsible for themselves and, above all, on whether they have the competence to manage their lives. To these questions, liberals give more pessimistic answers than conservatives. These very personal issues underlie the deepest disputes in domestic affairs, although older differences over the scale of government continue.

My greatest debt is to my critics, especially William Julius Wilson and David Ellwood: By arguing that the poor could not work or earn enough to escape need and dependency, they forced me to develop my presuppositions about poverty and politics more fully. Bill Wilson has a genius for asking good questions in antipoverty research, even if my answers to them differ from his. I have also learned a great deal from a number of conservative experts on poverty, especially Douglas Besharov, Ron Haskins, Kevin Hopkins, and Charles Murray.

As before, New York University provided me with a superb base. I am especially grateful to the dedicated staff of the Department of Politics—Marilyn LaPorte, Lisa Baum, Valerie Downey, and Stephen Faulkner—and to a number of talented research assistants—Joseph Chan, Ann Doherty, Neil Iovino, and Bridget Marks. My chairmen and dean graciously allowed me to devote more time to research than teaching. A number of colleagues—Mark Lilla, Bertell Ollman, Ted Perlmutter, Mark Roelofs—also provided astute comments on different chapters. At the library, Susan Shiroma solved all my documentary problems. Several foundations generously provided funding, among them the Lynde and Harry Bradley Foundation, the John M. Olin Foundation, and the Sarah Scaife Foundation.

I received feedback from a number of other scholars besides those already mentioned—Henry Aaron, David Blankenhorn, Richard Brody, Sheldon Danziger, Dan Friedlander, Judy Gueron, Harry Holzer, Christopher Jencks, Harvey Mansfield, Joel Schwartz, and Jim Sleeper. Historian Michael Katz sensitized me to the continuities between today's dependency issues and the timeless themes of "welfare politics." Various chapters were reviewed by Samuel Beer, Philip Harvey, Frank Levy, John Schwarz, James Sundquist, and Ray Wolfinger. David Ellwood, Ron Haskins, Kevin Hopkins, Ted Marmor, and James Q. Wilson read all, or virtually all, of the manuscript, for which I am especially thankful. It should not be inferred that any of these people agree with me; but while responsibility for the argument remains mine, they saved me from many errors.

At Basic Books, Martin Kessler has been a wise, and a patient, editor. His judgment about how to shape, and reshape, the manuscript has been unerring.

Herbert J. Spiro was my first teacher of political science, at Amherst College. Herb has been a theorist of comparative and international politics, a pioneering student of African politics, a member of the planning staff at the State Department, and a United States ambassador. His interests know no limits. His greatest gifts to me, however, were those of a master teacher—provocative ideas, an open mind, and a sincere interest in what his students had to say. It was largely because of Herb that I went into political science, and I have always been glad I did. In heartful gratitude, this book is dedicated to him.

Lawrence M. Mead
New York, November 1991

CHAPTER

1

Introduction

St. Paul's injunction—he who does not work shall not eat—is the basis of the political economy of the West.
—MICHAEL HARRINGTON
THE NEW AMERICAN POVERTY

THE problem of entrenched poverty in the United States has caused a sea change in American politics. Since poverty first became a leading issue thirty years ago, the questions that most bitterly divide Americans have shifted from how to secure working Americans more of the good things of life to how to cope with the problems of seriously poor and dependent Americans, most of whom do not work. Once, the most divisive demands on government were inspired by the working class; they now arise from the nonworking underclass. The New Deal and union rights used to be fighting words. Today, controversies over the homeless, welfare, and "law and order" are more bitter.

Some say the nation has become more conservative. The poor do receive less attention from government today than they did fifteen or twenty years ago. The Reagan administration cut some social programs, and the "kinder, gentler" Bush administration has declined to initiate much of any new antipoverty policy. The idea of throwing money at social problems is decidedly passé. But the nation has not moved very far to the right in the traditional sense. For all Ronald

Reagan's persuasion, big government is still popular with the voters, and overall social spending—for the poor and middle class alike—went right on growing in the Reagan years, albeit more slowly than before.

The very meanings of right and left have changed. The public wants government used to combat the disorders of the ghetto. Republicans have made that appeal their own, and ridden it to the White House, while many Democrats have resisted. That has altered what the parties stand for. Today conservatism still means smaller government, but it also means using government more vigorously against crime, welfarism, and the failure of ghetto children to learn in school. Liberalism still means bigger government, but it also connotes resistance to enforcement and a greater tolerance for disorder, dependency, and ethnic pluralism. The two sides now differ more sharply on questions of social authority than they do about the scale of government.

Up through the mid-1960s, an era that I call progressive,[1] the leading question was how to help ordinary Americans obtain advancement. Liberals favored greater government intervention in the private economy, while conservatives favored less. The underlying dispute was over economic class—whether to accept the unequal rewards meted out by the marketplace or to try to equalize them by raising wages and giving public benefits to workers and their families. In the new era, which is characterized by what I call dependency politics,[2] the leading issue is how to respond to the disorders of the inner city. Conservatives usually want to repress nonwork and crime, while liberals continue to seek solutions mainly through providing benefits. The focus of politics is now conduct rather than class.

The new agenda goes back to the later 1960s, when the welfare rolls doubled, crime soared, and riots erupted in the ghettos of major cities. These episodes raised issues of order and propriety much more sharply than had the earlier class politics. Ever since then, the closely linked problems of poverty, welfare, and the inner city have dominated the domestic agenda. The claims of broader groups, including minorities and women as well as workers, have not gone unnoticed, but they no longer command center stage. Classes and economic interests still jostle for advantage in Washington, yet the deepest concern is disadvantage. Issues of dependency and dysfunction, not equality among workers, now preoccupy our affairs.

This has happened not because concern for the poor is lapsing, but because efforts to help them in the old ways achieved little. The fact that policies to promote new opportunities, by both the right and the left, failed to integrate the urban poor inevitably shifted attention from social change to the personal capacities of the needy. It has become harder to find social barriers that explain why so few poor adults work regularly—the immediate reason most of them are needy. Whether one sees barriers at all increasingly hinges on judgments made about the personal capacity of the poor rather than social inequities. Liberals are the readiest to see further impediments and call for more programs, because they see the poor as victims without ability to proceed on their own; conservatives doubt that there are barriers because they think the poor can take care of themselves as well as other people.

I do not mean to say that dependency issues are entirely new. How to cope with the poor has been an issue for centuries. But in American politics the question was largely a local one. At the national level, poverty and the problems tied to it have a prominence today that they never had before. Progressive-style battles among classes and economic factions continue even during the dependency era, but they no longer set the tone of national politics at the highest levels. In domestic affairs, presidential and party programs mostly revolve around how to overcome urban decay or to regenerate the economy. Prosecuting the old battles of business versus workers is secondary.

It is true that Democrats and liberals still seek a redistribution of income, while Republicans and conservatives resist. Economic inequality has recently increased, and some think a new age of conflict between rich and poor is upon us.[3] Short of an economic collapse, I find that difficult to imagine. Most Americans are a lot more afraid of rising crime, welfarism, and declining schools than they are of their employers. Government is perceived as having failed to solve today's social problem. Until it succeeds, it will receive no new mandate to tackle the older problem of unequal fortunes.

For the left, nonworking poverty has been a political disaster. Only people who try to help themselves, above all by working, are seen as deserving by most Americans; only they can be the objects of a reform crusade or the recipients of mainstream benefits such as Social Security or Medicare. Thus, when poverty became largely nonworking in the 1960s and 1970s, support fell for governmental social change. That is a major reason why conservatives have controlled the presidency and the national agenda for most of a generation.

Dependency politics is growing in importance not only in the United States, but in the West as a whole. In Europe, disputes over the social behavior of low-income groups, often immigrant minorities, have become more contentious than traditional conflicts between organized labor and capitalism. As in the United States, the claims of workers are being shoved back on the agenda by controversies over groups at the periphery of society.

THE WELFARE ISSUE

Progressive debates revolved around employment and its rewards. The question, in today's parlance, was how to generate the most "good jobs at good wages" as well as support workers when they were unable to work. Liberals looked to achieve these aims through government programs, conservatives by relying on the private sector. That battle has largely ceded to questions of providing for those outside the economy altogether. The most important welfare program is Aid to Families with Dependent Children (AFDC), which supports poor, mostly single-parent families with a combination of federal and local funding. Since the 1960s, the leading question in social politics has been how to reform AFDC so as to minimize dependency by people who many feel could support themselves.

Welfare dependency has displaced labor issues as a question presidents feel they must address. Ronald Reagan, for example, took office as a conservative of the old school, his main purpose being to cut government spending and taxation. But if voters wanted cheaper government, they also wanted something done about urban disorders. Fortunately for him, Reagan also took tough stands on crime, welfare, and education. He asserted that moralism about "values" which is the conservatives' key resource in the new politics. In the end, despite his preferences, Reagan may have had more impact on social than economic policy. His cuts in federal spending barely slowed the growth in government, and his tax cuts will probably be reversed over time due to the budget deficit. But if Reagan did not cut the size of the welfare state by much, he did begin to change its character. It became marginally less generous, but also more demanding. Reforms passed under Reagan for the first time seriously required that able-bodied welfare recipients work or prepare for work in return for support.

Like the public, the Washington governing class has come to worry more about urban social problems than the scale of government. Government experts and analysts endured the Reagan spending and tax cuts, which put some of them out of work. They responded much more avidly when, on 4 February 1986, in his State of the

Union address, the president announced a new study of welfare to try to achieve "lasting emancipation" from the "spider's web of dependency."[4] In the antipoverty community, pent-up concern broke out as if a dam had burst. Over the next eighteen months, a flood of new studies of poverty and welfare poured forth from groups of every political persuasion. Great attention was paid to the new and apparently successful state-level work programs authorized by Congress in 1981. On 13 October 1988, Reagan signed the Family Support Act (FSA), the most thoroughgoing reform of welfare ever, whose key provisions will expand work programs.

FSA was a triumph, but it also signaled the passing of Reagan's economic politics from center stage. Congressional debate turned not so much on questions of benefits or costs as on the expectations to be made of the dependent in return for support. Were the poor to be held morally responsible for helping themselves or not?

THE WORK ISSUE

The welfare debate already suggests the most fundamental difference between the old politics and the new: Progressive politics was about how to advance *working* people, while dependency politics is largely about how to cope with *nonworking* people. Nonwork—by which I mean a failure to work or look for work by the employable—is the immediate reason for destitution and dependency among most of today's working-aged poor, who are the most controversial of the needy.[5] For mysterious reasons, poor adults no longer work as regularly as they once did, a fact too often neglected. Nonwork persisted even in the face of steady economic growth in the 1980s, and it has resisted all solutions, whether of the right or the left.

In *How the Other Half Lives*, a classic of social reportage, the journalist Jacob Riis described New York's Lower East Side at the turn of the century. Then, whole families of immigrants living in fetid tenements slaved long hours in sweatshops for the lowest wages merely to survive. It is still true today that new immigrants are among the hardest workers in the city, taking the lowest-paid jobs in an effort to get ahead.[6] An atmosphere of hustle and hard work can still be felt in the new immigrant areas of New York or Los Angeles, but in the poorest sections, bustle is much less evident. A great many native-born New Yorkers do not work. At the height of the recent boom in 1988–89, unemployment fell to 3.9 percent in New York City, compared to a national rate of 5.6 percent. Yet only 56 percent of adults in the city were either working or looking for work, a figure 11 points below the national norm. Among youth—those aged sixteen to nineteen—only 23 percent were in the labor force, less than half the rate for the nation generally. The situation is similar in other large cities. Somehow many poor people do not connect with the jobs that are available. "Analysts say it is a paradox that so many people should be habitually out of work while there is a blizzard of Help Wanted signs throughout the region," wrote one journalist. "We don't get the kind of behavior we expect," said Samuel Ehrenhalt, regional commissioner of the Bureau of Labor Statistics. "It defies all the rules."[7]

Nonwork has devastated large sections of New York. Formerly working-class neighborhoods like Spanish Harlem lost their aspiring character during the 1970s and 1980s, when welfare and the drug trade replaced legitimate employment as the economic bases of the community. When older residents look back, what they remember is "People worked hard." There remain many hardworking, self-reliant people in East Harlem, but, with over a third of the residents on welfare, workers no longer set the tone. People barely survive, despite the wealth all around them. One woman laments, "All those generations on welfare! There is no respect any more because people haven't worked."[8]

The poor in Riis's day lived mostly in two-parent families, and children worked alongside their parents. The answer to poverty was higher wages, which economic growth eventually provided. Today we see mostly female-headed families living on welfare and single men, among whom not even the adults work regularly. On the whole, the immigrant poor of old were poor *despite* work, while the current poor are needy for *lack* of it. Wages in low-skilled jobs may still seem too low to support families, but, as I will show, poverty is very uncommon among adults who work usual hours at *any* legal wage. The "working poor" are considerably outnumbered by the nonworking. The leading domestic issue has changed from how to raise wages and benefits for working people to how to turn more poor people into workers.

Politicians still believe in the traditional progressive solution of generating more opportunity for the jobless. Michael Dukakis, like Ronald Reagan, made that aim a centerpiece of his campaign for the presidency, but Dukakis's own state shows that growth is no panacea. In Massachusetts, the boom of the 1980s created large numbers of new jobs, even for the unskilled, and the unemployment rate fell to 3 percent, the lowest in the nation. Yet the number of nonworking adults in the state actually rose, as did applications for welfare. Nationwide, while unemployment fell to 5 percent, 10 to 20 million employable adults, many of them poor or dependent, remained without work.[9]

THE DECLINE IN WORK EFFORT

Since the 1960s, when poverty became a major public concern, work effort among the poor has dropped sharply, a trend that has received too little attention. Falling work levels have operated as an undertow, defeating the government's best efforts to overcome poverty. Table 1.1 details the changes, with the poor defined as those families who fall under the federal poverty line. In 1989, less than half the heads of poor families had any earnings at all, a drop of nearly a fifth

TABLE 1.1
Work Experience of Heads of Poor Families,
1959–89

Percent of all heads who:	1959	1975	1989
Worked at any time in year	67.5	50.4	48.9
Worked full-year, full-time	31.5	15.9	16.2
Did not work	30.5	49.1	50.8
Percent of single female heads who:			
Worked at any time in year	42.9	36.5	41.6
Worked full-year, full-time	10.9	5.6	8.8
Did not work	57.1	63.5	58.4
Percent of all other heads who:			
Worked at any time in year	74.9	61.5	56.8
Worked full-year, full-time	37.6	24.2	24.1
Did not work	22.5	37.5	42.6

NOTE: "Full-year" means at least fifty weeks a year, "full-time" at least thirty-five hours a week. "Other heads" are mostly men, with or without spouses, but include some married women. Proportions working and not working do not add to 100 because heads in the armed forces are omitted.

SOURCE: Calculated from U.S. Department of Commerce, Bureau of the Census, *Characteristics of the Population below the Poverty Level: 1984*, Series, P-60, no. 152 (Washington, D.C.: U.S. Government Printing Office, June 1986), table 4; idem, *Money Income and Poverty Status in the United States: 1989*, Series P-60, no. 168 (Washington, D.C.: U.S. Government Printing Office, September 1990), table 23.

since 1959, when over two-thirds were employed. The proportion in full-time, full-year work has dropped by half, to only 16 percent in 1989. Correspondingly, the share of heads of poor households without work has risen from less than a third to over half.

Much of this reduction comes not from the same persons working less, but from shifts in population. The poor as a percentage of the U.S. population dropped substantially in these years, from 22 percent in 1959 to 13 percent in 1989, mostly as a result of economic growth, which raised what wages could buy and thus enabled working families to lift themselves above need. The working poor left poverty, and the poor became almost by definition nonworking. Rather than ask why so few poor people work, we might as well ask why we still have so many poor.[10]

One can also categorize the poor as those who are needy relative to normal family income. Table 1.2 shows work levels among all families and among those in the top and bottom quintile, or fifth, of the distribution of family incomes. If we take the poor to be the bottom fifth, the poverty line is not fixed, but rises with earnings. This means the needy do not separate as cleanly from the rest of the population over time as in Table 1.1, but a difference in work effort

TABLE 1.2
Equivalent Number of Full-Time, Full-Year Workers
by Income Quintile, 1970–86

	1970	1978	1986
All families at all incomes	.76	.75	.76
Families with children	.91	.94	.97
Married couples	.98	1.05	1.12
Single mothers	.36	.40	.42
All families in top income quintile	1.23	1.25	1.25
Families with children	1.28	1.36	1.42
Married couples	1.31	1.37	1.45
Single mothers	.75	.91	.92
All families in bottom income quintile	.19	.15	.18
Families with children	.42	.33	.27
Married couples	.63	.62	.61
Single mothers	.05	.03	.03

SOURCE: Congressional Budget Office, *Trends in Family Income: 1970–1986* (Washington, D.C.: U.S. Government Printing Office, February 1988), table A-15. Entries are based on tabulations of Current Population Survey data, 1971–87.

remains apparent. In 1986, working hours, measured in units of full-time, full-year workers, were almost seven times as great among the top fifth of incomes as among the bottom. There is not much change in overall work levels in either the top or bottom quintile,[11] but there is among families with children, which account disproportionately for the needy. Work effort among such families rises in the top fifth and falls in the bottom fifth, among both female-headed and two-parent families. These work differences go far to explain the radical income differences among families at the top and bottom of society.

As this book will emphasize, it is not at all clear how to explain the decline. One might suppose that the poor are working less because fewer of them are working-aged. Traditionally, the poor were composed mostly of children and the elderly, since the working-aged could use earnings to escape need. The overall American population is, in fact, aging, but the working-aged proportion of the poor population is rising, not falling. Between 1959 and 1989, the share of the poor aged sixty-five or over fell from 14 to 11 percent, while the share under age eighteen fell from 44 to 40 percent, leaving 49 percent of the poor of working age.[12] The main reasons for these changes are that most of the elderly and disabled have been lifted out of poverty by rising Social Security payments, and poor Americans, like the better-off, are having fewer children than they once did.

Today's poor are mainly found among female-headed families and single adults. In both groups, the great majority of adults are nonelderly, yet they work less often than the intact families that previously predominated among the poor. Between 1959 and 1989, the total number of poor Americans dropped from 39 to 32 million, but the number of poor living in female-headed families grew from 7 to 12 million and the number of poor single people grew from 5 to 7 million. Together, the two groups comprised 30 percent of the poor in 1959, but 58 percent by 1989.[13] The fact that both groups grew absolutely, not only as a share of the poor, shows that the work decline is not just an artifact of the fall in poverty.

Some might blame the decline on the upsurge in female-headed poor households, on the argument that mothers abandoned by their husbands must inevitably work little because of their child care responsibilities. Much of the decline is indeed related to the fact that more poor families today are female-headed. Since such families typically work less than two-parent families, the shift lowers the overall work level among the poor.[14] But as Table 1.1 shows, there has been a substantial work decline among heads of family other than single women, due apparently to male workers withdrawing from the labor force. Some of these are elderly men retiring earlier due to higher Social Security, but fewer working-aged, low-income men also work today to support families. The economists Sheldon Danziger and Peter Gottschalk estimate that the proportion of employable men heading poor families with children who worked at least forty-eight weeks a year dropped from 72 to 46 percent between 1967 and 1984, while the share not working at all jumped from 8 to 17 percent. Meanwhile, the proportion drawing government income benefits of some kind more than doubled, from 17 to 38 percent.[15]

The decline in employment has been especially great among black men, a principal reason why poverty today is much higher among blacks than whites. In 1960, 83 percent of both white and black men were working or looking for work. By 1988, the white rate had dropped to 77 percent, the black rate to 71 percent.[16] Black unemployment rates, which typically run twice those for whites, reached 20 percent during the 1980s, and among black male teenagers an astounding 49 percent.[17]

Although female-headed households have lower family incomes, it is too simple to say they must be poor or dependent. For the population as a whole, as Table 1.2 shows, work effort by mothers, married and unmarried, is increasing. About half of all female family heads are working, nearly three-quarters of them full-time. Among those not dependent, the work rate is about 85 percent. Somehow, welfare mothers differ. Their numbers have doubled since the 1960s, and only 6 percent of them work at a given time, even part-time.[18] One might suppose that they suffer special impediments, such as large numbers of children or a lack of child care. But, as I will show, this does not seem to be the case.

Even if one exempts many of the adult poor as unable to work, a decline in work effort is clear. Setting aside the elderly, students, the disabled, and mothers with preschool-aged children, Danziger and Gottschalk found the share of poor households headed by adults who might reasonably be expected to work rose from 37 to 47 percent between 1967 and 1984, yet the share of these heads actually working at least forty-eight weeks a year dropped from 54 to 32 percent in this same period. Meanwhile, the share not working at all rose from 22 to 32 percent. By 1984, 91 percent of these employable heads of households lacked sufficient earnings to keep a family of four above poverty.[19]

THE FAILURE OF REFORM

The appearance of nonworking poverty is one great fact driving the emergence of dependency politics. A second is the failure of the progressive approach to social reform to raise work levels. Traditionally, government's response to any social problem was to try to expand opportunity for the downtrodden. For Democrats, this meant extending the protections of government; for Republicans, cutting them back and relying more on the free market. Both approaches have been tried. The Great Society sharply expanded antipoverty benefits and programs, and the Reagan administration somewhat reduced them. If either policy had integrated the poor into the larger society, American politics would probably still revolve around questions of class and economic equality, rather than personal conduct. But neither approach worked. The poverty rate, after falling sharply through the 1960s, bottomed out at 11 to 12 percent in the 1970s. It rose and then fell in the 1980s, ending in 1989 at 13 percent.[20] Just as important, social conditions among the poor radically deteriorated, with family breakdown, crime, and drug addiction becoming epidemic in America's inner cities.

Many social causes for nonwork among the poor have been proposed—low wages, lack of jobs or child care, racial discrimination, disincentives to work generated by welfare. But while each has some influence, my judgment is that none of them, individually or together, can explain nonwork on the scale now found among the poor. Most experts, left and right, agree that the causes of poverty remain mysterious. The reader must take this conclusion on faith now—later chapters will explore the evidence.

I do not mean to say that social barriers are unimportant. Differences in opportunity explain much of the inequality in American society. People with less privileged backgrounds, particularly less education, do have less of a chance to succeed in our competitive society. But such differences mainly explain *inequality among workers*, not *failure to work at all*, which is the greater problem among today's poor. It is the failure of most poor adults to work steadily in *any* job, not the inferiority of their positions, that largely explains their predicament.

Trends in the society should have resulted in higher work levels among the needy, not lower. Since the 1960s, opportunities have grown for the low-skilled. Their education levels as well as the number of jobs have risen. Racial discrimination has fallen, as have welfare disincentives, with the failure of AFDC benefits, since the early

1970s, to keep pace with inflation. Yet, mysteriously, work levels have declined and remained low. Whatever outward causes one cites, a mystery at the heart of nonwork remains—the *passivity* of the seriously poor in seizing the opportunities that apparently exist for them.

It is true that the economy has shown some negative trends, paralleling those among the poor. After 1970, the country suffered several economic shocks: the baby boom generation flooded the job market, productivity stagnated, and foreign competition destroyed many manufacturing jobs, especially in the Northern and Midwestern cities where many poor and dependent people live. The decline of factory jobs and the shift toward a "high-tech" economy, among other factors, have increased inequality among workers. Many liberals contend that a mismatch between the remaining jobs and low-skilled job seekers largely explains nonwork in the inner city.

But research has failed to confirm these theories. Economic trends may have reduced wages for those with the least skills; they cannot explain why so many of the poor fail to take the jobs still available. The decline of the factory has been offset by an explosion of employment in service trades. While the high-tech economy does reward advanced education, the vast majority of jobs do not require it. Most of the inner-city poor appear able to find jobs, albeit not of the quality they would like. The clamor of immigrants from all over the world to come to the United States strongly suggests that opportunities for the unskilled are still abundant here.

To explain nonwork, I see no avoiding some appeal to psychology or culture. Mostly, seriously poor adults appear to avoid work, not because of their economic situation, but because of what they believe. To a detached eye, opportunity may appear to be available to the low-skilled, but nonworkers typically do not believe this. A combination of resistance to low wages, pessimism about long-term prospects, the isolation of the ghetto, and group memories of a harsher past cause many to turn aside from the chances to work that exist. Thus, the poor remain economically passive in a society where other low-skilled people find abundant opportunity.

CAUTIONS

In mentioning these disturbing facts, I do not seek to be partisan, in terms of either the old or the new politics. I will not argue that the answer to poverty is either more government, in the simple sense of more spending or programs, or less. Like other conservatives, I am cautious about assuming that government has the answer to social problems, but I also believe that the degree to which government should intervene in society is a political question that I have no special competence to decide. It is an issue to be fought out in the progressive arena among functioning citizens.

My point is to stress the crucial importance of the work problem in shaping today's politics. It may not be clear how large government should be, but it is absolutely clear that employment is essential to being a functioning citizen. Only adults with a work connection have moral standing to demand either more government or less. Thus, once the nonworking poor became a presence on the national stage, the proper role of government could no longer be the central issue in politics. Instead, moralistic disputes about personal conduct came to the fore.

I will also not take a hard-and-fast position on the newer issues of dependency politics, which have to do with the moral responsibility and competence of the poor. I do not believe society is responsible for poverty to the extent it once was. At the same time, I believe that the poor as they now are need help. The poor may not be responsible for themselves at present, but they must become so. Competence cannot be the assumption of social policy, but it must be the goal.

It is too simple to say that conservatives are concerned about the disorders of the inner city while liberals are not. Liberals, too, disapprove of crime, nonwork, and welfarism. But they seek to overcome these problems by assuaging what they see as the underlying causes, rather than through imposing standards. It is also too simple to say that liberals are concerned about the poor while conservatives are not. For liberals, in their hesitation to levy expectations on the needy, reflect a less sanguine view of their capacities than most conservatives assert.

Whether the often-alleged social barriers explain poverty remains a matter of judgment, especially if one is seeking to generalize from a large body of technical research, as I do here. There is no rigorous way to sum up the various influences on poverty: low wages, racial discrimination, lack of jobs and child care, and so on. Some might say that these factors in combination, if not individually, can account for nonwork. I can only say that I find that conclusion unreasonable. It assumes that the explanations are all independent, each one accounting for a separate piece of the puzzle. In fact, the theories are largely competitive, each claiming to explain the same central mystery—the passivity of the long-term poor. I urge readers to weigh the evidence themselves. While I write for a general audience, I provide documentation that I hope will convince experts.

In what follows, I define the "poor" as the government does—those Americans whose income falls under a threshold calculated to provide a minimal living standard. The line varies with family size and is fixed in terms of purchasing power; it rises each year with inflation, but not economic growth. Many objections have been raised to this definition, by both liberals and conservatives,[21] but it shows the trends in poverty and their connection to the work problem, which is sufficient for my purposes.

The poor differ widely among themselves. Most are not on welfare. Some do work, and many who do not, including children, the elderly, and the ill, would not be expected to by any humane society. These groups may need and deserve more assistance than they get. I concentrate on the working-aged, employable poor simply because they are the most controversial and thus, politically, the most significant. They have also proved the hardest to help. When the public, as opposed to government, thinks of "the poor," it is usually thinking of them.

Poverty is often transient. Most Americans who become poor also escape poverty within two years,[22] and there is little reason to view them as distinct from the population in general. I focus on the long-term poor—the 6 to 7 percent of Americans who are poor for more than two years, and especially the 4 to 5 percent who are employable, that is, not elderly or disabled.[23] This is a narrower group than all the poor, but it is also broader than the homeless or the underclass, meaning the most dysfunctional poor. Within it, experts agree, there are two crucial subgroups—long-term welfare mothers and nonworking single men—and I will focus mainly on them. The initial reason for most working-aged poverty is simply that fathers in ghetto areas tend not to provide for their children, while the mothers usually go on welfare rather than work themselves. Whether the parents, both fathers and mothers, could work more than they do, and why they do not, are the leading questions in social policy today.

Nonwork, also, is only one of the many social problems afflicting poor Americans. Some argue that crime, drug addiction, failure in school, or unwed childbearing are more fundamental causes of poverty than nonwork. The needs of weak families and poor children, especially in inner-city ghettos, are certainly pressing. Disputes about how to solve these problems are as much a part of dependency politics as the work issue. They dramatize the embarrassing, *personal* nature of today's social dilemma, even more than nonwork. Tragic spectacles such as "crack babies" abandoned by drug-addicted mothers have even more power than panhandling men to drive the claims of working Americans off the front pages.[24]

Politically, however, nonwork is much the most significant aspect of poverty. Except for crime, it is the behavior of the poor that most offends the nonpoor. It has prompted the most sustained policy-making at the federal level, more than either crime or family problems. It is the problem about which research has taught us the most, though mysteries remain. It is also the respect in which the condition of the poor is most clearly deteriorating. Levels of crime and unwed parenthood appear to have peaked in the ghetto, but nonwork continues to increase.[25] Nonwork constitutes the core of the social problem, if not the whole of it.

Nonwork is the aspect of poverty that has the widest political implications. Crime and family problems arise initially mostly from private causes; employment problems have much more evident connections to social opportunities. Work is public behavior for which society has always accepted some responsibility. Employable workers who are idle for long periods become a political issue to which government must respond. The failure of traditional reforms to solve the work problem, therefore, has effects that reach beyond social policy. It suggests the bankruptcy of the entire progressive tradition—of our image of self-reliance as central to American politics. More than any other development, nonwork explains the appearance of a new politics focused on dependency rather than the claims of workers.

Much of the discussion that follows is framed as a debate between liberals and conservatives. Sometimes I speak of experts on poverty or intellectuals, sometimes of politicians. To speak only of two alternatives is, of course, a gross oversimplification; many viewpoints fall between these extremes. But I seek to dramatize the essential structure of the debate, not capture every nuance, and for this purpose simplification is essential. I also use "liberal" and "conservative" interchangeably with "left" and "right" and "Democratic" and "Republican," terms not always congruent, but close enough for the national-level, social politics that concerns me here.

My main point is to define the essence of the new dependency politics and contrast it with the progessive past. Secondarily, I will argue that dependency issues are now more important than older, progressive disputes. By this I mean that they control the commanding heights of politics, that is, the national agenda and, to a great extent, presidential elections. Admittedly, the progressive and dependency periods overlap in time. The former was not without issues of the dependency type—such as temperance—where social standards were more in question than equality. The latter still witnesses important, progressive-type clashes of economic interests and disputes over the role of government. Thus, progressivism and dependency shade into one another. The terms, as I use them, refer both to two political eras that came together in the 1960s and to two contrasting political styles that may be seen, to some extent, in every era.

Even if one doubts that dependency issues now dominate American politics, they have clearly become a major theme in national affairs. The shift from the working class to the underclass as the main social issue is a watershed in America's experience, and increasingly that of the West as a whole.

PROGRESSIVE POLITICS

The baseline for the change I discuss is the progressive era. By this I mean the period up through the mid-1960s when politicians debated primarily how to advance the *progress* of ordinary, working Americans toward greater wealth and status. Next only to preserving basic law and order, promoting broad-based mobility has been the overriding purpose of American domestic government since the nation's founding. Most politicians have shared Lincoln's belief that the purpose of democracy is to "elevate the condition of men" or, as Richard Hofstadter phrases it, "to provide opportunities for social ascent to those born in its lower ranks."[26]

The issues in progressive politics were structural, having to do with the basic organization of society. Politicians differed, above all, over whether the economy should be guided more by government or the marketplace. While American leaders, like the people, have always believed in capitalism, they have disputed how far government should interfere in the free economy to promote this or that economic or social interest. Especially they differed over whether more or less government was best for the hopes of working Americans to support their families and advance their position in the world. The meaning of social reform was impersonal: it meant to re-form society by adjusting the relationship of government and the economy.

The term progressive usually connotes governmental measures to protect workers (the minimum wage), redistribute income (the income tax), or provide support to those unable to work (Unemployment Insurance, Social Security). Progressivism as I use it also includes proposals by conservatives to attain the same ends with less government, through greater reliance on the free market. The American right has served the interests of business, but in the belief that unfettered capitalism also served the interests of ordinary people. Both sides claim to provide more "opportunity." For liberals that word suggests public benefits and protections from the marketplace, while for conservatives it means faster growth, and hence more and better jobs, in the private sector. The first choice provides more security and equality in an immediate sense, the latter stronger incentives to work and invest and hence, it is argued, greater wealth and opportunity in the long run. Each philosophy makes a genuine appeal to the interests of ordinary people, and each has enjoyed greater support at different times.

This debate dominated domestic affairs throughout the Western world for two centuries. The kind of economic interventions that Americans call liberalism have, taken to greater lengths, produced socialism in Europe and communism in the Soviet bloc. In Europe as in the United States, a period of ambitious governmental growth has lately been followed by retrenchment. Many nations are struggling to find the mix of public controls and market incentives that will best promote growth and affluence over the long haul.

The former Soviet Union represented one extreme of the progressive continuum. The statist Soviet economy guaranteed employment, and wages had little connection to effort. There was little incentive for workers to produce or managers to economize. Consumers, too, were protected from the market by subsidies for food and housing. As one Soviet economist remarked candidly, "the Soviet Union is a good place for people who don't like to work hard."[27] But if the people were secure, the nation was poor. In the American economy, much closer to the market extreme, incentives to effort and efficiency are much stronger, but there is also more risk that workers will be unemployed and investments will fail. The chance of greater wealth and growth comes at the price of greater insecurity.[28]

Alongside the decentralization of power now going on in the U.S.S.R., governments there and in Eastern Europe are proposing to cut back government protections for workers and consumers and move toward a more free-market economy. This restructuring, or *perestroika*, is meant to make workers, managers, and consumers a good deal less secure, in order to make the countries richer. More people will now have to perform for their income and face market prices. It is not at all clear that the change will be popular, as the cost in insecurity is real.[29]

At home, the progressive meaning of social reform retains considerable appeal. Demands for greater opportunity, earlier made by distressed workers and farmers, were picked up by blacks and women in the 1960s and 1970s. The civil rights and feminist movements were the last expressions of progressive claim making to obtain salience in American politics. They succeeded as movements of working people seeking greater opportunity within the mainstream economy. The fact that both groups were seen as functional was one reason their leading demands were granted. The effect of reforms, as designed, was to expand the black middle class and advance women in business and professional life.

The limitation of progressivism is that it assumes employment. Both liberalism and conservatism in their traditional meanings were theories on behalf of *working* people. The big-government and the free-market visions of society disagree about how much government workers require, but each presumes that ordinary people can and do work. Only the employed and their dependents benefit from labor regulations such as the minimum wage or qualify for mainstream social benefits such as Social Security or Medicare, which are more generous than welfare. It is also the employed, and those seeking work, who benefit most from the free-market economy. Both left and right assume that most of the help ordinary people need to get through life can be provided by expanding the rewards of employment.

Progressivism can deal with nonwork only if the problem is traceable to some reformable impediment outside the jobless. Some feature of society—economic depression, low wages, an unfair labor market—must be keeping people out of work or depressing the quality of jobs they can get. Only then does the progressive remedy of altering the scope of government apply. This is so regardless of whether one thinks the answer lies in expanded or reduced controls on the economy.

For a long time, this limitation went unnoticed. Over the course of American history, government and the economy together have succeeded mightily in improving the material situation of ordinary Americans. The combination of growing wages and government benefits has raised the incomes of workers and their families to levels undreamt of a century ago. As recently as 1938, probably two-thirds of Americans were poor by today's definition.[30] From World War II through the 1960s, poverty was driven down rapidly by growing wages and benefits earned by the still-numerous working poor. But after that, the decline first slowed sharply, then reversed. Due largely to nonwork, the remaining poverty no longer responded much to either government programs or a growing economy. Before these facts, the progressive tradition stood disarmed.

THE COMPETENCE ASSUMPTION

The progressive approach took for granted a goal-oriented view of human nature. The traditional left and right shared the assumption that the individual is willing and able to advance his or her own economic interests. Not just the businessperson, but the ordinary citizen is a maximizer, seeking not just survival, but advancement, in material terms—supporting one's family and propelling oneself to a higher station in society. "In America," writes Richard Huber, "success has meant making money and translating it into status, or becoming famous."[31] Americans are *in motion* toward *economic* goals. As an advertisement for a vocational school in the New York subways put it, "It's not where you are—It's where you're going."

This view of human nature, which I call the competence assumption, has permeated all conventional American political thinking. The Declaration of Independence reckoned the pursuit of happiness as an essential human right. This reflected the view of the Founders, according to Hofstadter, that the "rapacious" pursuit of self-interest was among the "necessary qualities of man."[32] There was no need to spur people to seeking their own advantage.

Competence here means all the qualities that allow a person to get ahead in economic terms—not only intelligence, but foresight, energy, discipline, and the ability to sacrifice for the future. It did not mean that people were moral, that is, willing to serve others before themselves, only that they were effective in pursuing their own interest. To reconcile the individual interest with the general interest was society's problem. A harmony might be achieved either through the invisible hand of the marketplace or through the visible hand of government.

Both varieties of progressivism assert this view of human nature. They differ almost entirely over the organization of society. Liberals have a more favorable view of government, conservatives of the marketplace, but each conceives of ordinary citizens as self-reliant. Traditionally, conservatives may have had a more confident view of personality than liberals, who are quicker to assert that people need some insulation from the market, but the difference is small. Even liberal measures, for example to subsidize higher education or home mortgages, presume that the beneficiaries will earn the money they need to make good use of these opportunities.

The vigorous pursuit of economic advantage has widely been seen as the keynote of American society. In the early 1830s, Alexis de Tocqueville noted that Americans put much more energy into both work and politics than was usual in Europe. All was "activity and bustle," he wrote, "everybody works," and no store was set on "idleness," even among the elite. There was no other country where "all those who work are so keen on making themselves prosperous."[33]

The United States has been known for a severe work ethic and, correspondingly, a suspicious attitude toward the poor. Intellectuals are typically critical, believing that a democracy should be especially tolerant of the needy. Tocqueville concluded, however, that democracy fostered a strong work norm. Economic effort was a way people earned the respect of one another in a society with few ascriptive distinctions. "Among democratic peoples where there is no hereditary wealth, every man works for his living, or has worked, or comes from parents who have worked. Everything, therefore, prompts the assumption that to work is the necessary, natural, and honest condition of all men."[34]

Intellectuals also say that Americans insist on too hard a line between government and the economy. They worship the free market and resist government interfering even to help the vulnerable. But it would be more accurate to say that the hard division is between groups who are seen as deserving and those who are seen as undeserving. Typically, people who can claim economic interests based on employment get some assistance from government; those without economic functions do not. In America, this moral distinction is a lot clearer than the separation of the public and private sectors.

Historically, there never was a time when American government was not involved in the economy. Almost from the founding, the idea developed, wrote Vernon Parrington, that "a democratic state stands *in loco parentis* to the economic interests of its citizens."[35] Throughout the nineteenth century, government at all levels showered subsidies on entrepreneurs and others seeking to develop the country. It helped finance turnpikes and canals, donated land for railroads, levied tariffs to protect growing industries, and provided infrastructure and services to farmers and industrialists. Most of the largesse went to well-connected businessmen, but homesteaders received land, Civil War veterans received pensions, and the retainers of politicians received government jobs.

The New Deal marked the high tide of this sort of intervention. Government regimented the private economy as never before, and major benefit programs were enacted for the unemployed, aged, and destitute. Academics write of the United States establishing a welfare state on the European model, one that shielded the needy from the marketplace, but, in fact, the traditional tie between aid and economic function was preserved. The most generous of the new benefits—Unemployment Insurance and Social Security—limited eligibility to people who had earlier paid payroll taxes. True to the American tradition, claimants on government must first of all be workers.

If the progressive tradition neglects anyone, it is people outside the economy. The political problem for today's poor is precisely that they usually are not workers. They cannot make the same demands on a helpful government as people with a work history. They do not satisfy the competence assumption. Some argue that the destitute should get more from government to compensate for their failure to get much from the economy, but the moral logic of American political economy is just the opposite: Workers get more from the economy *and* from government than nonworkers do, because they are seen as more deserving. If today's poor worked more, they would be seen as more, not less, deserving of government aid, even though they would be less needy.

DEPENDENCY POLITICS

In essence, dependency politics arises when the competence assumption comes into question. How does one cope with people who seem unable to advance even their own interests, let alone society's? That is the essential problem in domestic policy today. We debate less and less how to reform society and more and more whether the poor can be responsible for their own conduct. Progressive politics, a battle of ideologies, has given ground to moralistic disputes over individual behavior.

During the last three decades, most antipoverty policies paid homage to the competence assumption by assuming that the poor would get ahead if they were given the chance. That was as true of liberal training and service programs for the disadvantaged as of conservative reliance on economic growth. But the progressive assumption that opportunity was enough to overcome destitution proved invalid. Work levels actually fell among the poor, and many social programs came to operate in practice, if not intention, as substitutes for employment.

In the old politics, it was never doubted that individuals, even the poor, were responsible for their personal probity, if not for their economic fortunes. In the new era, the question of moral responsibility has become intensely divisive. Liberals deny that the poor are responsible for nonwork, crime, or family problems, on grounds they face a hostile society; conservatives defend responsibility and seek to enforce it.

In the old era, the political extremes disagreed about the organization of society but agreed that ordinary people could take care of their own interests, if not other people's. In the new era, the situation reverses. The two sides disagree less sharply about the role of government but more sharply about the competence to be expected of the poor. Liberals assert that the needy want to work and obey other mainstream mores, but are unable to in practice. Conservatives tend to doubt, not the competence, but the morality of the poor.

The rhetoric of dependency politics often uses progressive categories to debate the new issues. Liberals still talk of social barriers keeping the poor from working, while conservatives doubt this. But because the impediments cited are usually much more limited than those of thirty or fifty years ago, the debate is less impersonal than it seems. It is one thing to say people cannot work because of a literal lack of jobs or rigid racial bars to all employment—impediments that are rarely found today. It is quite another to say that lack of skills, transportation, or child care prevent work, since these are difficulties that a great many low-skilled people overcome every day.

When liberals appeal to such problems, they implicitly assume a lesser competence in the poor than do conservatives, who think opportunity is available. *Every view of barriers rests on a view of competence, usually unspoken.* Although the debate may be couched in the most arcane statistics about whether jobs or child care is available, the real difference is about human nature. Are poor people able to organize their lives to assume the burdens of employment? Or are they helpless victims of whom nothing can be expected? The very exhaustion of the more obvious barriers to employment brings these issues to the fore.

The drift of antipoverty policy during the 1970s and 1980s was away from social reformism of either the left or the right and toward efforts to reorder the personal lives of the poor. Work programs in welfare are the leading instance, but the same idea underlies recent reforms in law enforcement and education. The chief aim is no longer to enlarge opportunity by changing social structure, but rather to help make the poor more able to take advantage of existing opportunities. The new measures are more paternalist than liberal or conservative in the traditional sense. They do not reorder society, but neither do they dismantle protections and throw the vulnerable into the marketplace. Rather, they seek to build a structure around the dependent that will conduce to more functional behavior.

The practical question in social policy is the proper character of this new regime. Should it be indulgent or demanding? Liberals still want to help people in the style of the Great Society, with voluntary programs such as special training and education. The tendency of policy, though, has been toward the conservative preference, which is to enforce social standards. I see no speedy end to these differences as long as social conditions among the poor continue to deteriorate. To restore progressive politics will take a long struggle to raise work levels. Only then could personal responsibility and competence once again be taken for granted.

A LOOK AHEAD

The chapters that follow deal with both the nature of entrenched poverty and the political changes it has produced. I attempt to show how the social problem has proved resistant to traditional reformism and how this has forced politicians, experts, intellectuals, and the public to argue instead about dependency. Chapter 2 sets the stage by showing how the eruption of nonworking poverty in the 1960s shattered the progressive alliance of workers and the poor, dating from the New Deal. The condition of the inner city became a dominant issue, and prescriptions from either left or right failed to resolve it. These were important reasons why Republicans displaced Democrats as the dominant party in presidential politics. Chapter 3 explores in more depth why falling work levels had such power to undermine progress against poverty and weaken political support for generous social policies.

Chapters 4 to 6 document that it has proven impossible, in the main, to blame the work problem on reformable social barriers. I examine, and refute, arguments that low wages, lack of jobs, or other barriers to employment, including welfare disincentives or lack of child care, can explain the extent of nonwork now found at the bottom of society. But in every case, the verdict whether there is an impediment ultimately rests on a judgment about personality: *On an assumption of normal competence*, there do not appear to be prohibitive barriers, but there may still be if one assumes less capacity than that, as liberal analysts tend to do.

Thus, the debate about opportunity in America really comes down to opposed philosophies about the human nature of the poor. What sort of people are they? Chapter 7 assesses several interpretations found on both right and left. It seems implausible either that the poor are acting rationally when they decline to work or that they lack an ability or desire to work. My own, moderate view sees the poor as dutiful but defeated. There is a culture of poverty that discourages work, but the poor will work more regularly if government enforces the work norm. The policy history supports this interpretation (chapter 8). Antipoverty policies aimed at barriers or the self-interest of the poor have failed to raise work levels, while work requirements linked to welfare may succeed.

A final section concentrates on the politics of dependency. The question of how to reform welfare has gradually changed from a progressive to a dependency issue (chapter 9). The cost and benefits of welfare have become less contentious, work requirements more so. In Europe, as well as in the United States, the eruption of dependency issues concerning the behavior of out groups is transforming politics. This implies the end of an entire Western tradition in which the self-reliance of ordinary citizens was taken for granted (chapter 10). Lastly, I return to the American scene for a look ahead (chapter 11). I believe dependency politics will persist, and will continue to give the advantage to Republicans in national politics. But it is conceivable that work levels could rise, returning politics to a progressive focus on equality among workers.

This book ultimately asks a single question: Why do the seriously poor, who are so weak and so few in number, have such a power to preoccupy national affairs? Why are most affluent Americans more disturbed by the spectacle of welfare mothers who appear to do nothing to help themselves than they are by unions striking for higher pay, even though the latter have much more power to threaten them? Somehow, the very incapacity that gets dysfunctional people into trouble also enables them to dominate our common life.

CHAPTER

2

The Crisis of Reform

"The very rich are different from you and me."
"Yes, they have more money."
—ERNEST HEMINGWAY
THE SNOWS OF KILIMANJARO

THE progressive approach to social improvement assumes that government and the individual will work together to produce advancement for average Americans. Both the regime and the individual are presumed to be economically competent—the one generating chances to get ahead, the other seizing them. All successful social reform in the United States has ridden those two horses. That formula continued to work during the thirty years of New Deal politics that followed the Great Depression. It ceased to be effective in the 1960s for the poorest Americans, primarily because they worked less.

The combination of a more intractable social problem and the failure of conventional solutions discredited the earlier politics. Working people no longer allied with the needy, as in the New Deal, but rather feared them. Republicans capitalized on that sentiment, among other factors, to dominate presidential elections. Entrenched poverty blocked ambitions for large changes in the scale of government on the part of both left and right. The social problem now seemed more urgent than earlier concerns for economic equality. Politics turned toward the moralistic disputes—about behavior, responsibility, and competence—that mark the dependency era.

THE NEW DEAL AND AFTER

With the New Deal, government accepted more responsibility for employment than it ever had before. Individuals, it was now understood, could not master blind economic forces on their own. The Depression proved, according to Gardner C. Means, an advisor to Agriculture Secretary Henry Wallace, that "Anybody who is unemployed isn't necessarily unemployed because he's shiftless."[1] Government had to manage the economy so that jobs would be available to working people.

Yet the New Deal honored the competence assumption by attaching its new protections to employment. The designers of the major new benefit programs as well as the subsidies extended to agriculture, transportation, and other industries assumed that the beneficiaries would receive their reward through employment. Some critics characterize these benefits as "middle-class welfare," no different from AFDC, but the programs never just *gave* people money. Instead, they raised the incomes of people already working. In fact, the New Deal was rather strongly antiwelfare, as was public opinion. In the early 1930s, there was tremendous pressure to get the jobless back to work, but opposition to creating a dole. The Roosevelt administration initially paid out cash to the destitute, but this was widely unpopular. Roosevelt hastened to replace relief with public employment programs such as the Works Progress Administration, but even these were suspect. The new federal welfare programs were markedly less generous than the contributory programs meant for workers (Unemployment Insurance and Social Security) and hedged around with moralizing restrictions.[2]

Economists still dispute whether the New Deal really did much to overcome the Depression. Perhaps World War II accomplished that. Yet the economic recovery, as well as winning the war, is remembered as a triumph for government. With the return of full employment and peace, Americans turned their back on the Depression as on a bad dream. Servicemen said, "When I get back, I'm going to get a good job, a house and a car, some money in the bank, and I'm never going to worry again."[3] That is just what they did. Nevertheless, the postwar era derived much of its optimism from the memory of effective government. The suburbs expanded on the strength of individual efforts, but with the aid of further progressive programs. Veterans went to college on the G.I. bill, bought houses with government mortgages, and sent their children to public schools, then public universities. Their parents retired on Social Security. A growing economy supported higher wages and higher benefits alike. As earlier in American history, within the world of the "deserving," no contradiction was seen between private effort and public subsidy. The dual capacity of the individual and government never seemed so adequate to produce progress.

Progressive issues continued to dominate federal politics. Democratic presidents Truman and Kennedy sought to extend Roosevelt's social measures, for example by raising the minimum wage and implementing federal health insurance. Medicare, or health care for the elderly, was finally enacted under President Johnson in 1965. These measures were resisted by the business community and many better-off voters. Republican presidents—Eisenhower and Nixon—halted liberal reformism for a period, but could not reverse it, and neither made the fundamentalist criticisms of social programs that would be heard under Ronald Reagan. The progressive formula remained too successful.

Later movements—for civil rights, feminism, the environment, consumers—extended the reform tradition. All made demands in the name of functioning citizens for some new government protection, and all gained some success. As earlier, liberals promoted the new goals, while conservatives said the same ends could be achieved at less cost through the marketplace. In that era, both sides were right. New government social policies were instituted, but they succeeded largely because of the effort the beneficiaries put forth on their own behalf. Nothing has validated the competence assumption like the rapid advance of blacks and women to higher income and status in the 1960s and 1970s following equal opportunity reforms in their interests.

THE NEW POVERTY

After 1960, urban poverty and decay gradually displaced the concerns of working groups atop the national agenda. It was when destitution became uncommon, after the rapid income gains of the 1940s and 1950s, that it became an anomaly, in need of explanation and redress.[4] As an issue, poverty also became separable from the concerns of the working class, since few steady workers were now poor. However, poverty that was exceptional also changed its character. Traditionally, destitution had been widespread but was seen as impersonal; the causes lay in a downturn in the business cycle or the decline of a particular region or industry. Poverty was also transient for many, passing as prosperity returned. Before the Depression, probably no more than a quarter of poverty could be attributed to personal problems.[5] After 1960, destitution became more personal in character, hence harder to solve. It was often chronic rather than episodic, persisting through generations, even in the midst of prosperity. This was because it was now usually due in the first instance to the personal difficulties of the poor themselves, and only secondarily to their environment. The poor became an "other America," Michael Harrington wrote, set apart from the mainstream. They were "maimed in body and spirit" by lives of disadvantage and thus unable to "help themselves," even when opportunity beckoned. Above all, they could not work regularly as society expected.[6] They did not satisfy the competence assumption.

Some of this more passive poverty was genuinely new; it also became more visible as the rural poor migrated into urban areas, where more affluent Americans could notice. Blacks migrated from the rural South to Northern cities, Hispanics from Latin America and Puerto Rico to the cities and the Southwest. Like earlier immigrants from overseas, the newcomers had difficulty adjusting to American urban life. For obscure reasons, the new groups proved less assimilable than the old. The lower echelon of black and Hispanic society succumbed to extreme disorganization in the same years that better-functioning members of these groups made unprecedented advances.

The differentness of the poor only increased with time. The ghetto riots and a sharp rise in crime occurred amid major civil rights reforms and the 1960s boom. This timing showed that the usual progressive mechanisms—opportunity measures and economic growth—no longer sufficed to advance those at the bottom of society. The riots were followed by the welfare boom: Between 1965 and 1975, the number of recipients of AFDC more than doubled, from 4.4 to 11.4 million.[7] The causes included higher benefit levels, which made more needy people eligible, greater family breakup among the poor, and a breakdown in the stigma against welfare. The upsurge was greatest, not in areas with the worst hardship, but in Northern cities with the most liberal welfare policies.

The boom sharply reduced work effort by the poor in urban areas, as more people lived off benefits, fewer off legitimate employment. In New York City, 7 percent of all adults, or 318,000 people, were on welfare by 1970, and the massive growth of AFDC between 1960 and 1973 coincided with a fall in the labor force in the city by as much as 65,000.[8] By 1988, according to Senator Daniel Moynihan, there were 64,000 adults living on welfare in New York City who had never worked at all, and 45 percent of the city's schoolchildren were on welfare.[9] More than any other change, the boom was a watershed that permanently raised dependency issues to the center of national attention.[10]

Since the mid-1970s, the size of the welfare rolls has changed little, and attention has shifted to a more disturbing manifestation of poverty—the underclass. The term denotes the most disordered urban poor, including not only long-term welfare families but non-working men and youth, many of them school dropouts involved in street crime and drugs. The currency of the term reflects the upsurge of urban crime and troubled schools in ghetto areas in the 1970s and 1980s, when poverty was seen to involve not only welfare dependency but broader forms of dysfunction.

From the earliest analyses, the underclass was seen as a demoralized group unable to get ahead because of a lack not so much of opportunity as of personal organization. Inadequate jobs and residual racism were sometimes causes, according to one journalistic account, but more important was a lack of the "schooling, skills, and discipline to advance."[11] The underclass is not large, only 2 to 8 million people (0.9 to 3.5 percent of population) depending on how it is defined.[12] It may or may not be growing,[13] but because of its distressing ties to crime and welfare, it has come to dominate other Americans' image of the social problem.

In the 1980s, dysfunctional poverty acquired a still more unsettling face—widespread homelessness. The homeless are even fewer than the underclass—600,000 or less—but even more obtrusive. These poor no longer stay in low-income areas, but camp out in public places like railroad and bus stations, where the better-off are forced literally to step over them en route to homes in the suburbs. The homeless appear even less "deserving" than the underclass, as mothers and children comprise less than a quarter of their number.[14]

Advocates contend that the homeless are the victims of impersonal social barriers, particularly a lack of affordable housing, but investigation has shown that these are seldom "ordinary people down on their luck." Most have serious personal problems, including substance abuse and mental illness. Above all, few work, and this is often the immediate reason they are homeless. Most homeless parents are single mothers of the type society now expects to work, while a third or more of homeless men could be considered employable.[15] However, 60 percent of homeless adults have not had a steady job in over a year, a third in over four years, and only a quarter report any earned income in the last month.[16]

Beggars have also appeared in large numbers on city streets, mostly working-aged men, only some of them homeless. No greater outrage to the competence assumption can be imagined than these men subsisting on handouts as a busy society rushes past them. The public at large feels intense conflict. It hears claims that the panhandlers are victims, and some people give them money. But people also cannot help asking whether these men could work, and why they do not. As one local businessman observed, "When you look at these characters sitting out in the middle of the day when everybody else is working just to survive, you don't get a lot of sympathy."[17]

Political attention has shifted from low-paid workers and the short-term poor, who largely reflect mainstream society, to the long-term, urban poor, who seem much more alien. During the New Deal, the stereotypical poor person was a hardworking, usually white farmer or artisan in need of a break. Now it became a long-term, usually black single mother subsisting on welfare in the cities.[18]

Left and right espoused different approaches to social reform, yet both had understood it as a celebration of basic American values—freedom and individualism. After the 1960s, that confidence was no longer tenable. Perhaps inevitably, the focus of debate shifted to efforts to restore the personal competence that earlier reformism had taken for granted. This inevitably was a less hopeful task than expanding opportunity for functioning citizens:

> Americans like to think of their country as a place where people don't have to beg, don't have to starve. But the bedrock that idea rests on—that not to work is a disgrace, that any job is better than sitting there with your hand out—has been eaten away by the same corrosives that are destroying the slums. Attacking the beggars is easier than attacking the poverty, ignorance, and addiction that put the cups in their hands. No one knows how to make people *want* to get off crack, go to school, put in a good day's work, care about their own lives.[19]

THE POLICY RESPONSE

Besides the appearance of the new poor, the other great force behind the emergence of a new politics was the failure of progressive-style reforms to overcome poverty. The War on Poverty[20] arose initially because President Kennedy wanted to carry the old reformism to a new stage. The New Deal had opened new prospects for workers and farmers, and civil rights was in the process of doing the same for blacks. The "poor" were simply another group that Democratic thinkers said deserved government attention.[21]

The earliest antipoverty policies followed the progressive tradition. The "Kennedy tax cut" of 1964 and growing federal spending maintained full employment, while the civil rights reforms opened doors for nonwhites who were employed or in school. As the national economy expanded through most of the 1960s and early 1970s, growth, in combination with reduced discrimination, drove poverty down sharply, particularly for blacks, then heavily represented among the working poor. Fifty-five percent of blacks were poor in 1959, only 30 percent in 1974.[22] It turned out to be the last successful application of the progressive formula. After the early 1970s, progress against poverty virtually halted. A more troubled national economy was one factor, but equally important was that rising nonwork and other social problems made it harder for the remaining poor to utilize the available opportunities.

These trends shaped the War on Poverty. Its activities included a number of programs for children and youth as well as community action—efforts to organize the poor to help themselves by pressuring local government to improve services. These programs were aimed at poverty generally, but soon became associated with inner-city, mostly black poverty. The war was widely seen as an extension of civil rights.[23] The programs were implemented under the shadow of the urban riots, so they seemed to cater to the special problems of the ghetto.

The issue of competence became unavoidable. In an important speech in 1965, President Johnson declared that social policy had to move "beyond opportunity to achievement." It was insufficient, the president said, to secure equal rights for blacks if, due to past racism, they lacked the capacity to compete equally with whites. They had to be assured "not just legal equity but human ability."[24] The speech was applauded at the time, but its implications were sobering: It amounted to saying that reformers could no longer take the ability of the poor to seize opportunity for granted.

The War on Poverty and the larger Great Society tried to enhance competence by improving individual skills. The thinking was that if "low labor market productivity" could be overcome, reductions in poverty would follow.[25] Washington launched preschool and remedial education programs such as Head Start, meant to help disadvantaged children do better in school, and training programs such as the Job Corps, intended to enhance the wages poor workers could earn.

Critics say the emphasis on changing the poor themselves rather than the surrounding society reflected the conservatism of the war.[26] However, neither liberals nor conservatives in the New Deal era had focused on skills; they looked instead to control or decontrol the economy. The question of competence really was new.

Unfortunately, the compensatory programs had little effect. They did somewhat raise the skills and earnings of clients, but usually not enough for recipients to obtain high-paying jobs.[27] This left no way for the poor to overcome poverty in most cases except to take lower-paying jobs or work more hours in them. Unable to solve the employment problem, federal planners turned in the late 1960s and early 1970s toward the idea of defeating poverty by transferring more money to the poor. Plans to guarantee a minimum income to all Americans were defeated in Congress, but other income programs expanded to provide a de facto guarantee, allowing many more poor to live without regular employment. This was partly because benefits were liberalized, partly because more of those eligible claimed them. The explosion of AFDC was the most important instance, but other, newer programs such as Food Stamps and Medicaid, which provided groceries and medical care to the needy, also grew sharply. While these developments did reduce the incidence of poverty and allevi-ated nutrition and health deficits among the poor, they exacerbated the political issue posed by nonworking dependency.

Cash welfare such as AFDC is largely confined to women and chil-dren, but many nonworking men were able to carve a sustenance out of Food Stamps, disability benefits, and nonfederal assistance pro-grams. Some employment programs provided allowances to clients to support them during training, and these often became a form of welfare for men. That was especially common under the Compre-hensive Employment and Training Act (CETA), which during the 1970s financed government jobs as well as training on a large scale. Since the positions usually paid more than the recipients could com-mand in the private market for the same skills or effort, they often amounted to welfare in disguise. Income and training programs had been meant in the progressive spirit as adjuncts or aids to successful employment. They often became instead substitutes for employment, sustaining a largely passive, nonworking society apart from workaday America.

The shift from work to dependency was sharpest for black Ameri-cans. During the 1930s they had gained from New Deal opportunity and benefit programs as employees and farmers, not as blacks. There was no work problem among them then. They would "fight" for private jobs even at the lowest wages, employers recalled, and, lacking those, strongly preferred government jobs to relief.[28] The 1920s and 1930s were an era of intense black competition with whites for jobs, and the problems of blacks were perceived as those of working men.[29] Civil rights organizations of the time pushed an employment approach to black advancement, fearing that welfare-oriented strategies would offend the work ethic. In the 1960s, the emphasis reversed. Civil rights organizations endorsed the War on Poverty, but it was aimed largely at children and youth, not underemployment among adults. Black leaders faced pressure from the welfare rights movement to support a guaranteed income for the poor. They found themselves defending controversial antipoverty programs and liberal versions of welfare reform while work-oriented measures fell into the background. The shift occurred just when poor blacks were enrolling in welfare in record numbers, damaging antipoverty policy and, even more, the political image of blacks.[30]

Whether by accident or design, other aspects of federal policy also contributed to segregating less functional groups. Bilingual education programs and social workers shielded Hispanics and other immigrant groups from much of the pressure to learn English that earlier immigrants had faced. The Voting Rights Act of 1965, as amended and interpreted by the courts, instituted a kind of electoral affirmative action. Literacy tests were abolished and legislative districts were drawn to deliberately enhance minority representation in Congress and state legislatures.[31]

High levels of crime, nonwork, and other dysfunctions inevitably separated the needy from mainstream society, whatever benefits were given to them. Battles over dependency and nonwork soon eclipsed those over the extent of aid.

THE POLITICAL RESPONSE

The initial political effect of the new poverty was to destroy the alliance between the needy and better-off Americans that had supported the New Deal. In the Depression, only a quarter of working Americans had actually been jobless at any one time, but Franklin Roosevelt was elected four times because a majority of voters endorsed his measures to reshape the society. A coalition of workers and much of the middle class outnumbered conservatives. Power and income were redistributed on a new scale, and business was subjected to unprecedented controls.

Most Americans found much less to identify with in the plight of the new poor. This is evident from Studs Terkel's interviews in the 1960s with veterans of the New Deal. "During the Depression, we were all more or less engulfed," recalled one artist, but, "Today when people say poverty, they turn their head." Above all, it was the welfarism of the new poor that set them apart. The needy of the Depression "had to work sixteen hours a day," remarked a restaurant owner, while today's poor were "paid by people that works [sic]." They weren't "guilty" about it, "just sick, mentally sick." A housing administrator from the 1930s recalled, "At that time, when we said relief, we meant relief. Everyone then you assumed was an able and willing worker, simply out of work"; but today, many of the poor were "*almost* unemployable—'welfare people.' "[32]

In the South civil rights had been a movement largely of working people and students. In the Northern cities, the race issue took on a different and less attractive face. Whites saw poor blacks moving into their neighborhoods, bringing crime and other social problems with them. They easily fastened on the work issue to justify resistance. In Yonkers, New York, people opposed court-ordered residential integration in the name of the work ethic. In the words of one resident:

> All of us have worked for our homes.... We are not anti-integrationists. Show me some black guys who are working, and I'll go out and get people here to sell them houses.
>
> But we don't want any free rides. We're talking about a subculture of poverty—the crime-ridden, nonworking poor, people with lesser values that we don't share.

Residents complained that their city was damaged by public housing projects that brought in jobless blacks. "That was a transition," said another man. "It was no longer working poor, it was welfare poor. It wasn't color, it was the way they acted."[33]

The charges had special force because many of these whites were the descendants of immigrants, only one generation removed from poverty themselves. They had memories, perhaps idealized, of how hard they and their parents had worked to escape the slums of New York for suburbs like Yonkers. They demanded that today's poor do the same. Said an Italian construction worker in Canarsie, a Brooklyn neighborhood threatened by ghetto expansion: "We're working men, and we don't bow our heads in humility. We fight and say to blacks, 'Keep out of our neighborhood.' " Said a city employee: "These welfare people get as much as I do and I work my ass off and come home dead tired."[34]

American politics in the 1960s and 1970s shifted its focus from economic questions toward battles over assorted moral and social issues. The leading protagonists were no longer industrial interests—unions and business—seeking material advantage, but activists challenging public policies and social values on principled or cultural grounds. In various ways, those on the left sought, not so much to redistribute economic power, as to challenge conventional beliefs about personal and social discipline. They wanted a society that was more inclusive but also more individualist, and less insistent on the work ethic, law abidingness, and the conventional family.[35]

Not all of these issues had close ties to poverty. The black power movement erupted among radical civil rights activists, student demonstrators paralyzed major universities and opposed the Vietnam war, the feminist movement demanded expanded opportunities for women, various ethnic groups celebrated their identities, and those favoring and opposing abortion battled in courts and legislatures. Many of these disputes, however, proved short-lived. The student movement declined with the end of the Vietnam war, while feminism and ethnic pride have largely been accepted. Change could be rapid because these issues arose largely from clashes of opinion within the middle class. Differences in background and life-style between those on the two sides of these questions were not extreme.

The more enduring moral issues, however, did have a tie to poverty, race, or the inner city. In one form or another, tension between urban ghettos and the surrounding society has been constant ever since the 1960s, though the conflicts took more dramatic forms—riots, community action, welfare rights—then than they did later. Disputes over crime, welfarism, and the other problems of the ghetto have not been resolved because they spring, not simply from differences of opinion, but from a profound division in the society. Poverty is the perennial that has marked the new cultural politics from the beginning, and has lasted throughout.

The inner city also was the issue that, more starkly than the student movement or the hippies of the 1960s, dramatized where a relaxation of social discipline might lead. The new social liberalism was a lot less popular than the older economic liberalism. Political support for the War on Poverty was perilously thin; the programs originated from experts operating within the government, not broad-based demands.[36] The poor were no longer seen as workers in economic trouble, but as outside workaday society, even a threat to it. They could no longer lose themselves in the mass of employed Americans. Their interests were no longer carried forward by that mighty host.

REALIGNMENT

These shifts in the nature of the social problem, and in the public reaction, seem to be the greatest cause of the seismic change that hit American politics in the later 1960s. Federal politics took a conservative turn, and the public became notably alienated from politics. Some consider the change to be a realignment, meaning a large and lasting shift in the balance of power in politics. The significance of the shift is not yet clear. Although it is most often described as a movement to the right in conventional, progressive terms, I believe, rather, that it signals the emergence of dependency as a pivotal controversy in presidential politics.

Realignment, as political scientists usually use the term, has two dimensions: First, there is a change in the dominant issues, the questions that especially divide both the parties and the public;[37] second, there is a significant shift in the balance of public support underlying politics. It is not enough that the party holding the White House or Congress change; there must also be a sizable and permanent shift in the proportions of the electorate identifying with the major parties.

In the progressive era, the chief issues concerned the role or extent of government, particularly the degree of public intervention in the economy. These questions dominated federal politics through the mid-1960s and the enactment of Medicare and the civil rights reforms. Then domestic policy shifted toward dealing with urban decay. The most divisive battles now occurred over community action, post–civil rights racial issues (busing and affirmative action), the financial needs of cities, declining schools, crime, and welfare—all issues closely tied to entrenched poverty.

The older issues concerning economic management and fairness among classes did not disappear. The troubled economy of the 1970s and early 1980s and the Reagan spending and tax cuts helped keep them alive. Much of federal politics still involves battles over government regulations, subsidies, or spending. Health care and the environment are important questions, but in general, these economic issues were shoved off the front burner of politics by social crises that seemed much more pressing. There was no way the demands of, say, striking unions could compete with the crime epidemic or the child abuse crisis produced by recent drug addiction. Even the recessions of the 1970s and early 1980s, which crushed manufacturing industries and drove unemployment to the highest levels since the Depression, provoked no sense of crisis comparable to that of the 1930s. As long as the new poverty was so visible and traumatic, distressed workers and farmers simply could not get Washington's undivided attention.

A shift toward dependency concerns is visible at the level of public opinion. Between 1935 and 1960, when asked what was the most important domestic problem facing the country, people stressed economic problems, such as unemployment and inflation. In the 1960s, concern shifted sharply to issues linked to race and the inner city. In the period 1963–65, civil rights was the most important domestic issue, while from 1966 to 1973, social control issues such as crime took the lead. Economic questions recovered their primacy during the later 1970s and early 1980s, no doubt due to the recessions of those times, but always with concerns over social order close behind. In the late 1980s, social issues reached parity with economics as homelessness and the drug epidemic distressed the public.[38]

The shift toward poverty concerns is even clearer among policymakers. During the progressive era, theories of economic management were central to policymaking, as government's chief task was to maintain steady economic expansion. By the 1970s, however, worries about cohesion and competence at the bottom of society displaced economic issues at the head of elite agendas. The leading policy theories in Washington today are those that promise to cure poverty or dependency. The Reagan administration had its favored economists— Milton Friedman and Arthur Laffer—but the most cited conservative guru of the era was Charles Murray, whose *Losing Ground* exemplified the administration's antipathy to the liberal welfare state.[39]

During the election year of 1988, former presidents Carter and Ford assembled experts to advise the incoming president on the national agenda. In its report, the group gave greatest stress to "the critical issues of chronic poverty." The need to recover economic competitiveness received emphasis, but this was itself related to the social problem, because declining schools were seen as the main barrier to producing a "world-class workforce." The central enigma of domestic affairs, the authors wrote, was the presence of "two Americas, one increasingly wealthy, one tragically poor, a land of opportunity for most and of idle hopelessness for too many."[40]

The new president, George Bush, was interested mainly in national security, but the concern among other politicians and the press forced him to develop a domestic program focused on education and the recovery of competence. Journalists wrote of a "missing agenda," of the need to "address such long-neglected problems as the deterioration of public education, the inequities of our system of health care, homelessness, and the rise of…an urban underclass." A similar concern appeared among the public: In 1990, 72 percent of Americans thought poverty was worse than a decade before, and 77 percent thought Bush had done little to address the problem.[41]

A SHIFT TO THE RIGHT?

The second dimension of a realignment is changing electoral patterns and voters shifting to new party loyalties. The clearest sign here is that Republicans have come to dominate presidential elections, taking over an office that, but for the Eisenhower interlude, Democrats had owned since 1932. After 1968, only Jimmy Carter broke the string of GOP victories, and the Republican majorities seem increasingly secure.

The immediate reason is that the South currently votes as solidly for Republican presidential candidates as it once did for Democrats, and other groups central to Democrats' earlier dominance—Catholics and blue-collar workers—have tended to defect to the GOP. It has become difficult to imagine a Democrat winning the White House, except someone like Carter, a Southerner and relatively conservative for his party. The Republicans also made inroads in Congress, winning control of the Senate in 1980.

Some analysts dismiss these changes as superficial. They believe that Reagan won because he was a compelling candidate or because economic conditions favored him—he beat Carter in bad times, then won reelection in good—rather than because the voters endorsed his party or his philosophy. Certainly, public alarm over stagflation had much to do with Reagan's initial victory in 1980.[42] They also note that Democrats remain dominant in politics below the level of the White House, commanding a clear majority in Congress, where they recovered control of the Senate in 1986, and in state and local government.

Candidate qualities and economic management are not matters on which the parties differ systematically, however. The first is largely a matter of chance, while the second involves at most a difference of emphasis, with Republicans likelier to push the control of inflation at the expense of higher unemployment, Democrats the reverse.[43] In practice, every president tries to ward off recession, and none has much actual control over the economy, even though he is held accountable as if he did.[44] In the eyes of experts and voters, neither party has a clear answer to the country's long-term productivity problems.

To explain the long-term Republican dominance, one has to look to policy areas where the parties do differ. There is something about the Republican stance on presidential issues that the public prefers. The public did favor Reagan as a strong leader, and favorable economic conditions in the 1980s did help carry him and later George Bush to victory. However, voters also endorsed more conservative policies, both domestic and international, in the 1980 election. Later, they turned to the left on some issues, but they also expressed satisfaction with the more conservative policies Reagan had established. Further—and this is the acid test for realignment—the voters shifted their party identification sharply toward the Republicans, almost wiping out the edge in allegiance that Democrats had enjoyed for over fifty years.[45]

All depends on how this turn toward "conservatism" is interpreted. One view holds that the public is still voting largely on economic, size-of-government issues inherited from the progressive era; voters are simply taking a more conservative view of these questions than formerly.[46] Democrats' perceived economic failures in the 1970s probably have made the public more willing to identify the GOP as the party of prosperity. It is true that support has fallen for the notion, central to liberal progressivism, that government should guarantee a good job and a good standard of living to everyone. Fifty-nine percent of the public endorsed that purpose in 1960, only 24 percent in 1986. Meanwhile, the proportion who said people should be left to get ahead on their own rose from 24 to 47 percent.[47]

The public, however, is also reacting to new issues. Since the 1960s, the New Deal issues have been crosscut by the moral questions mentioned above—first civil rights and the Vietnam war, later a wide range of social issues. Politicians usually avoid some of these questions—abortion, religion, free speech—as too divisive, but others—crime, welfare, drugs—tend to unify the public in its dissatisfactions. These issues mobilize the voters against a federal regime, perceived as liberal, that fails to maintain order. They are often more keenly felt than the economic disputes because they touch deepseated feelings about right and wrong. It is mainly on these social issues, mostly linked to poverty, that Republicans have challenged Democrats for national primacy, if not yet displaced them.[48]

Much of the change in sentiment clusters around the race question. In part, race can be seen as a progressive issue, a struggle between blacks and whites for advantage within the same society. Civil rights was a classic progressive movement, and the parties' fortunes were shaped by how they responded to its claims. From the mid-1960s, Democrats became the party of civil rights and later of more controversial steps to advance blacks such as busing and affirmative action. Affirmative action pits the claims of black and white workers for advantage against each other in a classically progressive manner. Thus, one interpretation of the conservative shift is simple backlash. Republicans opposed the advanced race policies and gained the adherence of white defectors, particularly among Southerners and white ethnics. This exposed Democrats to losses in presidential elections, though they remained the largest party.[49]

The race issue has, however, changed over time and now lies mostly within dependency politics. Though most whites oppose affirmative action and busing, they have accepted the essential black claim for equal opportunity. Public support for nondiscrimination toward blacks has actually grown since the 1960s.[50] When whites oppose black claims today, the reason is usually not the old racist belief that blacks are inherently inferior, but rather, hostility to the social evils with which poor blacks have become associated.[51] Despite sharp clashes over some race policies, the parties differ most deeply over whether government should shield less functional blacks from social standards such as work or law-abidingness, or enforce them. The race issue today is largely the poverty issue in disguise.[52]

Some argue that the appeal of social issues was transient. Perhaps Republicans gained from public impressions in the late 1960s and early 1970s, years of the riots and the antiwar movement, that Democrats were soft on crime and communism, but Democrats recouped by taking a harder line on crime, forestalling a realignment.[53] I think it is more probable that the image of Democrats was permanently damaged by the reputation for permissiveness the party acquired in the 1960s due to its stands on race, crime, and poverty, just as the GOP suffered for decades from public blame for the Depression. The Democrats' image of softness revived in the 1980s, when the social issues returned to the fore and Reagan exploited these with skill. The combination gained the Republicans a permanent shift in public loyalty, although the balance of partisan power remains even.

Appeals like Reagan's work particularly well in presidential elections, where a concern for social values prevails. The public has not rejected big government or the welfare state, and it elects Democrats to Congress largely to keep these benefits flowing. At the same time, it elects Republicans to the White House because it wants a more assertive foreign policy and more conservative positions on crime and welfare than most leading Democrats feel comfortable with. Concerns about cultural issues, traditional morality, and crime, alongside older economic issues, played a pivotal role in the election of George Bush.[54]

Like the Democrats before them, Republicans may dominate presidential politics without winning every election. It is still imaginable that Democrats could win in years when the GOP suffers the stigma of scandal or bad economic conditions. Jimmy Carter won for these reasons in 1976, and, due to a stagnant economy, George Bush may be beaten in 1992. But even if that happened, it would not change the fact that Democrats are disavantaged in contemporary politics because of the distrust they have earned over the social problem. For them to capitalize, economic problems must now reach a much higher threshold than was true before the mid-1960s.

Democrats remain vulnerable on the social issues because of the makeup of their electoral coalition. The party appeals to affluent, educated elites who are relaxed about divergent life-styles, such as drug use and unmarried parenthood, as well as to groups who see themselves as outsiders to the society, including homosexuals, some feminists, black and Hispanic representatives, and welfare advocates. The combination means that Democratic leaders and analysts often suggest a tolerance for social problems that the wider public does not share. They tend to treat behaviors such as welfare dependency, crime, or drug use as regrettable personal choices that government should understand and change, whereas the majority of voters sees them as moral evils to be repressed. Democrats easily appear to condone challenges to fundamental values, to favor disorder and "cultural diversity" over order and integration.[55]

Politics today is still about justice, but the meaning of that issue has changed to the advantage of conservatives. The progressive era presumed that politics involved choices between fundamental values, especially between the market and government as the basis of social organization. Such divisions persist, but arouse less passion. The more contested question today is whether society is fair in practice, especially to blacks and women. Is it responsible for their disadvantages in income and preferment? At issue is not whether the United States should have a collectivist or a free-market economy, but whether equal opportunity is achieved.

The old size-of-government issues aroused a roughly even division of opinion, although liberals predominated. The division on the newer social and fairness issues is much more lopsided, to the right. Most Americans think society is fair, although they are not entirely sure. Primarily racial minorities and feminists say otherwise. The division is not so much within the public as between it and liberal elites and groups with special influence in the Democratic party. Republicans, therefore, can command a much larger majority on the social issues than they could on New Deal questions of government intervention in the economy.[56]

If there is a realignment, it is around these race-linked issues of morals, public authority, and fairness. "Big government" is not the issue that defeats Democratic presidential candidates, since big government remains popular. Rather, it is that, in deference to racial sensitivities, Democrats are less willing than Republicans to enforce the civilities and institutions that have broken down in cities. Thus, forces of opinion linked to dependency issues have overridden the old size-of-government issues and ushered in a new presidential party.[57] That shift in partisan advantage, however, is less significant than the larger change in the national agenda away from economic and class issues, and toward dependency. This change has transformed politics for Republicans and Democrats alike.

THE PARALYSIS OF REFORM

The disappointing results of antipoverty policies together with the new moralism about social issues put an end to the rhythms of progressive politics that prevailed through the 1960s. Earlier, the size or trajectory of government shifted back and forth as first liberals and then conservatives gained the upper hand in Washington. This is what one would expect from the dominant debate, which was primarily about the proper scale of government. The reform era at the turn of the century and the Depression years of the 1930s exemplify periods of government growth, the 1920s and 1950s, periods of consolidation. The new poverty cast doubt on the efficacy of progressive reformism, whether of right or left, making it more difficult to categorize the Great Society and Reagan eras in these terms.

The Great Society of the 1960s and 1970s is known as an era of government expansion, and in some ways it was. Federal legal protections for minorities and women sharply increased. The 1970s saw costly controls on industry, for environmental and health reasons, that were new at the federal level. However, unlike the New Deal, which created a welfare state for large groups in the population, the Great Society made no major additions after the period 1964–65, when Medicare was added to the middle-class insurance programs and Medicaid and Food Stamps were added for the poor.[58] The many special education and training programs that helped build a separate polity for the poor were small and cheap—the common notion that means-tested programs took over federal social programming in the

1960s is exaggerated. To this day, the United States conspicuously lacks benefits common in European countries—guaranteed income, universal health care, government child care, and training programs for the general population.

It is true that spending for social benefits vastly expanded. After 1960, government at all levels spent much more for social programs of all kinds. Total public spending for social welfare was $52 billion in 1960, $593 billion in 1982, an elevenfold increase (fourfold allowing for inflation). In those years, the share of national wealth spent for social purposes almost doubled, from 10 to 19 percent. But most of the money went for social insurance programs for the middle class. In 1982, the government spent over $300 billion on social insurance, primarily Social Security; all of welfare cost only $81 billion.[59] Most of the insurance spending was due to incremental increases in benefits; other than Medicare, the social programs added in the 1960s and 1970s never amounted to more than a fifth of the federal social budget.[60]

Proposals to extend entitlements were defeated, together with their advocates. Lyndon Johnson, the sponsor of Medicare, was driven from office by the Vietnam war, and Hubert Humphrey and George McGovern, his ideological heirs, were defeated by Richard Nixon. McGovern's proposal to guarantee every American an income never got to Congress, while welfare reform plans from Nixon and Jimmy Carter were defeated there. During the 1970s, various proposals from the White House or Congress to extend health or child care coverage also failed. In part, the plans were simply too expensive. Carter did significantly expand the use of government jobs to employ the poor, but these programs were ended by Ronald Reagan.

The view of the Reagan years as an era of smaller government, a swing of the progressive pendulum to the right, is equally exaggerated. In reality, Reagan did little more than trim the edges of earlier economic controls and benefit programs. He made sharp cuts in the education and training programs aimed at the poor, lesser cuts in welfare. He terminated a small number of minor programs, but increased social insurance benefits. The trimming and refinancing of Social Security in 1983, though very difficult politically, involved small dollar changes relative to the huge size of the program. Reagan's successes were also transient. Most of the cuts came in 1981, the administration's first year, after which congressional resistance toughened; through 1985, Reagan cut social spending by less than 10 percent below projections.[61]

Neither the Great Society nor the Reagan years, then, saw the sharp change in government effort on behalf of workers connoted by the tradition of progressive reform. Since 1965, there have been no new New Deal and no *perestroika*. Part of the explanation is simple politics: There has been little demand for major change. The country was too prosperous during the 1960s to contemplate the radical steps suggested on the left, such as a "freedom budget" for blacks or guaranteed employment for all jobless. Nor were the economic problems of the 1970s serious enough to give Reagan a mandate to gut the welfare state. Another factor was inertia: As social programs became established, sharp changes became more difficult to justify. Cost concerns inhibit large expansions, but the public is too used to the benefits to countenance sharp reductions.

A more important reason for the paralysis of reform was the failure of either version of progressivism to deal well with the new poverty. Neither approach solved the most worrisome social problem, so neither obtained a mandate for larger changes in society. The inner city became the great barrier blocking either larger *or* smaller government. Cost aside, what discredited social liberalism was its inability to stem the tide of crime, dependency, and school problems that engulfed American cities in the 1960s and 1970s. The rising tide of social spending did reduce poverty in economic terms, but it did not ameliorate the behavioral problems of greatest concern to the voters.

The most serious objection to proposed welfare extensions was that they would have aided people whom the public had come to think of as undeserving. There was much less public pressure to do something for the destitute than there had been in the 1930s. Expansions of welfare were proposed anyway, due to advocacy within Washington, such as the Nixon and Carter plans, but they did not include work requirements that Congress could sell to the public. This proved fatal.[62] The shadow of welfare darkened prospects for liberal reformism of any kind.[63]

The pattern of Reagan's spending cuts confirms the view that a failure to solve poverty constituted the main indictment of bigger government. The reductions were severe in means-tested education and training programs for the poor, much smaller in the middle-class insurance programs, even though the latter were vastly more expensive. David Stockman, Reagan's budget director, and other conservatives attacked the antipoverty programs as uniquely wasteful because they achieved little while isolating the poor in a separate world of agencies and care givers.[64] This view was shared by many liberal analysts and congressional staff members. Accordingly, the cuts met little resistance, and few localities chose to make them good with their own funds.[65] Social Security and Medicare had much broader support, and they were much tougher to call unsuccessful, so they survived almost unscathed.

Just as surely, poverty sandbagged Reagan's attempts to reduce the scope of government. The administration was forced to preserve a "safety net" for the poor: Benefits and eligibility in AFDC, Medicaid, and Food Stamps were only slightly reduced.[66] Again reflecting public opinion, Congress was as unready to dismantle welfare as to expand it, and Reagan's cuts in antipoverty spending, though marginal, earned him more public censure than anything else he did. Strong majorities of the public accused him of neglecting the needy, and many believed—falsely—that he left them entirely unprotected.[67] Most Americans resented the disorders of urban poverty, yet most did not want to force the helpless to shift for themselves. American politics simply could not accept a reduction in social protections on the scale now going on in the Soviet bloc. Such a change assumes a population of working poor or those who could become self-sufficient under pressure. This is not the case for many of today's long-term needy in the United States.

Reagan's own social policy was no more successful than the Great Society. True to the conservative tradition, the administration claimed that economic growth in the private sector was a better way to defeat poverty than overwhelming it with cash. Following the recession of 1981–82, a boom ensued that lasted for eight years. Most working Americans realized higher incomes, although the gains were distributed less equally than in earlier decades. The poor benefited much less, again because most of them were nonworking and thus outside the economy. Between 1982 and 1989, the unemployment rate fell by nearly half, from just below 10 percent to just over 5 percent, but the poverty rate fell only from 15 to 13 percent.[68] And, due to the crack epidemic, social conditions in the ghetto deteriorated still further.

In the eyes of many, chronic poverty had discredited reductions in the federal government as much as expansion. By the end of the 1980s, there was talk in Washington of a need for renewed social programs to help the poor; this was one of the impulses behind the Family Support Act, Reagan's last welfare reform, which will channel more money toward work and service programs for the dependent. The market, evidently, could not do it all. As one Washington planner remarked, "Competition by definition is for those who can enter the market. You can't promote competition in any field unless you take care of the poor. . . . That was the Achilles' heel of this Administration, and that's why their philosophy is not going to keep."[69]

THE CAPACITY OF GOVERNMENT

The new poverty and the frustrations of social policy put an end to the easy confidence about government that the country derived from the Depression and war years. Traditionally, political battles in America had been over the direction of policy, over what government ought to do or not do. The regime itself was assumed to be the honest, competent instrument of whichever candidate or party should gain the people's trust. In the 1970s, for the first time, it was seriously asserted that government was incompetent, that it simply could not achieve certain goals.

One reason for doubt was the economy, where government proved unable to maintain the prosperity the country had known for a generation. After the early 1970s, a train of recessions, along with longer-term difficulties with the balance of payments and productivity, devastated popular confidence.[70] A deeper cause for doubt, however, lay in the intractable problems of the inner city. These provoked intellectuals on both left and right to question the efficacy, as well as the wisdom, of government, as they had seldom done before. Many radicals now said that race and poverty, more than class, were the denied reality in American politics, the problem that the system was unwilling or unable to face.[71]

Neo-conservatives also tried to persuade those in official circles of the inherent limitations of government.[72] The traditional criticism of big government from the right had been that it overburdened the free economy, and the new conservatives questioned the sharp growth in social spending on this ground. Their strongest contention, however, was that federal programs aimed at poverty were doomed to fail—that social programs necessarily reward and promote the very evils they aim to solve. Nor, conservatives argued, can government administer such programs effectively, given the inherent inefficiencies of bureaucracy.[73]

As liberals have noted, the indictment was overdrawn. The federal government is hardly a failure in all respects, nor is there any clear relationship between social spending and economic growth or productivity.[74] Some antipoverty programs produce good effects, and the costs of the federal health and environmental legislation of the 1970s were well justified.[75] Nevertheless, these successes failed to lift the gloom. Government's oldest mission, the one most vital to its legitimacy, was still to achieve social advancement for the least advantaged, and in this it had signally failed. That disappointment, like no other, hit progressive government at its heart.[76]

Comparable feelings seem to have hit Americans at large. The public's faith in government fell, as can be seen not only in the turning to the Republicans, but in signs of disillusionment with politics. Fewer American voters espoused an allegiance to either party. Between 1960 and the 1970s, the proportion of voters claiming to be independents rose from a quarter to over a third. Voters cast their votes more on the basis of individual issues—including social issues— and less according to party. The majority of voters came to distrust government and to feel that it was unresponsive to them. Election turnout dropped—from 63 percent of eligible voters in 1960 to only 51 percent in 1988.[77]

Both the meaning and the cause of these changes are contested,[78] but clearly public discontent with politics and government has grown. While the economic slowdown is probably the major explanation, disappointments in social policy were also significant: Surveys date the turn against government from the mid-1960s, before chronic economic problems appeared. The catalyst seems to have been the social disorders and contentions of 1964 and ensuing years, mostly linked to poverty and race. Already by 1972—well before the energy crises and the double-digit inflation of the Carter years—voter distrust and antipartisanship ran high.[79]

The public did not lose faith in the main institutions of government, but it came to doubt whether Washington could solve the country's economic and social difficulties. The public wanted government to do more about the inner city, but also questioned whether policymakers knew what to do.[80] The public objects not so much to the cost of programs as to their ineffectiveness.[81] Ronald Reagan reversed some of the decline of trust in government with his leadership qualities and the country's improved economic performance.[82] He found no answer to poverty, and skepticism remains.

When progressive reformism faltered, dependency politics was born. In the new era, government downplays the goal of advancing low-income people and instead seeks to re-create the preconditions of progress. Increasingly, policy no longer assumes competence in the poor, but seeks to instill it. Unfortunately, fostering competence in individuals has proven immensely more difficult than expanding opportunity for competent citizens. That is the chief dilemma faced by American politics today.

3

The Costs of Nonwork

Work, work, work. That's how we'll make a name for ourselves.
—BANK ADVERTISEMENT IN THE METRO, WASHINGTON, D.C.

In the real world, it's what you do that counts.
—ADVERTISEMENT FOR CITY VOLUNTEER CORPS
IN NEW YORK CITY SUBWAY

IT may be that nonwork has paralyzed fundamental social reform in the United States, but why concretely should we worry about it? Very simply, need and dependency among the working-aged result very directly from a lack of earnings. Mothers go on welfare because they lose their husbands, but also because they do not work themselves. Employment is even more important for getting out of poverty than getting in. People may become poor for many reasons, but they become nonpoor primarily by going to work. Nonwork is, of course, only one of many problems afflicting the racial ghetto and the long-term poor, but it is the most fundamental. Nonparticipation in the economy, for whatever reason, is the main reason why today's long-term poor, unlike yesterday's, show little sign of progressing into mainstream American life. Lack of earnings would still set today's long-term poor apart, even if their separate schools and neighborhoods were broken up by governmental fiat.

The costs of nonwork are more than economic. By infringing the work ethic, nonworking adults close the door to much of the government help they might otherwise obtain. The public likes to help the poor, but it also wants to defend the competence assumption. It wants to give benefits to working adults, not the nonworking. If anything, that demand has increased in strength recently, since nonpoor Americans are working harder today than ever before. Given the work ethic, people with jobs are also likely to be better off than nonworkers psychologically, even if they are financially unsuccessful.

ECONOMIC COSTS

That nonwork should cause poverty is only common sense. Perhaps it is the common sense of an earlier age. In an affluent society, where poverty is the exception rather than the rule, its causes come to seem invisible, or capricious. Analysts tend to treat poverty as a misfortune inflicted on people by nameless social forces. They play down nonwork as a cause of poverty in favor of absent breadwinners, low wages, or the vagaries of government grant policies.[1] Nevertheless, even in the world's richest country, most people's income, short of retirement age, comes mainly from earnings, and most government benefits assume a history of working. Thus, if people do not work, they will often be poor. My point here is to highlight that fact. Later chapters consider other influences on poverty and the impediments that may explain failure to work.

Table 3.1 shows the proportions of those who did and did not work in 1989 among all individuals aged fifteen and over, heads of family, female heads of family, and other individuals not in families. The figures dramatize the extent of employment among adult Americans: Two-thirds or more were employed in 1989, even among women heading families. Roughly half worked all year, and 40 percent or more also worked full-time. Only a third or less did not work. Among the poor, however, less than half worked at all, a fifth or less worked all year, and the share working full-time and full-year was only 6 to 16 percent. If I had separated long-term poor from the short-term and compared them to the nonpoor, rather than the entire population, the contrasts would be even greater. Data not shown demonstrate that the pattern varies little by race. Among all blacks and Hispanics, work effort is almost as usual as among whites, but among the black poor, only 35 percent worked, while 65 percent did not—virtually reversing the figures for the population as a whole.[2]

The biggest difference between the general population and the poor is in the share employed full-year, suggesting that the main cause of the work problem is erratic work, not a lack of all employment. Many poor adults occasionally work, but they seldom put in

TABLE 3.1

Employment Status of Persons Aged 15 and Over,
1989

All income levels	All persons	All family heads	Female heads	Unrelated individuals
Worked at any time in year	69.2%	76.6%	65.0%	66.3%
Full-year	47.7	61.4	45.0	47.6
Full-time	41.8	58.0	39.9	43.3
Part-year	21.5	15.2	20.0	18.7
Did not work	30.3	22.3	35.0	33.6
Income below poverty				
Worked at any time in year	41.1	48.9	41.6	38.7
Full-year	14.0	20.9	14.5	11.4
Full-time	9.2	16.2	8.8	5.7
Part-year	27.1	28.0	27.1	27.2
Did not work	58.7	50.8	58.4	61.3

NOTE: "Full-year" means at least fifty weeks a year, "full-time" at least thirty-five hours a week, "part-year" one to forty-nine weeks a year. Proportions working and not working do not add to 100 because heads in the armed forces are omitted.

SOURCE: Calculated from U.S. Department of Commerce, Bureau of the Census, *Money Income and Poverty Status in the United States: 1989*, Series P-60, no. 168 (Washington, D.C.: U.S. Government Printing Office, September 1990), tables 22–24.

the steady hours, week after week, that keep most other people out of need. Although only 6 percent of welfare mothers work in a given month, higher proportions have some earnings over a year, and they often combine welfare with earnings and other sources of income.[3] Over time, they can accumulate a fair amount of work experience,[4] though less today than before the 1981 AFDC eligibility cuts. They work many fewer hours than comparable women not on welfare, however, and they work more erratically.[5] For these women, earnings are at best an addition to welfare income, not something they seriously try to live on.

Table 3.2 shows how sharply these work differences affect poverty levels. Without work, the poverty rate is one-fifth for all individuals and over half for female family heads. Among the working, that figure drops by about two-thirds, and with full-time, full-year work, it drops into single digits, far below the overall poverty rate for the groups shown. The drop is especially sharp for unrelated individuals, many of whom are working-aged single people who do not qualify for income benefits given to single mothers and the elderly. As in Table 3.1, steady work is the key to the reduction in need: On average, there is little reduction in poverty from part-year work versus not working, but an enormous decrease from working full-year.

TABLE 3.2

Poverty Rates by Work Level of Persons Aged 15 and Over,
1989

	All persons	All family heads	Female heads	Unrelated individuals
Overall	10.7%	10.3%	32.2%	19.2%
Worked at any time in year	6.3	6.6	20.6	11.2
Full-year (50–52 weeks a year)	3.1	3.5	10.3	4.6
Full-time (35 hours/week or more)	2.4	2.9	7.1	2.5
Part-year (1–49 weeks a year)	13.5	19.0	43.6	28.0
Did not work	20.7	23.4	53.7	35.1

SOURCE: U.S. Department of Commerce, Bureau of the Census, *Money Income and Poverty Status in the United States: 1989*, Series P-60, no. 168 (Washington, D.C.: U.S. Government Printing Office, September 1990), tables 22–24.

Poverty levels run higher at each work level for female heads of families, who have dependents to support, and for single adults, many of whom are unskilled or disabled, than for adults in general; according to data not shown, the levels also run higher for blacks and Hispanics than for whites, an indication that minorities suffer from relatively low wages as well as low working hours. Nevertheless, within each group, need drops sharply with work effort. The poverty rate in 1989 was 45 percent among blacks who did not work, but less than 5 percent for those working full-year and full-time.[6] The problem for poor minorities is precisely that regular work has become less usual for them. The worsening condition of the black and, even more, the Puerto Rican poor is directly connected to the fall in their earnings in recent decades.[7]

The tables show only gross differences in work levels and poverty. Many factors not considered affect who works and who is poor, including how much people can earn and what government benefits they receive; the figures for family heads also do not control for differing numbers of workers per family, which has a powerful effect on poverty.[8] If those differences were allowed for, poverty would not vary as extremely with work effort as shown here.[9] Nevertheless, it is clear that employment has a potent effect on need.

These figures apply to the poor in a single year, but the influence of work on poverty is equally apparent over time. Studies that track workers over years find that many dip in and out of poverty, but the trend in incomes is generally up for those who work steadily.[10] Most of the movement up and down is due to life-cycle changes, with young workers advancing to higher incomes, then losing income as they retire. Full-time workers at any age are seldom poor.[11]

Work effort also has a powerful impact on dependency. People go on welfare because they lack other means of support, especially earnings. Those who work steadily usually have incomes well above the eligibility levels set by states for AFDC. In the period 1977–81, 71 percent of female family heads were poor if they did not work, only 6 percent if they worked full-year and full-time. The figures for receiving AFDC are almost the same—66 percent for those without work and 7 percent for those who work full-year and full-time.[12] Quite simply, single mothers who work regularly have a good chance to avoid poverty and dependency, while those who do not work have to go on welfare.

The figures reveal the elemental connection between nonwork and poverty. Since poverty levels among people working conventional hours are so very low, poverty among the working-aged is almost synonymous with low working hours. If poor adults worked steadily, poverty levels would again drop rapidly, as they did in the 1960s. The implication is that *working-aged poverty is an employment problem*, at least in the first instance, and *the causes of poverty must be sought among the causes of nonwork*.

THE UNDERGROUND ECONOMY

One point to establish at the outset is that the low work levels that surveys find among the poor and dependent are real. Some have speculated that many poor adults who seem to be unemployed or outside the labor force are actually working in the "underground economy," that is, in activities not recorded by government. If this were true, they would be less different from workaday Americans than they appear.

Businesses that operate by cash transactions, such as street vending, can easily avoid government taxes and regulations. Working "off the books" also hides earnings that would disqualify recipients for means-tested benefits such as welfare. These jobs may be legitimate, aside from the failure to report earnings; other underground activities, such as drug running and organized crime, are illegal per se.

Some liberals believe that the underground harbors many poor blacks without skills, as they find it "the only possibility for earning income" in a society that denies them opportunity.[13] Conservatives, for their part, assert that poverty levels are overstated because of the underground. Unreported income, if known, might lower the unemployment rate and raise the work rate, poverty might be as low as a quarter of its reported level.[14] The best evidence for this argument is that poor families appear to consume almost three times the income they claim to receive, a ratio that has risen sharply since the 1960s. Even reported incomes among the lowest fifth of incomes increased 16 percent over the period 1970–77, although the value of welfare benefits fell with inflation.[15]

It seems unlikely, however, that much of this income originates from employment, even off the books; crime and donations from absent fathers, relatives, and friends are more likely sources.[16] Early, alarmist estimates put the underground economy at as much as a quarter of the national income as officially measured;[17] later surveys suggest no more than 10 percent.[18] This activity, moreover, seems mostly to involve small businessmen and retired or unemployed people who conduct transactions in cash. Most of these workers also hold, or once held, regular jobs; few are poor or dependent people outside the regular economy entirely.[19] Thus, the joblessness that seems to exist in the inner city is no mirage.

WORK EFFORT VERSUS FAMILY BREAKUP

To some, the reason for nonwork and poverty is very simple — increasing breakup among American families in general and especially among the poor. Work levels have fallen, it is said, because so many mothers have lost their husbands or never married the fathers of their children. Because of a need to care for children, these women cannot work as men do, so many become poor or dependent. In this view, there is no way to overcome poverty except to forestall breakup, promote marriage (or remarriage), or simply transfer more money to broken families.

The breakup or nonmarriage of parents is undoubtedly epidemic. Between 1960 and 1987, the share of families headed by women rose among whites from 8 to 13 percent, and among blacks from 21 to 42 percent. In the same period, the share of children born out of wedlock increased from 2 to 17 percent for whites and from 22 to an astounding 62 percent for blacks.[20] The trends are especially pronounced among the poor. Poor, female-headed families accounted for 37 percent of all poor people in 1989, compared to 18 percent in 1959.[21] There is no doubt that family breakup has precipitated much of the long-term poverty and dependency in the United States. According to one recent study, 19 percent of children live in poverty before their parents separate, 36 percent four months later.[22]

Nevertheless, the argument that breakup necessarily causes poverty or dependency is unpersuasive. Breakup certainly lowers earnings and increases economic inequality, since one parent cannot, on average, earn as much as two. It rarely forces a family into poverty or onto welfare—unless the parents fail to work conventional hours. As shown in Table 3.1, the majority of women heading families work, most of them full-time, and that is the main reason most of them avoid poverty and welfare. Family poverty has risen mainly because poor single mothers fail to work regularly, and their departed spouses do not contribute to their support.

Most analysts have seen breakup as the leading reason why families enter poverty, with loss of earnings second,[23] but the most sophisticated study rates the two about equal in importance. Mary Jo Bane and David T. Ellwood estimate that about half of all periods of poverty begin through a loss of earnings in the family, about half from breakup or other family changes. The largest single cause is loss of earnings by the family head (38 percent). The pattern does differ by the type of family: Earnings loss precipitates 58 percent of all poverty spells among male-headed families, only 14 percent among female-headed families, among whom the loss of the husband is the more usual cause.

Work is critical for both family types for getting out of poverty. Fifty percent of spells of poverty end through higher earnings by the family head and another 23 percent through earnings by other family members. The share of spells ending through the head's earnings is highest for male-headed families (64 percent), but even in female-headed families, 33 percent of spells end through higher earnings by the head, only 26 percent through the mother remarrying. All told, changes in earnings account for half of all entries into poverty, but three-quarters of all exits. Bane and Ellwood conclude, "It is simply not the case that the only routes out of poverty for women family heads are marriage or transfers," meaning welfare.[24]

When a woman goes on AFDC, three-quarters of the time the reason is that she separated from her spouse or bore a child out of wedlock; in only 12 percent of cases is it loss of earnings.[25] Yet, according to David Ellwood, work counts for more in escaping dependency, just as it does in getting out of poverty. When mothers leave AFDC, the reason is remarriage in 35 percent of cases, earnings increases in 21 percent. But earnings may play a contributing role when mothers leave the rolls for other reasons, so the share of exits attributable to earnings may run as high as 42 percent.[26]

In another study, Mary Jo Bane argues that lack of earnings plays a larger role in family poverty, and breakup a smaller one, than has been realized. Even if the incidence of female-headedness had not changed since 1959, poverty would be little lower than it is, since breakup changes the economic circumstances of parents only if they are employed. Too commonly today, poor parents are not employed, and poverty due to nonwork is also likely to last longer than poverty arising from breakup. Lack of earnings, not breakup, explains virtually all of the increase in poverty in the 1980s.[27] Poverty among children has grown even among families that remain intact, because their parents earn less.[28]

The employment problem also explains most of the enormous difference in family poverty between whites and blacks. While breakup and nonmarriage are much higher among blacks, these factors less often make them poor. Among blacks living in poor, single-parent families, the loss of the father was the initial reason for poverty in only 23 percent of cases, compared to 51 percent among whites. Most poor black families were needy before the split as well as after. This is because these families seldom had earnings, so the departure of the father made little economic difference. In 1980, even reducing their rate of female heads to that of whites, the poverty rate among black families would still have been 23 percent versus 8 percent for white families, simply because black earnings are so much lower.[29]

Even where breakup is linked to lower earnings, it is unclear which is the cause and which the result. Fathers who fail to provide for their families are more likely to leave them or to be ejected by the mothers. And mothers who acquire their own income, from either employment or government benefits, are more likely to separate from their spouses. For mothers, going to work has been a response to breakup, but it can also be a cause, as women discover that they can support their families by themselves.[30]

There may be little society can do to reverse the tide of instability in American families, especially among the poor. The causes lie in cultural shifts toward greater tolerance for divorce and for working women. These changes are desirable, at least in part, and in any event government could not reverse them.[31] The moral, in Mary Jo Bane's words: "The problem of poverty should be addressed by devoting attention to employment... rather than hand-wringing about the decline of the family."[32] Raising work levels among poor parents, whether or not they are married, could assuage the worst consequences of breakup.

THE MOST IMPORTANT SOCIAL PROBLEM

To some students of poverty, this focus on employment will still seem narrow. They may admit that nonwork is the immediate cause of need in many cases, but they see more fundamental causes. Family-oriented experts say poor parents do not work because many were born out of wedlock, poorly parented, given inadequate health care and education, and otherwise prepared for lives of failure. In turn, they themselves bear children out of wedlock, and the "cycle of disadvantage" continues. The problem for poor mothers is not so much that they are single, but that they cannot cope with life.[33]

Nevertheless, employment is the best single indicator of competence. People who work steadily are more likely to marry and stay married, and to function well as parents; employment either fosters these abilities or results from them. If the adult poor were commonly employed, rather than jobless, it would be difficult to imagine an underclass.[34] It is workers, not nonworkers, whom government has much the most power to help, and who also have the most power to help themselves.

Other analysts say racial segregation is the real cause of poverty. While bias against blacks in education and employment has largely ended, residential segregation has proven difficult to overcome. Because few blacks really live with whites, the argument goes, their neighborhoods never command the same resources as white areas. They cannot finance good schools and other community institutions, and their children lack the advantage of an integrated upbringing.[35] The experience equips them only for dependent lives.

However, living together is not what integration has usually meant in America. Different races and nationalities have always lived in distinct neighborhoods and gone to separate schools, especially in Northern cities. In this respect, the experience of blacks coming North from the South was the same as that of Jews and Poles coming from Eastern Europe. Rather, integration takes place through politics and employment. Groups may live separately, but they learn to speak English, vote in the same elections, and, above all, work in the same economy. Commonality in the public world compensates for separation in private. Eventually, the children of immigrants leave urban ethnic enclaves for more integrated suburbs, but to this day, ethnic groups remain more distinct in their identity and life-style than many people appreciate.[36]

The notion that residential integration is essential seems to reflect the deep conviction among blacks that they have to "get things from white people" if they are to live a decent life.[37] But black communities lack resources today mainly because so few lower-income blacks work steadily, not because they live without white people. Functioning parents are worth infinitely more to black children than going to school with whites. Black neighborhoods seem impoverished today not so much because they are segregated, as because most blacks with jobs have moved out.[38]

If poor blacks functioned better, whites would show less resistance to living among them. Blacks would also have less need for whites. They would have the income to develop their own neighborhoods, as ethnic groups have traditionally done. With higher incomes, they would be more likely to vote and thus exercise greater political clout. As one observer of New York black politics has written, "Most people master the skills of political or labor organizing only by working— that is, by getting out of the house, taking the subway, collaborating with others on the job."[39]

Thomas Rush is a black man who makes a good income as a senior skycap at a Chicago airport. He demands, and gets, respectful treatment from whites on the job ("The day of the shuffle is gone"), but, as he told Studs Terkel, he has no desire to live with whites. Instead, he speaks with pride of his own middle-class black community, where he and other skycaps live. "Every one of the fellas on my shift own[s] their own home," Rush says. He believes he and his group are well able to form their own community. The neighborhood is actually in better shape than before blacks moved in. "Most people are surprised when they come out here," Rush says. "I wonder why."[40]

POLITICAL COSTS

The economic costs of nonwork are severe, but they are no more serious than the damage done to the political standing of the poor. If the poor worked and still lacked money, government would probably give it to them, as it has to the elderly and disabled. Without work, the poor become "undeserving," lacking claims to income from either the marketplace or government.

Few systematic studies of social attitudes toward the poor and antipoverty programs exist,[41] but this much is clear: Government's refusal to give a living income to the working-aged does not spring from any generalized hostility to the needy. Americans and their leaders refuse to redistribute incomes on a broad scale, but neither will they abandon the vulnerable.[42] As noted above, the public criticized the Reagan administration for the cuts it made in the antipoverty effort. Such is the concern, according to one recent poll, that 75 percent of the public thinks the poor can hardly get by on what they receive, and 59 percent want government to spend more on helping them. Close to two-thirds overestimated the current poverty level, usually by a considerable margin.

The hitch is that people also want to defend the competence assumption, the notion that individuals normally can and should advance themselves. In the same poll, 74 percent of respondents said individuals are responsible for their own well-being, only 26 percent that government is.[43] The implication is not to deny all public responsibility for the needy, but rather to require that people show effort on their own behalf before receiving aid. To satisfy this emphasis on "deserts," those asking for assistance must be able to show that they are needy for reasons beyond their control.[44] Americans want to mete out assistance by the degree to which a group needing aid is responsible for its own predicament. The elderly, disabled, and children rank ahead of working-aged adults, including welfare mothers, unless it is clear that jobs are unavailable. These attitudes differ little between rich and poor or across social groups, and they have changed little over time.[45]

Current federal income programs reflect these priorities. They cover the elderly and disabled the most generously, on grounds that such persons should not need to work, while generally denying aid beyond Food Stamps to poor but employable men, who are presumed able to work. Locally funded general assistance programs cover some single men, but the benefits are low. Family welfare reflects the contradictory feelings the public has about poor children and their parents. People want to help the children while holding the mother (and the absent father) accountable for not supporting them. The compromise is that AFDC covers needy families, but benefits in most states are meager.

The generosity of welfare is directly related to judgments about "deservingness." Benefits tend to run higher in liberal states, such as New York and California, where recipients are more likely to be seen as victims, than in Southern states, where attitudes are more stringent. While the public might like to give higher benefits than now, it would also modulate support according to the effort recipients were making to help themselves. Higher benefits would go to parents who were looking for work, lower benefits to those who were not looking or were avoiding minimum-wage jobs.[46]

Welfare as it now exists is intensely unpopular, evoking bitter denunciations from voters of every background and race. People say that many recipients do not really need welfare, that it promotes dependency, and that too much is being spent on it. They also demand to know why the working poor do not take a second job, and whether their spouses work.[47] Although such attitudes sound punitive, the objection is not to the principle of aid, but rather to the "abuses" with which welfare has become associated, especially cheating and nonwork by welfare parents. Feelings have hardened in the last twenty years, apparently because welfare is more associated with irresponsibility than any other program.[48]

Americans would prefer to get away from welfare entirely, to guarantee the poor employment rather than income, because then there would be no doubt about deservingness. The intention is not to save money but to uphold the competence assumption. According to polls, 80 percent of the public would cut the able-bodied off welfare entirely, but a similar majority would guarantee public jobs for those who could not find private-sector employment—a position much beyond what even liberal governments have attempted in the United States. The public would do this even if the cost— due to the needed child care and other services—were greater than it is now. In the words of Daniel Yankelovich, "The public's emphasis on work and on helping people to become self-supporting can hardly be over-emphasized."[49] As one Senator put it, the goal is "...not that we somehow punish welfare recipients but that we provide a means so that men and women work to support their families."[50]

Such attitudes explain why there is powerful support for workfare, that is, requirements that adult welfare recipients work or look for work. Voters embrace such programs, only slightly deterred by the knowledge that they are difficult to implement. In one poll, 69 percent of respondents favored the idea, and only 25 percent opposed it. The results were much the same for Democrats (65 to 29 percent) as for Republicans (70 to 24 percent). White support (71 to 23 percent) was only a little stronger than nonwhite (54 to 39 percent), even though the majority of aid recipients who would be affected are black or Hispanic.[51]

Solving the work problem is undoubtedly the key to improving the image of welfare. Increased benefits for the working-aged poor will be difficult to justify until work levels rise. When advocates bemoan rising inequality or "family poverty," but ignore nonwork, they implicitly expect that the poor should receive higher income without employment. Politically, this is hopeless. The public would like to help children in need, who are certainly deserving, but it will not give families more cash as long as undeserving parents would also benefit.[52]

Working poor people, however, tap into a much more generous set of attitudes. The public loves to help poor people *through employment*, so they can claim to have earned what they receive. A common attitude is that adults should be assured of a job in which, if they work conventional hours, they can support their families without undue strain.[53] This suggests that nonwork is a much more fundamental problem than dependency. Without work, the poor can get little from either the economy or government. For the employed, both sectors could work together to provide support, and the precise mix of public and private provision is much less important.

Policy analysts tend to measure inequality in terms of income or wealth and say Americans have too little of it. To the voters equality is not so narrowly economic. It means to participate in a bundle of rights *and* obligations that people associate with being American. Access to opportunity is one of these rights, but a duty to work is the corresponding obligation. Americans hardly understand equality other than among workers, for only they are seen as real citizens. The poor must *become unequal* through holding available jobs before they can claim to get a better deal from either their employers or government.

None of this implies that poor adults are expected to accept unattractive jobs passively. To complain about one's job is as American as apple pie. Such claims were and are staples of progressive politics, with workers maneuvering through unions or lobbying to improve their situation. It is not American, however, to complain about one's job without doing it. Only workers *in* jobs, or at least with steady job histories, have full standing to protest the conditions of their employment. Claims to equality cannot be pressed from outside the work force.

Liberal analysts tend to see in popular feeling simply a rejection of responsibility for the poor. When voters criticize welfare, in this view, they are asserting an absolute duty of self-reliance and denying the communitarian side of the American tradition; there is no hope but to wait for the political pendulum to swing back toward greater tolerance for collective provision.[54] Among political elites, the social question often is framed in these New Deal terms as a battle between more government and less.[55]

But this interpretation cannot explain why the many forms of middle-class reliance on government go unquestioned, or the popular criticism of the Reagan cuts in social spending. The self-reliance voters ask for does not necessarily imply independence from government. It is accepted that people in difficulties have a claim on the public. Rather, the demand is for effort. People seem to be concerned that the poor lack the discipline needed *either* to be self-reliant *or* to share in the communal side of American life. Only workers are qualified even to enter into the progressive debate about what the precise balance of government and the marketplace should be.

At bottom, the public concern is about attitudes. What disturbs people most is the passivity of today's entrenched poor, their curious reluctance to help themselves in many ways. To average Americans, competence connotes not just working but a more general quality of "motivation" or "initiative" about life. They fail to see in today's poor that desire to improve oneself and one's family that has marked American society. Only when poor adults show a clearer commitment to "getting ahead" will other Americans be able to identify with them and feel more generous toward them.[56]

Most Americans will accept poverty as an economic condition, and will do something to help, but they will not accept defeatism. The poor, if they are to be "deserving," cannot simply give up. They must "try," and working or attempting to work is the great badge of that effort. Unfortunately, defeatism is precisely what a lot of poor adults seem to feel. The paradox is that Americans prefer those who assert themselves to those who do not, even though the assertive may be formidable competitors. We would rather be exploited by people out to make a buck than struggle with helping people who exploit only themselves. As one frustrated citizen exclaimed, "Why don't these people fight for themselves?"[57]

THE WORK ETHIC TODAY

Another force operating to isolate the poor is that even as they work less, other Americans have been working more. Employment never meant so much to so many people as it does today. Inevitably, nonworkers who seem not to share that dedication risk becoming outcasts in their own society.

As late as the 1960s, it was thought that employment would play a receding role in American life. John Kenneth Galbraith and other prophets foresaw affluence allowing ordinary people to cut back their working hours and retire ever earlier. Machines would take over many jobs, and society would accept a much greater degree of nonemployment, even by the working-aged. Increasingly, income would be divorced from work effort.[58]

The reverse is what happened. The standard work week was reduced to forty hours in 1940; it has fallen no further. Recently, Americans have been working more hours, not fewer. Between 1973 and 1988, the average work week grew from forty-one to forty-seven hours and leisure time plummeted by 40 percent. Mandatory retirement has been eased, and people are working longer into old age.[59] Most important, the proportion of Americans working has risen sharply, chiefly because more women, including mothers, have flocked to the labor market. The share of the adult population working or seeking work rose from 59 percent in 1960 to 66 percent in 1988,[60] the highest level in history.

The major reason for this shift was the chronic economic problems the nation encountered in the 1970s and 1980s. With frequent recessions and stagnant wages, families needed more members earning wages to keep up with inflation. The baby boom generation that entered the economy in the 1970s was forced to work long hours because the huge size of that cohort created intense competition for preferred careers. Driven by electronic communications, computers, and foreign competition, the finance and business worlds picked up their pace and became more demanding as well.[61]

People also found work more meaningful. A higher proportion of Americans than ever before appear to derive much of their satisfaction in life from their jobs. Employment has become a dominant source of personal identity and meaning as well as income. Many people value the sense of community they gain from coworkers, perhaps as a replacement for the increasingly unstable family. In surveys, around 80 percent of workers express satisfaction with their jobs.[62]

If any cultural force is driving the work explosion, it is women's liberation. One consequence of that movement has been the decision by many women to find their major satisfactions in employment rather than family life. They are driven not only by a need for income, but by the rising unpredictability of marriage. It may be, as one young woman told Studs Terkel, that "love is a woman's occupation," but in a world where half of marriages fail, "You can't depend on love. Oh, love is quite ephemeral. Work has a dignity you can count upon." The sentiment that "Your work is your identity"[63] is now one women assert as well as men. The proportion of women who say they would choose to work even if they were free to stay home has risen from 35 to over 50 percent since the late 1970s.[64]

There is dissatisfaction with work, but it increased only marginally between the 1950s and 1970s. It occurs in only about a quarter of the work force, mostly the young. The nature of the unrest suggests, furthermore, that people see *more* involvement with their work, not less. In keeping with a rising individualism, people want to direct their own work, take on interesting tasks, and feel more engaged in their jobs; they also want to be held accountable for performance on an individual basis. The shifts were greatest among the educated and affluent, but they occurred among the unemployed, blacks, and low-income workers as well. Very recently, the desire has risen among hard-pressed parents to spend more time with their children, and there is pressure on business to adjust work schedules accordingly.[65] However, in work life, there is little sign of the withdrawal of interest and involvement seen in politics.

The increasing importance of employment in American society means that nonworking poverty is likely to be even less palatable politically in the future than in the past. In the 1960s, when the country was affluent but less work-oriented, one could imagine simply giving the poor money, and this is essentially what the welfare reform plans of that era proposed. But after 1970, with a troubled economy and much higher work levels, passive poverty became unconscionable.

Most of the liberal welfare reformers of the 1960s could remember the Depression, World War II, and the long, apparently endless surge in affluence that followed. That sense of growing plenitude motivated their generous proposals. Today's culture, however, is dominated by the baby boom generation, born after the war. The boomers have had an almost opposite experience, being raised in the affluent 1950s and 1960s, then entering adulthood during the much more precarious 1970s and 1980s. In their working lives, incomes have not grown surely or steadily. They fear that they will not achieve even what their parents did, let alone be able to pass it on to their children.[66] The left says the boomers care too little for the poor, but they feel they have lived through a depression of their own. Much of the venom aroused by the new poverty comes from these younger adults, concerned that the foundations of a prosperous society are crumbling. The reception given to claims by the nonworking poor is not likely to grow warmer.

PSYCHOLOGICAL COSTS

It is easy to say that this new, tougher line on work is unfair. A love of labor comes a lot easier to the affluent, who typically have interesting, comfortable jobs, than to the less privileged, who usually have much more menial, pedestrian work, and who do it more for money than for meaning. Perhaps the work ethic is only cant that the lower orders have to endure from their betters.

It is true that few Americans want to work in just any job. Rather, they seek "better" positions, those with middle-class incomes and career prospects. They scramble for the education and other qualifications needed to enter white-collar careers. Many believe that menial jobs should be left to recent immigrants to the country, including illegal aliens. As one expert commented, "The attitude of many young people is that this is the dirty work of society and that people born, brought up, and educated in the U. S. shouldn't have to do it."[67]

But are less privileged Americans less attached to their jobs than other Americans? Surveys do not find this. Satisfaction with work varies remarkably little with social status. People working in less prestigious jobs seem, on average, to be about as content with them as those who are more successful. There is also little difference by race; working blacks are, if anything, more pleased with their positions than whites.[68] The real division, again, is between the nonworking poor and the rest of the population.

People without jobs, or at least a work history, are psychologically much worse off than the employed. They feel the stigma of being competitively unsuccessful, but a worse stigma from failing to work at all. A norm of reciprocity is pervasive in society, and though it is not enforced well in welfare, it takes a psychic toll. Either dependent people make an effort to work in return for support, or they have to regard themselves as less than full members of society. They must pay for welfare, that is, either in work effort or in the coin of diminished self-esteem.[69]

At a psychic level, the work ethic means accepting responsibility for oneself, whatever one's fortunes. It means avoiding that despondency, that refusal to cope, that the public finds so frustrating about the poor. Some might call despair a justified response to the depressed place the poor hold in our society, but denying responsibility is self-destructive, whatever one's station. People who believe they control their fate are happier than those who feel helpless in the face of outside forces. This is true for rich and poor, successful and unsuccessful, alike.[70]

Much of the reduction of black poverty since the 1960s is accounted for by intact families in which both parents work. Because black women are, on average, more employable than black men, the wives in such families often have better jobs than their husbands. It is a difficult situation for these men, but those who endure it are clearly better off. Those who cannot endure low-skilled jobs are those who never achieve anything, who succumb to the marital conflict, crime, drugs, and other tragedies of the ghetto.[71]

To satisfy the ethic means to work, but also to identify with one's task. Unsuccessful workers who only go through the routine of their jobs, without commitment, derive much less protection. Consider the lament of a salesman who, due to personal reverses, had to become a custodian:

> I don't have any interest in furthering myself, but I just can't see myself doing this the rest of my life. I almost get to the point that I might be on welfare. I ought to chuck it all and just not do anything.... I'd be free if I could say I'm a janitor.... If I could only say, "I'm Tim Devlin and I enjoy what I'm doing!"

Workers who can affirm their jobs can also live with their fortunes. A restaurant waitress who was proud of her work told of beating back the condescension of her customers:

> When somebody says to me, "You're great, how come you're *just* a waitress?" *Just* a waitress. I'd say, "Why, don't you think you deserve to be served by me?" It's implying that he's not worthy, not that I'm not worthy.... I don't feel lowly at all. I myself feel sure. I don't want to change the job. I love it.

A black parking lot attendant, seeking to stand equal to his more successful friends, found a democracy in common work effort that overrides differences of status:

> When people ask what I do, I tell 'em I park cars just like any other job. Only thing you got is a white collar, that's okay with me. Working behind a typewriter, that's fine. You're a doctor, that's cool. I got man friends, teachers. We meet sometimes, have a drink, talk. Everything is normal. Everybody got a job to do. My friends never feel superior to me.[72]

"Everything is normal. Everybody got a job to do." If today's poor adults could affirm that and work at higher levels, progressive issues would once again dominate American politics.

CHAPTER

4

Low Wages and Hard Times

Our city is threatened by the spreading blight of a
poverty even crueler in some ways than that of the Great
Depression half a century ago.

—ANDREW STEIN
"CHILDREN OF POVERTY: CRISIS IN NEW YORK"
NEW YORK TIMES MAGAZINE, 8 JUNE 1986

THE costs of nonwork are many-layered, but so far I have said little about causes. *Why* do today's poor so seldom work regularly? It is the supreme question in social policy today. All depends on how it is answered. Many conservatives treat nonwork as prima facie evidence that the poor are not trying, but what if one believes, with liberals, that nonworkers can get no jobs, or none worth taking? Even Charles Murray admits, "Presto: The portrait can be made to flip completely, and the nation becomes once more a country with structural poverty woven inextricably throughout the economy."[1]

There have been essentially four explanations for nonwork, and the next several chapters will consider them in turn. The first theory proposes that the poor earn such low wages that there is little point in their working (chapter 4); the second, that they are barred from work by a lack of jobs (chapter 5); the third, that jobs exist but there are other "barriers" to employment such as racial bias or a lack of child care (chapter 6). The fourth finds inner barriers, in the psychology of poverty (chapter 7). I believe the evidence mostly supports this last thesis. External barriers enter into the employment problem mainly by affecting wages, that is, the degree of equality among workers. None of them, individually or together, account for the sheer *lack* of work now found in the inner city. To explain that, some appeal to attitudes is unavoidable.

My conclusion remains hostage to the competence assumption, however. Conservatives and many economists typically assume that the poor are economic optimizers like other people, interested in getting ahead, and it is on this basis that it is hard to find prohibitive obstacles to employment. If liberal politicians and many analysts persist in believing that the poor cannot work, it is because they doubt, not so much that opportunity exists, but whether poor adults have the capacity to seize it. The expert debate shifts, that is, from the nature of society to human nature, the same shift that has occurred in politics at large.

This debate about barriers is one that continues among researchers, government officials, and others who deal with poverty professionally.[2] These disputes are often arcane, caught up in quibbles about statistics and analytic methods that only experts understand. The underlying political issues, however, are the same as those the public or politicians face as they grapple with the dilemma of poverty—are the poor to be seen as responsible and able to manage their lives, or not?

First, in this chapter, we will consider the effect of wages. It is true that low pay can explain part of poverty: Some workers who labor steadily remain poor. Yet the working poor are considerably outnumbered by the nonworking. Another contention is that recent hard times have produced nonwork and poverty. Yet the data show only somewhat greater inequality among people already working. Thus, low pay cannot explain most poverty. But this conclusion finally rests on a judgment about personality. All depends on whether one believes the poor should respond to hard times by working more or working less.

THE WORKING POOR

Those who doubt that work is the answer to need point to the shocking reality that not everyone who works escapes poverty. The "working poor" have become a synonym for the "deserving poor," a term that also connotes two-parent families that are intact but needy. We readily contrast such families, where at least one parent usually works, to poor, female-headed families, most of which live on welfare without working.

It is true that 41 percent of the adult poor, or 8.4 million people, worked at some time during 1989 (see table 3.1). Many could not increase their work effort. In that year, there were 1.9 million workers who labored full-year and full-time and yet lived in families that were poor. Another 5.5 million poor worked less than full-year. Among heads of poor families, 1.1 million worked full-year and full-time, 1.9 million worked less than full-year, and 3.3 million worked at some time.[3] Furthermore, 54 percent of poor families had at least some earnings, and 48 percent of the income of all poor families came from earnings.[4]

David Ellwood defines as adequately employed all families in which one worker, or a combination of workers, works full-year and full-time. On that basis in 1984, 44 percent of the two-parent poor families were fully employed, and another 35 percent were partially employed or looking for work. The poverty of the working poor appears due mainly to low wages and involuntary joblessness rather than lack of effort. "In most of these families," Ellwood concludes, "someone is working or trying to work. These families *are* playing by the rules." Nevertheless, "they are not making it in America."[5]

The working poor look a lot more like mainstream society, and a lot more "deserving," than the inner-city groups that have come to dominate the popular image of poverty. Most of the working poor are white, not black. About half of them are men, not women living on welfare, and most live outside metropolitan areas. Indeed, almost half of them live in the South, a legacy of the era, going back a century or more, when that region was the most backward in the country. These are the same characteristics found among the poor as a whole in any given year, even if the long-term poor are notably nonwhite.[6] If the majority of the poor were working, poverty would raise far fewer questions about competence.

However, the working poor are considerably outnumbered by the nonworking. There may have been 8.4 million poor who worked in 1989 if one includes everyone with any earnings, but there were 12.0 million who did not work at all. As table 3.1 shows, only 9 percent of poor adults worked full-year and full-time. Among poor family heads, who have responsibility for others, work levels ran higher, but the 3.3 million who worked at any time in the year were still exceeded by the 3.4 million who did not work.[7]

Liberal analysts sometimes classify as "working" all families in which anyone works even briefly during the year. That conveys a false impression that poverty and work at conventional levels may easily be combined. A more reasonable definition would limit the "working poor" to families with members working over half the year. That threshold is important. Among poor adults working half-year or less in 1987, 18 percent were poor, but among those working more than half-year, only 4 percent were poor. Among family heads, the comparable figures were 31 and 5 percent.[8]

Even among Ellwood's working poor, few are putting in what could be called normal hours. In the fully employed families headed by married couples, two-thirds of the husbands and 15 percent of the wives worked full-year and full-time, levels comparable to those for such families in general. But among those not fully employed, work levels are dramatically lower for both husbands and wives. As a result, for poor, two-parent families overall, only 30 percent of the husbands worked full-year and full-time; 40 percent worked part-year or part-time, and 30 percent not at all. The comparable figures for wives are 7, 33, and 60 percent.[9] It is the partially, not the fully, employed who largely account for "working poverty."

THE MINIMUM WAGE

Many believe that the minimum wage is an important cause of poverty. Congress has set a floor under wages for most workers since the passage of the Fair Labor Standards Act in 1938. Recent increases in the minimum wage have failed to keep up with inflation; it reached a peak in purchasing power in 1968 and has fallen since. Congress raised the minimum to $3.35 in 1981 and to $4.25 in 1989, effective in 1991, only partially recouping the loss. The level has also fallen relative to typical wages. The minimum wage was formerly worth about half of average hourly earnings, but by 1985 the ratio had slipped to 39 percent.[10] Perhaps the main thing poor people need in order to get out of poverty is a raise.[11]

However, the minimum wage has a lot less to do with poverty than most people realize. Most minimum-wage workers are not poor. The poverty rate was only 19 percent for workers at or below $3.35 in 1985, and two-thirds of such workers actually had family incomes at 150 percent of poverty or higher. Nor do most of the poor work at the minimum wage. In 1985, only 26 percent of poor workers were paid at the old $3.35 level or below. In fact, 34 percent received between $3.36 and $4.35 per hour, and 40 percent received $4.35 or above. Differences in hours worked, not in wages, principally determine whether workers are poor. As one moves to a higher wage rate, poverty drops less sharply than it does if one moves from not working to working full-time and full-year.[12]

Critics of the minimum wage commonly calculate what it would pay over a year's time and show that this is inadequate to support a family. Anyone who worked full-time and full-year (forty hours a week for fifty weeks, or two thousand hours) at the $3.35 minimum in 1989 earned $6,700. This figure is below the official poverty threshold in that year even for a family of two,[13] suggesting that the minimum wage falls well below a living wage. But even if we include all workers earning $6,700 or less, at any wage, the proportion in poverty in 1985 was actually only 31 percent. The figures for blacks (35 percent) and Hispanics (33 percent) hardly differ from that for whites (31 percent).[14]

How can workers with poverty-level earnings so often escape poverty?—because whether a person is poor depends on the total income of the family, not just on his or her earnings. Though many minimum-wage workers might be poor if they had to support their families alone, other family members typically also work, and the combined effort lifts the family over the poverty line. The poverty rate for workers at or below $3.35 was only 8 percent in 1984 if there were other workers in the family, but 45 percent if there were not.[15]

The rhetoric of the minimum wage typically pictures a head of household struggling to support a family alone on $3.35 or $4.25 an hour. *Very* few minimum-wage workers are in that position. In 1986, less than 1 percent of workers at or below $3.35 were male heads of family, less than 7 percent female heads. Only 710,000 such workers in 1985 were the only workers in a poor family, and only 120,000 were working full-time, year-round in a poor family. Even fewer, presumably, were the sole workers in their families, working full-time, full-year, and still poor.[16]

Most minimum-wage workers are secondary workers, that is, members of families in which the head is already working. Usually they are young or the spouses of the heads, and they usually work less than full-time. In 1986, 37 percent of workers at or below $3.35 were teenagers, 59 percent were under age twenty-five, 20 percent were wives, 52 percent were other family members, 66 percent were female, and 66 percent worked only part-time. The corresponding figures for all workers earning hourly rates were much lower.[17] Are low wages for these workers a serious problem? We can assume they or their families need the money or they would not be working, but work for teenagers is rarely as critical to a family as work for parents, nor are a wife's earnings usually as critical as her husband's.

In any event, the minimum wage has become increasingly irrelevant to actual wages, even for the low-skilled, because of the shrinking labor supply (see chapter 5). Whatever the government requires, employers usually find they must offer more today simply to attract workers. The media depict employees at the bottom of the economy "working at McDonald's" for the minimum wage, but in New England during the recent boom, McDonald's and other fast-food outlets were paying $5 to $8 an hour. Congress voted a new $4.25 minimum in 1989, but even as implementation began in early 1990, businesses all over the country had to pay $4.50 or more to obtain unskilled labor.[18]

LOW WAGES

It seems clear that wages are generally high enough to avoid poverty by the government's definition. As we have seen in Table 3.1, poverty falls to very low levels for workers who are steadily employed. But what about workers at low wages? If one defines as low-wage those workers earning less than half the average private-sector wage, the share of such workers who were poor declined from 42 percent in 1959 to 18 percent in 1984. In the same period, the share of such workers heading poor families fell from 24 to 7 percent. Poverty rates just for those working full-time and full-year would be lower still. By 1984, the remaining poor, low-wage family heads numbered only 1 million, or 1 percent of all wage and salary workers. They remained poor mainly because they worked fewer hours than the nonpoor and because fewer members of their families also worked.[19]

It is true that many low-paid workers escape poverty only because other members of the family also work. Most people would not see that as unfair, now that it has become usual for both parents of families to be employed among the high- and low-income alike. But is it fair for single mothers, who must usually support families unaided? Their situation is the acid test of whether wages are adequate. Should we expect such mothers to work to support themselves rather than go on welfare? Much of the debate about the rewards of employment comes down to this.

Liberal analysts assert that single mothers usually cannot work their way off welfare even if they try. In most cases, welfare pays them more than employment would, given the low pay and benefits they are likely to earn, particularly in cities with relatively high welfare and living costs.[20] The conservative position is that the mothers can almost always escape dependency and need if they exploit their opportunities. By one calculation, a single mother had a good chance to support two children above welfare and poverty in every state in the union in 1987, even working at the minimum wage, provided she worked full-time and full-year and claimed other government benefits still available to her.[21]

Whether the mothers can get off welfare mostly depends on their own effort, secondarily on how much help they get. The study considering the most factors found that single mothers who work full-time, receive child support from fathers, and pay no child care costs escape welfare (AFDC plus Food Stamps) in 82 percent of the cases and poverty in 72 percent. At the other extreme, only one-third of the mothers who work only half-time, receive child support, but have to pay for child care half the time will escape welfare. Provided they work full-time, 54 percent of mothers can probably exceed their welfare income even if they pay for child care and receive no child support payments.[22]

The issue, obviously, turns on one's view of competence. How hard should single mothers have to work? For most of them, working full-time is the key to escaping dependency or need,[23] but it may be unreasonable to make full-time work a norm for welfare mothers, given their child care responsibilities, in which case most of them would still need aid. On the other hand, many mothers start working part-time, then are able to shift to full-time and escape the rolls after all.[24]

The point here is that increasing working hours does a lot more for overcoming poverty than raising wages. It might be a good idea to take further steps to raise the rewards of employment, but we should not imagine that doing so holds the key to solving nonworking poverty in America. The key lies, rather, in finding out why poor adults so seldom work normal hours.

HARD TIMES

The contention that the economy causes poverty reaches further than arguments about wages. Many on the left believe that the American economy has gone through a quiet depression since the early 1970s, in some ways repeating the 1930s, and that this explains the nation's persistent poverty. Here we will consider that argument in general terms, and in the next chapter look more closely at whether jobs are available to the poor.

"Hard times" means the inflation and repeated economic downturn that stretched from the late Nixon years through the recession of the early 1980s. The immediate causes might lie in circumstance (higher energy and food prices) or in failed economic policies, but in the background looms the fact that after 1973 the productivity of workers in the American economy virtually ceased to improve, for reasons that remain unclear.[25] This resulted in intensified foreign competition and deindustrialization. As imported products flooded the country, manufacturing firms failed all over America, especially in the industrial Midwest. Many factory workers lost their jobs, often well-paying, and had to take positions at sharply lower pay. The media portray them as "going to work at McDonald's." Communities were devastated as plants closed, destroying not only private incomes, but the tax base of local and state governments. Some workers were forced to migrate to more prosperous areas in the Sunbelt, which then suffered the strains of excess growth.[26]

Leftist critics blame more than recessions and long-term economic decay. They see the economic structure of the country permanently changing to the disadvantage of ordinary people. The widespread prosperity after World War II was based on a broad middle class, much of it supported by well-paid jobs in manufacturing industries. Often, these positions paid well because they were unionized, not because they were demanding or difficult to fill. In large companies like General Motors, the great majority of jobs paid enough to support a family and buy a house in the suburbs. The system required steady economic growth and little price competition, so firms could raise prices to cover lofty wages and benefits. When recessions and foreign imports hit in a serious way in the 1970s, managers demanded cuts from unions and moved plants overseas to obtain cheaper labor. They diverted profits to industries outside manufacturing and failed to build the new facilities necessary to keep America competitive. These steps, as much as other problems, caused deindustrialization and the decline of wages.[27] So sharp was the shift of expectations that wage increases hardly recovered even during the good times of the later 1980s.[28]

The old system had rested on a tacit social contract: Management conceded high wages and benefits in return for labor peace. Companies also made a commitment to workers for the longer term. They would invest in employees and their skills and equipment so that high wages could be justified by high productivity. Workers were not merely cogs in an impersonal industrial machine. But as economic pressure grew, managers abrogated the contract and sought to reduce workers' compensation and maximize short-run profit.[29]

After 1970, the jobs offered by the economy less often ensured a middle-class life-style. Jobs were available, but of lower quality than workers had come to expect. Most of the new openings were in low-paid retail sales or "services," a catchall that includes work in hotels, fast-food outlets, health care, and temporary office work. In the 1980s, nearly 60 percent of the new jobs were in services; in 1986, they paid less than $14,000 a year on average, well below usual union wages. A rising share of jobs were part-time and, as a result, frequently lacked benefits such as pensions and health insurance. Many of the new jobs were of a kind that women customarily held.[30]

In a much noted study, the economists Barry Bluestone and Bennett Harrison claimed that the creation of good jobs virtually ceased with the election of Ronald Reagan as president. Between 1973 and 1979, only 20 percent of net new employment was low-paid, 64 percent paid middle incomes, and 16 percent was high-paid by the standards of 1973. But between 1979 and 1984, fully 58 percent of net new positions were low-paid, only 48 percent were middle-income, and high-paid jobs actually *fell* by 6 percent. The shift hit virtually all groups of workers and all industries and regions.[31]

It was a painful reverse for workers who had come to expect a well-paid job almost as a birthright. Said one displaced steelworker:

> No matter how you cut it, with all the people looking for jobs, there're not enough jobs. We all have to compete with each other, unemployed people against each other for a shrinking pie. What's happened in this economy is that higher wages have been busted down—everyone pushed down to a lower wage, even a minimum wage. Yeah, there are people back at work, but what kind of money are they making?[32]

INEQUALITY

Economic change produced a less secure America. Without higher productivity, average real earnings did not improve much at all after 1973, since workers who do not produce more cannot be paid more. Of course, wages went on increasing in nominal terms, but so did prices. Many believe there has been an absolute loss in real earnings and in family income, or at least no gain.[33] The "major economic story of the postwar period," the economist Frank Levy has written, was that the steady growth in incomes which the country had known since 1947 virtually stopped.[34]

Although ordinary workers suffered, many managers and professionals did better than ever. When the Reagan boom began, it was Wall Street financiers, property developers, and other speculators who profited. Along with low-paid service industries, "high-tech" industries such as computing and telecommunications burgeoned, with pay well above average. Thus, the best- as well as the worst-paid openings are increasing in number—threatening, as some believe, the middle class and even the stability of American democracy.[35]

Economists find that the distribution of men's earnings, from lowest- to the best-paid workers, grew less equal in the later 1970s and 1980s, reversing earlier trends.[36] Affluent workers are making markedly more money, although the low-paid are not making less. The reason is partly higher unemployment and the shift of jobs from manufacturing to services, which means a decline in relative wages for the low-skilled. Inequality is also rising within industries, together with the premium earned by the college-educated. Another cause is the weakened positions of unions.[37] The income of families has also become more unequal, in this case with the worst-off suffering losses in absolute terms, not only relative to the rich. By one reckoning, between 1973 and 1988, the poorest fifth of families lost 6 percent of real income, while the most affluent fifth gained 15 percent. As a result, the share of all family income claimed by the poorest fifth, only 4 percent in 1973, fell to 3.5 percent in 1988, while the share claimed by the most affluent fifth jumped from 44 to 47 percent.[38]

Liberal analysts connect these changes directly to conservative public policies. The trend to inequality accelerated in the 1980s, in their view, because a major objective of the Reagan administration was to shift income and wealth toward the rich. Reagan is said to have accomplished this through a combination of tax giveaways to business and Wall Street, shifts toward a more regressive tax structure, cuts in programs for the poor, looser regulation of industries, and a combination of lower inflation and massive debt that bid up returns to investors. It was a triumph for the classic procapitalist, antigovernment position that conservatives take in progressive politics.[39] Some liberal politicians would like to restore "smokestack America" to its position of primacy in the economy, shift the advantages of tax and benefit policy away from the affluent, and, above all, restore steady growth in earnings and family incomes. It is no accident that Michael Dukakis's most consistent promise during the 1988 presidential campaign was to create more "good jobs at good wages."[40]

THE SKEPTICS REPLY

Many economists find the indictment in the last section overdrawn. They regard slowed productivity as serious, but believe it may prove transient. They believe that the problem is partly due to the baby boom generation and larger numbers of women going to work, introducing many inexperienced workers into the labor force. The baby boomers crowded the labor market in the 1970s, bidding wages down. As these workers mature and gain skills, it is argued, productivity and wages are likely to improve,[41] although to date there has been little evidence of this.

The other problems are less substantial, and the plight of workers thrown out of work by deindustrialization has been exaggerated. U.S. Department of Labor surveys of workers displaced during the period 1979–85 showed that they numbered only 5.1 million workers, or less than 5 percent of the average labor force in these years. Sixty percent or more were already reemployed at the time of the surveys; only a quarter or less remaining unemployed. Reemployment rates for former manufacturing workers and the hard-hit Midwest fell only slightly below the norm. And while many workers did have to take wage cuts to get new jobs, the majority of full-time workers made as much money in their new positions as in the old.[42] In the later 1980s, manufacturing actually revived and showed the highest productivity gains of any sector, although manufacturing employment and wages have not returned to prior levels.[43]

The trend toward more part-time jobs goes back to 1973 and is largely benign. The reasons for it are mostly noneconomic, not a lack of full-time jobs. It is true that part-time employment grew rapidly during the recession of 1981–82, but as the economy recovered, full-time employment again became the norm.[44] Secondary workers such as teenagers and wives want flexible schedules to accommodate school or homemaking duties. In 1985, less than a third of part-time workers held such jobs involuntarily, and only 12 percent did so because they could find only part-time work.[45] Wages for part-time work seem only slightly lower than what the same workers would earn full-time; for women, they may even be higher. The main drawback is less coverage by health and pension plans.[46]

There is little reason to blame the expansion of services employment for recent low wages. This sector often pays low entry-level wages, but it also includes the lion's share of managers and professionals in the economy, who are usually well-paid. Services appear less desirable mainly because of the prevalence of part-time work, which, again, is mostly transient and voluntary. Indeed, service industries have dominated the economy ever since World War II. They became controversial when income growth stopped in the 1970s, but in fact, that problem had little connection to services.[47]

After various technical corrections, most economists now see some growth in family incomes after 1973, though certainly less than in earlier years. Growth fell in the late 1970s and early 1980s, but returned in the late 1980s.[48] Median family income rose 20 percent between 1970 and 1986, although fortunes varied widely among families, with the elderly, families with steady workers, and the affluent doing much better than female-headed families, the nonworking, and those with lower incomes.[49] In addition, other indicators of well-being, such as standards of health, housing, and nutrition, continued to improve through the 1970s.[50]

Income per capita has risen more quickly than earnings per worker, because more members of families have gone to work to keep up with rising prices, while the size of families has fallen. Especially wives and other women have taken jobs in record numbers, allowing the majority of families to keep ahead of inflation. Of course, when both parents work, the upbringing of children receives less attention. Some of rising income is financed out of debt, and there is less saving. In these senses, the nation is borrowing against the future, but in the short-term it is better off.[51]

While a drift toward inequality is undeniable, the extent is disputed. Assessments of the trend are sensitive to the assumptions made; by some methods of calculation, the wage distribution shows little polarization, only an across-the-board trend toward better-paying jobs. While high-paid manufacturing workers clearly were humbled, the troubled years also abolished a great many low-paid jobs, for instance in textiles, apparel, and agriculture. And while high-paid, high-tech occupations are growing rapidly, they remain as yet too small to spread out the earnings distribution very much. If male workers are becoming less equal in earnings, women are becoming more so.[52] Recessions accentuated inequality, and the further the economy got beyond the downturns of the 1970s and early 1980s, the better the situation looked. In the period 1983–89, the years of the Reagan boom, both the richest *and* the poorest fifth of families gained about 12 percent in income.[53]

Rising inequality appears to be a problem concentrated in a few groups of workers, especially men aged twenty-five to thirty-four with no more than a high school education[54] and workers in the states most impacted by the decline of manufacturing after 1979. For these workers deindustrialization means a district loss in earnings and status. Withdrawal from work by the least-paid workers explains nearly all the trend toward higher unemployment since the 1960s. For the rest of the labor force and the economy, the trends are much more ambiguous, and the future more hopeful.[55]

The prophets of polarization have overgeneralized from the plight of the smokestack industries. "To some extent," says Robert Samuelson, an economic journalist, "the experience of auto and steel workers has been magnified into a false metaphor for the entire economy." The problem is not so much greater inequality in present incomes as an "inequality of prospects." As young workers look to the future, many doubt they will ever experience the steady increases in wealth that their parents enjoyed.[56]

HARD TIMES AND POVERTY

Whatever the extent of hard times and inequality, do these developments affect poverty? Very little, the facts suggest. Critics on the left too quickly conflate the problems of poverty and dependency with those of the declining factory. Both workers and the poor are too easily taken for victims of economic collapse and the Reagan administration. In the words of one radical economist:

> The joint appearance of fleets of stretch limousines and hundreds of thousands of homeless in the streets of our major cities in the 1980s is an indictment of a failed economic program—a program that promised to stimulate productive investment... and well paying jobs. The widening income gap between the rich and the rest... is paralleled by a disturbing rise in racial tensions and [a]... reversal of black gains in access to jobs and education.[57]

From this traditional viewpoint, workers and the poor are both victims of a lack of opportunity, just as they were in the Depression. The new poverty is really no different from the old.[58]

It is true that the poverty rate fluctuates according to economic conditions, rising during recessions and falling during recoveries. The poverty rate for the nonelderly fell during the 1960s, changed little during the 1970s, then rose during the early 1980s—all in step with trends in prosperity and family income. Together, movements in the unemployment rate and wages predict movements in poverty quite closely, and this is true for single- as well as two-parent poor families. The poverty rate, it would seem, is "basically tracking the performance of the economy."[59]

However, this means only that sufficient working poor still exist so that overall poverty levels react to the economy. It does not mean that hard times explain the bulk of poverty—that the rest of the adult poor only await "good times" to go to work. To mix a metaphor, the working poor are the icing atop a large and nonworking cake. By conventional economic logic, lower real wages should mean expanded employment for the worst-paid workers, because they become less costly to employ; in reality, these workers show higher jobless rates than better-paid, costlier workers, including those most exposed to deindustrialization.[60] The main determinant of whether disadvantaged workers are employed is not the unemployment rate, it is factors outside the economy, such as the size of a person's welfare benefits and whether the individual did well in school or had working parents.[61]

Much the same is true of welfare dependency. Economic conditions exert only a minor influence. Applications for welfare have risen in the current recession, most typically for people in temporary economic trouble,[62] but the bulk of the rolls at any given time are composed of longer-term cases with little connection to the economy. Dependency was much more responsive to economic conditions before 1960, when levels of working poverty were higher. As Daniel Moynihan first noted, the close link of the AFDC rolls to unemployment was broken in the 1960s, when dependency exploded even though joblessness was low. Since the early 1970s, the rolls have remained at 10–11 million people, varying little in good times or bad.[63]

If hard times were a serious cause of poverty, we would expect to find a large overlap between workers who encounter employment problems and the poor. We do not. Less than 17 percent of workers experienced unemployment in 1985, and of these only 21 percent were poor. Conversely, of all poor adults in the same year, only 15 percent reported any unemployment. Less than a third of employees who worked part-time in 1985 did so involuntarily, and only 19 percent of these were poor. Less than 6 percent of full-year, full-time workers earned less than the minimum wage, and of these less than a third were poor. Poverty is not much higher even among workers with multiple and lasting work problems.[64]

The overlap between dependency and work problems is also quite limited. Only 19 percent of people receiving cash welfare reported any labor market difficulties in 1985, most often unemployment. Conversely, of all those reporting such problems, less than 6 percent were on welfare. Indeed, only 41 percent of those with employment problems received government assistance of any kind, most usually Unemployment Insurance.[65]

The reason employment difficulties have so little to do with poverty or welfare is that in order to encounter such problems, one must at least be trying to work. Since most poor or dependent adults are not working or seeking work, they are less likely to encounter these difficulties than the more affluent. They, and the nation, would be better off if they had *more* problems trying to work than they do.

The poor, particularly, are seldom victims of deindustrialization. Displaced industrial workers rarely become the jobless poor of the inner city. It is true that fewer displaced blacks than whites found new employment easily, but even that gap has closed over time.[66] Few very poor or homeless men in the cities held good jobs before falling into destitution.[67] Deindustrialization of whites and blacks alike appears to be going on over the heads of the poor. They have hardly participated in the struggle over industrial America. The contestants are mostly better-off workers who, whatever their problems, are seldom poor or dependent for long periods.

Differences in work effort explain much of the economic inequality among families, and also why inequality has grown.[68] Among individual workers, greater inequality seems to derive mostly from growing differences in wages paid, not in working hours.[69] Among families, however, the main problem seems to be increasing numbers of adults not working at all. The major reason family income has become more unequal, according to one calculation, is that the bottom fifth of families earned 11 percent less in 1987 than in 1979 while the top fifth earned 13 percent more, a change that dwarfed all other changes in income, including shifts in government benefits and taxes.[70] The reduction in work effort in turn is linked to increasing breakup of families and withdrawal of men from the labor force, especially among the poor. Low-skilled men are most frequently unemployed and outside the labor force for reasons unrelated to the fluctuations of employment conditions that we associate with the business cycle. These trends go back to the prosperous 1960s and show no clear relationship to the economy.[71]

White Americans typically earn more than blacks for many reasons, among them higher skills and wages, but a divergence in work effort appears to be the main reason that gap persists. Between 1960 and 1970, black median family income rose from 55 percent of white median family income to 61 percent, as working blacks gained from equal opportunity reforms and a growing economy. By 1980, the proportion fell back to 58 percent, mainly because average work levels among black families fell, largely due to increased breakup of families and nonwork among the poor. The figure has since changed little, despite the recession and boom of the 1980s; it was still 57 percent in 1988.[72]

The polarization that has occurred among blacks is directly tied to employment. With strenuous work effort, better-off blacks pull themselves into the middle class. Among black families with both parents, three-quarters are actually in the upper three-fifths of the income distribution,[73] chiefly because both parents work. The bottom third of black society remains poor mostly because it contains the lion's share of long-term welfare mothers and nonworking men.

PROSPERITY AND POVERTY

If hard times were the fundamental cause of poverty, we would expect better times to be the solution, but they are not. As noted earlier, the poverty rate dropped only 2 percentage points during the Reagan boom, to 13 percent. Not only conservatives counted on growth to reduce poverty. It has long been an article of faith among Washington economists, most of them liberals, that "Slack labor markets and poverty tend to go hand in hand." The 1980s created a distinctly tight labor market. When poverty fell only slightly, the same experts expressed surprise.[74]

Reports from around the country dramatized how easily the return of prosperity bypasses the new, nonworking poor. In New York City, the poverty rate actually rose, to nearly a quarter of the population, between 1986 and 1987, despite forceful economic growth. Milwaukee has rebounded from deindustrialization, increasing employment by 83,000 jobs since 1979, yet unemployment and welfare have actually risen in ghetto areas; black men stand idle on street corners saying they cannot find work, while all around them other people hustle to their jobs.[75] The most remarkable case may be Atlantic City, New Jersey, where billions of dollars have been invested in new hotels and resorts since casino gambling became legal in 1976. In that time, 41,000 new jobs have been created—more than the entire city's population. The city should have become affluent, yet it has collapsed from within. Crime is rampant, and, as residents flee, the population has shrunk 20 percent. The number of homeless people has exploded. Dependency has risen to the point where half the remaining population is on welfare.[76]

Growth, to be sure, is not without good effects. In a city like Boston, which for much of the 1980s enjoyed an exceedingly "hot" economy, poverty declined and minorities made gains in employment. In 1988, the jobless rate for black men dropped below 6 percent in Boston, compared to 15 percent nationwide, and 71 percent of black men were working in the city, compared to 60 percent nationally. These rates approached the national rates for whites.[77] Joblessness among teenagers and the young does respond to economic conditions.[78] Between 1983 and 1987, unemployment among youth with no more than a high school education, who were out of school, dropped 10 percentage points in cities where the general unemployment rate was under 4 percent. For blacks in this category, the fall was a startling 33 points, from about 40 percent joblessness to 7 percent, and blacks also made the sharpest growth in earnings.[79] Some have taken these findings to show that a strong economy is, after all, the answer to poverty—that "a rising tide lifts all boats."

But nearly all of the impact was on youth who were already looking for work, and who therefore were unlikely to be poor. The rate at which youth participated in the labor force did not change much; it actually fell in most cities during the period 1983–87. Only in the case of blacks in cities with unemployment under 4 percent did the rate clearly rise, and only by 6 percentage points, to 79 percent; thus, 21 percent were not even looking for work, and these were the youth most at risk of poverty and dependency.[80] Economic conditions matter, but they account, at best, for a third of the large employment difference between black and white youth.[81] A growing economy can do only so much to solve the social problem.

THE RESPONSE TO ADVERSITY

Poverty and dependency do not, apparently, follow directly from low wages or hard times. A changing economy seems to depress some wages, but not to keep many people out of jobs long-term. Indeed, it is unclear even in theory whether hard times should produce more work effort or less. Falling wages, economists say, have two contrary effects, one tending to produce more work effort and the other less. Work becomes more necessary but less worthwhile. Lower wages reduce a family's income, generating pressure to work more hours to make up the difference, but at the same time employment pays less per hour worked, creating an incentive to work less. The first is called the income effect, the second the substitution effect. The effects reverse direction if wages rise; higher incomes mean less pressure to work, but employment pays more if one does work.

The notable fact about recent economic history is that the income effect dominated for the middle class, the substitution effect among the poor. Middle-class Americans reacted to stagnant earnings in recent decades by working harder. American workers today put in more hours of employment, and take fewer hours off, than employees in most other industrialized countries. Women increased their effort even more than men. Among middle-income couples with children, the share of income coming from secondary workers (usually wives) rose from 14 to 21 percent in the years 1970–86. Middle-income single mothers relied even more heavily on employment: Their earnings accounted for 48 percent of their income in 1970, rising to 62 percent in 1986, while the share coming from welfare fell from 22 to 16 percent. At the same time, low-income single mothers were working less. The share of their incomes coming from earnings fell from 33 to 21 percent during the period 1970–86, while the share coming from welfare rose from 45 to 65 percent, despite the fact that the value of welfare benefits fell. The worst-paid male workers reacted to falling wages by reducing their working time 16 percent since the late 1960s.[82]

The middle class and the poor appear to exemplify two different economic personalities. The first has responded to adversity with greater effort, the other with less. Why would poor adults *reduce* their work effort in hard times, especially if dependency is the price? One welfare mother explained:

"I'm not happy about being on AFDC...but I need it for him," said Rhonda Jackson, 25, of West Oakland, as she cuddles 2-year-old Montay while waiting for her welfare check to arrive in the mail. "I've had a few small-time jobs, but I quit them because I couldn't even make ends meet. So I just try to make it the best way I can and trust in the Lord."[83]

Why does one *quit* work when one cannot make ends meet? It is not a reaction that struggling middle-class Americans are likely to understand.

These different responses dramatize the real issue behind the ongoing debate about low wages and hard times—competing judgments about human nature. Liberal interpreters tend to take the response of the poor to disappointing wages as the natural one. They say, in effect, that poor adults fail to work consistently because of a sense of relative deprivation. The "dirty," low-paid jobs they can get are worth so much less to them, in both pay and self-esteem, than the jobs of the better-off that they end up working little or not at all. It is low wages *in combination* with this sort of demoralization that produces nonwork. As Patricia Spakes says, "How does one . . . lower the aspirations of a person and convince him or her that a low-paying, dead-end job is all he or she can expect, without destroying that person's motivation to work at all?" Disappointed people cannot be expected to behave rationally and take the available jobs. Instead, they may well injure themselves with crime or pregnancy. According to Ruth Sidel, "If a young woman's realistic choices are between working as a waitress . . . or in a sweatshop . . . or behind the counter in a fast-food restaurant, who can blame her for choosing or just happening to have a baby?"[84]

Conservatives, in contrast, take the response of the middle class as normal. They see the poor as potential economic maximizers who could and should buck up and work harder. The poor, conservatives believe, are as motivated as other people to make money and advance themselves. They can do this by making the best of whatever opportunities come to them. They should not compare themselves to the more fortunate, but simply seize the best jobs available and escape poverty and welfare. They should not be disheartened but keep "getting ahead."

Note that both assumptions about personality are independent of whether opportunity is meager or generous. The poor could feel relative deprivation no matter how good their jobs were, provided only that other people had better jobs. Conversely, they might behave as self-reliant optimizers in any kind of society, no matter how unjust. If one believes the poor are competent in this sense, one will suppose they could make it even in the most backward Third World country. Milton Friedman's favorite image of capitalism is Hong Kong, where hardworking Chinese, many from peasant backgrounds, have diiven themselves to prosperity under a laissez-faire regime.[85]

It is clear that low wages and hard times fail to account for most poverty unless one credits the poor with less capacity to help themselves than most Americans assume. A poor class too demoralized to work has daunting implications. Social progress in America does not depend on prosperity. The national project—advancing ordinary people—goes forward in bad times as well as good. It may simply go forward more slowly. If the economy does not achieve mobility, government may well try to do so. However, progress absolutely depends on the poor being employed. Only then can they gain from the economy or from whatever government does to improve earnings.

Are Jobs Available?

Almost every unemployed person can now find a job in
a very short time.
—MARTIN FELDSTEIN
"THE ECONOMICS OF THE NEW UNEMPLOYMENT"
THE PUBLIC INTEREST

I came to this country [in 1983], and the next day I was
working.
—DOMINICAN IMMIGRANT CAB DRIVER
NEW JERSEY, JULY 1989

LOW wages, that is, job quality, are one possible cause of poverty.
Another possibility is job quantity—could the poor work even if they
took jobs at any level? In a word, are jobs "available"? Among experts, this issue draws even more attention than the decline of good
jobs at good wages.[1] If jobs are lacking, nonwork by the poor is
an indictment of society. If jobs exist, but are simply not taken, the
current drift of social policy toward regulating the behavior of the
poor becomes unavoidable. As one critic observes, the availability of
jobs is the "empirical centerpiece" of the argument for workfare.[2]
Certainty is elusive, but most of the evidence suggests that at least
low-paid work is usually readily available, at least to those seeking
work at a given time.

The public tends to believe that jobs exist. It sees stable welfare
rolls in an age when the employed proportion of the population
is the highest ever and many employers are strapped for unskilled
labor. In New York City, I watched an older black man hustle past a
younger one, who was panhandling. "If I can get a job in this town,"
the older man muttered under his breath, "he can too. I've been

a super [an apartment house custodian] for twenty-five years. Why, in my home town [Durham, North Carolina], if you can't get a job, they have a work farm where they'll put you to work."[3] That kind of feeling explains why the public thinks workfare is such a good idea.

But among experts and in Washington, the assertion that jobs are available remains controversial. As in the last chapter, "facts" do not settle the issue. The underlying issue is again competence. What is a "job" and who is a "worker"? The right and the left tend to define these terms so that one side finds jobs are plentiful, the other scarce.

WHY THERE IS DOUBT

Since the availability of jobs seems a critical issue, one might expect government to collect statistics on the subject. It does not. It gathers data on unemployment, that is, on workers without jobs, but not on jobs without workers.[4] According to a few special surveys, vacancies comprised something less than 1 percent of all jobs in the early 1970s, and a little over 1 percent in the early 1980s.[5] At a point in time in this period, for every vacancy, 3 to 5 unemployed people sought work. Only national unemployment rates in the 3 to 4 percent range—much lower than actual—would bring the two figures into line.[6] The disproportion increases if one adds to the unemployed, who are seeking work, and other groups who might be expected to work, such as welfare recipients.[7] There is some evidence that the labor market became tighter over the 1970s.[8] Findings like this give reason to doubt that all the jobless poor could go to work at once even if they wanted to.

All depends, however, on the turnover in the vacancies and in those seeking them. If fresh jobs came on the market every month, but the number of jobless did not change, the openings would soon occupy all the jobless even if the latter were initially much more numerous. Conversely, if jobs did not increase while the jobless turned over as people gave up looking for work, the disproportion of job seekers to openings would be even greater than it seems to be. In other words, how fast the hiring queue moves is more important than its length. What counts is not how many people appear to be competing for jobs but how long they actually remain jobless. As I will show, time out of work is short for the great majority of unemployed.

In addition, the evidence indicates that when more people seek work, additional jobs are created. When available jobs are taken quickly and held, more wealth flows into the community, and the resulting spending creates further jobs. Employers will locate in areas where willing but underemployed workers are known to exist. The supply of labor, therefore, tends in part to create its own demand.[9]

What about the unemployment rate, so prominently reported every month? This measures the percentage of the labor force (defined to include those working plus those looking for work) that has taken active steps to obtain work in the previous four weeks but remains jobless. Politicians and liberal analysts tend to regard rates up to about 3 percent as healthy, due to normal turnover as workers change jobs, but higher rates suggest a job shortage.

Unfortunately, unemployment as officially defined tells us very little about job availability. To qualify as unemployed by the official definition, the jobless need only be looking for a job. They do not have to accept offers that come to them. They could be offered any number of positions, but decline them for inadequate pay or conditions, and remain classified as unemployed, provided they keep looking. Thus, the unemployment rate may overstate the proportion of job seekers for whom jobs are completely unavailable. On the other hand, the rate may understate the proportion, because "discouraged" workers, who want jobs but have given up looking, are regarded as outside the labor force, rather than unemployed.[10]

Without systematic information, the dispute over job availability falls back on anecdotes. On the one hand, when government agencies or large firms hire workers, hundreds of people often line up to apply. In New York City in 1987–88, openings for teacher's aides, nurse's aides, and manufacturing workers were vastly oversubscribed. Critics of the economy take this as proof that sufficient jobs do not exist for the low-skilled. On the other hand, jobs in some government programs have gone begging. "A recent ghetto renovation project in Newark, New Jersey," reports one conservative journalist, "couldn't attract local workers at $5 or $6 an hour and ended up importing union labor from the suburbs."[11] Defenders of capitalism take that as proof that the poor could find jobs, but will not take them.

Judgment ultimately hinges on how one reads the intentions and capabilities of the jobless. Do they seek out new work in an urgent, dutiful way, rapidly accepting the best job they can find, as politicians commonly assume? If so, then any substantial unemployment would indicate a lack of jobs. But what if the jobless demand better jobs than the economy offers them or are simply too incompetent to hire?

Then the same unemployment rate becomes an indictment of the workers instead of the economy.

The public, it is interesting to note, gives some credence to each of these possibilities. In a survey taken in 1982, 51 percent of respondents said the main reason for unemployment was lack of jobs (it was a recession year), but 26 percent said job seekers did not want to work, and 21 percent said they lacked skills. In a later survey, during better times in 1988, only 37 percent said private-sector jobs were lacking for the poor, 49 percent that they were available.[12] Far from settling the jobs issue, the unemployment rate is a conundrum that may or may not allow us to trace nonwork to impersonal causes.

Certainly, the poor have much higher unemployment than average. In March 1990, the unemployment rate among poor heads of family was 20 percent, compared to only 4 percent for all family heads. Liberals take this as prima facie evidence that the poor cannot find jobs as easily as other people. To conservatives, however, it is more notable that so few of the poor family heads were even in the labor force, that is, either working or looking for work—49 percent compared to 75 percent for the population at large.[13] Was this because they could not find jobs and stopped trying, or because they would not or could not take jobs available to them?

TRENDS IN THE LABOR MARKET

Given the paucity of data, analysts infer what they can from broader trends in the labor market. Each side has an argument, but the conservative viewpoint is more plausible.

Job pessimists argue that the repeated recessions since 1970 caused high unemployment. In the 1970s, with the energy crisis and stagflation, the boom of the postwar era came to an end. The recession of the early 1980s, the most severe since the Great Depression, gave the *coup de grace* to the confident prosperity Americans had come to assume. The jobless rate for the general population, only 3.5 percent in 1969, rose steadily thereafter, reaching nearly 10 percent in 1982 and 1983. While the Reagan years fostered a kind of recovery, it rested on weak foundations—a huge spending deficit and borrowing from abroad.

Just as worrisome was the enormous growth in the labor force due to the surge of women coming to work, the maturing of the baby boom generation, and the rise in the rate of labor force participation. The number of Americans working or looking for work grew by 13 million in the 1960s, then by an astounding 24 million in the 1970s, and another 18 million in the 1980s—rates of increase of 19, 29, and 17 percent. Over thirty years, the labor force rose by 55 million or 79 percent—an unprecedented increase.[14]

According to the pessimists, the economy could not absorb such a horde; the unemployment rate shot up and remains unacceptably high. The labor market, according to sociologist Fred Block, is "dangerously overcrowded." A burgeoning labor force competes for a more slowly growing number of jobs. It is a struggle the poor inevitably lose, as they have the fewest skills and thus stand at the back of the hiring queue. The market is slack as well, according to economist Bradley Schiller, because of "low levels of aggregate demand," and as long as this persists, "we must expect high unemployment rates and the resulting poverty." A "labor shortage," wrote Michael Harrington, "...would probably do more to eliminate poverty...than all other policies combined."[15]

Job optimists say, to the contrary, that jobs are plentiful. The doleful picture painted by the pessimists is exaggerated or passé. The very fact that labor force participation increased among adults in recent decades proves that jobs were widely available. While the recession of the early 1980s was indeed severe, the subsequent boom reduced unemployment almost to 5 percent, the lowest level since 1970, and below what many economists consider full employment. The increase in work effort by women has about reached its limit, and the "baby bust"—the smaller cohort of young workers resulting from lower birthrates in the 1960s—has succeeded the baby boom. Relative to the recent past, the flood of new workers has slowed to a trickle.

At the same time, the economy has generated jobs on a scale never before seen anywhere in the world. Employment grew 20 percent during the 1960s, 26 percent during the 1970s, despite all the troubles of that decade, and a further 19 percent in the 1980s. This prodigious job creation almost equaled the enormous growth in the labor force in the same period. Unquestionably, the labor force outpaced employment during the 1970s and early 1980s, but employment grew considerably faster than the labor force in the late 1980s. The growth came mainly in small- and medium-sized firms and was one benefit of deindustrialization. There may be fewer well-paid factory jobs than before, but there are a lot more nonunion jobs at low and moderate wages. As a result, employers can afford to hire many more people with limited skills.[16] To have absorbed so many new workers was a stupendous achievement for both government and society, one Americans take too much for granted.[17]

Demographic trends point toward a tight labor market in the future. The Labor Department projects that the labor force and employed workers will each grow by 21 million between 1986 and the end of the century. That correspondence is no accident. Jobs cannot grow more rapidly than the number of workers available to fill them. Slower growth in the labor force has already begun to crimp the growth of the economy.[18] "For the first time in two decades," remarked Samuel Ehrenhalt, the Department of Labor commissioner for New York, in 1988, "the help-wanted sign has replaced the unemployment line as the dominant symbol of the labor market."[19]

The recent boom sparked many stories of labor shortages, particularly in New England and the suburbs. Jobs at all levels went begging, and economists worried that the shortage would cut economic growth or raise inflation as firms bid up wages to attract workers. Employers went to extraordinary lengths to find even unskilled workers, offering extra benefits, time off, and transportation. They took to hiring the elderly, underage teens, university students from Europe, and the retarded.[20]

The current recession has temporarily cooled the labor market, but the slow growth of the labor force has helped to hold the monthly jobless rate to below 7 percent, well under the double-digit level of the last recession a decade ago.[21] The main public complaint is no longer joblessness but rather stagnant incomes, due to the country's long-term productivity problem, which have pinched middle-class life-styles. It is a sign of the times that the current unemployment is hitting higher-skilled managers and professionals as much as or more than the low-skilled; they have become more expendable. A chronic shortage of jobs can be seen only in some rural areas, due to the depopulation of parts of the Midwest and the shift of population toward the coasts and the Sunbelt.[22]

Overall, the optimists have the better of the trends debate. In most times and places, the current labor market clearly favors workers. They have too many choices for employers to be able to crack the whip. In The Grapes of Wrath, Steinbeck's novel of the Depression, the Joad family journeyed to California desperately seeking any work it could find, even stoop labor in the fields. This image of unemployment as a calamity inflicted on willing workers by a hostile economy still prevails in politics. But today, apple growers in New York and Vermont must bring in migrant workers from Jamaica to harvest their crops. They attest to labor officials that "There is absolutely no local labor available to pick apples."[23]

IMMIGRATION

The Jamaicans bring to mind another fact—heavy immigration—that strongly suggests that unskilled employment is plentiful in the United States. More foreigners want to come to this country than any other, and they come mainly because the opportunity to support their families is widely available.

Immigration to the United States has lately returned to the high levels seen at the turn of the century, although the flow, then mostly from Europe, is now mostly from the Third World. More than 3 million foreigners were admitted to the country legally in the 1960s, more than 4 million in the 1970s, and around 5 million in the 1980s, when well over half a million people arrived every year.[24] Millions more entered illegally, mostly from Mexico and other Latin American countries. The illegals have been estimated at as high as 15 million, and there may be a million or more in the New York area alone.[25] The Census estimate is 2 to 6 million.[26]

It used to be thought that the illegals were mainly migrant workers like the Joads and Jamaicans, performing low-paid chores on the fringes of the economy. That may have been the case at one time, but due to the labor shortage, illegals are increasingly getting much better paid jobs in the cities. They are also often thought to be exploited—made to work below the minimum wage, for example, because they cannot claim the protection of U.S. law. In fact, their average pay is about 60 percent of prevailing wages, and only a quarter of them are paid less than the minimum, mainly in agriculture and domestic work.[27]

As every urban American knows, foreigners have taken over many of the low-skilled jobs at the bottom of the economy. One might imagine that high school dropouts should be driving taxicabs in American cities, since it is a job they could do, but today the drivers are often Arabs or Africans who can barely speak English. Seventy-seven percent of those applying recently for new hack licenses in New York City were born outside the continental United States. Other trades where aliens figure heavily include cleaning office buildings at night, kitchen work in restaurants, caring for the children of the middle class, and low-wage manufacturing employment.[28]

This situation might mean, not that jobs are widely available, but that the aliens have beaten the domestic poor out of the openings that exist. Some suppose that unskilled Americans cannot compete for jobs against illegals who, by the nature of their situation, are willing to do anything to get work. Some employers do see aliens as "superworkers," preferable to Americans, who are likelier to be uppity. Yet overall, there appears to be little conflict. Statistical studies do not find that blacks are losing jobs to aliens. Blacks are doing no worse in the areas where immigration is high, such as the Southwest, than in those where it is lower. Rather, by taking jobs that neither whites nor blacks want, immigrants appear to improve the economy for everyone[29]—another indication that there is considerable room in the labor market for low-skilled workers.

Employers agree that the aliens are indispensable. According to Edwin Reubens, "In New York City, businessmen in garment manufacturing, laundries, restaurants, and other fields have flatly stated that if it were not for the illegals, they would have to close up. Businessmen and their attorneys in Miami, Houston, and Los Angeles agree." Employers who are raided by the government for hiring illegal workers scoff at the notion of replacing them with jobless citizens. Declared one manager in the Bronx, "I can't recall one American coming in here and asking me for a job." According to another, in Brooklyn, "American citizens don't want to work for the minimum wage." The head of a furniture company on Long Island protested that "my unskilled jobs go begging if aliens don't take them."[30]

The public is guarded about immigration, with a plurality favoring restrictions, but concerns about employment are not uppermost. According to one poll, 34 percent of Americans say immigrants are taking jobs from citizens, but 52 percent say they are taking jobs Americans do not want. Only 15 percent say that they themselves fear job competition from illegals. The proportion with this concern was surprisingly low even among Hispanics (26 percent), blacks (29 percent), and people with low income (23 percent), the groups in the most direct competition with aliens.[31] If there were clearer signs of a struggle for work between immigrants and poor Americans at the bottom of society, the notion that jobs are lacking would be a lot more credible.

Pressure to restrict immigration largely reflects cultural concerns, especially the fear that a flood of Hispanics will turn the country into a bilingual society. In 1986, Congress enacted the Immigration Reform and Control Act, designed to restrict illegal immigration by penalizing employers for hiring illegals. But such is the pull of available jobs in the United States, along with enforcement problems, that the illegal tide has barely slowed. In 1990, business persuaded Congress to expand legal immigration by over 35 percent in order to bring in more workers with needed skills.[32]

The immigration experience disproves the contention that the U.S. economy systematically creates fewer jobs than there are workers to fill them. That is what is happening in the Third World, where stagnant employment cannot keep up with rapidly growing populations. In the United States, the economy is outgrowing the labor force, and immigration is a safety valve. With birth rates low among the native-born, the influx from abroad now accounts for much of American population growth.

The newcomers appear to have no doubt that jobs exist. One young man from El Salvador told James Fallows in Houston that "he could not understand all the talk about unemployment. Why, he himself was holding three jobs."[33]

THE NATURE OF UNEMPLOYMENT

It would be misleading to rest the case for job availability too heavily on the recent labor market. There will be recessions, as there is at this writing. When unemployment rises enough to become a political issue, are jobs still available? There is evidence they are, at least to those seeking work at a given moment. Much of joblessness is apparently voluntary, in the strict sense that job hunters often could find some job. However, they often feel free to decline available openings in hopes of finding better, or in favor of not working. They are *shopping* for jobs, with the option not to buy, rather than *searching* for them with the urgency suggested by Depression images of unemployment.

The decision to seek work often seems to reflect choice as much as necessity. Politicians speak of the unemployed as having been "thrown out of work" by impersonal economic forces, but on average, during the period 1970–90, only 48 percent of the unemployed had lost their jobs. The figure exceeded half only in recession years. Of losers, during the 1980s, a quarter or more were laid off with some prospect of recall, not totally separated from their positions. In contrast, 52 percent of the jobless became unemployed by choice, either because they quit their jobs (13 percent) or had just entered the labor force and begun to seek work (40 percent).[34] Transitions in and out of the labor force, not in and out of jobs, now largely determine the level of unemployment.

One could argue that people who leave the labor force but still want work should be counted among job seekers, but few such "discouraged" workers appear to have much commitment to working. When surveyed, only a third of them report holding a job, or even looking for one, in the previous year, and a year later over 60 percent are still outside the labor force. Rather than workers with a recent employment history, most of the discouraged are teenagers seeking their first jobs or women thinking about returning to work after a period of childrearing.[35]

A further fact that makes unemployment look soft is that it is usually transient. On average, during the period 1970–90, 44 percent of the unemployed, when surveyed, said they had been out of work less than five weeks, and nearly three-quarters said fourteen weeks or less. Only 26 percent had been out of work fifteen weeks or longer, and only half of those for over six months. The longer-term proportion rises in bad times, but even in the worst year—1983—less than a quarter of the unemployed had been out of work over half a year.[36] In fact, most job seekers find jobs so quickly that *almost 70 percent of them are never recorded as unemployed at all.*[37] This means either that jobs are available on demand for most workers or that they can postpone entry into the labor force until a position turns up that they like.

The Department of Labor did a special survey of the jobless in May 1976. The results shattered the involuntary image of unemployment dear to the political process.[38] We tend to presume that those looking for work often must scale down their wage expectations in order to get a job. Actually, the average job seeker demands a 7 percent *raise* to go back to work, and even those who have lost jobs demand 3 percent more. Demands drop below previous wages for most people only after they have been out of work a year or more. Excluding the job losers who want a raise from the unemployed would reduce the jobless rate by more than a point, more than three points for blacks.[39]

Another sign that work is often a choice, not a necessity, was that only 30 percent of the jobless would commute more than twenty miles to a new job, and only a third would move to one. Especially for married women, maintaining ties to one's existing home, property, and friends often took priority over employment. Most of the jobless in the 1976 survey also had the resources to hold out for an attractive job. They dealt with lower income mainly by delaying major purchases and reducing expenses, less often by relying on savings or unemployment benefits. More demeaning steps such as asking help from friends or relatives, borrowing, or going on welfare were much less common.[40] Similar conclusions emerge from government surveys of displaced workers in the 1980s. These workers, thrown out of work by plant closings and cutbacks, are clearly job losers, yet only 13 or 14 percent of them moved to a different city or county. The majority obtained new employment in their old location.[41]

TURNOVER

If unemployment is usually brief, so also is employment. A great many Americans work only intermittently, spending most of the rest of the time out of the labor force.[42] This might mean that the economy is inhospitable to job seekers, but it seems rather to indicate that these workers are not committed to steady employment.

As Robert Hall says, economists, like politicians, used to think that unemployment was due to "a simple shortage of jobs." The jobless, say economists Kim B. Clark and Lawrence H. Summers, were seen as a "stagnant pool...awaiting a business upturn."[43] Unemployment was seen as long-term and Depression-like. There is still truth to this image. A minority of the jobless are out of work for months or years, and they account for most of unemployment as it is officially measured.[44] At any given time, the rolls of the unemployed, like the poor or the welfare-dependent, are dominated by the long-term cases.

But for most jobless people, as for most poor and dependent, adversity is brief. Most job seekers go in and out of unemployment quickly, and many also leave employment or the labor force quickly. The turnover is most prevalent among the groups—such as teenagers, women, and minorities—that also have the highest measured unemployment. Whites, men, and older workers show much greater stability. It appears that disadvantaged groups have as great a problem keeping jobs as they do in finding them. These workers exhibit what Hall termed "pathological instability in holding jobs."[45]

Turnover seems to be the main reason why the share of the jobless who receive Unemployment Insurance—nearly 60 percent in the early 1960s—has since fallen to only a third. Liberal analysts regret this trend, which they attribute mainly to benefit cuts and tougher administration in the Reagan era. While these were factors, the greater cause is probably that most of the unemployed no longer fit the involuntary image of joblessness required to qualify for Unemployment Insurance. The system covers only job losers, not those who quit their jobs or enter unemployment from outside the labor force, and it demands that claimants show "attachment to the labor force" by having worked most of the previous half-year. Job losers today are only a minority of the unemployed, and many people work too sporadically to build up the work history needed to claim benefits.[46]

One theory is that rising turnover simply reflects changes in the labor force. In the 1940s and 1950s, the work force was dominated by males of prime working age, usually heads of family, who typically worked steadily and left jobs reluctantly. When, starting in the 1960s, women and teenagers flooded into the labor force, they needed work that they could fit around prior commitments to children, family, and education. Secondary workers, who also surged in number, felt less pressure to work steadily than heads of family.[47] These forces, which underlie the recent rise in part-time employment, also explain why unemployment has softened.

More ominously, the turnover phenomenon has widened the separation between whites' economic fortunes and those of blacks, among whom job instability is much more common. According to Hall, "Blacks are 73 percent more likely to become unemployed than whites, and, if unemployed, are 25 percent less likely to leave unemployment," even when other differences are taken into account. Turnover makes it much more difficult for them to get their feet on the economic ladder.[48]

THE DUAL LABOR MARKET THEORY

It is largely to explain the instability of low-wage employment that liberal analysts have developed new theories of the labor market. They reject the implication that unemployment is voluntary, especially for minorities and the inner-city poor, arguing that these groups work so much less than normal that conclusions from studies dealing with the whole population, such as those cited above, cannot apply to them. The poor *must* face some special constraint.[49] The discussion so far has concerned the supply side of the labor market—the willingness of people to seek work. Liberals shift their focus to the demand side—the willingness of employers to hire the disadvantaged.

One theory describes the labor market as dual, or segmented, with a primary sector consisting of government, nonprofit organizations, and large firms, in which jobs are typically long-term and carry attractive pay and benefits, such as health insurance and pensions, and a secondary sector based on small firms where jobs are less secure, more poorly paid, and usually lack benefits. This sector includes many of the service industries—fast food, hotels—that have provided much of the new employment in the economy. Allegedly, poor workers suffer higher joblessness mainly because they are confined to this secondary sector. Hiring is institutionalized against them. Preferred employers usually hire from within their organizations or through unions that are themselves exclusive. When employers search more widely, they use race, gender, or formal education as screens to exclude most disadvantaged applicants without assessing individual skills or potential. The poor, female, and nonwhite are left to work in unattractive, menial jobs that tend to be transient, and this explains their high turnover and unemployment rates.[50]

Unskilled workers certainly do obtain less pleasant jobs than the better-off, and there is a lot of turnover in these positions. However, it has not been shown that people are slotted into these jobs arbitrarily. Statistical studies demonstrate that differences in earnings mainly reflect differences in the human capital—education, skills, and work experience—that workers bring to jobs. The main reason youth, women, and minorities are usually paid less than prime-aged white males is that, on average, they are younger, less experienced, and less educated. Many women also interrupt their careers for child-rearing. There is little evidence that low-paid groups are treated adversely apart from these factors.[51] Remaining discrimination against nonwhites appears to occur mainly within the primary sector rather than in low-skilled positions.[52]

The heart of the dual market theory is the conviction that the structure of employment is set by the economy before employees ever appear, and job turnover is forced on the poorest workers. If that were true, we would expect to find job instability dependent mainly on the features of jobs, not workers' own features.

In fact, personal characteristics are much more important. Young, female, unmarried, and black workers show more turnover regardless of where they work. Wage, industry, type of job, and whether the job is unionized make much less difference. Indeed, because women and blacks work disproportionately for government, their jobs should be *more* secure than average. Yet they leave work more often than men and whites.[53]

In a segmented labor market, there should be little or no upward mobility for poor workers. Even if they work hard they could never escape the menial, secondary market and get a "good" job. As Bradley Schiller puts it, "A poor janitor who works hard stands a very good chance of becoming a hard-working poor janitor."[54] Studies of workers' fortunes over time conclude differently. Disadvantaged groups have not become more equal to the better-off overall, but neither have individuals been denied all advancement. There is considerable mobility—up and down—within the income and job hierarchy for workers at all levels, including blacks. According to several economists, "There is no evidence that there are secure, protected niches in the economy," or that low-paid workers are "locked into dead-end jobs."[55]

The notion of the dead-end job misrepresents the nature of mobility in the economy. Most jobs are dead-end in the sense that any given employer usually offers employees only limited chances for promotion. Most workers move up, not by rising within the organization, but by leaving it and getting a better job elsewhere. Mobility comes not in a given job but from a work history that convinces each employer that the job seeker will be a reliable employee. Advancement is something workers must largely seek out for themselves, not something given to them by employers.

Perhaps young workers would get on the ladder if they could get better jobs to start with, but in fact, whether black youth work is little affected by how good a job they can get, if education and other personal factors are controlled for. Nor would better jobs clearly reduce their absenteeism when employed.[56] The jobs they can get are actually not much different from whites', since both races have to satisfy the same local economy. Among employed teenagers in inner cities in 1975, 40 percent of whites had white-collar jobs, but so did 37 percent of blacks. Both groups found white-collar jobs harder to find outside the cities. Yet black teens were unemployed at twice the rate of whites.[57] That is not something that a dual labor market can explain.

THE MISMATCH THEORY

According to a second theory, jobs of any quality are simply unavailable to the poor because of global changes in the economy. The marketplace may not discriminate against inner-city job seekers, yet jobs are simply out of their reach, either in the suburbs, where the poor cannot easily move or commute, or because they demand education and skills that poor job seekers lack. A spatial or skills "mismatch" has made jobs increasingly inaccessible.

In the 1950s and 1960s, many low-skilled men, including blacks, were able to make a stable, middle-class life for themselves, even though they often had not finished high school, by working in urban factory jobs. After 1970, despite job growth in the economy as a whole, the major cities experienced large job losses as manufacturing firms declined or shifted operations to the suburbs, the Sunbelt, or overseas. Low-skilled employment continued to grow rapidly outside the cities, but within them the new openings were largely white-collar jobs in newer, high-tech industries, such as computing, that required more education than most poor adults possess.

The result was catastrophic joblessness in the inner city followed by damaging social changes. Employed blacks increasingly left the inner city for the suburbs, draining it of social and financial resources. The remaining inhabitants lost models for regular employment and networks of the employed that could help them find jobs. The proportion of inner-city men who could support families fell, in turn causing women to bear children on welfare rather than marry and weakening the black family. The other social ills of the ghetto largely followed.

The theory is imaginative. It connects America's two leading social problems—the declining factory and the inner city. It offers a key to the central mystery of today's labor market—how inner-city areas can remain jobless and depressed when all around them society appears to be employed and prosperous. Mismatch may explain why an old city such as Camden, New Jersey, is desperately depressed, given over to welfare and crime, while in nearby suburbs, the Chamber of Commerce reports, "There isn't a retail store where a young person can't walk in and become instantly employed for at least $5 an hour."[58] The theory explains how nonwork could grow even when equal opportunity reforms have done all they can to open doors to the disadvantaged. Schooling levels are seen in this theory as a valid measure of employment skills, not as a screen used arbitrarily to exclude the poor. Where the dual labor market theory blamed joblessness on unfair institutions, the mismatch theory blames geography and meritocracy—barriers that are harder to call unjust, or to reform.

The theory is most associated with the work of the sociologists William Julius Wilson and John D. Kasarda,[59] but the basic idea is so plausible that it is often heard in popular discussions of the work problem. In Atlanta, where the suburbs are strapped for workers while black youth languish jobless in the ghetto, businessmen reason, "The biggest problem we face is finding ways for economically disadvantaged people from the core city to get to the suburbs, where the openings are." When Samuel Ehrenhalt of the Labor Department announces new unemployment figures for the New York region, he often blames high joblessness among youth and minorities on the "mismatch" between them and the available employment. In the San Francisco Bay area, a labor shortage of 45,000 is anticipated in Contra Costa County in the next twenty years, yet thousands of potential workers sit idle in nearby Oakland. "It's absurd, isn't it?" remarked one business analyst.[60]

However, to date, proponents of the theory have failed to demonstrate a causal connection between economic restructuring and nonwork. They speak mainly of high-level trends in the economy, of blue-collar jobs leaving the cities and workers becoming more educated and white-collar while at the same time work levels fall among blacks and the poor. It is clear that the farther jobs are located from the inner city, the less likely blacks are to hold them. It is also clear that the shift of the economy away from manufacturing has, somehow, reduced black employment more sharply than white.[61]

But it is treacherous to assume that the economic changes really cause nonwork.[62] The fall in employment might result from the population abandoning older cities, especially ghetto areas, rather than factories abandoning workers. The fact that well-off people are leaving faster than the poor, together with increases in overall poverty, largely accounts for increasing hardship in these cities.[63] It is not clear that lack of jobs is a factor. In fact, the population loss much exceeds the loss in jobs, so that the ability of the remaining poor to find employment in the inner city may actually be rising.[64]

Falling employment by the unskilled may simply mean that, due to rising education levels, there are fewer high school dropouts today trying to find jobs. Rather than the economy forcing unskilled workers out of jobs, unpleasant ghetto social conditions may be driving firms out of the cities. It was Nelson Rockefeller's opinion as governor of New York that the migration to the North of Southern blacks unprepared for city life was causing the "destruction of urban industrial America."[65] In Chicago, the main focus of mismatch inquiry, the social decay of black neighborhoods occurred mostly before 1970, the loss of jobs largely after that.[66]

Mismatch proponents say blacks are hurt more than whites when manufacturing industries leave inner cities, but the studies they cite are specific to the Midwest (Chicago, Detroit, St. Louis).[67] Black work levels are low in other areas as well. New York never had as much heavy industry as the Midwest, and blacks in New York never were highly reliant on manufacturing for employment, although Puerto Ricans were. Yet work levels today are low for both groups. Sectoral shifts cannot explain the worsening work problems of blacks in the city.[68]

Among the displaced workers of 1979–85 discussed above, there were only 670,000 blacks nationwide, 40 percent of them women, or 11–12 percent of all displaced workers. The number was also small compared to the 5 million black men who were working or the 600,000–900,000 who were unemployed every year in this period, not to mention the 3.4 million nonworking black poor.[69] For deindustrialization to explain low work levels for blacks as a whole, one would have to believe that the ouster of some black factory workers somehow caused much larger numbers of blacks across the country not to work at all.

The link between employment and marital stability and dependency assumed by the theory is also doubtful. The marriageability of prime-aged black men has not changed enough to explain the very sharp rise in female-headed families among blacks. Marriage rates have plunged among black men, but this is true for successful and unsuccessful blacks alike. The unemployment rate shows little connection to whether black men become fathers or husbands. They appear to be having a much tougher time staying married than finding work.[70]

ARE JOBS OUT OF REACH?

In its spatial aspect, the mismatch theory asserts that the jobless poor cannot reach jobs outside cities, which everyone agrees outnumber jobs inside. In fact, a great deal of employment is still available in and near cities, even for the unskilled. A recent study of Washington, D.C., a mostly black city, discovered that 33 percent of jobs in that area were in the district itself and another 45 percent in the inner ring of suburbs.[71]

Jobs outside cities may be difficult to reach, at least in the short run. Suburban housing tends to be expensive, in part because multi-unit housing is restricted by zoning, often motivated by a desire to exclude the poor. Employers in these areas may be hurting for low-skilled workers, but residents do not want the apartment houses or public housing needed to house them.[72]

Mismatch theorists doubt that inner-city job seekers could commute to jobs in the suburbs, but the evidence shows that they can and do. Working low-income people appear to have access to automobiles,[73] and most likely, lack of earnings explains any lack of cars rather than the other way around. People who get jobs find ways to commute, such as car pools, until they earn enough to buy their own cars. In some regions, suburban businesses are so desperate for workers that they have taken to busing workers out from the urban core or subsidizing their travel expenses.[74]

Bus and subway service tends to be well-developed in the declining older cities. In 1969, two-thirds of urban low-income households lived within two blocks of a transit line leading to a central business district, and only 9 percent lacked access entirely. Yet mass transit does not seem critical to employment. Transit operators say that low-income workers rely on buses or subways mainly to arrange a job and during the first few weeks at work, after which they join car pools or buy cars.[75] Experimental transit lines to the suburbs were instituted in several cities in the late 1960s, on the supposition they would reduce inner-city joblessness, but few workers used the services, and still fewer jobs could be traced to them. Largely as a result, the experiments were discontinued.[76]

Although the spatial mismatch theory is over twenty years old,[77] a series of researchers has found only limited support for it in statistical studies.[78] It is true that blacks who live in the suburbs earn more than those who live in the center city, but the reason may be that they are more skilled, not that access to jobs is easier for them. Maybe people find work in the suburbs and then move there, not vice versa. It is also true that the movement of industry to the suburbs has reduced earnings in the city, but whether this shift has caused nonwork and other social problems or the other way around remains unclear. When lower-income blacks move to the suburbs, their employment gains are marginal at best.[79]

The strongest determinants of whether people work in and around cities are race and education. Blacks work at lower levels than whites in all locations, as do people with less schooling, compared to those with more. Some studies have found that proximity to jobs affects whether blacks work, but the influence seems to be secondary. Black youth are less likely to work when they have to commute longer to jobs, but the difference between their commuting times and those of white youth is too small to believe that it really explains why they work at levels so much lower than whites. Such effects are sizable only in some cities and not among older workers.[80]

The mismatch theory is most plausible for the most depressed Eastern and Midwestern cities. Wilson has concentrated his research on Chicago, which, along with New York, Philadelphia, Newark, and Detroit, accounted for two-thirds of the growth in high-density urban poverty between 1970 and 1980. Detroit and Cleveland have lost half or more of their white population since 1970, and their city governments have been reduced virtually to receivership.[81] In these cases, mismatch may explain *part* of the inner-city work problem.[82] But these tragic instances do not typify American cities, and in any event, all urban high-poverty areas house only 9 percent of the poor.[83] Serious poverty seems rooted much more in the personal lives of individuals, wherever they live, than in economic geography.

There is some evidence that the departure of jobs from cities has accelerated during the 1980s, so the mismatch may be more true today than earlier.[84] On the other hand, the labor market has grown much tighter for the unskilled than it was a decade ago. Inability to reach jobs, therefore, appears to play only an incidental role in the problem of nonworking poverty considered nationally.

ARE JOBS TOO DEMANDING?

The idea of a skills mismatch may have more validity. Are poor workers being driven out of employment by a more sophisticated economy? Many disadvantaged workers, particularly youth, have such obvious limitations in skills that many analysts conclude that this must explain their employment difficulties as well as other social problems.[85] It hardly matters where jobs are located if the poor, in any event, cannot qualify for them.

This too is implausible. Demanding jobs are rising rapidly in number, but the entire "high-tech" sector is still too small a part of the economy to make employment, overall, much more demanding than it was in earlier decades. Government projections for 1984–95 show that professional and technical jobs are the fastest growing, but lower-skilled trades are vastly more populous and, because of that, are still adding many more jobs to the economy even though their rate of growth is smaller. Substantial growth is expected even in production and manufacturing employment, the traditional bastion of the low-skilled but well-paid job.[86]

New York, the nerve center of the new computing economy, saw the greatest rise in entrenched poverty between 1970 and 1980, yet a detailed study of the local labor market found that between 1972 and 1981 the proportion of jobs requiring low skill dropped hardly at all—from 58 to 57 percent. During the later 1980s, blue-collar jobs actually increased in New York by 140,000, to a fifth of all employment, despite the decline in factory work. Admittedly, jobs today more often call for literacy, less often for manual dexterity, than in the past. But unless we regard literacy as an advanced skill, the labor market is not much more demanding today than it ever was.[87]

It is also difficult to blame limited education for the work problem when rising schooling has done little to reduce differences in work levels among the races. The share of all adults aged twenty-five and over with at least a high school diploma soared more than 30 points between 1960 and 1986, to 75 percent, and among blacks it more than tripled, to 62 percent. By 1980, the median years of schooling completed was about twelve years for blacks and Hispanics as well as whites,[88] but in this same period, the racial gap in work levels widened. The jobless rate is at least twice as high for blacks than whites at all education levels,[89] just as it was before the education boom.

This suggests that the quality, not quantity, of black education is the problem. Today's minorities differ from other ethnic groups mainly in the far greater difficulty they have in school acquiring the skills to be employable. Employers demand more schooling for some jobs than they used to, but partly to compensate for falling educational standards. If one cannot be sure that high school dropouts can read, one demands high school graduates, and if necessary college graduates.[90] Some firms have given up on the schools and shouldered the task of teaching employees themselves.[91]

They are teaching the three Rs, not computing or higher mathematics. Employers accept that, as needs change quickly, they will have to teach specific skills. They complain rather about the lack of very elementary capacities. They ask for employees able "to reason, to follow written instructions and to articulate their thoughts to teams of co-workers," to "exercise a sense of responsibility," be "fair and honest," "demonstrate self-control," and "function well in groups." The lack of such skills is a problem even for black youth working at McDonald's, and it would have posed a problem in the old economy as well as the new. Indeed, employers who are still hiring for factory work voice the same complaints as those in newer industries—workers "fail drug tests" or "simply have little notion of what is involved in holding any job."[92]

To the extent there is an educational mismatch, it seems to be to the disadvantage of the society rather than the jobless poor. There is a mismatch between the low-skilled and jobs in the sense that the economy could well use higher-skilled workers than it has. Low skills are one reason for the failure of productivity to improve. The high-skilled inevitably have better opportunities than the unskilled, and their edge has probably grown. But there seldom is a mismatch in the sense that the low-skilled cannot find employment at all. To the contrary, employers in the current labor market are often forced to find some way to employ them, even, if necessary, through retraining. The attitude of managers seems to be, in the words of one observer, that "Business can't live with America's poor and it can't live without them. It can't afford the social and economic costs of their dependency. Nor can it afford the waste of labor as middle-class entrants into the work force slow to a trickle."[93]

Overall, the mismatch theory may help explain why the inner-city poor fail to find well-paying jobs, but usually not why they so seldom work at all. Poor adults, after all, are few in number. They are not in competition with the entire labor force. It may be beyond them to "succeed" in competitive senses, yet to find employment sufficient to get off welfare or out of poverty is probably easier today than ever before. These are the jobs the new immigrants are doing; they, rather than poor Americans, are treading the traditional path toward upward mobility.

WHAT THE POOR SAY

Finally, there is the testimony of the poor themselves. Few of them seem to think jobs are unavailable to them. The government survey that generates the annual poverty statistics asks people who worked less than full-year in the previous twelve months what the main reason was. Table 5.1 shows the work levels of various groups, both poor and nonpoor, and, within each, the share of those not fully employed who gave inability to find work as the main reason. The figures for work levels show again the large differences in employment between the poor and nonpoor.

TABLE 5.1
Work Levels and Lack of Work in Persons Aged 15 and Over,
1987

Percent that	All adults	Poor adults	Poor blacks	All men	Poor men	Poor black men
Worked at any time:	68.3	39.6	32.7	77.0	49.8	35.9
Worked full-year and full-time:	40.9	8.8	6.2	52.2	13.3	7.1
Worked less than 50 weeks:	21.6	26.6	23.3	21.2	32.4	26.6
Percent of these for whom the main reason was inability to find work:	30.3	37.8	41.3	41.0	49.2	47.9
Did not work:	31.1	60.2	67.1	22.0	49.7	63.6
Percent of these for whom the main reason was inability to find work:	3.3	8.7	13.2	4.9	13.5	15.8

ᴏᴛᴇ: Some percentages do not add to 100 due to rounding or employees in the armed forces.
ᴏᴜʀᴄᴇ: Calculated from U.S. Department of Commerce, Bureau of the Census, *Poverty in the United ᴀtes 1987*, Series P-60, no. 163 (Washington, D.C.: U.S. Government Printing Office, February)89), table 10.

Differences in access to jobs are not the main explanation for that gap. The shares of poor and nonpoor working less than full-year are not grossly different, nor are the proportions of these workers who cite lack of jobs as their main problem. Lack of full-year work was the greatest single reason for working part-year, but even it was cited by less than half in all the groups, even the most disadvantaged. It is the proportion not working at all that clearly differentiates poor from nonpoor. Total withdrawal from the labor force is the main reason for low working hours among the needy.

If the problem were the economy, we would expect high proportions of poor who were not working to blame lack of jobs, yet only 16 percent or less did so. Other reasons—disability, education, and tending children—were considerably more important. Nonworkers mostly feel they could find employment if other concerns did not keep them out of the work force, and much the same is true of people on welfare. Among nonworking welfare recipients in 1985, 23 percent in rural areas gave inability to find work as the main reason for not working, only 14 percent in urban areas.[94]

More notably, black youth report that jobs are fairly easy to find. This group regularly records the highest of all unemployment rates, usually over 40 percent. No other statistic lends such credence to the view that jobs must be lacking. To explore the question, in 1979–80 the National Bureau of Economic Research conducted a special survey of disadvantaged young black men in the ghettos of Boston, Chicago, and Philadelphia. (The last two cities are particularly good candidates for the mismatch theory.) The respondents did not report prohibitive employment conditions. Only a minority were employed, yet 46 percent of the nonworkers said it was very easy or fairly easy to get a job as a laborer. An equal percentage said it was difficult, only 8 percent that it was impossible. A higher proportion — 71 percent — said it was easy or very easy to get a job at the minimum wage, while 23 percent said it was difficult, and 7 percent said impossible. In a later survey in Boston in 1989 — admittedly a very favorable labor market — nearly 90 percent of white and 75 percent of black out-of-school youth said job opportunities were plentiful. The youth apparently know about such jobs; there is little support here for the proposition that they lack the contacts to obtain them.[95]

When poor people leave big cities for outlying areas, as many are doing, the major reasons they mention are to escape crime and other threats to their children, not to find employment. The goal, by one account, is "to find a better school, a setting where there were fewer drugs and fewer chances to get entangled with the gangs." They say that they can get more and better jobs after moving, that they feel more motivated to work in suburbs or small towns, where employment is more usual. They do not say they could get no jobs in the city. For them, crime is the overwhelming problem of the ghetto, not lack of jobs.[96]

HIDDEN ISSUES

It is hard to avoid the conclusion that at least low-paid work is readily available to many, perhaps most, of the jobless poor. Again, we do not know that there are enough jobs for all nonworkers, only for most of those seeking work at any one time. Martin Feldstein estimated in 1973 that the share of the labor force that truly could not find work might be half the reported unemployment. Today, on the other side of the baby boom, the judgment seems at least as valid. In the words of one recent review, "Except perhaps in the depths of a recession, people who want jobs can get jobs."[97]

Yet this conclusion is controversial. Apart from lingering doubts about the extent of available jobs, the main reason appears to be that issues other than availability are involved. One is the question of what a "job" consists of. The literature reviewed here mostly defines jobs narrowly, as employment paying at least the minimum wage and meeting other government conditions. This definition is favored by conservative analysts. Liberal analysts tend to qualify "job" with terms like "good," "decent," "suitable," or "meaningful"; for them, typically, a job is not really a job unless it pays enough to support an average family on one income, offers promotion prospects, health and pension benefits, and is interesting and affirming to do.[98] Obviously, such jobs are a lot less available than the menial positions accepted by immigrants but declined by many of the nonworking poor. The question of job quality harks back to progressive controversies about what level of pay and benefits workers deserve, an indication that these issues are far from dead.

Even more important to the jobs issue appears to be differing views of whether the poor can actually do the available jobs. Even the most rudimentary positions demand the abilities to get to work on time, take orders, and get along with coworkers. Conservative analysts insist that society is obliged to provide jobs only for people who have these capacities. They also believe many nonworkers lacking basic discipline would speedily develop it if society did not indulge them with welfare and other escapes from work. As the plan for a recent, rather hard-line workfare program in Illinois stated: "Program participants must be viewed as adults who have a wide range of abilities. . . . Any other view of the recipient is inaccurate and at best patronizing, if not demeaning."[99]

Liberals remain doubtful. They tend to think all nonworkers have a claim on a job, even the least skilled. At the same time, they fear that many would be rejected by private employers on any terms, even if there were more open positions. According to Christopher Jencks:

> [Employers] think [illegal aliens] are more diligent, less uppity, more pliable, less likely to demand promotions, etc., etc. Thus, it is not clear . . . that the fact that such workers get jobs proves anything about the availability of jobs for . . . unskilled or semiskilled blacks. The fact that illegals with the "right" personality traits can get jobs proves no more about the availability of work to people with the "wrong" personality traits than the availability of jobs for B.A.'s proves about the availability of jobs for dropouts. . . . You might respond, of course, that in a market economy if blacks have such "undesirable" traits from an employer's viewpoint, they will have to settle for even less than illegal Hispanics. But it is not clear that such jobs exist. I don't think you can get a job pouring water and clearing dishes in a restaurant by offering to work for less than the Hispanics who now do the job. The restaurant owners don't want "bad" workers at *any* wage.

Hence, jobs may not really be available to many of the low-skilled, whatever the appearances. Some of these workers simply "can't make it on their own, because their skills or behavior [are] too atypical or incompetent [for them] to make their way in a competitive market economy." If society wants these people to work, it will have to provide them jobs through government.[100]

The evidence we have tends to support conservative expectations—and liberal fears. Employers do set a minimum on employability. They resist hiring workers they regard as unreliable, even at low wages. There is a particular resistance to workers who are both demanding and unskilled, a frequent combination among ghetto youth.[101] A number of government subsidies and tax credits have tried to persuade employers to hire more such workers, largely in vain. Job applicants who are eligible for such credits are *less* likely to be hired than others. Involvement in the program apparently stigmatizes the job seekers in the eyes of employers.[102]

Assumptions about worker quality, like those of job quality, determine conclusions about job availability. If one defines acceptable jobs broadly, but employability narrowly, as conservatives do, jobs will seem widely available; if one sets more demanding standards for jobs, but lower ones for workers, as liberals do, jobs will seem lacking, notwithstanding the fact that a great many low-skilled people find work in the United States.

Often, when liberal analysts say barriers explain nonwork, they really refer to some difficulty in working *combined with* some lack of personal discipline. That is, employment makes some demand on job seekers, but it is this in conjunction with an inability to cope that actually causes nonwork. The mismatch theory, for instance, is a lot more persuasive as an explanation of nonwork if combined with the demoralization of the poor than on its own: The poor work less when attractive jobs disappear *and* they are less ready to do unattractive ones.[103]

The jobs question, thus, comes down to the demands one feels society should make on the nonworking poor. If they can be expected to behave like the nonpoor, there is no reason why they should not get ahead in the current economy just as immigrants are doing. But if one thinks they have special, personal disadvantages for which society is responsible, then virtually no job market will seem to provide enough, or good enough, jobs for them. Either way, the debate shifts from the economy to the character of the poor themselves.

CHAPTER
6

Barriers to Employment

By and large we expect that people will take jobs [if]
we eliminate the barriers that have stood in the way of
employment.

—GEORGE SHULTZ
CONGRESSIONAL HEARINGS ON SOCIAL SECURITY
AND WELFARE PROPOSALS, 16 OCTOBER 1969

WHETHER the poor can work depends on more than the availability of jobs; there might be barriers that keep people from taking the jobs that exist. Nonwhites might be victims of racial bias. Welfare recipients may face "disincentives"—the fact that they may "earn" nearly as much by living on welfare as they could by working. Personal incapacities, including low skills, may simply make working impossible for them.

Much of the dispute here revolves around welfare mothers. Perhaps most single mothers could in principle escape poverty and welfare by working, but can they work in practice? The answer depends not only on the structure of the economy but also on the special burdens the women face as mothers. Many analysts have supposed that single mothers cannot work outside the home, that they must tend to children essentially full-time. But times have changed. The great majority of single mothers not on welfare are already working, undercutting the argument that welfare mothers cannot do so. Again, as in the previous two chapters, the issue hinges on the capacity one attributes to the poor. Do we expect disadvantaged welfare mothers to overcome obstacles to employment as effectively as middle-class women? Do we see them as vulnerable victims, or as capable optimizers able to get what they want from life?

RACIAL DISCRIMINATION

The oldest and simplest explanation for nonwork is racial bias. Most of the long-term poor and dependent are nonwhite. Perhaps they are poor simply because white society will not allow them to work. Given the historic subordination of blacks in America, the hypothesis must be taken seriously. Many opinion makers believe, in the words of the Kerner Commission report, that "White racism is essentially responsible" for the social problems of the ghetto.[1]

The trouble with this view today is that in the 1960s, national policy decisively changed. The civil rights acts mandated equal opportunity and an end to discrimination against minorities in voting, public accommodations, education, and employment. The shift was backed by public opinion, as rising majorities of whites—often over 90 percent—endorsed the principles of equal treatment. Most whites say they have abandoned prejudice in its traditional form—the belief blacks were innately inferior regardless of personal attributes.[2] The bureaucracy and courts have even interpreted civil rights, via affirmative action, to require a degree of preference for nonwhites.

After 1960, minorities rapidly advanced in status, one indication that bias actually did recede. Blacks' representation among the professions and other high-paying jobs sharply increased. Their average earnings rose as a proportion of whites'. In 1940, the average working black man earned 43 percent as much as the average white; in 1980, he earned 73 percent. By 1980, 29 percent of working black men actually earned more than the typical white income.[3] While younger, college-educated blacks gained the most, and black women gained more than men, the black advance was broadly based. The majority of blacks were once working-class, at best. Today, probably two-thirds are working- or middle-class.[4] Since these gains occurred at the same time as the decline of work effort among poor blacks, it is hard to blame the latter on bias.

Blacks recognize that times have changed. In a poll taken in 1985, a large majority of them strongly disapproved of the Reagan administration, yet two-thirds believed that blacks were making progress in America, and only a quarter believed that white people wanted to keep them down. Sixty percent said they never had experienced discrimination in applying for employment, and 82 percent said young blacks could expect to get ahead if they worked hard enough, in spite of the prejudice they might encounter. Indeed, black morale actually improved during the Reagan era. Blacks appear to have bought into the American belief in opportunity, though they are still more cautious about it than whites.[5]

American society has hardly become color blind. The great failure of integration has been in housing. Blacks and whites appear to enjoy roughly equal access to higher education and employment, but they seldom live together, and for that reason, public education is also largely segregated. It does not appear that whites oppose living next to blacks as such. Polls since the 1960s show that whites have accepted more contact with blacks on a personal and neighborhood level, and in integrated schools.[6] Rather, the problem seems to be that when middle-class blacks move into a white area, poorer and more threatening blacks often follow. Whites cannot confine their interaction to blacks more or less like themselves, as they can in more selective settings such as employment; they therefore resist integration in housing much more than on the job. They either oppose all black entry into white neighborhoods or flee once it occurs—making their fears self-fulfilling.[7]

Residential segregation is a tragedy and an injustice. Evidence of bias in housing is a lot stronger than in other areas of American life, with blacks seeking homes or apartments often refused openings or steered by real estate agents away from white areas. The Open Housing Act of 1968 was the weakest of the civil rights measures, and in 1988 Congress acted to strengthen it.[8] But, as discussed in the last chapter, without more evidence that exclusion from white areas explains low work levels among blacks, we cannot regard it as an important cause of poverty or dependency. Blacks work at much lower rates than whites no matter where they live. There is little reason to suppose that merely to intermingle black and white residences would change this. Indeed, there is more reason to argue the other way, that to raise black work levels would do much to break down white resistance to living with blacks.

Some believe the white commitment to equal opportunity is two-faced. White Americans may have given up overt racism, but most continue to oppose strong measures to promote integration, such as school busing and affirmative action. There is much more acceptance of the principles of equal opportunity than of mixing with blacks on a personal level. One interpretation is that whites remain racists at heart, another that they merely oppose government intrusion into their private lives.[9]

I believe most whites are fearful, not of nonwhites as such, but of the social evils—crime, welfare, decaying schools, and so on—that have become linked to low-income blacks. "Racism" today usually connotes, not support for the Ku Klux Klan, but a defense of social standards against the perceived disorders of the ghetto. Whites simultaneously believe in racial fairness while asserting that blacks, compared to other people, are more likely to be violent and "lazy" and to live on welfare.[10] Given the preponderance of blacks among violent criminals and the long-term poor and dependent, those characterizations are not inaccurate, although they do not apply to the majority of blacks. The drift of white attitudes is away from denying the potential equality of blacks and toward criticism of their shortcomings in the common society.

The feeling expressed by most whites is that the competition for success should be racially blind, but also that traditional standards of excellence should apply. A black person may become a doctor or a lawyer or make a lot of money, provided that he or she can perform the tasks these callings require, a capacity to be proven in impartial competition with white aspirants. Mainstream people do not want the unreliable personal style associated with lower-class blacks to take over the workplace, and they oppose special advantages for blacks as such.[11] As a result, equal opportunity for blacks will not quickly produce equal outcomes. Even without bias, blacks would be disadvantaged in fair competition with whites because of lesser education and different backgrounds, in part due to past prejudice. These limitations are a lot tougher to change than the attitudes of white people.[12]

The end of Jim Crow, however, does mean that blacks usually can find some employment, provided they have the most basic skills. Much of the gap in earnings between blacks and whites may still be attributable to discrimination.[13] It is less likely that bias can explain why so many lower-income blacks fail to work at all. Studies in which equivalent white and black applicants approach employers find slight preferences for whites, but not of an order that could explain why black youth are unemployed and outside the labor force at rates far above those for whites.[14] The erratic work histories of black youth do not seem forced on them by bias, since black male heads of household, most of whom are older and steadier workers, are actually underrepresented among the long-term jobless.[15] Equally important, black single mothers are just about as able to work their way off welfare as whites.[16]

It is true that many employers dislike unskilled male black applicants, but they usually say this is because they have had bad experience with the group, not because they believe black men to be innately inferior. They complain that the men lack the fundamental motivation, reliability, and honesty for employment, that "They don't want to work." They infer these qualities at least partly from the race, ghetto origin, and limited schooling of the applicants. Such beliefs may cause them to practice some "statistical discrimination,"that is, to dismiss some capable men who happen to have adverse labels. However, employers also consider attributes that are more individual and job-related—the men's lack of polish and articulation and their erratic prior work histories. They make fairly sophisticated distinctions among blacks who possess or lack good work habits. Black employers express the same reservations as whites.[17]

Employers appear to prefer hiring women to black men, apparently because they see them as more cooperative. The flood of women into the labor market is thus one reason that many black men have withdrawn.[18] But since black women benefit along with whites, this again does not reflect prejudice in the traditional sense that asserts black inferiority. The sentiment against black men appears, unfortunately, to be well earned, and it is difficult to believe that many competent black workers are being denied opportunity.

Discrimination of the old kind, unrelated to deserts, still exists, but it seldom denies people all employment. The limited information we have suggests that the victims are mostly those blacks who have made the greatest progress in America, not the poor. The black middle class is advancing because it has seized white-collar careers in large corporations and government agencies in which the rules have become fundamentally fair. Some resistance remains to blacks rising to leading positions.[19] Minorities and women make up 30 percent of middle management in big corporations, but only 1 percent of top management.[20] In journalism, there are many black reporters but few editors. Frustrated black journalists claiming bias won a lawsuit against the *New York Daily News*.[21] Black and Hispanic agents sued the Federal Bureau of Investigation, obtaining judgments that the agency engaged in racial harassment and discrimination.[22]

This sort of treatment is much more furtive, and more racist, than the suspicion employers show toward the black poor. Here, the black aspirants have much the same education and background as their white rivals, so they cannot be dismissed as unqualified on nonracial grounds. Compared to the poor, their presence forces more real change in the remaining white prejudice, and is thus more likely to arouse it. These successful blacks seem to encounter prejudice more often than the worse-off precisely because they are moving ahead. They have more everyday contact with white people and thus more opportunity to encounter bias than the black poor, many of whom live today in all-black neighborhoods.[23]

For this reason, perhaps, the black elite is more conscious of prejudice than blacks as a group. Whereas 40 percent of the black population says it has experienced discrimination in seeking employment, 74 percent of black leaders say they have. They are notably less sanguine about progress for the group. Yet the leaders themselves are highly successful by any measure—80 percent are college graduates, and 59 percent have graduate degrees. No doubt for the same reasons, black political leaders are also much more liberal on race issues than most other leaders or ordinary voters, including blacks.[24]

The black poor evidently have more trouble holding any job steadily than in dealing with traditional racism.[25] It appears that the remaining bias in America would be unlikely to keep them out of jobs unless, like the low wages discussed earlier, it demoralized them so that they did not work at all. Unquestionably, racism and the fight against it continue; but, like the battle over deindustrialization, it is being fought largely by working people over the heads of the poor.

WELFARE DISINCENTIVES

Another common supposition has been that the welfare poor, especially women, fail to work because they lack an incentive to do so. Perhaps they could support themselves, but why should they make the effort when their welfare grants would be reduced by whatever earnings they made, leaving them no better off? This reasoning may explain why single mothers like Rhonda Jackson (see chapter 4) choose to rely on welfare rather than look for a job. Welfare creates a similar disincentive against marriage, since usually only single mothers and their children are eligible, not families with both parents.[26]

The theory is inherently plausible. Politicians easily pick up on it. President Reagan frequently commented on all the benefits that government programs offer to people who decline to work or marry, the respectable routes to upward mobility. "Under existing welfare rules," he declared, "a teen-age girl who becomes pregnant can make herself eligible for welfare benefits that will set her up in an apartment of her own, provide medical care, and feed and clothe her. She has to fulfill only one condition—not marry or identify the father."[27]

Analysts also give credence to this theory. If welfare recipients work, they suffer a reduction in numerous government benefits: housing, medical care, and Food Stamps, as well as income grants. Economists believe the cuts can add up to a prohibitive "tax" on earnings that prompts some recipients to decline employment. Conservatives conclude that welfare must be narrowly limited to the unemployable,[28] while liberals seek to restructure welfare benefits to reduce the disincentive.[29] Recently, some conservatives have contended that disincentives to work and marry can explain the entire demoralization of low-income America. According to George Gilder, welfare, by assuming responsibility for families, preempts the proper role of the father, leading to family breakup and all the ills of the ghetto. Charles Murray says that the sharp deterioration of poor black society after 1970 resulted directly from the buildup of welfare and other benefits for the needy. Misguided generosity changed the "rules of the game" to reward dysfunctional rather than responsible behavior.[30]

Research confirms that welfare and other benefits reduce work effort among recipients. States are free to vary AFDC benefit levels, and comparisons among states show that work effort is relatively lower in states with higher benefits. Effort falls, as well, when the "tax rate" on income (the proportion of wages deducted from the grant) is increased.[31] Under Unemployment Insurance, claimants stay out of work 25 percent longer than they would without the benefits, and unemployment measures perhaps a point higher as a result.[32] Social Security and the Disability program have similar effects on the aged and disabled, but these attract less attention, because these groups are not expected to work.[33] Much of the decline in male labor force participation in recent decades, especially for older workers and blacks, may well be due to the attractions of Disability.[34]

But if a work disincentive due to benefits is clear, it is also limited. The broadest estimate is that all income programs together probably reduced work hours for the population by 5 percent in the late 1970s, prior to the Reagan cuts. Within that total, AFDC had a smaller effect than either Social Security or Disability.[35] Among welfare recipients, the work reduction appears larger, about 30 percent. During the period 1967–77, work levels of welfare recipients fell by 40 to 60 percent in the South as benefits rose, and wives and single mothers reduced their work effort substantially in government experiments where they were guaranteed an income.[36]

However, these work reductions occur from a very low base. Welfare mothers would apparently work an average of only ten to nineteen hours a week even without AFDC. Welfare attracts people who would find it harder to work in low-paid jobs than other people in any event. Ninety-five percent of dependent mothers would still work too little to be ineligible for AFDC even if they were off the program. Conversely, it is rare for a mother to deliberately work less to get on the program. Women on and off welfare appear to have distinctly different attitudes to work. This accounts for virtually all of the difference in work effort that appears due to the disincentive.[37] Work effort is also low among poor men, who get little welfare, and among black youth, even though their earnings are not deducted from their families' welfare grants.[38]

Of course, welfare confers benefits other than cash, chief among them health coverage. AFDC families have access to Medicaid, the federal health program for the poor. While the better-off usually receive health benefits from their employers, low-wage workers often do not. Many analysts and welfare officials suppose that single mothers stay on welfare for fear of losing health protection for their children.[39] In fact, this effect is small. Single mothers with health problems are more likely to go on welfare than others, but the majority of welfare women are little influenced. To get health coverage, therefore, is not an important reason why people become or stay dependent.[40]

Benefit levels also exert little effect on recipients over time. One might suppose that for the caseload as a whole work effort would rise or fall as the real value of benefits changed. Actually, the fall in work effort among the poor appears to predate by some years the sharp rise in social spending in the late 1960s, and it has occurred even among groups, such as single men, who never received much welfare. Work effort by women on AFDC has apparently changed very little since 1967, even though the real value of benefits first rose and then fell during that time.

Benefit effects on family behavior also appear to be limited. Higher benefits do promote somewhat higher dependency on AFDC as well as somewhat higher family breakup; higher illegitimacy is more doubtful.[41] One estimate that seems reasonable is that the presence of welfare might explain 20 to 30 percent of the growth in lower-income female-headed families between 1955 and 1975.[42] The trends in family problems, as in work effort, do not clearly follow the trends in benefits. Illegitimacy, crime, and problems in the schools went on getting worse in the inner city during the 1970s, even though welfare benefits fell.[43]

In sum, the disincentives of welfare remain important, but insufficient to explain the extent of nonwork and female-headed families that we now find among the poor. The main causes of those developments must lie elsewhere.[44]

CHILDREN

It has been widely supposed that welfare mothers cannot work outside the home because they must care for their children. Indeed, this was the presumption behind AFDC when it was first established in 1935. Welfare was supposed to take over the breadwinning role for mothers without husbands, so the women could devote their energies to childrearing.

Until then, however, single mothers had been expected to work. Government might have an obligation to provide them with relief, but they were supposed to do sewing or laundry or take in boarders to help support themselves and their children. That expectation relaxed only between the turn of this century and about 1960, as most states enacted pensions for mothers and AFDC became a mainstay for unwed mothers. Even these programs were narrowly drawn at first, intended to support widows and the wives of the disabled, not the unwed or "undeserving."[45] Only after 1960 did AFDC broaden into the mainstay of inner-city America.

Today, the work expectation has returned with full force. One reason is that the vast majority of welfare mothers appear "undeserving" by the old rules. In 88 percent of AFDC cases in 1988, the father was missing or not committed to the family, and in 52 percent he had never married the mother,[46] a vast increase from fifty years ago. The norm that mothers should stay home has also changed. Today, the great majority of mothers, whether married or not, participate in the labor force. In 1988, 57 percent of wives were working or looking for work, as were 61 percent of women separated from their husbands and 76 percent of the divorced. The figures for women with children under age six were little different—57, 53, and 70 percent, respectively. All the numbers have risen sharply since 1960.[47]

Accordingly, the public today rejects the idea that it is unfair or harmful to children to expect welfare mothers to work.[48] It is true, as both liberal and conservative analysts point out, that most wives do not work full-time, nor do most mothers of preschool children, and it may be unreasonable to expect welfare mothers to do so.[49] Work effort of any kind, however, is unusual on welfare. Overall, single mothers today work at the same levels—about half—as single women without children.[50] Welfare mothers are the great exception to that pattern.

The difficulties that children pose for working mothers appear to be more manageable than is often supposed. Many people think welfare mothers are barred from working by large families, and it is true that they are less likely to work the more children they have. However, the finding has limited importance because the size of welfare families has fallen sharply. Only 27 percent of welfare mothers had more than two children in 1988, down from 53 percent in 1967.[51] It has also been thought that children too young for school keep their mothers from employment, but two-thirds of mothers who escape the welfare rolls by working have children under age six, a higher proportion than for welfare mothers overall.[52] Young, usually unmarried, mothers now dominate the rolls, but, in David Ellwood's words, "The presence of young children, per se, does not seem to be the cause of their especially long expected duration of welfare dependence."[53]

Opponents of work requirements often assume that children suffer if the mother must take a job. The evidence suggests rather that disadvantaged children, at least, tend to gain. They are likely to think better of themselves and do better in school if they see their mother functioning in the world outside the home. It appears best that the mother divide her time between child care and working in order to provide this example, though of course, it would be better if there were two parents, able to tend to both work and children more fully.[54] Many welfare women who go to work find their children are their first admirers: "We're proud of her," they say. "She no longer stays home all day."[55]

CHILD CARE

Even if work for welfare mothers is accepted in principle, it is commonly believed that in practice they cannot work for lack of child care. Advocates assert that work levels cannot be raised until the supply of care is vastly expanded, preferably in the form of child care centers financed and regulated by government.[56]

Without question, finding child care is a challenge for working mothers. As work levels by mothers have soared, the need to arrange care has loomed larger in American life. A patchwork system has emerged in which children are tended by a mix of family members, friends and neighbors, employers, government programs, nonprofit organizations, and for-profit child care chains. A widespread belief among consumers as well as advocates is that there is a "child care crisis" and government should do something.[57]

Government already does. Washington spent $6.2 billion on child care in 1987, more than double the amount in 1972 even allowing for inflation, and several expensive new child care programs were authorized by Congress in 1990. To be sure, $3.5 billion of this money went for tax reductions offsetting the costs of child care arranged by middle-class parents and their employers, most of it informal care by relatives and friends rather than in centers. Only $2.7 billion went directly to child care programs such as Head Start and the care given to welfare families.[58] The new programs voted in 1990 continue this pattern of diffuse subsidy.

While specific programs are targeted mostly on low-income families, the federal government has never accepted any general responsibility to fund child care for the poor, let alone the bulk of the population, as some other advanced countries do. The nearest it came was in 1971, when an omnibus day care package sponsored by Senator Walter Mondale and Representative John Brademas passed Congress but was vetoed by President Nixon. Advocates say that defeat left a permanent hole in the American social safety net, accounting for many of the problems of rich and poor mothers alike.

What the decision really meant, however, was simply that the marketplace rather than government met most of the burgeoning child care needs of the 1970s and 1980s. Huge expansions of care occurred under private auspices, with government playing a secondary role. The growth in organized facilities was not behindhand. Between 1969 and 1985, the share of children aged three to five attending nursery schools or kindergartens jumped from 35 to 55 percent. Between 1976 and 1986, the number of child care centers more than doubled, to nearly 40,000, and the share of preschool children they could serve grew from 16 to 23 percent or more.[59] According to a detailed study of three localities, enough slots have already been created in centers and family day care homes to serve about half of all children from birth through age four. Existing facilities were far from full, with centers operating at 92 percent of capacity and family care homes at 46 percent.[60]

Overall, the care system is overwhelmingly private and informal. In 1987, only 9 percent of all primary child care arrangements made by working mothers involved child care centers or nursery schools. Even for children under age five, who are not yet in school, the figure was only 24 percent, and for mothers with the greatest needs—those working full-time with children under age five—the figure was only 28 percent. Most care, rather, is provided informally, through friends and relatives, or, for older children, through the schools.[61]

The great majority of parents express satisfaction with their care arrangements. In a national survey in 1975, all forms of care were approved by at least 64 percent of users. Care by relatives in one's own or another home received the highest ratings—around 80 percent. While organized forms of care outranked informal care by non-relatives, they also recorded some of the highest levels of dissatisfaction. In the study of localities cited above, most mothers who wanted to change their mode of care wanted to change to organized centers, mostly so their children could learn more. Yet dissatisfaction was still so low that less than a third of mothers would have changed even if all alternatives had been free.[62]

Another common belief is that working women face serious risks of their child care arrangements breaking down.[63] Some suppose that the informal care that most women use is less reliable than centers. While that is true, breakdown in any kind of care is uncommon. Among working mothers in a given month, only 7 percent lose time on the job because of a failure in child care arrangements. According to one study, low-income women suffer such problems less often than the better-off.[64]

In the last decade, younger, better-off working mothers have shown a greater preference for organized forms of care, and they are the main force behind the upsurge in centers. Of those who used day care centers in 1975, 69 percent did so mainly in order to work or seek work, a figure higher than that for any other form of care. It is mothers who are college graduates or have professional or technical jobs, and who are working full-time with children under age five, who show the highest reliance on organized care—34 to 35 percent in 1984–85.[65] The reasons probably are that these women demand care with an educational component, and they find informal care arrangements difficult to make, due to their long working hours and frequent lack of friends and relatives close to home.

Is child care a barrier to employment for poor women with low work levels? Disadvantaged mothers do use organized forms of care relatively heavily, especially if they are working and their children are young. The proportion of children under age five with working mothers who use day care centers or nursery schools reaches

16 percent for the poor, 28 percent for blacks, and 30 percent for single mothers. Nevertheless, more informal, home-based arrangements still predominate. Among working welfare mothers, reliance on centers is around 21 percent; they can usually find informal care and prefer it.[66] Indeed, when free or subsidized center-based care has been offered to such mothers as part of government programs, there have sometimes been few takers.[67]

Because low-income groups use organized care relatively heavily, one might infer that they need it to work and could use more, but one could also conclude that they already receive more of this kind of care than average and any barrier to work must lie elsewhere. Black children are enrolled in preschool programs at very similar rates to whites, and at higher rates in publicly funded programs. Black mothers with lower incomes use preschool programs more heavily than whites, as do black single mothers whether or not they are working. Most likely, trends in organized care have little to do with whether mothers are seeking to work.[68]

Despite the widespread perception of difficulties, most mothers find child care fairly easy to arrange. When nonworking mothers are asked whether they could arrange for care if they decided to work, two-thirds say yes, only 14 percent say no, and there is little difference by race. Of those saying no, only half say the reason is that care is unavailable or too costly. In the three localities mentioned earlier, mothers needing child care spent on average one-third to one-half a day to arrange it.[69]

Even if more centers are not essential, it has been assumed that government must pay for child care if it wants poor women to go to work, as they cannot afford it themselves. Stories abound of child care costing hundreds of dollars per month, or even per week. But child care is less expensive, on average, than most people think. Costly, center-based care is not the norm. In 1987, only a third of working women using child care had to pay *anything at all* for it, and of those who paid, the average cost was only $49 a week. The costliest care was for children up to age four, but even here only 53 to 59 percent paid, and the cost averaged $51 to $58 a week. These expenses averaged less than 7 percent of family income, 25 percent for the poor, counting only those who paid. Among working welfare mothers with preschool-aged children in 1984–85, only 40 percent paid for care, and the typical cost for those who paid was only $22.50 a week.[70]

The case that lack of child care is still a barrier to employment rests mostly on the fact that as many as a quarter of nonworking mothers say they stopped working due to problems finding suitable

or affordable care, and even more—60 percent in some studies—
say they would seek work if assured satisfactory and affordable care.
Disadvantaged mothers—young, black, unmarried, uneducated—are
the likeliest to say this.[71] The trouble with taking the statements at
face value is that the care the mothers need is probably already available to them. In the three localities discussed earlier, the capacity was
already in place to serve the children of the mothers who said they
might work, although the openings were mostly in family day care
homes rather than centers. Many more mothers said they would work
if suitable care were provided than said they had had to stop work
for lack of it. Some said cost had been a problem in the past, but the
prices they said they could pay were close to those actually charged.[72]
The problem is probably not that care is unavailable, but that these
mothers have not looked for it. They are expressing an aspiration to
work rather than recounting problems they have encountered trying
to work.

Mothers who actually work seem to decide to do so and then find
the care that is most practicable for them. Some prefer more formal,
some more informal arrangements, but they take what is available,
and they pay what they can afford. Arranging care is usually an
aspect of going to work rather than a barrier to it.[73] We seldom find
mothers who locate jobs and then are blocked from taking them by
lack of child care.

Several studies have questioned whether the availability of care
has much to do with whether poor mothers take jobs. The differences in the adequacy of care available to working and nonworking
mothers, like other barriers, are simply too small to explain the large
difference in work effort between the groups. An increase in child
care availability could produce at most a 10 percentage point rise in
the share of low-income women working or seeking work, leaving
them well short of the norm for the population as a whole.[74]

The current child care system seems generally adequate for purposes of employment. More government funding seems justified
only for the few localities where supply may be insufficient or for
goals other than employment. Some argue there are too few care
centers for very young children, or that the quality of care is un-
acceptable. The recommendation often made is to replace informal
care by friends and relatives with care that is more regulated and
professionalized, which usually requires centers and higher costs. A
related argument is that enriched care could overcome some of the
educational handicaps of poor children by preparing them better for
school. Head Start might be expanded to serve all the disadvantaged

children eligible for it, rather than only one-sixth. Finally, some contend that to express a broad commitment to the family, Washington should fund a national care network as other Western governments do, without reference to impacts on specific social problems.[75]

These purposes, unlike employment, would require a larger government presence in child care. Although the ends are worthy, they are politically less pressing than raising work levels, and some of the claims made for expanded care are dubious. Given the limitations of large, bureaucratic programs, government probably cannot do much more to raise care quality or the abilities of disadvantaged children, and more centers might well weaken rather than strengthen the family.[76] In any event, child care is evidently not central to overcoming poverty. Whatever it does for children, it has all too little effect on the functioning of parents, and thus does not reach to the heart of the social problem.

EMPLOYABILITY

One conclusion of the last chapter was that a great deal of work remains for the unskilled to do. But are poor single mothers actually able to perform even unskilled jobs? Burdened with children, themselves often high school dropouts, they would seem to offer very little to employers. It is easy to summon up a specter of such women competing hopelessly for jobs against better-prepared applicants.[77]

To judge from statistics, however, welfare mothers are a good deal less constrained than they once were. Not only do they have fewer children, they are younger than they used to be—55 percent were under age thirty in 1988, compared to 41 percent in 1969. They also have noticeably more education: In the same period, the proportion lacking a high school diploma dropped from 60 to 20 percent.[78]

Equally important, these demographic features have only limited influence on whether the mothers in fact work. If one considers all single mothers, those who are working are noticeably more advantaged than the nonworkers; they have more education and fewer children, and are much less likely to have a child under age six.[79] These differences account for a lot more than work status, however. The working mothers include many better-off women who are more than competent in the minimal sense I mean here; they are successful in competitive terms. Confining comparisons to those nearer the bottom of society, where poverty and dependency are more widespread, a lot less difference appears between single mothers who work and those who do not.[80]

If one asks only whether single mothers escape poverty, then much the strongest determinant is simply whether they work substantial numbers of hours. Race, education, marital status, and age of children are all less significant. Considering only poor single mothers, the demographic differences between those working and not working are remarkably small, and sometimes to the advantage of the nonworkers. In 1984, 53 percent of poor single mothers who did not work lacked a high school diploma, but so did 39 percent of those working full-time. Forty-two percent of the first group was black, but so was 48 percent of the second. Forty-four percent of the nonworkers had three or more dependents, but so did 53 percent of the full-time workers.[81]

Statistical studies also suggest that demographic differences have little to do with whether welfare mothers leave the rolls through employment. As mentioned above, black mothers are about as able to work their way off as whites, and the effect of children, while significant, is limited by the small size of today's welfare families. Older, as opposed to younger, mothers and single, as opposed to divorced, women have similar chances of working off. The characteristics that make a difference are those that indicate an ability to accomplish something outside the home—a high school diploma and recent work experience. Demographic differences have much more effect on whether women leave welfare via remarriage or reconciliation with their former spouses.[82]

The message is not that all welfare mothers are employable. One can identify a subset—young, black, unmarried, uneducated, with young children—who suffer from so many disadvantages that employment clearly would be difficult for them.[83] Yet, more striking is how dependent welfare mothers are, how unlikely to work steadily, regardless of their attributes.[84] Personal characteristics, like welfare disincentives, simply do not reach to the heart of why poor women so seldom work.

DISABILITY

A final issue is whether significant numbers of the poor could be viewed as disabled, that is, so physically or mentally impaired as to be unemployable. Many poor and dependent people do suffer from health problems. Health may be the characteristic of welfare mothers that best predicts whether they will work or not, and mothers with health problems are more likely to go on welfare than others. Thirty-one percent of the heads of poor families in a given year claim some degree of disability, as do 39 percent for the long-term poor, compared to only 11 percent for the population. Figures for the heads of welfare families are similar.[85]

Yet disability does not seem to cause poverty or welfare to this degree. In 1989, 13 percent of poor adults claimed they did not work because of disability or ill health, as did 12 percent of poor family heads; the equivalent figures among the nonworking poor were 22 and 24 percent. There is clearly a difference from the population in general, in which all these rates run much lower.[86] However, disability is a judgmental condition that, like unemployment, may or may not constitute an actual barrier to work. What proportion of the disabilities mentioned by nonworkers actually prevent unemployment is unclear. Among people claiming illness or disability, many fewer among the poor work despite their problem than is true for the population in general.[87]

The first form of disability to come to mind might well be mental illness, as this is a serious problem for the homeless, currently the most visible of the poor. Around a quarter of the homeless have at some time been institutionalized, and as many as a half have significant psychological problems.[88] But among the poor and disadvantaged generally, the problem is less notable. Twenty percent or more of poor children probably have mental or adjustment problems, compared to 12 or 13 percent for the population in general, with perhaps half of these disorders amounting to handicaps.[89]

It is notable that there have been various economic and social theories to explain poverty, but no psychological theory. No one has seriously contended that poverty or dependency can be explained in any broad way with reference to mental illness. Initial research along this line in the 1960s petered out in the 1970s, no doubt in part because this approach to social problems is politically sensitive. A more fundamental reason, though, is simply that no close association was found between poverty and mental illness as clinically defined.[90]

While the poor clearly are more impaired than the population, the difference is not enough to explain the much greater divergence in their economic status. Many experts accept at least tacitly that welfare work programs could at best employ perhaps two-thirds of welfare mothers; the rest have too many personal problems, mental and otherwise, to work.[91] But two-thirds is still far above the proportion that is regularly working or involved in work programs now.

Disability might be an attractive solution to the work problem, since current policy accepts that society should support the disabled without a work obligation. Unfortunately, the proportion of nonworkers that reasonably could be exempted from work on this ground is too small to resolve the work controversy. The caseloads of programs supporting the disabled have risen sharply since the 1960s, but the reason is that eligibility had been defined more generously and administration has been lax, not that the population is more impaired; actual health conditions probably have improved. Doubt about whether beneficiaries were in fact disabled led to controversial attempts under the Reagan administration to exclude the employable. There have even been slight moves toward requiring beneficiaries to work, much as in welfare. Thus, the disability approach does not avoid the work issue, but re-creates it in a new form.[92]

VULNERABILITY

On balance, the impediments to poor women working do not seem prohibitive. We should expect many more poor women to be working steadily than, in fact, we find. Alternatively, we should expect much less family poverty, since steady employment would lift many women out of need. I do not mean that work is easy for single mothers. It is difficult for anybody. It is more difficult for single mothers than for most people, especially mothers on welfare. But the impediments poor mothers face in working do not seem unusual.

The underlying issue, again, is competence. Conservative analysts generally believe poor women can and should go to work, regardless of difficulties; that is, they ought to exhibit the same masterful mentality middle-class women display in maximizing their income.[93] Liberal analysts attribute to the poor a much more vulnerable identity. They argue that welfare women want to work, but constantly face crises such as the loss of a welfare check, eviction from their housing, the breakdown of day care, or the sickness of children. They are already "overwhelmed by failure," and to require them to work might just bring more defeats and "reinforce a poor self-image."[94]

Does weakness confer an exemption from normal functioning? Short of outright physical incapacity, should one be excused from routine expectations, such as work, because they are too difficult? Welfare mothers are usually not incapacitated—just distracted and overburdened. Are these sufficient excuses for not working? To these questions, most liberals reluctantly answer yes. Conservatives, on the contrary, believe that individuals who feel overwhelmed should not be excused from work, but should rather correct their weaknesses. Welfare recipients, Peter Ferrara says, "need to learn...how to fail and overcome it, as the rest of us have."[95]

People more easily seem competent if one views them from the outside, impersonally, as the marketplace does, and this is the conservative standpoint. Liberals take a more interior view, trying to get inside the head of the poor and sharing their fears. Hard-eyed observers may say that the mothers are employable; liberals ask whether they feel they are. A mother says, "I get so nervous and scared going out looking for a job.... Meeting all them strange folks, you know. And I never know how to talk to them." Liberal analysts readily sympathize—"We all remember the anxiety in getting our first job."[96] If one focuses on such inward fears, few nonworking adults will appear employable.[97]

Such judgments govern whether one thinks severity or solicitude is the best way to combat the dysfunctions of poverty. Will toughness or tenderness best motivate the dependent to take charge of their lives? In Michigan, the authorities prosecuted two single mothers for bearing children while addicted to cocaine. Like other conservatives, they thought that this would give the mothers a "strong incentive" to change. "Our attitude is, 'Hey, let's stop it now!'" said one police sergeant. "It's a form of caring." But outraged social workers and defense lawyers replied that a mother would bear an addicted child only because of "the severity of her disease." To prosecute the mothers would only "undercut their fragile self-esteem."[98]

This debate of "hard" versus "soft" is eclipsing the old disputes over the proper scale of government. Liberals tend to blame nonwork on adversity and claim that making life easier for nonworkers would raise work levels. Conservatives take an opposite line, believing that nonwork has come of making life too easy for the poor, and that reducing the alternatives to working would make people try harder. The serious difference is not over the impediments to work but the personality imputed the poor.

SOCIOLOGISM

To what extent is behavior determined by environment? This is the question that stands behind all the disputes about jobs and employment, and indeed behind all of dependency politics. Are the dysfunctions of the poor, including nonwork, to be blamed on social forces, or can the poor themselves be held responsible for them?

Progressive politics already posed the question whether economic fortunes could be blamed on society. Conservatives held workers responsible for whether they were able to make money and get ahead, while liberals said class and economic structure were largely responsible. The left was always more willing than the right to shield ordinary people from capitalism—to raise wages and provide income outside the market. The liberals of the 1930s and 1940s, however, never made working or poor people appear helpless. They invoked social forces largely to explain low wages and economic depression, but they assumed that workers were capable of getting through school, managing their personal lives, staying on the right side of the law, and above all, working for a living.

When dependency erupted as an issue in the 1960s, liberals extended their social analysis in a way that brought personal competence much more into question. The problem was to explain how social forces could still cause working-aged poverty in an era that was vastly richer and fairer than the thirties. One had to account for the dysfunctional personal behaviors—dropping out of school, early pregnancy, crime—that were now the immediate cause of most sustained poverty. This required a new understanding that was much more determinist than the old. The old liberalism spoke of social forces that were blunt and mostly impersonal. Workers were trapped in an economy where market forces drove wages and job security down below what workers needed to support families. The answer was unionism and government controls on business. The new liberalism spoke largely of subtler forces that crippled the capacity to cope at a formative age. People were poor because they were brought up in weak families, given inferior education, consigned to dead-end jobs, and forced to live in ghettos. As President Johnson announced at the dawn of the Great Society, "Men are shaped by their world," by the "hundred unseen forces" that do or do not give them the "ability" to realize their goals.[99]

This diffuse, determinist style of analysis, which I have termed sociologism, construes the personality as essentially passive: The poor are seen as inert, not active. They are spoken of in the passive voice. They are people who *are* or *have been* disadvantaged in multiple ways. They do not *do* things but rather have things *done to* them. They are the objects, not the subjects of action. They are not to blame for conditions such as dropping out of school, AIDS, or drug addiction, but rather "at risk" for them. They "experience" behaviors such as crime or illegitimacy rather than commit them. That exceptive voice became the hallmark of the new liberalism, just as assertive claim making on behalf of deserving workers was the voice of the old.

The basic mechanism of sociological thinking is objectification. Springs of behavior that a conservative might locate within the individual are projected onto the environment. Causes of problems that are initially personal are lumped together with social causes. To the sociologist Genevieve Carter, dependency is due not only to economic conditions and welfare policies but "ethnicity, or culture" and "responsibility for child care." To David Ellwood, the ghetto is the product not only of "deprivation, concentration, isolation, discrimination, poor education" and the departure of jobs but "crime, drugs and alcohol, the underground economy, and welfare."[100]

Inevitably, sociologism brings competence into question, as traditional liberalism seldom did. The implication is that the poor are no longer to be held responsible even for personal behavior. However destructive they may be to themselves or others, the blame lies outside them. They live, in Michael Harrington's words, "beneath moral choice." "These violent men and 'immoral' women" are actually "social products," and "society is responsible for the evil it has imposed upon them."[101]

Liberals do not deny the value of personal competence and responsibility, but they hold society responsible for whether people attain these virtues. According to the sociologists Loïc Wacquant and William Julius Wilson, the shiftlessness others see in jobless black men is really an attribute of the economy. The men see no "objective probability of achieving a socially rewarding and stable life," so they do not attempt it. They "experience . . . long and repeated spells of unemployment, or a succession of low-paying, dead-end jobs," so they lack "a strong attachment to the labor market." Self-reliance is not given to them, so it is "simply not a reality."[102] Conservatives, in contrast, hold individuals responsible for behaving well, rather than the environment.

In the liberal view, society ought to provide the resources, social as well as economic, to permit character to develop. According to Wilson, "a youngster who grows up in a family with a steady breadwinner and in a neighborhood in which most of the adults are employed will tend to develop some of the disciplined habits" required for employment. James Coleman, another sociologist, says that children need "social" as well as economic capital, or relationships they can draw on for support and guidance when they are in trouble.[103] In contrast, conservatives say that people have a duty first of all to behave well, and if they do they will acquire social and economic resources.

By blaming society for personal, as well as impersonal, problems, the left states a powerful claim to aid, but at a cost. The claim is made, so to speak, by the disassembly of the personality. By disowning personal responsibility, sociologism assigns the moral capacity of people to the environment. Only a diminished self remains. The individual is reduced to a set of impulses that succumb to temptations without thought of the consequences. Conservatives, on the contrary, aggrandize the individual at the expense of the environment. They say people have the power to work and, generally, control outcomes beyond themselves. It is as if opportunities fly to them, as metal flies to a magnet, by the sheer dynamism of their personalities. That assumption effectively absorbs aspects of the social structure within the personality.

Sociologism provides a theory for helping people, but not for making them independent. Liberals speak of "empowering" the poor, by which they mean helping them do difficult things. To be "empowered" to work is to receive aid in working, for example, special training or child care.[104] To a conservative, the idea of *giving* people power is self-contradictory. Power, as conservatives understand it, is not something anything outside a person can give. To help people to work may well *free* them from a burden, but to be *empowered* they must become able to shoulder the burden themselves. If only government makes work possible, then only government is powerful.

Conservatives find sociological thinking demeaning, precisely because it leaves competence in the hands of outside forces. A person who is only an expression of social pressures is not a person at all. In the progressive era, conservatives resisted the collectivization of the economy. In dependency politics, they find themselves fighting a condescension that would turn the passive poor into wards of the state. As Ronald Reagan remarked near the end of his presidency, the partisan battle was now about "moral" more than "economic" issues. His administration had fought to restrain the size of government, but above all it had resisted the "determinism and despair" of liberal social analysis.[105]

Progressive politics concerned the proper boundary of government and society. Dependency politics is about the boundary between the poor individual and personal surroundings. In the earlier era, the central issue was the proper extent of economic freedom; in the current era, it is the strength to be imputed to disadvantaged selves. That is a profound reorientation for both right and left. People are no longer seen as literally "free," as conservative ideology often pictures them, nor can they be made free as liberal reformism aspires. Rather, they exist in tension with their environment. The question is whether they can make headway against it. Do the problems of working— finding a job, child care, transportation—constitute prohibitions or challenges?

That is not an issue that facts can resolve. It is only clear that many poor adults have difficulty with work-related tasks. It is not clear whether the difficulty is that they cannot cope or that the demands they face are unusually severe. That doubt exists in any situation where human beings are defeated by their environment. This is why, in principle, one can always attribute a social problem to either the individual or society, even when, as is usual today, it arises in the first instance from the behavior of the "victims."[106] Where the blame lies hinges on one's view of the human nature of the poor. Are they victims or victimizers? Judgments about social barriers are always *relative* to some judgment about personal competence.

MOVING AHEAD?

Barriers to opportunity do exist in American society. People who have to work at low-paid jobs because of limited skills or education are necessarily worse off than the higher-paid. That is why the progressive debate about how to improve jobs or equalize rewards remains important. But social forces do not appear to explain the extent of nonwork now found at the bottom of society. The barriers that exist for the poor seem to be more the result of employment than impediments to it. Few Americans are literally barred from work, but those who do work become more aware of practical problems than those who do not. It is working blacks, not the nonworking, who most often feel the remaining racism in America. It is working women, not jobless welfare recipients, who complain most that they get a raw deal from low wages, inadequate child care, and so on. Active people, not passive, are those who feel resistance from their environment. It is bodies in motion, as Newton said, that provoke an equal and opposite reaction.

CHAPTER

7

Human Nature

There are literally hundreds of thousands of people in
this city who think their options are limited to fast-food
service or welfare.

—WILLIAM J. GRINKER
NEW YORK CITY WELFARE ADMINISTRATOR
NEW YORK TIMES, 15 MARCH 1989

IN the absence of prohibitive barriers to employment, the question
of the personality of the poor emerges as the key to understanding
and overcoming poverty. Psychology is the last frontier in the search
for the causes of low work effort. Opportunities to avoid poverty and
dependency seem abundant in America. Why do the poor not seize
them as assiduously as the culture assumes they will? *Who exactly are
they?* While the poor are diverse, the debate here hinges on the two
elements most central to long-term, working-aged poverty—welfare
mothers and the nonworking men of the inner city. The psychology
of these groups is so important that a number of poverty experts
have recently written statements about it. I take as optimists those
who see the poor as fundamentally rational, as willing and able to
work if only the constraints around them change. Pessimists say the
reluctance to work is more deeply ingrained.

My own view is a moderate one. It rejects the position that nonwork is sensible behavior for the poor, and also the view that the poor
are fundamentally flawed or opposed to work. I see them rather as
dutiful but defeated. They do harbor attitudes that discourage work,

as pessimists say, but the origin of these feelings lies mainly in the difficult histories of the most disadvantaged ethnic groups, not in the injustice of the current society. To a great extent, nonwork occurs simply because work is not enforced. Overall, I think conservatives have the better of the barriers debate—the chance to get ahead is widely available. But liberals have the more realistic view of the psychology of poverty—the poor do not *believe* they have opportunity, and this still keeps them from working.

OPTIMISTS

Optimists about poverty psychology say that the poor are rational about their self-interest, but are deterred from working by their situation. They have essentially the same attitudes and abilities as other people, but welfare disincentives or barriers to opportunity make it unprofitable for them to seek employment. Conservatives like Charles Murray argue that poor adults are tempted into dysfunction by the welfare system, which in effect pays them not to marry or work. In *Losing Ground*, Murray explicitly rejects the idea that any sort of "culture of poverty" is needed to explain the differentness of the poor. In his analysis, there is "no 'breakdown of the work ethic'... no shiftless irresponsibility... no need to invoke the specters of cultural pathologies or inferior upbringing." Rather, poverty and dependency result simply from "people... making the decisions... that maximize their quality of life" in the welfare system.[1]

Seeing that policy positions are "decisively affected by the analyst's conception of human nature," Murray went on in a later book to state his psychological presuppositions more explicitly. His *In Pursuit* sets forth the argument that ordinary people are perfectly able to realize their own happiness, alone and in voluntary association with others, if only government ensures basic security and refrains from meddling.[2]

While most optimists are conservatives, the group also includes some liberals. These experts, typically economists, also believe that more of the poor could well work, but they find the main constraint in the meager rewards of employment compared to welfare. According to a government study of poverty psychology headed by David Ellwood, the main reason few welfare mothers work is that "it is hard to earn one's way off of welfare" without higher wages and benefits than low-skilled people typically earn.[3] In the words of Bradley

Schiller, another liberal economist, the poor "share middle-class goals and await improved opportunities to pursue them."[4]

A related idea, which goes back to Durkheim, is that aberrant behavior results from conflicting pressures. Society teaches that everyone should get ahead economically, but it does not provide the worst-off with the skills or opportunities necessary to do so in socially prescribed ways. The disadvantaged fall back on illegitimate means, for example, crime. According to poverty researcher Leonard Goodwin, "A poor youth who cannot obtain money from his family or from a job may engage in petty theft, not because he really likes it, but because it is the only way he can think of to get enough money."[5]

Previous chapters have already questioned the presumption underlying the optimists' argument, that the poor are surrounded by unusual constraints. So it seems unreasonable, in most cases, to construe welfare dependency as rational behavior. Work levels on welfare respond very little to changes in benefit levels, as the last chapter showed; they respond little more to the wages the mothers are able to earn.[6] But even if not working were rational in some narrow sense, it would involve other costs. Many women with dependent children reasonably resort to welfare briefly, due to the loss of a spouse or a job, but to stay on welfare for the long term is damaging. We may be able to understand why poor teenagers give up on school and go on welfare for years, but it is not sensible behavior. Such mothers are much less likely to marry well or obtain satisfying jobs than those who get through school and avoid welfare.[7] As even Ellwood admits, "It is not rational to get pregnant at 17, no matter what the alternatives appear to be."[8]

The rational model also suggests that unskilled men and youth choose crime over work because it pays more, or is more available, than legitimate employment. This seems improbable. Crime is not strongly related to the unemployment rate, as one would expect if the theory were true.[9] Nor does crime seem a rational choice for unskilled workers. While it may appear so in the short run, over a year or more crime pays less on average than regular employment, even at low wages. The income poor people get from crime is in fact limited.[10] Many have supposed that the recent surge of cocaine addiction in the ghetto has meant a bonanza for drug sellers, and it is true that the crack epidemic of the 1980s made more poor youth than before think that crime paid better than legitimate work.[11] But in fact most dealers involved in the drug trade make very little money.

They also face serious risks of arrest and incarceration, violence from superiors or rival dealers, and becoming addicted themselves.[12]

How can nonwork be rational in the usual, economic sense if work raises income? That is the problem the optimists fail to solve. Under current conditions, if the poor were rational in the usual sense, they would probably not remain needy for very long in the first place. They would seize on available opportunities to earn money, and most would soon be nonpoor, if not middle class. The puzzle is that poor adults seem less responsive to economic incentives than the better-off, even though they need money more.

One can claim that the poor calculate the consequences of their actions only over the short term, not the long. So, as Charles Murray argues, they will decline to work or marry because this seems to pay under the current "rules of the game," even though such behaviors are "traps" in the long run.[13] One can also argue that in not working, they are maximizing some other value than income, for example "leisure" or taking care of children. To use "rational" in these senses, however, is an abuse of language. Unless rationality involves foresight, it is not distinguishable from impulse, and unless the goal maximized involves material gain, then all behavior becomes rational, in the sense that *some* purpose lies behind it.

The idea that incentives or disincentives could explain poverty largely accounts for the prominence economists have had as interpreters of poverty. They have dominated antipoverty policy-making for over twenty years, but in retrospect their influence is surprising. Theirs is a science of market behavior, while the poor today are a largely nonmarket group. There is simply no way to reconcile the rapid job turnover and long-term joblessness found among the needy with the supposition that they are maximizing their income.[14] Some economists admit that "We still understand very little about the basic causes of poverty." The entire tradition of explaining poverty or dependency in terms of incentives or disincentives is bankrupt.[15]

Nevertheless, the rationalist approach to poverty remains attractive to politicians and others because it is the truest to the competence assumption. It is comforting to many to believe the poor have the same motivations as the better-off, as this minimizes the seriousness of the social problem. All society needs to do is change the incentives controlling poverty behavior, and work levels will rise. It is hard to accept that an economic theory that describes what happens on Wall Street, and to a great extent on Main Street, cannot explain why the passive poor remain on the sidelines of American life.

CAPABILITY

More pessimistic readings of poverty psychology are readier to conclude that the poor are different in some way. But how? In the past,
such theories were often racist. It was a common belief in the nineteenth century that blacks would inevitably be poor, even if they were
liberated from slavery, because they had an innate inability to compete with whites. According to historian J. R. Pole, they were seen
as "defective in those hard, acquisitive, and competitive characteristics which undoubtedly dominated the world of ... business." A lesser
but similar suspicion greeted the waves of immigrants from Southern
and Eastern Europe—Jews, Italians, Greeks, Russians, Poles—when
they flooded penniless into the country at the turn of the century.[16]

Such theories have been discredited by the advance of all racial
groups toward mainstream status. Most of the turn-of-the-century
immigrant groups have risen to parity, or near parity, with the rest
of the population in income, occupation, and status. In the wake
of the civil rights movement, a sizable black middle class has done
the same. Variation in income or status is now much greater within
racial and ethnic groups than between them.[17] The black advance
debunked genetic theories of black inferiority just as it did the view
that discrimination prevented all black progress.

Blacks have recently found success in the business world that the
earlier theories said was too tough for them. Whites may still raise
eyebrows when they discover that their boss or their account executive is black, but this has not stemmed the growth in the ranks of black
executives. While most black businesspeople work in firms owned by
others, the number of black-owned businesses rose by 38 percent
between 1982 and 1987, compared to 14 percent for all firms.[18] A
few blacks have already won business distinction of the highest order,
for instance Reginald Lewis, a leading financier on Wall Street, and
Richard Parsons, chief executive of the Dime Savings Bank of New
York.[19] Past theories of racial differences cannot account for their
success.

At the other end of society, the poor population includes all races.
While the long-term poor and the underclass are mostly black, there
are also entrenched poor white populations, notably in Appalachia.
The nonwhite face of poverty is exaggerated if we look only at the
major cities; in smaller cities, the white poor are more significant.[20]
The most dramatic collapse of social functioning in America has
occurred among Puerto Ricans, most of whom are white. Between

1960 and 1985, the share of Puerto Rican families with female heads exploded from 16 to 44 percent; the women mostly went on welfare instead of working, and their poverty rate soared.[21]

The idea that racial inferiority could explain poverty rests mainly on the fact that blacks typically score 12–15 points lower than whites on IQ tests. While that difference seems ominous to many, its implications are limited. Blacks have much the same range of intelligence as whites; only their average is lower.[22] The black deficit seems rooted more in black children failing to realize as much of their potential as whites, due to weaker families and schools. Arguments for a genetic difference are dubious.[23]

Intelligence seems to be changeable over history. Some immigrant groups, such as Jews and Japanese, initially performed poorly on IQ tests and in school, then did markedly better as they achieved higher social status. IQ thus may reflect the success and morale of a group as much as inborn potential.[24] In any event, intelligence as measured by tests has less to do with economic success than abilities to influence people and get things done.[25]

As noted previously, women who live on welfare for extended periods seem to have proclivities for dependency not accounted for by measurable characteristics, but these leanings do not seem connected to race. While blacks, on average, are more often dependent than whites, the association disappears once one controls for conditions that dispose people to welfare, such as low education and numbers of children.[26] Women who grew up on welfare are only slightly more likely to go on welfare themselves than otherwise similar women without this experience.[27]

One can also focus, not on race as such, but on dysfunctional groups such as criminal offenders or the long-term dependent. James Q. Wilson and Richard Herrnstein find that violent criminals tend to display an aggressive and impulsive temperament as well as low intelligence from a young age, characteristics they attribute to heredity and parental influences rather than later social influences. Less extreme antisocial traits may cause nonwork.[28] Serious criminals are far fewer, however, than nonworking men.

Even if inborn differences between races or classes do exist, they would—like the barriers considered earlier—explain inequality better than nonwork. They would imply only that blacks or the poor will typically have low earnings and fail to succeed in competitive senses. They could not explain why the poor fail disproportionately to work at all.

My own conclusion is that the *nature* of poverty is not racial at all. It is not necessary or inevitable that most of the poor should be non-white. Rather, the *politics* of poverty is racial. Unlike any other group, blacks can point to a history of slavery and officially sanctioned bias. This makes it easier for them to call for government redress, and more difficult for whites to call for black self-reliance. But the social problems poor blacks experience are not in themselves distinctive.

VALUES

Another tradition in pessimistic interpretations of poverty has been to doubt that the poor want to work or observe other mainstream civilities. This would be the simplest solution to our problem, for if poor people do not want to work, then nonwork is easy to explain. In disputes about dependency, conservatives have been the readiest to question the values of the poor, just as liberals are the readiest to disbelieve their competence.

The public doubts the poor believe in the work ethic. According to a recent study, most voters think of welfare recipients as "able-bodied and indolent people who take advantage" of government assistance, and do not share the national belief in "the importance of hard work." In the words of one respondent, "How are we going to educate these people to think our way?"[29] If one infers values from the low work levels now found among the poor, that conclusion easily follows.[30]

Some studies suggest that work indeed has a low priority among the needy. In this view, welfare mothers are not tortured by their joblessness. They simply do not think of themselves as workers. Their role in life is to keep house and raise children; other people should support them—a husband if available, welfare if not. The stigma of welfare bothers them less than it does people who are not on welfare.[31] Detachment from work also emerges strongly from some firsthand accounts of low-income life. In poor neighborhoods, according to sociologist Elliot Liebow, a sympathetic observer, "Men, women and children spend much of their time on the street, on corners, sitting 'on the front,' or leaning out of windows." Life revolves around "Lovemaking, mate seeking, gambling and drinking." Getting ahead is secondary.[32]

But these studies are based mostly on unstructured observation of the actual behavior of the poor. When asked about their attitudes, poor people express the same desire to work as other people. Leonard Goodwin concluded, after comparing work attitudes of those on and off welfare, that "The poor and the nonpoor, blacks and whites, the young and the old, feel the same way about work." All strongly affirm it. Jobless men and women in federal employment programs also say they want to work, not only for the income, but for prestige and self-respect.[33] Poor people also affirm other middle-class norms such as law-abidingness, maintaining stable marriages, and getting through school. However aberrant their life-style may be, it does not signify a counterculture. In their thinking about how life should be, they are part of the larger society. They simply live by these norms less consistently than the better-off.[34]

How does one reconcile what the poor say with their low actual work levels? In part, they may profess the work ethic because they know that this is what interviewers want to hear. The unpleasant jobs they are usually able to get must make them ambivalent about work. My judgment, nevertheless, is that their answers in surveys are essentially sincere. Most poor people probably do want to work at some level, even if doing so is often not an immediate priority. The costs they incur for not working are too heavy for them to feel otherwise.[35] More concretely, as the next chapter will show, they respond positively to programs that require them to work.

At the heart of any definition of competence is the notion of consistency, the idea that one does what one wants to do. This is the psychology that the middle class assumes. The poor, however, are inconsistent. They challenge conventional values without asserting others. They *offend* mainstream society while *clinging* to it, even seeking greater entry. That contradiction is probably what exasperates better-off Americans about poverty as much as anything. It would be easier to understand bohemians who offended society without seeking to join it, or radicals who sought a new society without identifying with the old.

PESSIMISTS

Today's pessimistic theorists of poverty psychology do not say that the poor are inferior or opposed to work, but they do believe, contrary to the optimists, that the poor defeat themselves in some way. To understand nonwork, we require a more complex psychology than rational calculation. Inconsistent behavior must result from attitudes that keep the poor from working even though, in principle, they want to.

A sociologist like Christopher Jencks involves "culture" in the explanation of poverty. The seriously poor have troubles in their family and work life that most other people avoid. The explanation, in Jencks's view, is that society no longer clearly endorses traditional mores such as the ideas that illegitimacy and divorce are wrong. The elites who shape the culture have abandoned these prejudices. But while a liberated life-style involves few costs for them, it has proven disastrous for the poor, who have far fewer resources.[36]

Jencks himself is doubtful of the mismatch theory, which, as we saw earlier, offers deindustrialization as the central problem for the poor. Another liberal sociologist identified with this theory, William Julius Wilson, also appeals to counterproductive attitudes as part of his explanation of inner-city problems. The damage caused by economic change, he says, is reinforced by the "social milieu" of the ghetto, in which role models for success are lacking and people suffer from a "low perceived self-efficacy" that discourages employment.[37]

In Wilson's view, the blame still accrues to society. In his Godkin Lecture at Harvard and in other statements, he has attacked the "individualism" of American social policy. Conservative analysts persist in attributing poverty to the merely personal failings of individual poor people. They blame the deficient "*moral fabric of individuals*" instead of the "*social and economic structure of society.*" Poverty should not be blamed on a "welfare ethos" in isolation, Wilson argues, but rather on "the cumulative structural entrapment and forcible socioeconomic marginalization resulting from the historically evolving interplay of class, racial, and gender domination, together with sea changes in the organization of American capitalism and failed urban and social policies."[38]

The long words reflect the sociologism of liberal analysis, the conviction that poverty, however personal in its immediate causes, must always be traced to social forces outside the self. But if most of the pessimists are liberals, there are some conservatives who say much the same thing. Another government study of poverty psychology, headed by Kevin Hopkins, concluded that poverty is rooted mostly in the failure of the seriously poor to develop habits of self-reliance. For lack of strong families and schools, the dependent do not learn at a formative age how to achieve goals like work. The main difference from the liberal view is that the blame is laid on ineffective social programs rather than on the limitations of the economy.[39]

RESISTANCE

One attitude that deters work is resistance to available jobs. A considerable number of the poor, particularly men, seem not to work because they reject the jobs they can get as inadequate in pay or conditions. The implication is not that they do not want to work at all, but that they will work only *if* the jobs they get allow them to live a mainstream life. The behavior is noneconomic because it arises from moral revulsion rather than calculations of self-interest; the motive is to save one's self-respect or make a political point, even at the cost of lower income.

Commentators on both the right and the left have asserted this theory. According to sociologist Nathan Glazer, the essential cause of today's mass dependency is that "various kinds of work that used to support families" have become "undesirable to large numbers of potential workers."[40] According to Frances Fox Piven and Richard A. Cloward, work levels fell after the 1960s when young blacks came to feel that the "bitterly hard life" society offered them in menial jobs was "neither inevitable nor legitimate."[41]

Resistance to unpleasant jobs apparently does reduce work levels. Disadvantaged black youth are unemployed or out of the labor force twice as often as whites, and a quarter to a third of that gap is due to the wages they demand in order to work. The pay they expect is no higher than whites' demands in absolute terms, but it is higher relative to their qualifications and the jobs they can actually get. Their refusal to lower their demands thus helps keep them jobless. Work levels are also higher among black youth with higher career aspirations, who see working as hopeful, than among those with lower ones.[42]

Welfare mothers also commonly reject low-paid positions. While most want to work and many do so sporadically, they do not "care for menial jobs."[43] Substantial proportions of welfare mothers oppose working as maids, and some say they would decline such work if offered, even though this is often the only kind of job they can get. They want "better" positions that pay more and confer prestige, even though these require more education or training than they have. Such feelings appear to have strengthened in the last thirty years, and that is one reason work levels have fallen. In 1950, two-fifths of black women worked as domestics; in 1980, less than 5 percent did.[44] Welfare, for many, has become a substitute, and of those welfare mothers who do work, few hold menial jobs.[45]

When asked, many nonworking men express strong aversion to low-skilled employment. They describe the jobs they can get as "hard, dirty, uninteresting and underpaid."[46] Some welfare mothers say the same. One who used to be a maid told Studs Terkel, "I don't want my kids to come up and do domestic work. It's degrading." "Mighty few young black women are doin' domestic work. And I'm glad.... There's no more gettin' on their knees."[47]

The resistance can take on a political aspect. The public believes welfare recipients should return to the menial jobs they used to do, and much of the pressure behind workfare stems from this.[48] At congressional hearings on welfare reform, AFDC mothers rejected the idea that they work as domestic help rather than live off the public. "Poor women want to work," declared one mother, "but we do not want to work for slave wages."[49] Meanwhile, the continuing sight of so many adults standing around idle in poor neighborhoods exerts remorseless pressure on government and experts to solve the work problem. It is as if nonworkers have been carrying on a demonstration. From the viewpoint of getting attention, nonwork would have to be called a success.

Nevertheless, the resistance has been costly. Rebellious attitudes mean that low-skilled job seekers often cannot get and keep jobs even when they want to. Even fair-minded employers must expect that workers perform, but many youth bristle at the demands and thus end up quitting or getting fired. Successful blacks such as Richard Parsons tell youth, "Don't let the fact that life isn't always fair stop you from working hard."[50] But many are too alienated to comply, to their own cost.

DEFEATISM

Some pessimists argue that many of the poor fail to work consistently because they find the demands of work to be overwhelming. Thus, many welfare mothers would accept available jobs, but they have given up trying to manage all the logistics involved—finding a job, arranging transportation, setting up child care, getting to the job every day, and so on. The desire to work succumbs to defeatism.

Disadvantaged people without jobs find no end to reasons why working is impossible for them. The jobs they can get pay little compared to welfare, society is racist, they can never get training—the whole litany of barriers imagined by liberal analysts. They avoid personal responsibility and blame circumstances beyond their control, arguing that government must find them a job, arrange training, child care, and transportation, then reassemble the pieces whenever anything goes wrong. While some of the feeling springs from injured pride, as discussed above, the stronger note here is helplessness, a sheer disbelief that one ever could work on one's own.[51]

This theory approaches the classic idea of "culture of poverty" developed by the first generation of antipoverty researchers in the 1960s. The keynote of that theory was that the poor accept mainstream values such as working in principle, but feel unable to achieve them in practice. The implication is not that they are behaving reasonably under constraint, as the rationality theory would have it, but rather that they have lost control of their lives. They find themselves unable to live by the values they profess, and that very fact accounts for much of their depression. They have to give up the idea that mores are binding. Work and other norms come to be felt as aspirations but not as obligations.[52]

Another implication missing from the rationality theory is that the feeling of helplessness is ingrained: Due to prior failures to work and succeed, nonworkers have so internalized helplessness that they seldom seek work, even if opportunity becomes available. Jobs may be declined even if offered, to avoid the risk of further failure.[53] By this means, nonwork can persist even under conditions of full employment. For government to offer help may only exacerbate the problems, by ratifying the conviction of the defeated that they can manage only with outside help.[54] The attitude can be passed on from one generation to the next. Children may feel as helpless as their parents did, even though their chances to succeed are really greater.[55]

Another divergence from the rationality theory is that, faced with a hostile environment, the poor take actions that are self-defeating. This supposition better accounts for poverty behavior than the notion of short-term calculations. Inability to withstand present frustration makes later life futile. Completing school is hard, so teenage girls drop out and have babies, which relegates them to lives on welfare. Supporting oneself in low-paid jobs is hard, so men quit and hustle drugs, which gives them a criminal record and little chance of better-paying jobs. Feeling trapped, Michael Harrington says, poor people are "driven to hurt themselves." They say, according to William Julius Wilson, that "I know this is wrong but there's nothing else I can do."[56] Thus their belief that success is impossible becomes self-confirming.

Studies of attitudes find that whether poor people work does not depend on how strongly they believe in work, which is fairly constant, but rather on how confident they are that they can work and on whether they accept welfare as an alternative. The long-term poor adopt what sociologist Lee Rainwater calls a "depressive" style that aims only to survive. They lower their aspirations and do no more than the minimum to get by. They depersonalize failure, blaming it on outside forces and tuning out stigma. They feel welfare without work limits their commitments.[57]

The core of the culture of poverty seems to be inability to control one's life—what psychologists call inefficacy. From the earliest systematic research on poverty it was clear that the sense that one was responsible for consequences was strongly linked to getting ahead in life.[58] Statistical studies find that the poor and dependent typically are lower in efficacy than the better-off. Most likely, the connection is that confidence leads to employment and keeps people out of poverty, but success may also build confidence.[59]

Donna Van Name, a single mother subsisting on welfare in Boston, is typical. She used to be a clerk and wants to return to work, but feels she cannot, due to the cost of child care, low wages, and other problems.[60] To me, this story is not very plausible. Living in the tightest labor market in the country at the time, she probably could find an adequate job, and, by taking advantage of the state's very generous workfare program, she certainly could obtain quality child care. The point, though, is that a mentality is at work that refuses to believe that opportunity exists, even when it does. As long as mothers like this have so little inner sense of freedom, no reform in the outer pattern of opportunity can raise work levels very much. In a sense, such people *are* oppressed by the conditions around them, for those who lack a sense of mastery will inevitably be governed by their environment.

THE GHETTO

Resistance to low-wage jobs and a sense of defeatism appear to be the main deterrents to work in the minds of the poor. These are sentiments that could have dominated poor areas at any point in American history. Thirty years ago, employment was certainly less fair and probably less available than it is today. Yet the poor more usually worked then than now. While the ghetto does not appear to be isolated from the economy, as the mismatch theory contends, it is increasingly socially isolated. As a result, attitudes contrary to employment appear to have strengthened in the inner city, or to meet less reproof there.

Poor people are becoming more concentrated in the inner city. The number of poor living in urban neighborhoods with poverty rates of over 40 percent grew by 30 percent between 1970 and 1980, the result not of poor people moving in, but of the better-off leaving.[61] In ghetto areas, residents are notably less functional than outside. According to a study done in Chicago, blacks living in areas with 40 percent poverty have less education and less often own their homes than those in areas of 20–30 percent poverty. But the greatest difference is in work levels: In the 20–30 percent poverty areas, two-thirds of adults work compared to only 39 percent in the 40 percent poverty areas. As a result, 25 percent of residents are on welfare in the areas of lower poverty versus 58 percent in the higher-poverty areas.[62]

Institutions linked to dependency are a presence in and around the ghetto. Here is where homeless shelters and other custodial institutions tend to be clustered, in part because land is cheaper and community resistance less effective. Here, too, most public housing projects are built, and black youth who live in them or on welfare are markedly less likely to be in school or working than others.[63] Here is where welfare is most often long term, which also means it is nonworking.[64] Living in such neighborhoods does seem to add extra pressures toward dysfunction. Youth from heavily poor and black areas are somewhat more likely to drop out of school, become unwed mothers, and earn low wages, even controlling for personal characteristics. Less certainly, they are more likely to get into crime.[65]

The underlying cause appears to be that social authority breaks down in the ghetto. A generation ago, due to Jim Crow, most black middle-class and professional people, including clergy, lawyers, teachers, and government employees, lived in the same neighborhoods as less prosperous blacks. They offered models of work effort and success to the less fortunate, and they financed the churches and other institutions that helped to realize orthodox goals for the group as a whole.[66] But after civil rights reforms, much of the black middle-class took advantage of improved prospects to move to better neighborhoods, or to the suburbs, just as the white middle class had done before them. Their departure deprived poor blacks of leadership and social resources[67]; the hostile or resigned attitudes they always had toward employment then encountered less restraint.

The sanction of social disapproval seems essential for deterring antisocial behavior, and in any community, much of that pressure comes from the more substantial citizens.[68] Once they leave, an atmosphere of failure and disorder easily comes to dominate schools and streets. Now families who want to go straight no longer receive support from the society. Parents find it difficult to protect their offspring from crime or pregnancy. Socializing institutions that used to help them, such as churches, lose their grip on the community.[69] The desire for schooling, jobs, and social respectability remains, but is more and more divorced from actual life.[70]

ETHNICITY

The main limitation of the pessimistic approach as presented above is that it fails to explain why some ethnic groups—blacks, Hispanics, and American Indians—are poor at much higher levels than others. Since innate differences show little tie to poverty (the heavily poor groups are themselves racially diverse), the cause must lie in ethnic history. The difficult experiences of these groups over decades, even centuries, seems to be why their members today often doubt that they can get ahead in America.

J. R. Pole remarks that American social thinking assumes a "principle of interchangeability," reflecting the abstraction of American public culture, the separation of American citizenship from any particular background. Individuals of any ethnicity are seen as equally able to play any role in society, provided they receive the requisite training and experience.[71] But in fact, different groups have had very different experiences both before and after coming to America, and this leads to different propensities to prosper.

The most successful groups in economic terms have been those (such as Jews and Asians) that were already urbanized in their countries of origin, committed to remaining in America, and hardworking in school and on the job. Jews and Asians also avoided welfarism and had strong families able to prepare children for education and success in the new society. The least successful groups, at least initially, were those who came from rural or peasant backgrounds, sometimes came only for the short term, and were less diligent as workers. They also had weaker families and were more prone to rely on public assistance. These included Irish, Mexicans, and Puerto Ricans, as well as American blacks, whose shift from Southern farms to Northern cities was an internal form of immigration.[72]

One may argue that the differing economic cultures of the groups are the outcome, not the cause, of their fortunes. People who are systematically denied opportunity will inevitably be less provident.[73] I see much truth in this view, particularly for blacks and Hispanics.

From their long subservience to whites, as Thomas Sowell observes, blacks learned those "foot-dragging, work-evading patterns" that persist in poorer members of the group today. However, Jews and Asians encountered lesser degrees of prejudice yet have done remarkably well. Their success in school and their diligence as workers overcame their disadvantages.[74]

Though the groups each contain the entire range of temperaments, from the most self-reliant to the most dependent, they do, on average, exhibit sharply different stances toward getting ahead, particularly in their political postures. Jews and Asians have exemplified exactly the personality assumed and recommended by conservative analysts. They have been self-reliant optimizers, seizing chances for good schooling and careers with a minimum of claim making and appeal to government. They have chosen to ignore or endure bias, rather than, as Thomas Sowell says, "surrender to despair or exhaust themselves in trying to reform others." Blacks and Hispanics have more often shown the demoralization that liberal analysts see at the core of poverty. While most members of these groups have been self-reliant, black and Hispanic leaders speak mainly for the unsuccessful, constantly petitioning government to change the social rules in their favor.[75]

Hispanics face special problems of assimilation not shared by the European groups or by blacks. Partly because of bilingual education and social services, Hispanics have been slower than most earlier immigrants to enter mainstream culture, and especially to learn English. Since the Hispanic population is growing much faster than blacks, it may soon pose an even greater challenge to integration. "Mexicans, together with other Spanish-speaking populations," according to one observer, "are creating a bifurcation in the social-political structure of the United States."[76]

BLACK CULTURE

The culture of black America is the most significant for an understanding of today's nonwork and poverty. Although less than a third of blacks are poor in a given year, a majority of the long-term poor come from this group. Evidently, the worldview of blacks makes them uniquely prone to the attitudes contrary to work, and thus vulnerable to poverty and dependency.

Civil rights leaders and white liberals often suggest that the problems of poor blacks follow automatically from the injustice of American society today. Poor blacks seldom express themselves in such terms. I believe their condition usually arises in the first instance from their families, the lack of fathers and other problems spoken of by psychologists. Dysfunction does connect to social structure, but further back in history. Today's black poor function poorly because their parents did, and *their* parents did, a pattern that ultimately goes back to the black experience as a subordinate caste in America. Group memories of slavery and Jim Crow inculcate hopelessness more powerfully than any bias blacks are likely to meet at present.[77]

Other groups also experienced prejudice, albeit less intensely. Blacks are more distinctive in how they responded. They did not— with the exception of a few intellectuals and Black Muslims—turn away from white society and rely on their own enterprise to get ahead, as Jews and Asians did at first. Blacks did not, for example, flee the South in large numbers until well into this century.[78] They remained dependent on the white man, both economically and psychologically. They continued to look to white society for the solution of their problems. This paradoxical reliance on the oppressor to undo oppression would become one of the keynotes of dependency politics.[79]

The civil rights movement was one of the glories of progressive politics and an expression of considerable self-reliance. Yet at the culmination of the great March on Washington in 1963, Dr. Martin Luther King, Jr., spoke of justice for blacks as a "promissory note" on which America had so far defaulted. Blacks, he said, had "come to cash this check, a check that will give us upon demand the riches of freedom and the security of justice" and thus "make real the promises of democracy."[80] The metaphor reflects the deep-seated conviction, shared by blacks and many whites, that blacks are victims who can be saved only by outside forces.[81]

Blacks' own doubt about opportunity, as well as discrimination, are reasons they have put their strongest efforts into peripheral areas of American life. Black achievements have been conspicuous in the arts, sports, religion, and government service. Black educators have become symbols of the faith in education that all Americans share. In all these areas, blacks' presence is out of all proportion to their numbers in the population. In the performing arts, and especially in music, the black contribution has been so extraordinary that without it American culture would seem almost two-dimensional. Aside from government service, however, none of these endeavors can support large numbers. Until recently, blacks have played a much smaller role in the institution where other groups find their economic base—the private economy.

Black society sometimes appears polarized between a leadership of unusual distinction and a disproportionate number of poor people. The situation is exemplified by the life of Dr. James A. Forbes, Jr., a black clergyman who rose from humble origins to become a professor at the elite Union Theological Seminary in New York and then minister of nearby Riverside Church, an affluent, mostly white institution given to supporting social causes.[82] Union and Riverside, situated on Morningside Heights in Manhattan, look down upon Harlem, where large numbers of blacks subsist on welfare and drugs.

More important for black progress may be men like Billy W. Best, a dedicated industrial arts teacher who coaches fatherless black youth in the Washington, D.C., public schools. Best imparts basic skills, gives encouragement, and reproves indiscipline. His students say he "tells us what a man is supposed to do, what's right and what's wrong," and "how we're supposed to act when we go to the white man to get a job." His credo is that "all black men need to go to college and become self-employed." Just as important, Best is a steady husband and father who has raised two sons himself.[83] If there were many more Billy Bests living disciplined, workaday lives, black poverty and nonwork would not be the problems they are.

Among poor blacks, life-styles have developed that direct energies away from getting ahead. Middle-class blacks as well as whites presume that by working steadily one can at least become a stable family provider, if not successful in competitive terms. Disadvantaged blacks, however, tend to sacrifice such modest hopes to satisfactions in the present. Many develop what Lee Rainwater calls an "expressive life-style," oriented to verbal jousting and personal display rather than practical achievement. Unfortunately, employers reject this style as shiftless and irresponsible; workers who display it tend to be fired or quit in short order.[84] The display of "soul," one might say, comes at the expense of payroll.[85]

Blacks have had difficulty asserting themselves in conventional careers. They have, as black commentator Shelby Steele says, "a fear of self-interested action."[86] Their challenge is to seize chances to get ahead without giving personal offense. This requires conforming to common civilities and satisfying authority figures such as teachers and employers, yet competing for success in legitimate ways. That is what better-off Americans of all races understand. By offending the authorities yet dropping out of school and not working, poor blacks do exactly the opposite.

Where blacks have been properly assertive, they too have succeeded. Much of the reason for the extraordinary black achievement in the arts and athletics is that, in these fields, blacks work hard for success without expecting help from whites.[87] Blacks have also excelled recently in the military, where they now comprise 23 percent of the active forces, nearly double their proportion of the population. In the army, they comprise 32 percent of the force, 35 percent of the noncommissioned officers, and 11 percent of the commissioned officers. There are twenty-six black generals, led by Colin Powell, chairman of the Joint Chiefs of Staff. The reasons for this remarkable advance appear to be capable black recruits coupled with tough equal opportunity policies that convinced many blacks that the military was a place where they could strive and succeed.[88]

For the black poor, however, the challenge is to work hard in jobs that do not immediately convey much income or prestige. This is what a great many blacks during the progressive period were willing to do. They became the parents of today's black middle class. In that era, working hard and going to church were much of what black culture meant. Today, tragically, it is more likely to mean rock music or the rapping of drug dealers on ghetto street corners. That change, rather than any change in the surrounding society, seems to lie at the origin of the underclass.

THE THIRD WORLD

I also believe that the work attitudes of many of today's seriously poor were shaped, in part, by their origin in the Third World. The groups that initially formed American society came almost entirely from Europe. Today's immigrants come mostly from Latin America and Asia; and blacks, who have been latter-day migrants to American cities, have their origins in Africa. The important difference is not a racial one, since the non-European immigrants include all races. Rather, it is a difference in worldview.

One of the basic distinctions between the West and non-West is that, in modern times, only the former has consistently taken an activist attitude toward economic activity. Industrialism developed first in the West. People in the West commonly seek to justify themselves through material achievement, and Western societies have a dynamic, ever-changing character. The non-West has typically been less interested in economic progress, suspicious of individual striving, and slower to change. Except for Japan and a few other Asian countries, these societies are still "premodern" or "developing" in Western terms.[89]

The Founders of the United States were Westerners, and they gave the new culture an achieving, commercial stamp. As Herbert Croly wrote, "America has been peopled by Europeans primarily because they expected in that country to make more money more easily." Nineteenth-century schoolteachers told immigrant children that "the end was to get ahead, to make good."[90] The groups that have excelled in America are those that were most Western in orientation if not in their origins. Asians, Jews, and most other whites have pursued material advancement through goal-oriented action, including a willingness to save, stay in school, and sacrifice present satisfactions for future ones.[91] In contrast, one frequently hears contemporary poverty described as "Third World." The image expresses the widespread sense that today's degradation is different from the distress earlier poor populations suffered in the United States. It is much more passive and enduring.[92]

The origin of this resignation lies in the formative experiences of the heavily poor groups. History has not confirmed for them the Western faith in the possibility of individual achievement. Hispanic immigrants remember their roots in Latin America, where governments have often been predatory, the culture resists material progress, and upward mobility for the masses has been lacking.[93] Black demoralization is heavily due to the oppressions of slavery and Jim Crow, but it seems unlikely in any event that people coming from Africa would quickly have become economic individualists. For although African culture is in many ways highly evolved, it did not begin to develop in the Western, economic sense before the advent of European colonialism in the nineteenth century.[94]

The adjustment of American blacks to the Western style of life began seriously only with the end of slavery. Black history since then can be seen as a high-pressure education in an economically achieving way of life. The black migration from the South to Northern cities was also an entry into a new world where money was the measure of success and blacks had to compete with whites as never before. The majority of blacks did adjust, becoming working class and then, in many cases, middle class, a remarkable tribute to their resiliency. As Sowell writes, no other group "had to come from so far back to join their fellow Americans."[95] The minority that did not adjust, however, seems to have generated most of today's long-term poverty.

THE NEW IMMIGRATION

If Third World immigrants often have problems in America, how do we account for the advancement of many of today's newcomers? Some, notably Asians, have been conspicuously successful. The answer is that immigration often is a selective process that favors people interested in "getting ahead."[96] Immigrants may look poor and uneducated to Americans, but they are typically above average in education and ambition for the countries they come from. After a transition period, most newcomers become decidedly nonpoor. Middle-class or skilled immigrants, who are favored by current immigration law, often step quickly into high-paying jobs. Some critics accuse the United States of stripping Third World countries of their best and brightest.[97]

Many immigrants come to America because they want to live an achieving, American-style life, leading to the paradox of immigrants preaching self-reliance to poorer, native-born Americans. West Indians typically outstrip native-born blacks,[98] taking jobs that native-born black youths decline due to low pay. In Miami, American-born blacks accuse Cubans and Haitians of truckling to the white man, while the immigrants accuse the natives of lacking the pride to get ahead on their own. "The Haitians," confessed a local black psychologist, "have a sense that we complain too much, that our children are out of control, that we don't do enough for ourselves."[99]

Dawit Wolde Giorgis is an Ethiopian now working with the homeless in New Jersey. He says that his clients often lack the "skills" and "motivation" to "become self-sufficient in this competitive society." He preaches to them the possibility of controlling their lives: "I say, 'Look, where I come from, there is nothing you can do about what happens to you. Nature, God, the government, these are beyond your control. But here, you can work and fight to change things.' Still it is hard for them.... They are not aggressive." According to Mark Matha Bane, a black author born in South Africa, American-born blacks are simply not prepared to work hard and meet white standards. They suffer from "defeatism" and the conviction that "black people are not as good as whites."[100]

However, immigration is selective only if it is difficult to get to America. Newcomers display the upwardly mobile, "immigrant personality" when they have to surmount logistical or legal barriers to get here. Those hurdles select in favor of Western-style competence. If entry is easy due to geography or lax government controls, immigrants will more often display a passive, Third World temperament. Thus, Asians or Arabs who have to cross oceans to get to the United States are more likely to be upwardly mobile than Hispanics, for whom access is easier. Among Hispanic subgroups, in turn, Mexicans are more hardworking than Puerto Ricans; they need such a temperament to get to the United States—often illegally—and prosper there. Puerto Ricans have right of entry as citizens, and so the same selective process does not operate. As a result, they do much worse economically than Mexicans. For the same reason, Jamaicans who came to New York have done better than those who emigrated to London; the latter have less advantaged backgrounds,[101] probably because for years they had right of entry to Britain as members of the Commonwealth.

Immigrants also will be more mobile when they decide to come here as individuals. Groups that come unwillingly or *en masse* are more likely to preserve a peasant mentality. The troubled history of the Irish in their early decades in America originated in the massive exodus from Ireland precipitated by the potato famine of the 1840s, a movement that no doubt swept along many who did not want to leave home. Similarly, Vietnamese and other refugees from Southeast Asia are currently the least successful of the Asians, with many involved in welfare or crime[102]; government transported large numbers to this country after the Vietnam war, whereas the more successful Chinese and Japanese came individually.

Most native-born blacks also descend from involuntary Americans—slaves—but the clearest case of all is that of American Indians, who were already here. Europeans overwhelmed them with a different culture, and they never fully adjusted. Indians are the most radically dependent of all poor groups, with about a quarter of them living on reservations as virtual wards of the state.[103] Many Hispanic settlements, especially in the Southwest, likewise predate American settlement and control.

Immigrants have the advantage, not only of selection, but of having chosen to assume the burdens of this society. They compare America favorably to their original lands, so they bear its faults and injustices with some patience. In contrast, the native-born poor often feel that Americanism has been imposed on them, and they are inclined to define themselves against the competence ethic, even at their own cost. For newcomers, doing well in school is accepted as a practical necessity, whereas for poor blacks it is to "act white" and lose their identity. The same resistance keeps many Hispanics from learning English. According to one leader, they "didn't come to the

U.S., so the idea of coming to a new country and having to adapt to it is not part of the mentality of many Hispanics."[104]

A large part of the today's poor might well be described as people, or their descendents, who did not really choose to come to America. The idea of America as a melting pot of nations originated among Western or Westernized groups, but now the country must integrate a much more far-reaching pluralism, one that touches basic attitudes to life. There is nothing inherently superior about Western culture. It has its own pathologies, and much of progressive politics is about controlling them. The self-seeking individualism of American business poses significant threats to the environment and the well-being of vulnerable citizens, which government must constantly offset. But for better or worse, activism remains the way of *this* society, so the non-Western worldview faces profound resistance in America. Many of the newer immigrants feel, and display, fatalistic attitudes about "getting ahead" that are alien to the dominant culture. Their conflict with harder-working Americans will continue to fuel dependency politics.

AUTHORITY

A limitation of all the theories of poverty psychology discussed so far is that they focus too much on the individual, not enough on the collectivity. One way or another, they all say that the poor want to work but are inhibited. Yet if the poor do not challenge the work ethic, it stands to reason that one cause of nonwork must be a breakdown in the sanctions that normally support social norms.

The loss of the middle class from the ghetto is one reason mainstream mores are not upheld among the poor as well as they once were, but public institutions are also critical. The most immediate cause of nonwork and other disorders may be that, starting in the 1960s, government largely gave up enforcing orthodox behavior among the urban poor. The schools allowed educational standards to decline, the criminal justice system ceased to deter crime and drug addiction, and—most relevant for this discussion—the welfare system no longer required employable recipients to work.[105] The contention that public authority matters is the main reason my view of poverty psychology is more hopeful than that of the pessimists: all these public institutions might, through changes in policy, become more authoritative, and then work levels would rise.

I do not mean to imply that these relaxations were easily avoidable. The social problems posed by the new poor were evidently more serious than those government had earlier confronted. There was more doubt that the newcomers could cope with the demands of American society, and this increased pressure to relax social standards, especially from politicians and activists who identified with the poor. The result was a profound crisis for social authority in America. Whether, and how, to restore that authority is what dependency politics is all about.

Enforcement, or lack thereof, can affect the behavior of the poor precisely because they do not question conventional values in principle. Middle-class critics assume that the less privileged must be rebels against the society, as they themselves would be if they were similarly deprived. The evidence suggests quite otherwise. In Western countries, the working and lower classes may be liberal on progressive issues concerning government intervention in the economy, but they are more conservative than the better-off about the issues of social order that dominate dependency politics. They want orthodox values firmly enforced, in part because they have often known severe treatment themselves.[106] Indeed, they want norms enforced exactly *because* of their tendency to deviate. Such people value external controls on behavior exactly because their internal controls are less secure, mainly due to ineffective parenting.[107]

According to sociologist Walter Miller, the apparent resistance of disadvantaged people to social norms like work or law-abidingness is not to be taken at face value. They actually desire control, which they typically have not had enough of. Beneath their rebelliousness lie "powerful dependency cravings" that equate "being controlled" with "being cared for." Thus, they will actually seek out "highly restrictive social environments wherein stringent external controls are maintained over their behavior," for example the armed forces or prison.[108] Far from seeking a greater freedom, they experience liberation as *abandonment*.

The competence assumption presumes that people willingly and actively pursue the best chances they can find to get ahead. Reformers, left and right, are full of schemes to include the poor more fully in the society through some new dose of opportunity, for example, expanded suffrage or schooling or better jobs. But as the political scientist Harry Eckstein has shown, the poor tend to frustrate such plans. Typically, they take up the new chances very reluctantly. They are not excluded from the society; rather, they exclude themselves.

The authorities and orthodox values are not challenged, but they are accepted at a distance, with little personal involvement and without much effect on behavior.[109]

This withdrawal reflects distrust of the society, but it is seldom overt. Mostly, poor people are *passively* aggressive. Even violent criminals, who are dangerous and therefore thought of as active, are fundamentally inert. They have difficulty asserting themselves in effective ways—and for that reason break out in uncontrolled impulses.[110] Poor blacks, particularly, tend to express hostility by devious refusals to cooperate, a passivity that infuriates whites—as it is intended to—without challenging them directly.[111]

Studies of disadvantaged black students in school find them to be hostile to the institution, but at the same time, deferential and evasive. They may threaten teachers, but without truly questioning their authority. Higher-status students do question their authority, but also identify with them sufficiently to learn from them. Poor children, even at their most compliant, withdraw from true engagement, because they do not believe that the middle-class life the school promises can be for them. They are thus not available to learn, and their fears of failure become self-confirming.[112]

The passivity of the poor suggests why the problem in the ghetto is not simply one of "law and order." The answer to poverty cannot be simply to repress disorders such as crime and drug addiction, necessary though that is. The energies of poor people must also be mobilized more fully on their own behalf. To escape poverty, they must become less deviant but *more* assertive in their own self-interest, especially by working.

THE CAUSE OF NONWORK

To sum up our search for the causes of nonwork: Conservatives are largely correct that opportunity is available to the poor. It is rarely true in any gross sense that social or economic barriers deny opportunity to nonworkers. But liberals have the more credible view of the psychology of poverty. To view the seriously poor as self-confident maximizers, as conservative analysts tend to do, is implausible.

Put another way, the poor do not face unusual obstacles to work *if one assumes normal competence*, namely the confident, maximizing attitudes of the better-off. Workers actually encounter more practical difficulties with employment than nonworkers, which shows that competence, not social fairness, is the important variable. In my opinion, the liberal viewpoint overstates the obstacles facing the poor, but captures quite well how the poor themselves feel. It is often said that the right explains poverty by blaming the victim, the left by blaming society. Actually, each side seems to understand the other's subject better: Conservatives grasp that society is open, while liberals grasp the convictions poor people have that society is closed.

The various theories liberals have about barriers should be understood, not as literally true, but as parables of poverty culture. A "closed opportunity structure"[113] does not exist for most people in America—but it does for those who believe it does. The mismatch theory does not appear to be accurate urban economics, but it is a powerful metaphor of the despair that the inner-city poor project onto their environment. One review of William Julius Wilson's *The Truly Disadvantaged*, entitled "Prisoners of the Economy," featured a cartoon showing a black man and woman, as large as Gulliver, their arms and legs built into the masonry of the tenements around them.[114] That is apparently how many of the poor see themselves—trapped without any chance to get ahead on their own.

The great question in social policy is whether to enforce the competence assumption against all odds or accommodate the special inhibitions of the poor. Through nonwork, poor adults ask, in essence, for better or easier employment than the economy offers them. Most analysts support them, arguing, one way or another, for public provision of better or easier jobs for the nonworkers, or support unrelated to working. Most voters and politicians resist, in part on account of the financial cost, but also because they reject tampering with the traditional terms of belonging in the society. They want the poor to prove themselves in menial jobs before expecting better.

While other factors play a role, *that impasse is the essential cause of the work problem*. In dependency politics, this debate occupies center stage. It is a dispute over social standards much more than opportunity, however much the contestants argue about "barriers." The question is what degree of competence—meaning work effort—is to be expected of citizens.

CHAPTER

8

Policy

If you don't use a degree of compulsion, how do you
get...people to realize that they are so much better off
if they get training and get into suitable employment?
— WILBUR MILLS
*CONGRESSIONAL HEARINGS ON SOCIAL SECURITY
AND WELFARE PROPOSALS*, 16 OCTOBER 1969

I was tired of sitting at home. The first month here,
I didn't think I could do it, but it got easier.
— OKLAHOMA WORKFARE PARTICIPANT
NEW YORK TIMES, 19 NOVEMBER 1988

THE work problem has not gone unnoticed in Washington. Federal policymakers have been trying to solve it for thirty years. A
succession of programs have aimed to increase earnings among the
poor and dependent. I examine that history here mainly to ratify the
view of nonwork taken in the preceding chapters. I will not review
the programs in detail but rather glean from their history what they
can tell us about the nature of the social problem. The research cited
above is useful, but programs test more concretely how easy it is to
work in America.

Experience has driven policymakers toward my own conclusion,
that psychic inhibition, not a lack of opportunity, is the greatest
impediment to employment. Expanding opportunity by increasing
the rewards of working has failed to raise work levels. Workfare
programs with authority to require employment or training have
had much more effect. They raise actual work effort substantially,
although their economic effects have so far been limited. Experience
with such programs also confirms that lack of jobs or child care is
rarely a serious constraint on clients going to work. Clients seldom

volunteer for workfare, yet once involved, most approve of it—which confirms the ambivalent psychology discussed in the last chapter. Workfare exemplifies a broader trend toward more directive social policies. Driven by passive poverty, a paternalistic system is emerging that guides the lives of the dependent in many respects as well as helping them.

MAKING WORK PAY

The most popular approach to solving the work problem has been to make employment more remunerative for the low-skilled, on the supposition that the poor fail to work because they do not get enough out of it. If we "make work pay," liberal economists say, more poor adults will choose to work steadily.[1] This advice follows from the diagnosis offered by liberal optimists in the last chapter. Unfortunately, enhancing rewards does not raise work levels, and may even reduce them.

A traditional device is raising the minimum wage, as Congress last did in 1989. The intent is to help the "working poor," but in fact most of the benefit goes to the better-off, simply because most minimum wage workers are already above poverty.[2] A more efficient mechanism is the Earned Income Tax Credit (EITC), an earnings subsidy confined to low-income workers with children that goes back to 1975. In 1990, Congress raised the EITC substantially; in 1991 eligible workers received a credit against federal taxes of around 17 percent of earnings, or as much as $1,235 a year, and higher amounts in later years. Both measures raise the effective wages of low-skilled workers, which makes them better off. But they probably will not work harder. A higher minimum wage probably reduces work levels, because it eliminates some jobs, and this causes some youth to withdraw from the labor force. A higher EITC probably reduces work effort slightly, because workers who qualify can now make the same income with fewer working hours.[3]

Another approach to changing the payoff from work is to weaken the disincentives in welfare that many still believe deter the dependent from working. The conservative version is simply to cut back welfare coverage and benefits so that fewer low-paid families can substitute welfare for work. Along these lines, the Reagan administration cut AFDC benefits and eligibility in 1981, eliminating most higher-income recipients from the rolls.[4] But Congress is unlikely to go much further in this direction; some of the 1981 cuts have already been reversed. In any event, the effect would probably be more to reduce dependency than to raise work levels or income, since, as we have seen, benefit levels have little influence on work effort.

The liberal version of the same idea is to improve incentives within welfare. If recipients could keep some of their earnings, economists reason, rather than have their grants reduced by the whole amount, more of them might work. "Work incentives" were included in the federal income maintenance experiments, as well as most of the welfare reform plans debated in Washington in the 1960s and 1970s. Unfortunately, the device increases the cost of welfare, since people with higher incomes qualify for aid, now that much of their earnings are excluded from the calculation of their needs.

Worse, work incentives failed to show much impact on actual work behavior. The income maintenance experiments recorded only weak effects. Fairly strong work incentives were also instituted in AFDC in 1962 and 1967, when working recipients were allowed to keep about a third of their earnings plus work expenses. These rewards had no palpable effect on work levels among recipients. The Reagan administration eliminated most of the incentives in 1981—and again work effort did not change.[5] These disappointments caused most experts and politicians to turn away from work incentives as a basis for welfare reform.[6]

The incentives idea has lately been reborn in proposals that would reward youth in various ways for going straight. In 1981, Eugene Lang, a New York businessman, visited his old school in East Harlem. On an impulse, he promised sixty-one sixth-graders that, if they graduated from high school, he would pay their college tuition. His "I Have a Dream" movement has since expanded to thirty-one cities. Businesses interested in obtaining more capable workers have also promised jobs to students in local schools if they succeed in graduating.[7]

Some analysts have recently proposed "individual development accounts" worth $20,000 or more for young people to use for further education or training, provided they finish high school and avoid pregnancy and crime. The idea is to "foster individual responsibility" by motivating the youth to behave in provident ways and plan for their future.[8] But it is implausible that merely improving the returns to virtue will accomplish much. The incentives for youth to get through school and avoid trouble are already great. If poor youth misbehave, the main reason is not that their rewards are limited but that they are not in control of their lives. If they were, they would seldom be poor for long in the first place. Only 16 percent of Eugene Lang's students are still in school and on schedule to graduate; many more have succumbed to the behaviors—pregnancy, crime, dropping out—the program was supposed to avoid.[9]

"Making work pay" is popular because it suggests that the poor respond to the same suasions as the middle class. But the people who respond to incentives are mainly those who are already functional, already within the economy. No incentive has shown a power to pull many people across the line from nonwork to work. For that, stronger medicine is required. Incentives assume competence; the need is to create it.

VOLUNTARY PROGRAMS

Another frequent approach to improving employment has been voluntary training and service programs, which attempt to raise earnings through teaching nonworkers new skills or providing other forms of support, but without requirements to participate. Where the incentives devices try to improve rewards in available, low-skilled jobs, training and services try to equip the jobless to get better positions.

The most widespread federal training programs have been those funded under the Job Training Partnership Act (JTPA) and, before 1982, the Comprehensive Employment and Training Act (CETA). These offer a range of classroom and on-the-job training options for disadvantaged job seekers. There are several youth-oriented programs begun under the War on Poverty, of which the most important today is the Job Corps, an intensive rehabilitation program for disadvantaged youth. There are also social service programs, mostly tied to welfare, that provide counseling, child and health care, and other assistance to mothers and children. These services are also often included in work programs linked to welfare.

Evaluations suggest that the training programs have at best a limited impact on incomes.[10] Typically, clients improve their earnings by something less than $1,000 a year, with women gaining more than men. While these gains may be enough to justify program costs, they seldom lift people out of poverty. This outcome should not seem surprising, since the clients, few of whom succeeded in school, commonly lack the potential to improve their skills very much. In any event, skills are not central, because poverty is due mainly to low working hours rather than low wages. The way out of poverty for most nonworkers is simply to work more consistently in the low-skilled jobs they can already get. In fact, where earnings gains result from training programs, the reason is usually that the client worked more hours, not higher wages.[11] Voluntary programs may actually reduce earnings by encouraging clients to withdraw from low-paid employment to pursue plans for education or training.[12]

Disillusionment with voluntary programs may be one reason why support programs focused on families have lately received more attention. Another is that the family problems of the poor have worsened since training programs began in the 1960s. Many analysts now feel that unless that disarray is dealt with, poor children will hardly reach adulthood, let alone be capable of constructive activity once they get there. Advocates feel bound to argue that expanded social services would help the poor to work as well as in other ways, but experience has shown otherwise. Child care and other services in welfare were vastly expanded in 1962 and 1967 on the argument that this would raise work levels among recipients. Instead, the fall in work levels continued and the welfare rolls exploded.

Lisbeth Schorr and others have recently advocated a more ambitious form of program where services are more comprehensive and care givers interact more intensively with clients. Pilot efforts that have shown encouraging results include family planning programs to reduce teen pregnancy, health services aimed at prenatal and infant care, early childhood education, and crisis intervention to reduce family breakup and the need for foster care. The nation already has an early childhood education program in Head Start, but it is not fully funded. Some advocates would like to see such programs expanded into a much more comprehensive family policy.[13]

The intensive strategy aims, in effect, at replacing the parents in weakened families. The care givers "establish relationships [with clients] based on mutual respect and trust" in order to direct, as well as assist, the lives of both parents and children. An example is Upward Bound, a program for disadvantaged girls in Bridgeport, Connecticut, run by Bob and Aline Doss, a black couple. The girls undertake special college preparatory studies while playing on a championship basketball team, then are recruited by top colleges. The program seems to work because the Dosses are dedicated leaders who inspire loyalty and leave the girls in no doubt as to how they are supposed to behave.[14]

Taking over families is, of course, controversial,[15] and even if there were the political will for it, such programs would be extremely difficult to implement on a wide scale.[16] Even ambitious service programs can in practice be passive and bureaucratic, and fail to get the full attention of their charges. One example is Project Redirection, a program for disadvantaged teen mothers that provided comprehensive services, including family planning and parenting training as well as education and employment. Impacts were limited, probably because the clients used the program only briefly or intermittently, with many simply drifting away.[17] Without a requirement to participate steadily, little was achieved.

In all likelihood, one cannot help most disadvantaged children and youth without first reaching the parents. If the parents signal by their withdrawal that life is futile, no program is likely to teach the children otherwise. Intensive programs do seek to involve the parents. Head Start, for example requires them to help out in the program part-time. But without requiring the parents to do something to improve their own lives, particularly to work, children probably will not learn to identify with a life of self-reliance.

Some services advocates play down the element of authority that seems essential to overcome entrenched poverty. Probably the most effective proponent of expanded services has been Marian Wright Edelman of the Children's Defense Fund. She argues that the nation has to "invest" in child care and other benefits for poor children, lest it have to pay more to support them later in life. She says little about direction.[18] Skeptics doubt, with good reason, that services can do much for young, single mothers who accept no responsibility for themselves. Edelman was herself brought up in a strict, church-going family, and became a pioneering civil rights lawyer in the South. If her clients were like her, they would not need the benefits she advocates. Edelman herself admits to doubts. "What scares me," she says, "is that today people don't have the sense that they can struggle and change things." Passivity is alien to her. "In the sixties, in Mississippi, ... [w]e always had the feeling that there was something we could do, and that there was hope. We felt in control of our lives."[19] It is not clear that providing services in any way fosters that sense of control.

Most voluntary programs have been designed by liberals who want the poor to work but also harbor doubts about whether they are able to. This has meant that the programs, like work incentives, take motivation for granted, yet do nothing to enforce work effort. Conservatives, with their higher view of competence, regard such programs as too soft. They think training programs have to put pressure on clients to have an effect, and indeed the most successful efforts have been those that were the most demanding. The Supported Work demonstration program for the long-term jobless, one of the most effective, required participants to attend motivational sessions with peers and counselors in an effort to change their defeatist and dependent attitudes.[20] In the Job Corps, which has also worked well, urban youth are sent away, usually to rural locations, where they undergo a regime of discipline and study akin to a military academy. Such programs already point toward workfare, in which authority is used even more deliberately.

RADICAL REFORM

Another approach to inner-city problems entertained on the left is to fundamentally change the economy to enable the poor to work more easily. Proponents disdain the ameliorative policies discussed so far as mere Band-Aids applied to a life-threatening disorder. To raise employment, they argue, the entire labor market must be altered in favor of low-skilled job seekers. The government must guarantee every willing adult not only a job, but "a *good* job—one with decent pay, good benefits, and a reasonable prospect of security and advancement."[21] Modest versions, such as the recommendations of William Julius Wilson, would rely on planning to promote private-sector employment, with public jobs as a backup.[22] More radical versions would require government to compete with business in providing "better" jobs, on the model of the Civil Works Administration, an early New Deal jobs program that provided well-paid positions to large numbers of unemployed with few questions asked.[23]

Government employment was tried on a substantial scale in the 1970s, when a troubled economy made the view that jobs were lacking more credible than it has seemed before or since. Some experts contended that the experience of working for a brief period in a "good" job would increase recipients' commitment to private jobs thereafter.[24] President Carter's Secretary of Labor, Ray Marshall, was an expert on "public service employment," and under his aegis PSE under CETA grew to over 750,000 positions a year. Trainees in CETA jobs were placed throughout local government agencies and in the myriad nonprofit organizations that work as service providers for government welfare and training programs.

The outcome was disappointing. CETA was troubled by scandals. Local governments often used the slots for political patronage or to rehire displaced public employees, rather than give people with more serious work problems a chance.[25] PSE also had little impact on the intended clients, and this was more damaging in the long run. Its effect on earnings was marginal,[26] and more important, recipi-

ents were apparently no more likely to work steadily after holding
a government job than before. Few PSE workers "transitioned" to
private-sector employment.[27] For all these reasons, as well as cost,
even most liberal experts abandoned PSE, and it died in the Reagan
budget cuts of 1981.[28]

The other direction radical reform might take is to impose strong
racial preferences on hiring. While this would generate enormous
controversy, it probably would have little effect on the work problem.
Since the late 1960s, affirmative action policies have created greater
access for blacks to the public and nonprofit sectors most subject
to these rules, but the effect has been more to redistribute black
employment than to increase it. Blacks already working have shifted
toward the covered sectors, and only among the most educated have
wages increased. Apparently, they were not replaced by other blacks
in the private sector, as the fall in work effort by black men and the
poor continued throughout.[29]

Affirmative action is in part an issue of dependency politics. Government elites favor such policies to satisfy political pressures to find
some way to produce greater progress for poor blacks, few of whom
work regularly.[30] Yet in its operation, affirmative action is more a progressive policy, working mainly to shift advantages among groups of
workers who are already within the economy. Whites may resent affirmative action, in part, because of this contradiction. The policy is
supposed to help the downtrodden, yet the actual beneficiaries are
more competent blacks whom most white people do not think need
preferences.

Like other voluntary strategies, radical reform assumes competence rather than facing the motivation problem that lies behind
nonwork. In common with older progressive measures, this approach
would obligate society to help workers. It would not obligate nonworkers to become workers, which seems the greater problem.

WORKFARE

Since the late 1960s, the drift of antipoverty policy has been away
from providing opportunity and toward enforcing moral standards.
Increasingly, welfare recipients are not encouraged to work by special payoffs but required to work as a condition of eligibility.[31] It is an
effort to restore, through government, some of the social authority
that used to enforce the work ethic. The movement originated in
the disappointment over the outcome of voluntary programs and

the rising frustration of voters over the worsening work problem.[32] These new work programs vary widely, however, with liberal versions continuing to stress benefits rather than obligation.

Requirements that employable AFDC recipients work or look for work were first legislated in 1967, and they have become steadily more stringent. At first there was the nationwide Work Incentive, or WIN, program, which was supposed to place the employable in jobs or training. In 1981, Congress allowed states to replace WIN with more demanding programs of their own,[33] and in 1990, those programs as well as the remainder of WIN were subsumed by the still more ambitious Job Opportunities and Basic Skills Training Program, or JOBS.[34] With voluntary programs being cut, welfare work programs have become the most important enterprise in federal employment policy.[35]

The original purpose of "workfare" was to deter employable people from going on welfare at all. Adults were to receive no cash assistance, but only aid in return for working in an unpaid government job. Often seen in locally funded assistance programs for single men, mandatory work requirements cause 30 percent or more of such clients to give up assistance.[36] The public feels kinder toward mothers with children, and in AFDC workfare has been much less punitive. Here the goal is to promote work alongside welfare rather than instead of it, through assigning employable recipients to training or job placement, mainly in the private sector. While AFDC work programs may assign people to mandatory work, their purpose has been less to reduce the welfare rolls than to make the experience of welfare less passive. Here I use "workfare" in this broader sense.[37]

By the measurements evaluators use to assess employment programs, workfare looks more effective than voluntary training, but not much more. WIN raised earnings on average by less than $1,000 a year, and there is no evidence that it reduced dependency.[38] The state programs started after 1981 achieved comparable earnings gains, reduced dependency in some cases, and usually saved money for government. The gains were mostly confined to women.[39] In addition, workfare may make it easier for welfare women to marry, both because working makes them more eligible partners and because jobs give them opportunities to meet eligible (that is, employed) men.[40]

However, the distinctive purpose of workfare has never been to raise earnings for clients, although this is desirable, but rather to cause more adult recipients to work or prepare for work as an end in itself. It is here that workfare succeeds, and does so markedly more than any previous policy. WIN had little effect on work effort, mainly because only about a third of the employable clients were ever called to participate actively.[41] This was partly for lack of funding, and in part because program staff tended to work with only the most employable recipients while exempting the rest.[42]

The post-1981 programs were more demanding, and participation increased sharply. The number and proportion of recipients taking part in workfare annually approximately doubled between 1981 and 1985, from around 400,000 to about 1 million.[43] About half of the registrants participated in some work-oriented activity, including job search, public employment, or training, within six to nine months of entering the program. This activity was well above the WIN level and *at least twice as high* as that of equivalent clients not subject to the new programs.[44] In the most exemplary programs, in San Diego and West Virginia, the great majority of clients found themselves working or in training on a regular basis.[45] Three-quarters or more of clients in the new programs satisfied the work obligation either in this way or by leaving welfare.[46]

These results show more impact on *actual work behavior* than any other approach to the work problem. The dependent poor appear to react more strongly to *requirements* to work than to opportunities. Public authority has more effect on them than incentives, as we should expect, given the psychological dependence and deference discussed earlier. Workfare has the potential to change the passive nature of welfare, and this explains why it dominates antipoverty policy today.

BARRIERS TO EMPLOYMENT?

Experience with workfare has also confirmed that barriers to employment rarely prevent dependent adults from working. The evaluations of these programs seldom emphasize the sort of impediments that figure prominently in traditional explanations of the work problem.

Can welfare parents earn enough to get their families off welfare? In 1985, the average wage of clients entering jobs from the post-WIN workfare programs ranged from the then minimum of $3.35 to $6.56 an hour. The average was $4.14. While not munificent, that figure would, with full-time work, pay $8,280 a year, close to the poverty line for a mother and two children for that year. In the typical newer program, 52 percent of clients entering jobs earned enough to leave welfare immediately, while in states still operating

WIN programs, the figure for 1984–88 was 61 percent. In affluent states, pay was often more than $5 an hour, and jobs often included benefits. In Massachusetts, for example, the typical starting wage was $5.50, and around half the jobs recipients obtained included health insurance, paid sick leave, and vacation.[47]

Are jobs available to workfare clients? They can be scarce in rural areas. The West Virginia program chose to rely on government jobs, due to a depressed local economy.[48] In such a setting, the involuntary, Depression-era image of joblessness propagated by politicians may still be valid. But in urban areas, where the vast majority of recipients live, the situation is very different. In New York, workfare staff commonly say that convincing employers to hire recipients is difficult; finding jobs is less so.[49] In Chicago, where the workfare program has filled 130,000 jobs in three years, the problem is not to find jobs but, as earlier research suggests, to persuade clients to stick with positions that initially pay little.[50] There is enormous natural turnover on the welfare rolls, and this alone suggests that a great many recipients can find work, often without assistance from workfare.[51]

Are jobs accessible? Transportation appears in most cases to be a minor problem. In WIN, only 5 to 10 percent of clients reported difficulties with transportation,[52] and newer workfare programs have had to devote only 7 percent of their budgets to this service. Some clients are too remote from work programs to participate, but while 30 percent of the new programs report this as a serious problem, most of these are small operations in rural areas.[53]

Is child care available? The most notable reversal of expectations has occurred here. The conventional wisdom has been that lack of child care is a serious constraint on expanding workfare.[54] On that argument, some states expanded child care sharply in preparation for new work programs, notably in California and Massachusetts, where huge sums were budgeted for this service.[55] In the event, child care proved not nearly this costly or difficult, mainly because workfare participants, like other working mothers, usually make informal care arrangements, and these are much cheaper than the subsidized care programs have geared up to provide. In WIN, only 8 percent of children aged twelve or under were placed in child care centers, two-thirds in more informal kinds of care.[56] In 1985, the typical post-WIN program spent only $34 per participant, or 6 percent of its budget, for child care—even less than for transportation. While most of the new programs report that some clients are prevented from participating by lack of care, only 17 percent find it a serious problem.[57]

Massachusetts's Employment and Training Choices program (E.T.) funded child care for workfare more lavishly than any other state, yet only 14 percent of participants asked for care from the program, the rest making their own arrangements. Transitional care was also offered to those finding jobs, but only 28 percent claimed it.[58] Even in a "saturation" program in San Diego, which tried to maximize participation, care remained abundant, largely informal, and cheap, and only 12 percent of clients even bothered to claim reimbursement.[59] In California's statewide program, known as Greater Avenues for Independence (GAIN), only 10 percent of the mandatory (that is, officially employable) participants used GAIN-funded care. Although 12 percent qualified for care after employment, only 2 percent claimed it. The use was so far below projections that in 1987–88, GAIN spent only $7 million of the $20 million it had budgeted for child care.[60]

Do low skills bar clients from jobs? The conventional wisdom has been that the dependent are so deficient in preparation for work that only the most employable should be placed in jobs at first. The others should be diverted to remedial education or excused. But staff running the better programs have learned that they cannot predict who is employable as well as the labor market. A lot of people who look unemployable in fact get jobs. It is better and cheaper to send most of the clients out to seek work, and then concentrate remedial activity on those who fail to find jobs. The philosophy in San Diego was that "a broad range of welfare recipients are appropriate for and will participate in group job search activities."[61]

Those who do not get jobs are sometimes assigned to mandatory, unpaid jobs in government agencies, usually low-skilled clerical or maintenance work. But even these clients appear to have fewer limitations than one might suppose. Their supervisors say they generally have the skills needed for their tasks, including reading and arithmetic where called for.[62] These are the sorts of positions that exist in large numbers and are generally filled by immigrants. Experience with workfare offers little evidence of any mismatch between such jobs and the skills of the poor.

The evaluators of the San Diego programs closely examined why some participants failed to join workfare activities or dropped out. The most important reasons were that they were already employed, no longer on welfare, or ill. The barriers long debated by analysts of the work problem played hardly any role. No more than 7 percent of the respondents, and usually less, said they had been blocked from participating by lack of transportation or child care.[63]

All people face practical problems in going to work. Workfare programs exist, in part, to help the poor overcome these. The experience of the programs, however, refutes the idea that the impediments nonworkers face in finding jobs are prohibitive or unusual.

THE NEED FOR OBLIGATION

For this reason, putting the employable poor to work is a problem in public administration, not social reform. It requires mobilizing clients to participate in work programs and providing them with necessary support services, after which employment is usually possible. Experts continue to debate whether participation in workfare must be *required* to accomplish this. Voluntariness is more attractive to liberal analysts and politicians; it honors the competence assumption by assuming recipients are already motivated to work. But, like voluntary training, voluntary workfare may really reflect a lesser view of competence than programs that make serious demands on the dependent.

I think obligation is essential to workfare's achievements.[64] Mandatory participation assures a higher participation rate. That is desirable, first, as an end in itself—welfare becomes less passive when clients do something to help themselves, as the public wants; and second, higher participation is also a means toward higher work levels—which the public also wants. The share of workfare clients that enters jobs is a direct function of the share that participates actively in the program. This is so even allowing for other factors that traditionally have been seen as deterring work, such as economic conditions, welfare disincentives, and the employability of the clients.[65]

High participation also improves workfare's impact on earnings and employment. Where involvement is low, a program "creams," serving only the most employable recipients, who probably would have gone to work anyway. To make a difference, a program must reach and serve more disadvantaged clients, which it can do only if participation is raised.

But must participation be mandated to reach high levels? Analysts usually say no. They think the onus to make a program effective rests with government. The program should attract clients by offering compelling benefits.[66] This is the position taken by the most publicized workfare program, E.T. in Massachusetts. E.T. is promoted vigorously to both recipients and employers, but the clients are left free to join in or not, in the belief that otherwise they will not be motivated to work.[67]

One might suppose, given recipients' evident desire to work, that they would respond voluntarily to programs, but only a small fraction does. Their response is more likely to be caution and avoidance. When California's GAIN began in 1986, staff assumed "participants would come rushing in" the minute the doors opened, but participation fell drastically short of projections.[68] E.T. sent mailings to recipients urging them to participate, but on average only 1.5 percent responded. In New York City in 1987, letters were sent to 100,000 AFDC clients urging them to volunteer for training and employment programs; only 1 percent participated.[69]

Without requirements to participate, programs reach, at best, the most employable third of the caseload. The biggest impacts come from serving the second third, while the bottom third often has too many problems to respond.[70] E.T. has funded training and child care lavishly, yet its participation rate is no more than about a third over a year's time,[71] about the same as in WIN. It is doubtful whether the program has much impact.[72] Voluntary programs generate many success stories about recipients who get attractive jobs, but with few clients involved, the bulk of the caseload remains unchallenged and the work problem remains. Only mandatory programs, it appears, can mobilize the reluctant clients and change the nature of welfare.

THE STRUCTURE OF COMPLIANCE

The operation of work programs confirms the psychology of poverty suggested earlier. The origin of the work problem is not that the poor oppose employment. They seldom resist the effort to enforce work overtly. Rather, they *withdraw* and evade. The major challenge in workfare administration is to counter that reflex, get people involved, and overcome their pessimism. After that, they typically discover they can profit, and they become less depressed. They participate more for reasons of their own, and enforcement is less necessary. Authority thus operates as the midwife, not the antithesis, of freedom.[73]

There is a considerable falloff between the share of recipients who are initially assigned to workfare and those that actually join in activities, what has been called the workfare "funnel."[74] In Chicago, for example, only 64 percent of the recipients called to orientation actually attended, only half were assigned to job search, and only a third finally participated. Of those who were supposed to go through both job search and mandatory jobs, only 23 percent were assigned to jobs, and only 7 percent actually entered them.[75] Some of this dropoff reflects administrative confusion and normal turnover, with many clients leaving welfare before they can participate in workfare. Much of it, though, is due to clients disappearing or declining to show up for required activities.

The sanction that enforces workfare is that noncompliers risk reductions in their welfare grants. In San Diego, 47 percent of noncompliance cases were for failure to show up for the initial workshop, while 24 percent were due to dropping out of the workshops and 19 percent for failing to show up for mandatory jobs. No-shows have also plagued California's GAIN, with a third or more of clients failing to appear for orientation.[76] It is this evasion that incurs the ire of workfare. More overt opposition is rare.

The behavior reflects the defeatism many recipients feel about work. Staff say the clients often are unused to "applying themselves." Many only "go through the motions" of attempting to work, for fear of the many obstacles they believe they might encounter, such as loss of welfare, leaving children in care, or getting fired. Thus, workfare personnel expect some initial resistance, and they see the requirement to participate mainly as a way of overcoming that. According to staff in Chicago, the mandate was "a way of waking them up." "We'd never have any clients in here, otherwise."[77] Most workfare staff think participation should be mandatory, and the need to get clients into the program is the main reason.[78]

Staff are more concerned about enforcing participation than they are about what clients do once they are in the program. Even in programs that emphasized high participation, as in San Diego and Chicago, officials could be quite accommodating about rearranging assignments or allowing clients excuses, once it was clear they had made a commitment to the program.[79] Staff operated like truant officers in the public schools—concerned that students attend school, much less concerned what they do there. The point is to demand that people participate fully in the opportunities of American life; what they make of them is much less critical.

The most effective programs have been those, like San Diego's, that forcefully monitored client attendance. The county achieved its excellent results not by penalizing people for noncompliance—though officials did not flinch from that—but by intense "case management." As much as two-thirds of staff time was devoted to tracking down no-shows with letters and phone calls.[80] Far from resisting such pressure, clients take it as a sign of concern. "They don't want anyone to fail," said one participant in New York's Westchester County. "They're always keeping an eye on you. They're behind you pushing."[81]

It is only when recipients become involved in workfare that they see its possibilities and participate more willingly. In San Diego, once clients had joined job search workshops, less than 10 percent dropped out except to take a job.[82] One welfare official asked a group of participants in California whether they thought the program should be mandatory—"And every single one of them raised their hands, and they said they wouldn't have been there had the program not been mandatory but once they got there, they saw the benefits that the program was going to provide."[83]

Much like the tax laws or the speed limits on the highways, workfare involves enforcement, not coercion. People do not contest the rules in principle, but they do not always comply with them in practice. Public authority provides a needed extra suasion. For the poor, satisfying the work ethic is a bigger problem than for the better-off. Workfare operates to close that gap. It provides the structure the dependents need if they are actually to do what they want to do, which is to work.

HOW CLIENTS REACT

Opponents fear that workfare will be repressive, dedicated only to keeping people off welfare.[84] Clients who become involved, however, are surprisingly positive about their experience, even those in mandatory, unpaid jobs, commonly seen as the most punitive assignment. According to surveys of these participants in recent programs, over 90 percent liked their jobs, and over 80 percent felt they were treated like regular employees. In most programs, large majorities viewed the work requirement as fair, were satisfied to be earning their welfare, and felt better about their dependency as a result.[85]

Critics say work requirements force new values on the poor.[86] Actually, the purpose is to enforce the values they already have, and for this they are usually *grateful*. It is not a response that middle-class intellectuals are likely to understand. Most Americans would resist being told how to live by government, but this is because they are more able to tell themselves. It is those who have internalized norms like work less fully who need the structure that workfare provides, and who welcome it. Requirements provide a control over their lives that benefits and services alone cannot give.

It is welfare activists, not recipients, who tend to oppose work requirements. Very few workfare participants come into conflict with the program. The rate of clients incurring sanctions for noncooperation is only about 5 percent.[87] My impression is that those who resist the program tend to be more self-reliant than the average recipient, not less. Some of them go on to become activists themselves. The activists claim to speak for the recipients, but their way of life is almost opposite. They defend entitlement in welfare and oppose work requirements, but they usually satisfy the work ethic themselves—few of them are on welfare. The recipients, in contrast, affirm the work ethic but usually fail to satisfy it. Thus, the first group defends a dependency it does not show, while the second exhibits a passivity it cannot defend.

Intellectuals of both the right and the left find a contradiction between "compassion" and "deterrence" in welfare. The effort to enforce work is thought to make welfare less available to the needy, or drive them away.[88] But that is to project a middle-class mentality on the poor, to assume that they are repelled by the work test and choose between it and independence in a calculating, self-reliant manner. In fact, the requirement apparently has little if any deterrent effect on would-be recipients.[89] If anything, workfare probably makes welfare *more* attractive. It provides the combination of support and direction that many poor people need and want.

ASSERTIVENESS

If workfare programs did no more than enforce norms, however, they would not truly solve the work problem. Something must be done to overcome the defeatism of the clients, to engage their own energies in the quest for employment. The poor must become more effectively assertive in their own interests, not less. As an administrator of the current Chicago program remarked, "You can give people some education and skills. You can even find a job for them. But if they don't have confidence in themselves, they probably won't make it."[90]

Effective programs, therefore, seek to be authoritative without being authoritarian. While they do penalize people who refuse to cooperate, they prefer to exert authority more informally. They give direction through a process of intense interaction with the clients that involves give and take.[91] Relationships grow up among the clients as well as between them and the staff, and these ties become the real means of motivating work effort, transcending the more formal authority that initially brings people into the program.

Extensive use is made of "job clubs," or workshops in which groups of participants, under staff guidance, learn and discuss how to get jobs. The groups are effective because they provide both reinforcement and guidance.[92] Members empathize with each other's struggles, but they also reprove one another for "shirking." In one of the San Diego programs, evaluators observed:

> When participants arrived the first day, it was evident that many had no desire to be there; usually, however, after that day's session, laughter and joking could be heard as the group moved through various warm-up exercises. By the end of the second or third day, the transformation was even more visible. An assemblage of formerly reluctant strangers had turned into a lively, responsive group whose members were interacting warmly. When one person found a job, the momentum of the group carried others forward in an attempt to achieve the same goal. Participants now had a sense of responsibility to each other, of not wanting to let the group down.

Participants' reactions to the group sessions were strongly positive,[93] explaining why few clients drop out of workfare activities once they become involved.

Workfare does not transform the economic situation of participants, but for many, it opens a wider world. One mother in an earlier Chicago program remarked that "She...liked having a place to go to every day, where she could be out among people and get her mind off the anxieties of...living on welfare." Said a mother in Oklahoma City, now working, "It gives me a reason to comb my hair in the morning." According to another mother in New York, who had found new confidence as well as a potential husband through the program, "The feelings that I am having right now, I should have had a long time ago."[94]

GOING FURTHER

Favorable experience with the newer work programs was the main reason why the most recent reform of welfare, the Family Support Act of 1988, aimed mainly to expand workfare. But in the framing of FSA, the authoritative version of workfare I have favored in this discussion was still disputed. Liberals contended for a much more benefit-oriented package.

The final act was a compromise. JOBS called for far more extensive training, education, and child care than earlier versions of workfare, but the conservative side of the act was more notable. Earlier workfare programs had usually classified mothers with children younger than age six as unemployable, which exempted most of the adult AFDC caseload from the work test.[95] FSA lowered the age of exemption to three, so that most mothers, at least in principle, have to participate. Most important, it instituted tough new standards for raising participation levels in the new JOBS program. State programs were required to achieve participation rates of at least 7 percent of employable recipients in fiscal 1990 and 1991, rising gradually to 20 percent in 1995, on pain of reductions in their federal funding. Those levels may seem low, but they must be achieved on a monthly basis. Given that even the employable cannot participate all the time, due to health and other legitimate reasons, by 1995 states will probably have to involve half or more of the employable over the course of a year. That level, considerably higher than in WIN,[96] is about what the better recent programs achieve.

These standards make a huge difference to the size of work programs. The initial Democratic proposals for JOBS lacked any participation standards, while the Republican plan had even tougher standards than were finally enacted. Estimates were that the House Democratic proposal would involve only 210,000 more recipients in workfare over five years, and in the same period would cause only 15,000 more families to leave the rolls. Projections for the Senate Democratic bill were even more modest—86,000 and 10,000. In contrast, the Republican plan generated 935,000 more participants and ushered 50,000 families off the rolls. Because the final act had participation standards, it too should have a sharp effect—estimated at 1,055,000 more participants over five years and 50,000 more families leaving AFDC.[97]

My current recommendation is simply to implement FSA fully. Some states are resisting, on grounds of cost, but funding is already sufficient to achieve the 1995 participation target.[98] After the FSA targets are achieved, I advocate raising participation levels to half, on a monthly basis, again with implementation phased in. "Participation" should be defined to require the involvement of employable clients at least half-time, either through training, looking for jobs, or actual employment.[99] It may be difficult to go further than this. To include recipients beyond half may be prohibitively costly, as the less employable cases require more support services, while to require mothers to work more than half-time is probably unreasonable, given their parental responsibilities.[100]

But if even half the recipients participated half-time, it could be said for the first time that work effort of some kind, rather than nonwork, had become the norm on welfare. This would change the politics of poverty. With more work, dependency and poverty would probably decline, and there would be more support for higher benefits for the remaining recipients, who—if working—would appear more deserving. Ultimately, higher work levels would have the potential to shift dependency issues off the agenda, and to return politics to progressive battles over equality.

If participation in workfare became more routine for the employable, other issues would arise, such as defining more precisely who is subject to the work test. The "employable," at present, are those who are not disabled, have no children under age three, are provided with child care and transportation, and are otherwise able to participate. Liberals suspect that states, under pressure to raise participation, will abuse the restrictions to get as many clients into their programs as possible. Conservatives worry that they will bend the rules to excuse as many recipients as possible, since those exempted are excluded from the participation rate calculations. Another question concerns what "participation" involves. Virtually all workfare programs include several options for participants, from immediate placement in private jobs, to public jobs, to training or education of various kinds. Liberals tend to emphasize a need to improve skills so clients can get "better" jobs, while conservatives, fearing that few clients will actually go to work, emphasize immediate placement.

So far, conservative fears appear more reasonable. To date, high-participation work programs have been strictly local. No state has yet used JOBS to try to raise workfare participation much above the WIN level. In California's GAIN, the largest program, a high rate of clients has been "deferred" on various grounds, and counties seeking higher participation levels have had to limit the practice. FSA favors education over immediate work, and a few states have emphasized education and training heavily. In GAIN, in the early stages, 60 percent of recipients were found to need remediation, slowing the flow into jobs to a trickle.[101]

The main priority at this stage should be to enforce participation and limit deferrals. Raising participation is crucial to workfare's success. It is much less important that clients go to work immediately, provided they participate in something. The different activities within workfare appear to generate much the same movement into jobs.[102] The reason for this is that workfare has its impact mainly through motivating the clients to organize their lives for regular activity outside the home. Once they have done that, it matters much less what precise activity they undertake.[103] FSA endorses this approach. It sets tough new standards for participation while allowing programs great leeway in how they assign clients.

Extreme outcomes seem unlikely. No program to date has overemphasized job placement, while programs that emphasize education and training, such as GAIN, face the limitation that most clients are more interested in getting a job than in going back to school.[104] The programs also face funding limits, since JOBS resources are not enough to finance training for more than a minority of the clients; job placement is much cheaper. It seems to me premature to limit these choices; if abuses emerge, that will be the time for closer regulations.

A WORK POLICY FOR MEN

Another frontier for work policy is to reach more of the nonworking men who stand beside mothers with dependent children at the center of the social problem. Men get less attention than single mothers because they are less often on welfare, and there is correspondingly less pressure to make them "earn" their benefits.

Workfare probably would be the best hope for raising male work effort, though programs instituted to date have had less impact on men than women. About a fifth of clients in workfare are already male, either unemployed fathers or teenage sons not in school. For work programs to affect more men, more welfare husbands would have to be on welfare and thus subject to the work requirement. Traditionally, AFDC covered mainly female-headed families; states could include two-parent families only if the husband were unemployed and working less than one hundred hours a month—only 7 percent of AFDC cases in 1988.[105] FSA required that states offer this coverage at least half the year but kept the hundred-hour rule. It also required that 75 percent of the fathers participate in work—not just training—at least sixteen hours a week by 1997, a much tougher work requirement than for the caseload generally. With these restrictions, the two-parent segment of AFDC is unlikely to grow much.

A better idea would be to eliminate the hundred-hour rule so that a welfare father, like a mother, might work substantial hours and still be supplemented by welfare if the family were still needy. In return, the father would have to work in a private job or participate in workfare full-time.[106] For these fathers, AFDC would become a wage subsidy, assuring them that they could support their families, at least at a minimal level, even at low-paid jobs. Thus society could express its commitment to help *working* people "make it." While this arrangement might attract somewhat more welfare fathers to work-fare, most would no doubt still be too demoralized to shoulder the responsibilities of fatherhood on a regular basis.

In all likelihood, institutions outside welfare will have to bear the brunt of achieving work among men. One means is enforcing child support requirements. Alongside workfare, there has been a move-ment toward tougher collection of the payments absent fathers are supposed to make to former spouses for the maintenance of their children. There is little chance that child support could take many welfare families off the rolls,[107] but it could save some money and provide a basis for requiring men to work who are not on welfare. Some states are experimenting with assigning men who owe child support to work programs, so they can earn the money to pay.

Otherwise, work will have to be promoted for men by less direct measures that increase confidence and close off nonworking ways of life. Most crucial is reforming the public schools to make them more effective in teaching disadvantaged children. If poor people learn as children the skills to support themselves in the regular economy, they will less likely choose welfare or hustling. A process of educational reform is already under way at the state and local level, with the main focus to date on enhancing teacher training and pay, and raising the standards students must meet to be promoted or graduate from high school. Equally important, but less advanced, are measures to make schools more effective as organizations, for example by giving principals and teachers more authority, and perhaps giving parents more choice among schools, to expose educators to more consumer pressure.[108]

Another essential is more effective law enforcement. One means to enforce legitimate work in the inner city is to shut down illegal alternatives, particularly the drug trade. Currently, the criminal jus-tice system is more adept at punishing and incarcerating offenders than at preventing crime. Typically, serious criminals commit mul-tiple offenses, but are eventually locked away for long periods. A system that incarcerated lawbreakers more certainly, but for shorter periods, would deter more crime, yet be more humane.[109] As in ed-ucation, a reform process has begun at the local level; it aims, among other things, to reduce discretion in the courts and make police more visible on the streets.

For adults on welfare, workfare provides a regime combining support with requirements to function. Together, schools, law enforcement, and other local agencies must do the same for disadvantaged people not on welfare. For poor men as well as women, the solution to the work problem seems to lie, not in freedom, but in governance.

THE NEW PATERNALISM

Workfare is only the most developed instance of a trend: Government is moving away from freedom and toward authority as its basic tool in social policy. Opportunity is no longer enough to overcome low income, given the dysfunctional character of serious poverty today. The ghetto has become to a great extent self-perpetuating, and, for many residents, there remains no alternative to society attempting to redirect behavior. A tutelary regime is emerging in which dependents receive support of several kinds on condition of restrictions on their lives.

The trend diverges from the intensive service programs considered earlier because there is a more explicit reliance on standards. Where the service programs invest in people and direct lives only tangentially, the new paternalism seeks openly to manage behavior. The movement differs as well from the out-and-out institutionalization seen, say, in mental hospitals. The problems it addresses have to do with social order, not health. And while the trend is away from institutionalizing the mentally ill, it is toward lesser forms of control over people whose problems are more behavioral than psychological.

In welfare, some localities have attempted to add other obligations beyond work. In Wisconsin, welfare families must prevent truancy by their children as well as satisfy work and child support requirements.[110] Some experts propose that single mothers live in supervised housing as a condition of aid. Some localities require that drug-addicted mothers enter treatment programs on pain of losing their children to foster care. In the public housing projects where many welfare mothers live, local and federal authorities are evicting tenants for drug selling or unauthorized gun possession.[111]

Shelters for homeless families sometimes exert even more control. In Andrew Cuomo's HELP program in New York, clients are subject to curfew, and drugs and guns are forbidden. "You have to see your caseworker, get into drug treatment or job training or whatever is called for," Cuomo says. "You have to make sure your kids stay in school. You have to make a commitment." And if the rules are broken? "You are out of here in seven seconds." But the result is safety. Says one director, "This is a sanctuary where the world cannot intrude."[112]

Men's homeless shelters police the lives of their inmates with varying effectiveness, hoping to keep out drugs and crime. At Phoenix House, a treatment center in the Bronx, all aspects of life—sleeping, eating, work, study—are regimented; monitoring is pervasive, there is "no privacy," and violations are punished by penalities or expulsion. Says the director, "We have to bring structure back to their lives." Such programs are usually voluntary, but in some cases patients are required to enter them, either through civil commitment or criminal sentencing.[113]

Public school reforms are not only stiffening standards and improving teaching, they are also asserting an authority over children that goes beyond academic learning. Too many children suffer from inadequate parenting, due either to poverty or, in middle-class families, both parents working. Around the country, teachers are shouldering the roles of parents, counseling students about personal problems, visiting their homes, and teaching parenting skills to the parents. Schools offer child care before and after school hours, among other programs; they are becoming omnibus social services agencies. "Parents just aren't there today," says one principal. "We still are."[114]

An idea that extends structure beyond school is national service. It is an American tradition that many youth who have been "in trouble" get "straightened out" in the army. But today the military is volunteer, and the most disadvantaged youth often cannot qualify. Some see national service as a way to give them the same kind of direction: Youth would perform public tasks for one or two years in return for education benefits or limited pay.[115] With a similar purpose, Mississippi, New York, and other states have created quasi-military corrections programs aimed at young offenders, such as the legions of drug dealers flowing through urban courts. Rather than languish in cells or conventional rehabilitation programs, the convicts undergo several months of "shock incarceration." The experience has deliberate affinities to boot camp—constant calisthenics, labor, and inspection by drill instructors. According to one corrections official, "We tear them down, then build them up, we hope, with a sense of responsibility, respect for others and a work ethic—things most of them have never had in their lives." According to one inmate, "I feel better about myself than I have since I was in the service."[116]

CUSTODIAL DEMOCRACY?

All of these proposals originate in the same realities that underlie workfare—intractable poverty and the failure of voluntary programs. They respond to the need to restore order in the inner city, but they are profoundly disturbing to many.

The new paternalism may place undue faith in public institutions. It assumes that government agencies can direct the lives of the disadvantaged better than they do themselves, and perhaps even change them for the better. However, over the course of American history, a number of new social institutions—the workhouse, the orphanage, the prison, and the mental hospital—have claimed that they could reshape adult personality. None has succeeded. Most began with lofty purposes only to subside into little more than warehouses for the unfortunate.[117]

Authority does seem to have the power to reshape behavior, for as long as clients remain subject to it. Rules consistently enforced do affect actions. The dependent poor today seem responsive, exactly because they accept mainstream values and are looking for direction. It remains doubtful, however, that programs like those described above can alter attitudes in any fundamental way, or even influence behavior once clients leave their purview. This is because clients, beyond the very young, seldom internalize the strictures deeply enough to affect their subsequent lives. Even prisons, the most rigid of institutions, produce little inner change.[118]

Workfare does improve earnings somewhat, and it can raise work activity substantially, but it has not yet shown much power to reduce the welfare rolls. If participation in workfare is stringently enforced, the passive nature of welfare may finally change. Then more recipients may go to work on their own, without waiting to enter workfare. Then dependency levels should fall. But hope, at this point, must be limited.

The new paternalism raises great disquiet on both the right and the left. To accept that so many adults need supervision undercuts the American social ideal of a nation of free and independent citizens. It is horrific to many conservatives that, in Charles Murray's words, "A substantial portion of our population...will in effect be treated as wards of the state."[119] Liberals express simliar fears.

The two sides would, however, change the character of the new regime in sharply opposed ways. These differences are another way to frame what dependency politics is about. What is the best hope for regenerating the dysfunctional—to be indulgent or demanding? Liberal policymakers were responsible for the separate polity created for the poor during the 1960s and 1970s, a regime that was decidedly permissive. Liberal politicians and many social service professionals would still prefer to help the poor only with benefits and services, and they will resist the new behavioral controls.

Most conservatives want a much more demanding regime. To them, it is patent that today's poor need order rather than indulgence. "The helping professions," remarks one expert, "seem stuck in an era when the challenge was to free people from overstrict consciences, while today's task is to provide children with coherent environments and limits, with adults firmly at the helm."[120] That urge lies behind most of the recent policies and experiments. Confronted by a dependent class that defeats itself, what can government do but restore order and hope that, over time, it rubs off?

So far, however, the new paternalism is only a side show. Proponents can point to innovative programs, but there are few clear functioning requirements yet stated in law. Workfare is still in its infancy. The presiding spirit of the welfare empire—AFDC and satellite programs such as Food Stamps, Medicaid, and public housing—is still that of entitlement. Few recipients must take active steps to justify their dependency. Conservatives would like to change that, while liberals resist. Politically, that is what the battle over workfare is all about.

CHAPTER

9

Welfare Reform

We must muster the forthrightness and the determination to insist that some of these people do something in their own behalf.

—RUSSELL LONG
CONGRESSIONAL RECORD, 21 NOVEMBER 1967

To track the changes in American politics caused by entrenched poverty, no subject serves better than the perennial question of welfare reform.[1] From the 1960s to the 1980s, that issue changed from a progressive one to the centerpiece of dependency politics. In the early years, politicians argued mostly over basic rights to support and the scale of spending and benefits for the needy. Later, questions of responsibility, competence, and program administration came to the fore. All the while, the work issue increased in prominence. Reflecting public sentiment, congressional conservatives insisted that employable recipients make more effort to help themselves as a condition of support. At first, federal planners did not take this demand seriously, and this is the fundamental reason why the reforms proposed by presidents Nixon and Carter were defeated, although high costs were also a factor.[2] By the time of the Family Support Act in 1988, a will to promote work was clearer, reflecting the success of new work programs at the state level, research that suggested the potential of workfare, and lobby groups' increasing willingness to face the work issue.

Talk of a new consensus on welfare, however, was premature. Scale-of-government disputes over the costs and benefits of the reform ended in compromise, but FSA almost foundered on the question of how demanding the new work programs should be. The authority of programs had become more contentious than their economics, and this was typical of the dependency era.

THE CHANGE IN ISSUES

Between 1967 and 1981, the leading issues in welfare reform shifted from questions of expense and federal control to issues of how to achieve social order. In the 1960s, the debate pitted reformers seeking to extend welfare against early advocates of workfare in a contest of basic principles. In the 1970s, the work issue remained important, but debate over how to raise work levels focused mainly on barriers that seemed to prevent work, in part because the economic troubles of that decade raised questions whether work was feasible. By the 1980s, how work programs would operate received more concrete attention, reflecting the emerging paternalism in social policy. Overall, the center of attention shifted from entitlement, to work obligation, to opportunity, to programming.

The 1967 Reforms

When the Johnson administration proposed in 1967 to enhance a number of programs for the low-income population, including AFDC, the battle began as a conventional one over benefits. The proposals came at the high tide of Great Society liberalism, and the idea that the poor deserved an income was in the air. Although President Johnson did not endorse guaranteed income, he did propose several incremental extensions of benefits.[3] Conservative and local government groups resisted increased federal control of welfare; "states' rights" was a principle of conservative progressivism.

Committees in Congress approved some of the new benefits, but, unexpectedly, they also suggested the first serious work requirement for AFDC. Recipients judged employable by welfare officials would have to sign up for work with the new WIN program. The very idea of a work test was attacked as an "atrocity" by liberal members of Congress and social welfare groups and, less strenuously, by the administration. Most liberals still treated the vast majority of adult welfare recipients as unemployable, blaming personal problems on a hostile environment in the classic sociological style. Recipients might want to work, said Representative Jeffrey Cohelan, for example, but they suffered from "inadequate physical ability, insufficient skills and education, discrimination, and the simple lack of job opportunities."[4]

By later standards, support for any work obligation was tenuous.[5] The right of a welfare mother not to work was still strongly defended. Opponents feared that the work test would limit access to benefits and, worse, that it could sidetrack the drive to expand welfare. The House Ways and Means Committee called WIN a "new direction" for welfare,[6] and the left felt distinctly threatened.

This was a battle over principles, not programs. Abstractions dominated the debate as the contestants struggled to establish or oppose the basic legitimacy of expanded welfare or a work requirement. Some arguments made against the work test, for example that it was unconstitutional,[7] would not be heard again. Much less attention was paid to how recipients might go to work if it was decided they should. Barriers to employment were loudly asserted, but not clearly specified. Nor did details of how work programs might operate receive much attention.

The Family Assistance Plan (FAP)

In proposing the Family Assistance Plan in 1969, the Nixon administration raised questions of entitlement as well as the work issue. The plan would have extended welfare coverage to all poor families with children, whether one or two parents were present. The most heat was generated by the question whether the effect would be to integrate the poor into mainstream society or make them more dependent. Extreme claims were still voiced on both sides. For the National Welfare Rights Organization, welfare was the "solution" to poverty, not a "problem," a view outrageous to most voters.[8] From Representative Watkins Abbitt, on the other hand, came the nightwatchman view that "The Government was never established to take care of the people" but only to provide a "climate" within which they could "make a living...without governmental interference."[9] Conservatives again resisted FAP's tendency to federalize welfare.

The work requirement also proved contentious, with a range of positions becoming apparent, just as on the size-of-government questions. FAP contained a modest work registration requirement, which the House Ways and Means Committee endorsed. Most of those who testified in hearings, however, accepted only the principle of work, and fiercely resisted actually requiring anyone to take a job. At the other extreme, the Senate Finance Committee proposed that the employable have to enter government jobs to get any support at all. Discussion focused intensely on exactly who would be subject to the work test, and what quality of job they would have to accept.

Conservatives raised questions about the conduct of the poor. Something had to be done, they believed, to cause the dependent to *behave* differently, whether or not they received more support. For liberals, that subject was too sensitive, and it distracted from their main objective, which was still to build up social spending and commitment to the poor. As in 1967, they countered with militant sociologism. Only after poor people were guaranteed a "living income," Congressman John Conyers declared, would they be "free to feel that they are directing their own lives" and thus able to work.[10]

The benefit and behavioral issues cut across each other, fragmenting support for reform. Members of Congress from affluent Northern areas, who in progressive politics might be conservative, were often liberal on welfare, believing FAP's benefits too low. Those from the poorer South, who were liberal on New Deal issues, opposed the Nixon plan over the work issue, partly for fear that the new benefits would destroy work discipline among Southern blacks. The plan succumbed to ideological confusion, with the opponents on both economic and moral grounds combining to kill it.[11]

The details of reform received more scrutiny than in 1967, but less than the principles. FAP's work incentives were criticized by Senate Finance, but otherwise were of interest mainly to economists. Other than welfare disincentives, barriers to work received little close analysis. Nor was much heed paid to the details of administration, other than the work test.[12]

The Program for Better Jobs
and Income (PBJI)

The Carter administration's main reform plan showed a further shift toward dependency themes. The Program for Better Jobs and Income, proposed in 1977, also would have broadened welfare, so it raised the progressive issue of the scale of government. Spokesmen for both guaranteed income and the abolition of welfare testified as before, but drew less response. Likewise, concern over the federalization of welfare reappeared, but was muted. The shadow of FAP was palpable. Everyone realized that the old extreme positions were no longer tenable. Welfare was not about to be abolished, nor driven out of Washington, but neither would it be extended without serious attention to employment.

The work issue was as pivotal to PBJI as it had been to FAP, but now it was dealt with more practically. The Democratic administration endorsed a WIN-like work test—a shift from its 1967 position—and liberal groups accepted it as politically expedient.[13] PBJI attempted to answer the fear that expanded welfare would reduce employment by an elaborate system of incentives, which rewarded recipients for working, together with an ambitious government jobs component. The plan, Carter's spokesmen insisted, "emphasizes work and incentives to work."[14] The concern over social barriers became more concrete, with a particular concern about lack of jobs in that time of relative employment scarcity. Liberal members of Congress and others claimed a "severe shortage of jobs." Due to deindustrialization, according to one community activist, "Jobs for the unskilled have just about disappeared forever from our country."[15] These fears help explain the unusual stress on public job creation in PBJI as well as CETA and other Carter initiatives.

At the same time, the dysfunctions of the poor were discussed more candidly. The Senate's expert on welfare, Daniel Moynihan, pressed administration witnesses to tell "the truth" about behavioral problems among those on welfare.[16] Alvin Schorr, an economist, made the first mention of the "underclass," a group he described as living in "a world of public clinics, welfare, and housing administrators, while the rest of us live with the free market."[17] A new concern about the fate of poor children also appeared, and would grow in the future. Solicitude for the unfortunate had overtaken the fears of group, race, and class conflict typical of progressive politics.

The program mechanics of PBJI received much more attention than had been the case for earlier proposals. This was partly because the plan was complicated, but it also reflected the emerging realization that welfare was a problem within government much more than the society at large. Solutions mainly involved organizing the lives of the recipients, through various benefits and requirements, so they could function better. Enough jobs for the dependent existed or could be created, said Secretary of Labor Ray Marshall. Claims to the contrary were "myths." The problem was mainly in "administration and delivery."[18]

This practical spirit was one reason why support services got much more attention from PBJI on. If one wanted more recipients to work, one had to give them the child care and other assistance they needed. Another reason was the eruption of the feminist movement. In 1977, Congresswoman Patricia Schroeder announced that welfare was a women's issue. Welfare reform would never be the same. The feminist movement was led by career women who viewed work positively. This made it much tougher, as Moynihan observed, for liberals to portray work requirements as punitive for welfare women.[19] At the same time, women's groups put a new stress on child care as a barrier to work. This shifted attention further from the principle of working to employment barriers.

The Reagan Reforms of 1981

Reagan's reform proposals dramatized the fading of the old issues and the emergence of the new. Reagan espoused the traditional conservative agenda for AFDC—cuts, restrictions, devolution to localities—but his main legacy turned out to be the expansion of workfare. States seized on the new authority they received in 1981 to develop their own work programs, and the success of these set the stage for the Family Support Act.

Reagan's cuts in AFDC and other programs in 1981 received little criticism. Even liberals now worried about the passivity of the dependent, and they allowed Reagan to kill several ineffective social programs. The main criticism made of the Reagan changes was over employment, not benefits. Experts feared—wrongly—that the near-abolition of work incentives in AFDC would reduce recipients' work effort still further.[20]

THE STATES REFORM

After 1981, the initiative passed to the local level. The Reagan reforms allowed states several options in workfare that WIN had not, including mandatory work. By 1986, about forty states had instituted new work policies of some kind. The new programs were usually WIN-like in stressing private-sector job placement and offering only minimal services to clients, but a few—notably California's GAIN and Massachusetts's E.T.—invested heavily in education and training.[21]

In crafting the new programs, states displayed the political patterns that would later be seen at the federal level. The key to establishing workfare was a concordat on older progressive issues. Liberals had to agree that it was not enough to give income and other benefits to poor people; promoting work was important too. Conservatives had to agree to enforce work, not just by cutting back welfare, but with service programs within the welfare system. The issue then shifted to how demanding the new work programs should be—the question most characteristic of the new politics. Should employable recipients have to go to work immediately in available private-sector jobs or in mandatory government jobs? Or should they receive extensive education, training, and support services to fit them for higher-paying positions?

The balance was struck differently in different places. Eastern states tended to be liberal. Programs in Maryland, Massachusetts, and New Jersey concentrated on encouraging clients to improve their skills, often at the expense of immediate employment.[22] Midwestern and Southern states took a harder line, reflecting a tougher work ethic; programs in West Virginia and Chicago, for example, directed as many of the employable as possible toward private-sector jobs or, if necessary, public ones.[23] Some states changed over time. In Massachusetts, a conservative governor instituted a strict, placement-oriented work program in the late 1970s. It was replaced in 1983 by E.T., which is voluntary and oriented toward services, following protests by activist groups and the election of Michael Dukakis as governor. Recently, conservatives in the legislature attempted to shift the program back toward mandatory work. In Chicago, the initial strict program also gave way, in 1985, to a more moderate one providing more education and training. In Wisconsin, a traditionally liberal state, a conservative governor is now pushing a tough form of workfare along with benefit cuts.[24]

The most elaborate politics occurred in California. As in Massachusetts, a conservative governor—Ronald Reagan—instituted a controversial mandatory work program in the 1970s. In San Diego, a highly efficient and tough-minded work program was developed, and its demonstrated effectiveness provided critical support for the workfare movement nationally. But the politics of the state and the welfare bureaucracy were generally more liberal. The GAIN program that emerged in 1985, in a compromise between the Democratic legislature and a Republican governor, is mandatory but oriented to education and training.[25] More recently, funding cuts have forced a move back toward a somewhat more placement-oriented program.

Everywhere, the danger of an impasse was real. Politicians had to agree on the old issues of scale and cost and then take on the new question of how demanding to make "workfare." The California negotiations were lengthy and difficult. In New York, the second-biggest state, the legislature remained divided for years. The state senate, controlled by Republicans, wanted a mandatory program dedicated to immediate employment, while the assembly, controlled by Democrats, wanted a voluntary system with much more generous services. There were tensions between conservative upstate regions and New York City and, within the city, between a conservative welfare bureaucracy and welfare activists.

The deepest division was not over spending or centralized control, the staples of the old politics, but over how much education workfare should allow clients to pursue before going to work. Democrats would have allowed them to attend regular four-year colleges, Republicans only two-year institutions. Agreement was reached only in June 1990, barely in time to comply with the new federal Family Support Act. New York's JOBS will be much like GAIN—mandatory, but emphasizing education and support services; postsecondary education, however, was limited to two years.[26] The difficulty in reaching this decision reflected a deep division about how to deal with entrenched poverty. "One side says that people on public assistance should do more to help themselves," said Michael Dowling, a senior welfare official, "while the other would say the only way to get them to help themselves is to greatly expand the programs and services we offer."[27]

Most states forged some agreement on new programs. This put governors in a position to offer national leadership, reversing the recent pattern in social policy, in which initiatives have come from Washington. Led by Governor Bill Clinton of Arkansas, the National Governors Association (NGA) along with the American Public Welfare Association (APWA) became the main lobbies pushing workfare as a basis for reform at the federal level.[28] The governors' message was twofold: work programs could be effective, and the politics surrounding them was manageable.

THE PUBLICS SPEAK

As reform came home to Washington, a more elitist politics took over. A number of advisory groups strongly influenced the next step. In the late 1960s, studies by similar groups had helped consolidate the consensus of that era, that the way to reform welfare was to combine income guarantees with work incentives.[29] Now the groups focused much more candidly on the behavioral problems of the poor, which had become more salient in the interim. Some groups found themselves changing position.

In 1967, APWA, the weightiest of the welfare lobbies, had endorsed guaranteed income, insisted that employment for recipients be "voluntary," and rejected the idea of forcing mothers with young children to work as "frightening." Thereafter, by degrees, APWA came to accept that employable recipients should register with work programs, and, by 1977, that they should have to "accept a bona fide offer of employment or training." By the time of the hearings on the Family Support Act in 1987, APWA avowed that "individuals bear the *primary* responsibility for their own well-being." Some welfare rights groups then broke with the organization, accusing it of seeking only to provide a "cheap work force" for industry.[30]

Black leaders also shifted. In the 1960s and 1970s, they had opposed any suggestion that poor blacks had any personal responsibility for the disorders of poverty; the onus lay entirely with whites. But, starting in 1983, fearing a total collapse in the ghetto, civil rights figures began to talk more openly about the black social problem. Eleanor Holmes Norton called for more self-help by blacks, and also for "far more disciplined" social programs designed to "overthrow...the complicated, predatory ghetto subculture."[31]

This change opened the way for a sharp shift in the elite wisdom about welfare. When President Reagan announced his intention to reform welfare in 1986, there was a new outpouring of studies.[32] As in the earlier era, the reports struck common themes, but these were very different from those of the earlier liberal economism. Past arguments about how much to do for the poor and the degree of federal control fell firmly into the background. The more liberal groups still asked for higher welfare benefits and more services for the poor, and conservatives spoke of greater devolution of welfare to local control. But, except for the "Hobbs Report," the Reagan administration's reform blueprint, named after Charles Hobbs, its chief author, which would have made experimental welfare and work programs run by localities the basis of reform, none of the advisory reports concentrated on these progressive themes.[33]

Instead, the focus was on dysfunctional poverty and what to do about it. The reports were much more candid about social problems than the earlier studies. One might expect this from Hobbs and the American Enterprise Institute (AEI), a conservative think tank; both these reports distinguished sharply between simple economic need and dependency brought on by the poor themselves. The more liberal APWA, however, also spoke of a "dependency cycle" extending over generations, while the Ford Foundation warned of the emergence of "an alienated, unproductive underclass."[34]

All the groups, to quote a task force convened by Mario Cuomo, the liberal governor of New York, wanted employment to be the "cornerstone" of reform. All endorsed expanded work programs in welfare, as well as tougher enforcement of child support requirements. All would have required employable recipients to participate in workfare. The AEI, Cuomo, and Ford reports even suggested limiting the time a woman could receive AFDC unconditionally, perhaps to two or three years, after which she would have to take a job or enter a work program to retain assistance—a position that would have been unimaginable to liberals in the 1960s or 1970s.[35]

The progressive era always saw greater economic opportunity as the solution to need among the working aged, but this assumed that the deprived were prepared and able to work. The new reports questioned that assumption. The "early confidence of the 1960s," said AEI, that "economic growth and equal opportunity" were enough to defeat poverty had proven unfounded. A tight labor market was no longer enough to raise work levels, said the Cuomo group, because today's poor commonly lacked the skills and motivation to earn adequate wages. "Economic growth" was still vital, "but growth must be linked to increasing the productivity of the labor force."[36]

All the studies emphasized the problems of youth and the family, not of workers. The social problem today does not arise predominantly from a grudging economy, the AEI group wrote, but from "an inability to seize opportunity even when it is available." The Ford report described the "multiple problems" of "troubled teenagers" that were so "much more difficult" to cope with than even twenty years ago. This "complex pattern of social disorder" had become "the Achilles heel of our society."[37]

The new reports talked nearly as easily of obligations for the dependent as the earlier studies had spoken of rights and claims. The AEI report was the freshest in this respect, boldly asserting that the duty to work was not degrading, but essential to the "self-respect," "moral dignity," and even citizenship of the poor. All the reports stressed the idea of "social contract" or "mutual obligations" as the conception that should underlie welfare. All affirmed, in the words of the Cuomo group, that "citizens have a responsibility to their fellow citizens to take steps toward self-sufficiency," while society has a "collective responsibility" to help them do that by providing opportunity and aid.[38]

The convergence appeared most clearly on the old questions of the scale of effort and federal responsibility that had dominated the progressive era. The character of the proposed new work programs was more contentious. As at the state level, liberals had expansive ideas; they wanted workfare to offer generous education, training, and child and health care, and they would have guaranteed public employment for recipients who did not find jobs in the private sector.[39] Conservatives wanted programs to stress employment in the private sector, with a minimum of coddling or preparation.

Behind this difference lay a divergence over how far to enforce social mores. Everyone agreed that policy had what the AEI report called "an ethical component, a signaling function"; it could not and should not be "value free." There was a need, the Ford and Cuomo experts recognized, to "send a new message" to the dependent about work, to create something "more consistent with American values than the current welfare system." The Ford group spoke of "personal responsibility" and even uttered a warning worthy of any conservative that "social programs must resist being exploited by people who will not try to help themselves."[40]

But in general, the conservatives were much readier to direct the poor. They spoke out confidently against the "moral disorder" of poverty. To tolerate it, they stated, was to show "misdirected compassion"; levying demands on the dependent was a "moral response." The liberals were much less ready to judge. They set forth mainstream norms, but without reproving contrary behavior by the dependent. They were vague about what would happen to recipients if they did not cooperate with workfare, while the conservatives discussed "sanctions" in considerable detail.[41] It was exactly such differences that kept the "new consensus" from reaching from the old politics to the new.

THE ROLE OF RESEARCH

A final influence on the coming welfare debate arose from academic research on poverty and antipoverty policies, a force that had been felt in earlier episodes of reform, but now attained new heights. The underlying reason was that poverty had become more mysterious. In the progressive era, and as late as 1970, it seemed reasonable to relate most deprivation among those of working age to racial bias or to obvious shortcomings of the economy—low wages or unemployment. Anyone could see the connection; expertise was unnecessary

After that it became less obvious why many employable poor stayed needy for long periods, and researchers with answers acquired unprecedented influence.

At first, little was known. John Gardner, secretary of Health, Education, and Welfare under Johnson, admitted "We still know very little about...reducing dependency," and "we need to know more about the relationship between income maintenance programs and the motivation to work."[42] Early evaluations of Great Society training and education programs, all of which were voluntary, showed that none had much impact on the work effort or earnings of the poor. This discredited some of these policies and helped set the stage for change.[43]

Simultaneously, there was a massive increase in research. Before 1965, few academics had cared about problems of low income per se. After that, one could hardly pick up journals in social science without finding articles on poverty or the closely related subjects of employment, inequality, or race. Researchers zeroed in particularly on the problems of the urban black poor, as these had the greatest political salience.[44] Policy was also intensively studied. Between 1973 and 1977, 3,400 evaluation studies were performed for federal agencies, mainly those dealing with social policy. Poverty and social policy concerns dominated the emerging fields of policy analysis and social experimentation, with the support of generous federal funding. Research spending by federal poverty-related programs rose from about $30 million in 1965 to around $300 million in 1980, accounting for half the growth in all social science funding over these years.[45]

This research recast the design and consideration of welfare reform. At the time of the Nixon and Carter welfare proposals, the conventional wisdom remained that "nothing works," so the influence of research was mostly negative. Congress hesitated to expand welfare when it seemed that government programs might actually exacerbate the poverty problem. Indeed, a finding from the last of the income maintenance experiments that guaranteed income might increase marital breakup among recipients helped to kill the Carter reform plan.[46] By the time Ronald Reagan announced a new effort to revamp welfare in 1986, the weight of research was still greater, and this was itself a spur to action. "We've got to move fast," said Daniel Moynihan, a welfare expert turned policymaker. "We're not going to know more than we know now, and we know a lot."[47] Moynihan's own hearings in the Senate on reform may have been the most academic ever; while the usual attention was given to politicians and welfare groups, the tone was set by experts who analyzed the welfare problem and how stronger work and child support programs might affect it.[48]

Broad conservative critiques of social policy such as George Gilder's *Wealth and Poverty* and Charles Murray's *Losing Ground* played an important role in setting the agenda for reform.[49] They were more confident and ranged wider than previous conservative attacks on the welfare state, and were widely seen as expressing the anti-welfare momentum of the Reagan administration. They made clear to the political class surrounding social policy—most of which was liberal—that important changes were unavoidable.

The actual content of reform, however, was more influenced by statistical studies of welfare dynamics and evaluations of the new workfare programs.[50] The congressional staff who did most of the drafting were experts on this research, and many members of Congress learned the basics as well. Thomas Downey, who led the Democratic effort in the House, defended his proposals by claims that they were firmly based on "...the studies. We have put them together in this bill."[51] To a great extent, that was literally true. According to Ron Haskins, a congressional staff expert, fifty-seven different empirical studies or compilations of research were referred to by members of Congress or witnesses during House hearings on FSA, and thirteen were cited during House floor debates, a remarkable currency for research that is often forbiddingly arcane.

The new findings gave more support to reform than had been the case a decade earlier. Two lines of inquiry had greatest influence. The first was the demonstration by several economists (Mary Jo Bane, David Ellwood, and June O'Neill) that long-term dependency was a serious problem. While turnover on AFDC is substantial, about half of welfare spells persist longer than two years, and the average welfare mother spends a total of nearly seven years on the rolls. The second key source was evaluations of post-1981 workfare programs by the Manpower Demonstration Research Corporation (MDRC). These showed that the projects generally had positive impacts on employment and earnings and saved money for government, and that the effects were greatest for the more disadvantaged clients.[52]

Together, these two results crystallized the expert consensus behind reform. They made change seem more urgent *and* more possible. The proof of long-term dependency discredited the long-standing liberal claim that welfare recipients were not distinct from the rest of the public, while the MDRC studies undercut the conservative contention that nothing could be done. In part, problems come on the public agenda, not when they are urgent, but when a solution can be devised for them.[53] Workfare became the theme of reform because it showed more impact on the passivity of welfare recipients than either work incentives or changes in benefit levels.

Just as important was what research did not show: the findings failed to demonstrate that the barriers often cited in earlier years were sufficient to account for nonwork on welfare. Dependency or poverty was evidently not due predominantly to disincentives, low wages, lack of jobs, racial bias, and so on, though each of these played a minor role. A few witnesses in hearings still contended that a literal lack of opportunity could explain nonwork, but most members of Congress, to judge from their statements, now found such arguments unpersuasive.[54]

The effect was not to end controversy, however, but to shift its focus from the character of society to that of welfare. If opportunity of a kind existed, then the priority was no longer to create more and better jobs, but to reshape welfare so recipients would take the jobs already available. Welfare reform became a programmatic issue instead of an exercise in social reform. The researchers concentrated mostly on the actual character of poverty and workfare, and on how specific services might raise work levels, setting aside fundamental disputes over entitlement, obligation, or the federal role. In this they gave a lead to politicians, and they reflected the change that had been going on in American politics since the appearance of the new poverty in the 1960s.[55]

THE FAMILY SUPPORT ACT

The debates on the Family Support Act of 1988 witnessed the full flowering of dependency themes.

The Reagan administration announced an intention to reform welfare early in 1986, and in December, it produced the Hobbs Plan to expand local experimentation with welfare. House Democrats countered in early 1987 with a plan that expanded work and child support programs but spent most of its new money on enhanced welfare benefits. In the Senate, Daniel Moynihan developed a more moderate plan that expanded work programs, child support, and support services, with only limited new benefits. Neither bill contained participation requirements. House Republicans, in alliance with the administration, demanded such standards as well as smaller benefit increases.

In its final form, FSA dropped new cash benefits except for a requirement that two-parent welfare coverage be offered in all states. Most of the new money went for work programs and support services, and child support was toughened. JOBS, the new workfare structure, was the centerpiece of the act. The program had a liberal stress on education for long-term recipients, but it also included the new participation standards insisted on by conservatives.

In the congressional discussions, the eligibility and entitlement issues that were so pressing in earlier years were quiescent. No one seriously proposed either guaranteeing income or doing away with welfare. Advocates and conservative groups that had earlier taken these positions were now less vocal. Intergovernmental issues were also dormant: the federalization of welfare was no longer in dispute. The initiative for reform now came largely from the states, not Washington, and all sides accepted that localities should retain substantial discretion in running the new work programs. The supposed barriers to opportunity also received less attention than in the 1970s. Few participants now contended that the poor were unemployable or without any chance to work. Some liberals still complained that available jobs were not good enough; according to Representative Augustus Hawkins, there was "a dearth of jobs *in the regular economy*."[56] But this lacked the force of saying there were no jobs at all.

Democrats as well as Republicans took employment as the touchstone of reform. The Democratic Leadership Council, a group of moderate officeholders, argued for a less claims-oriented approach to the problems of the poor and minorities. The chairman of the council, former Virginia governor Charles Robb, gave provocative speeches arguing for a new emphasis on "responsibility" and "citizenship" in social policy.[57] "Reducing welfare dependency by creating significant work, education and training opportunities" would be the "cornerstone" of reform, House Democrats claimed. Thomas Downey, chief architect of their bill, said that Democrats had "always believed" in work, "but we did not believe it as fervently as we do today." Republicans dismissed the change of heart as lip service, but Democrats protested their sincerity. Said Sander Levin, the bill "links welfare and work irretrievably. It crosses the Rubicon." Democrats used the new language of reciprocity freely. Downey called for a "contractual relationship" between clients and welfare, and Representative Barbara Kennelly spoke of "a new sense of mutual obligation." The same was true in the Senate, where the recurring theme of Moynihan's hearings was the need for a new social contract.[58]

Some private groups still resisted the idea of work tests, but the liberal front was less unified than earlier. Religious opposition had become less adamant. Lutherans and Mormons now endorsed the requirements in principle, and Catholics said they were open to "well-crafted" employment programs. Perhaps the stiffest resistance came from the American Federation of State, County, and Municipal Employees (AFSCME), afraid that more recipients would be assigned to jobs in government without pay, thus undercutting the pay and benefits of regular public employees.[59] Most elected and appointed officials, of either party, took it for granted that work requirements were fair and constructive for the recipients.

Attention speedily shifted from principles to practicalities. The detailed organization and operation of work and child support programs received much more attention than before. Entire hearings were devoted to these subjects, which in earlier reform episodes had been neglected or settled behind the scenes.[60] Above all, enormous attention was given to child and health care. According to various Democrats, there was a "'crying need' for safe, affordable, good quality day care," and the lack of it "creates an insurmountable barrier" to leaving welfare,[61] although there was little hard evidence for this. These sentiments explain the generous new funding for "transitional" child and health care included in the act for recipients entering jobs.

The disintegrating inner city was in the back of everyone's mind. Few policymakers imagined they were engaged, as in the progressive era, in redistributing advantages among functioning citizens. Rather, they were mounting what the Ford Foundation experts called a "salvage operation" for poor communities that were falling apart due to drugs, crime, and welfarism.[62] Members of Congress of both parties stated their goal candidly—to reverse the growth of the "underclass." The hope, George Miller, a liberal Democrat, said, was to save "the very social fabric of the country." The purpose, Daniel Moynihan declared, was to discharge "the central task of any society: to produce citizens."[63] A refrain heard throughout the hearings and debates was the need to "invest" more in the preparation of poor families for employment, so they could eventually be independent. "Stop thinking welfare," Moynihan told reporters. "Think children."[64]

The act emerged as the leading monument to the new paternalism in social policy. It embodied the most comprehensive regime yet devised for the welfare poor. The aim was to provide them new benefits and services, but also to order their lives in ways that prepared them for self-reliance and enforced mainstream social values. Under

FSA, a state is supposed to ensure that able welfare recipients are "encouraged, assisted, and required" to work.[65] It is a combination that the progressive era could never have imagined.

OLD ISSUES RECEDE

The congressional politics of the Family Support Act illustrates the paradox noted earlier—agreement about many of the old progressive issues, yet heated division over newer dependency issues, particularly what demands the new work programs should place on welfare recipients.[66] There was much talk of the new "consensus" that had appeared earlier at the state level and among the advisory groups. As Moynihan framed it, "Conservatives have persuaded liberals that there is nothing wrong with obligating able-bodied adults to work. Liberals have persuaded conservatives that most adults want to work and need some help to do so." Downey, his House counterpart, said that liberals had accepted the need for work programs in welfare, while conservatives had accepted that recipients need more child care.[67]

Conflict remained over the old questions, particularly in the House. Democrats pushed for a bill with greater costs and federal controls than Republicans wanted. They proposed new welfare benefits and services, especially child care, that the GOP regarded as wasteful and even counterproductive. But these traditional partisan positions were compromised or abandoned, indicating that they were not rigidly held. Both sides concentrated on crafting a work policy that might make a dent on dependency.

Welfare liberals had always objected that AFDC gave states total power over benefit levels, which permitted Southern states to set them far below the poverty level. The first version of the Democratic House bill set a floor under benefits; later, financial incentives for states to raise benefits were substituted. The liberal Education and Labor Committee drafted rules for work programs that made participation virtually voluntary, yet participants could go to college. But by the time the bill reached the floor, Downey had abandoned the benefit floor and incentives as well as most of the Education and Labor provisions in an effort to placate conservatives. Liberals were distinctly unhappy.[68]

On the other side, conservatives early gave up their hope to devolve welfare to localities. Reagan had proposed a radical devolution plan for welfare and other programs in 1982; Congress ignored it.

The Hobbs Plan was more moderate in that it transferred control over welfare to localities merely on a limited and temporary basis, and maintained federal funding, but even this proposal received little serious consideration. Some Republicans still hoped to restrain the growing cost of welfare; few believed that the federal role could be questioned.

Instead, the GOP took its stand largely on the participation question. Reports by the General Accounting Office showed that work requirements had not yet been seriously implemented.[69] Analyses by the Heritage Foundation, a conservative think tank, pointed out all the limitations on enforcing participation contained in existing policy and in Democratic proposals.[70] Meanwhile, welfare officials in the executive branch, realizing that the Hobbs Plan was doomed, put together their own ideas for reform. Based on these discussions, the Office of Management and Budget drafted a plan in early 1987 called Greater Opportunities through Work, or GROW, whose centerpiece was much higher participation standards.

That, everyone realized, had much broader appeal. Working with OMB, House Republicans assembled a bill centered on participation thresholds, which the administration then endorsed. Senate Republicans took a similar stance, and the shift proved decisive for the final legislation. FSA included no new devolution provisions, but it did include the toughest participation standards in the history of workfare. Charles Hobbs himself remarked, "We started from a much different position and we've come a long way."[71]

The parties also reached a compromise on costs. Republicans early gave up the ambition of the Hobbs Plan to spend no new money on reform, while Democrats kept cost below the levels that would have provoked a Reagan veto. To satisfy conservatives and budget pressures, Downey trimmed his bill to $5.7 billion over five years, far below the cost of earlier reform plans, and Moynihan kept his plan to only $2.8 billion. During the conference to reconcile the bills, the House twice instructed its conferees not to push costs above the Senate figure. The final tally was $3.34 billion,[72] comfortably below the Republican pain threshold, and Reagan signed the bill with enthusiasm.

The new tendency was to see the spending level, not as significant in itself, but as a means to finance practical new programming. Most of the new money went for JOBS and associated child and health care because, as Moynihan pointed out, "We must put in place the supportive services that will enable ... parents to train for, secure and retain jobs outside of the home."[73] Recipients could receive these new benefits only by entering workfare or a job. In the same spirit, Republicans accepted the Democratic insistence on extending welfare coverage to intact families once they had added a tough work test requiring most of the fathers to enter mandatory employment.[74]

The manner of reform was also largely bipartisan. Proposals tend to be most partisan when they originate from presidential leadership. Reagan had started the reform process with his 1986 address, but thereafter, the administration played only a limited role, partly because it fielded two different proposals, the Hobbs Plan and GROW. The details of FSA came largely from Congress, with both parties contributing. Only toward the end did the White House take a firm stand, and on an issue—participation standards—that had not been part of its original position. In Congress, Moynihan developed his bill in a highly collegial manner, signing up most of the Senate as cosponsors, eventually including eight Republicans, and negotiating with the administration.[75] In the House, there was more contention, but it arose as much over procedural issues as substance.[76]

Some might argue that partisan divisions were muted only because neither side proposed ambitious changes in the scope of welfare. Due to the budget deficit, fiscal pressures were much more constraining than in earlier reform episodes. The deeper reason, however, was that the character of the social problem had changed over the previous twenty or thirty years. Now that welfare connoted dysfunctional poverty, not simple economic need, it was much harder to argue that just spending more money—or spending less—offered any solution. While the new work programs cost money, they also promised savings through reduced grants as clients entered jobs. Spending levels no longer expressed well the nature of welfare, so they were less in dispute.

"I don't want to make a political statement," said Dan Rostenkowsky, chairman of the House Ways and Means Committee. "I want to get law on the books." Many shared this spirit, and the participants themselves remarked on the sobriety of their discussion. "The debate is more mature today," noted Robert Reischauer, a longtime Washington economist. "Virtually everyone" accepted government's duty to help the needy, yet they also accepted that just distributing "cash" was not in the "best interests" of the recipients. As the conference committee deliberations approached, Downey and Moynihan characterized the remaining issues as matters of "numbers," not "principle," and hence negotiable.[77]

NEW ISSUES APPEAR

If traditional partisan issues faded, however, the newer issues related to dependency aroused unexpected passions. Conflict did not really disappear—it shifted from economic, size-of-government questions to issues of authority and social standards. Agreement might be possible about the cost of welfare and the new work programs; "Gaping philosophic chasms,"[78] nevertheless, divided the parties over how much the new programs should demand of recipients. The differences emerged most sharply in the House floor debate on the Democratic reform plan in December 1987. There was agreement, said J. J. Pickle, a Texas Democrat, that there should be "some kind of workfare," but everything depended on what kind. As Sander Levin, another Democrat, put it, all accepted that "welfare and work should be linked"; the issue was the balance "within that structure" of "opportunity" versus "obligation."[79]

Liberals wanted a mainly voluntary program emphasizing new support services, education, and training. They wanted recipients to work, but believed they had to receive the new benefits before they could do that. Without help, liberals claimed, welfare parents could not "take advantage of the opportunity to work or go to school." "Work alone is not enough," asserted George Miller. To neglect "investment" in families would be "penny-wise and pound-foolish." Only training and education could enable recipients to get the good jobs needed to escape welfare permanently. Without it, said Harold Ford, "You're going to take 1.4 million people and run them through a carwash." To give them real prospects, government had to "follow them into the marketplace."[80] A cynic might say that Democrats were just trying, as they had in the 1970s, to use a "jobs" angle to excuse an expansion of the welfare state. No doubt, for some liberals, the new JOBS program looked like a chance to resurrect the vast CETA empire of services and public employment that Reagan had abolished.

Republicans insisted that work programs require employment in available jobs with a minimum of preparation or ongoing assistance. From the time of FAP, conservatives had questioned the "undue emphasis on basic education and other institutional training" in workfare.[81] This criticism now became a chorus. Republicans attacked the first plan offered by House Democrats over cost but, more intensely, because of the impediments the bill created to clients going to work: It raised benefits and hence disincentives to work, restricted authority to place clients in mandatory work or private jobs at low wages, and exempted mothers with children under age six.[82]

The battle came to focus, more than anywhere, on participation standards. Should Washington require that states enroll some minimum share of the employable clients in workfare? Democrats opposed this as coercive and because they feared larger enrollments would prevent programs from adequately serving clients. Republicans feared that without standards states would go on running token programs that did not touch the bulk of the caseload, exactly as they had done in WIN. For Republicans, participation standards became the acid test of reform, the question that revealed whether a member really wanted to change welfare.[83]

Democrats trimmed their new benefits and lowered the age of child exclusion to three, but refused to consider mandatory participation. When the bill came before the House, Republicans pounded away at this point. The bill did not "require one single welfare recipient to work" or even "look for a job," they said. It made work "optional." The GOP offered its own plan, which spent much less on new benefits and services, but included ambitious participation standards and thus drew many more recipients into workfare. The bottom line, said Hank Brown, chief architect of the bill, was that "We spend a fourth of the money and have four times as many participants."[84] The outcome was close. The procedural rule governing the floor debate passed the House by a bare 213 to 206, and the Democratic bill itself passed by 230 to 194, a narrow majority. *All* Republicans voted against the rule, and all but thirteen against the bill.

Participation standards were also contentious in the Senate. Moynihan's bipartisan style was normally accommodating to Republicans, but on this issue, he refused to budge. The White House, however, threatened to veto the bill if it did nothing to enforce participation. Democrats were forced to accept an amendment requiring most welfare fathers to enter unpaid jobs and instituting participation thresholds for all employable recipients. While the final vote on the bill was 93 to 3, the division on the GOP amendment was much closer. A motion by Moynihan to table it failed by only 41 to 54, with only three Republicans voting in favor.[85]

Participation then became the make-or-break issue in negotiations between the houses. While the conference committee spent most of its time on money and service provisions, it was the participation question that threatened to torpedo the legislation. Downey and House Democrats fiercely resisted the standards in the Senate bill, which violated their entire idea of reform; they yielded only to the clear threat of a veto. Then liberal House members led by Augustus Hawkins rebelled, denouncing the work tests as "slave-fare." Final agreement was possible only because Democratic leaders were prepared to strike a deal with the White House and abandon the liberals.[86]

The battle would be replayed one more time over the regulations to implement the new act. The rules devised by the Department of Health and Human Services defined "participation" for purposes of satisfying the participation thresholds. States could count as participants only recipients involved in workfare at least twenty hours a week—more than many states wanted or expected. MDRC cautioned that the standards were too ambitious. "The proposed rules," Delaware governor Michael Castle protested, "will actually force significant changes in current programs." This was precisely the point. Governors and social welfare groups, most of them liberal, preferred to involve in workfare only as many clients as they found it comfortable to serve, whereas the Republican administration insisted on sufficient participation to change the nature of welfare.[87] In progressive politics, liberals had wanted to get people into government programs, conservatives to keep them out. In workfare, at least, those roles virtually reversed.

UNDERLYING ISSUES

Underlying the open debate were many of the issues discussed in earlier chapters, such as authority and competence. In an inversion of the progressive pattern, Republicans were now more willing than their opponents to deploy federal power, at least to enforce mores.

Traditionally, Republicans had defended local governments against regimentation from Washington, but now Democratic governors and the American Public Welfare Association defended localities against the Republican participation rules. Local officials wanted "funding" and "flexibility" from Washington, not standards.[88] Moynihan had written his bill primarily to satisfy these groups. He saw himself as enfranchising a process of local initiative that was already under way, precisely the approach Republicans had formerly taken.

Even more controversial were federal demands on individuals. Liberals were distinctly loath to *require* the poor to work, even if they personally thought employment desirable. For example, Senator Barbara Mikulski, a liberal Democrat, thought the "opportunity to work" was the "right message" to send to recipients, but cautioned "Let's not punish those who are unable to work." Republicans, in contrast, wanted to "base our welfare program on the values we share," in the words of Representative Nancy Johnson. She and other Republicans called it "absurd and unfair" to exempt welfare women from work when most other single mothers labored to support themselves. Liberal welfare groups, however, distrusted the workfare movement exactly because it was "value driven."[89]

Republicans were willing to trade increased services for meaningful obligation, but found that no concession on benefits could ever get that agreement. The liberal conviction that the recipients were victims incapable of obligation was unappeasable. In one House hearing, Hank Brown pressed Gerald McEntee, the president of AFSCME, to say at what point he would obligate the clients to enter workfare. What if generous support services, then full funding, then mainstream earnings were guaranteed to the participants? Brown asked. McEntee resisted at every step, conceding only, "Well, in some far-off world, where everybody...went through an adequate training program and was provided with transportation, child care, and health care and promised a job in the labor market..., then I think maybe we could begin to look at the possibility..." of obligating the recipient. But, "...we do not see that happening for a long time."[90]

The Republicans went far beyond their traditional concern to defend private society against government. In the progressive era, business had been the target of federal control. Now it was welfare groups who expressed fear of "big-brother government." In a striking speech, Nancy Johnson came close to identifying Americanism with obligation rather than freedom. "Volunteerism" in welfare was contrary to "America's fundamental values," she declared. Americans did not believe that welfare "parents should volunteer to support their children." They should be "obliged" to do so the way other people were. This was big-government, not small-government, conservatism. Democrats and liberals cringed. "Where," asked Sander Levin, "are the profamily echoes that used to come from that side of the aisle?"[91]

By the end of the 1970s, among politicians as among experts, a language of "soft" and "hard" was driving out the traditional, economic terminology of left and right. In 1978, Daniel Moynihan complained that liberal welfare reformers suffered from "soft ideas" and were insufficiently "tough-minded." The Hobbs Report characterized welfare as a "tender trap" for the poor presided over by a "soft police" of social workers. The battle over participation standards in FSA was not a struggle over the scale of government, wrote journalist Mickey Kaus, but a battle between "Softs" (MDRC and the governors) who resisted standards and "Hards" in the administration who pushed for them.[92]

Liberalism came to mean, not so much doing more for the poor, as defending them from the new welfare requirements. It meant a solicitous tone of voice. "Most of these welfare parents need help, not sanctions," wrote one recent critic of workfare. "They need tutoring services, drug and alcohol abuse counseling, alternative educational programs for their children and additional resources to meet basic family needs." Conservatism now meant, not mainly smaller government, but a demanding tone of voice. Conservatives were those who thought poor adults should meet social demands without excuses. To expect less, Representative Dan Lungren asserted, would only undermine their "confidence in their ability to function."[93]

As the rhetoric suggests, the deepest difference is about competence, the core issue in dependency politics. Liberals are more sociological, that is, readier to project blame for dysfunction onto the environment. To Congressman Matthew Martinez, a liberal Democrat, people stay on welfare for "many reasons," including lack of "adequate" jobs, skills, child care, and "family or peer support." Conservatives assume greater competence and thus hold the dependent more accountable for behavior. Said Toby Roth, a Republican congressman, "We have to put a premium on the individual's ability to create a better life for himself or herself."[94]

Over the years, from 1967 to 1988, the liberal viewpoint became less vocal, the conservative more so. In the heady atmosphere of the 1960s, sociologism was a battle cry. Welfare liberals celebrated the helplessness of the poor because it created new claims upon society. Most recipients were "unemployable," they declared, yet "self-determination" was something society could "give" people by the right combination of benefits. Later, the tone became more practical. "People who want to work and cannot find a job are caught in a system that can...destroy lives," Michael Dukakis testified in 1978. If it wanted to reduce dependency, government had to help "move people from welfare to work." Some welfare groups now pleaded for assistance rather than demanding it. Said one, "give us real, long-term, self-worth counselling and honest, practical training for real jobs."[95] But throughout, the liberal conviction remained that the poor, without help, must be helpless.

As the political climate turned their way, conservatives asserted their belief in competence more and more confidently. Early on, they had questioned welfare in principle and remarked on the passivity of the poor only in passing. One Republican congressman in 1971 expressed amazement that "whole generations" could subsist on welfare "devoid of any drive toward self-advancement."[96] By the 1980s, bold conservative rhetoric about "responsibility" and "obligation" set the tone of the FSA debates. Throughout, the Republicans believed that the poor could take care of themselves if they were required to.

The parties' stances on dependency issues probably are more constant than the stands they take on progressive issues. The latter rest on impersonal doctrines of how best to organize the society, matters subject to some degree of argument and persuasion. Dependency positions, in contrast, reflect gut assumptions about the nature of morals, personal responsibility, and fortitude, attitudes that are both less changeable and more explosive. Such questions, quiescent during the progressive era, inevitably took center stage once the distressing new forms of poverty appeared. The parties can carry on their old argument about equality only when social order is not in question, not when it is.

The Wider Meaning
of Dependency

Wherever you turned you saw injustice. The issues stuck out as clearly as they did in a prison. You knew what was good and what was evil. Life was very exciting.

—SAUL D. ALINSKY
HARPER'S, JUNE 1965

Not long ago it could be argued that politics was the business of who gets what, when, where, how.... It has become...who *thinks* what, who *acts* when, who *lives* where, who *feels* how.

—DANIEL P. MOYNIHAN
MAXIMUM FEASIBLE MISUNDERSTANDING:
COMMUNITY ACTION IN THE WAR ON POVERTY

IN this chapter, I attempt to draw out some of the further implications of dependency for politics in the United States and beyond.[1] One of my purposes is to specify the differences between the style of dependency politics and that of the progressive era in more detail. I will draw a number of specific contrasts between the two periods. I also will defend the idea that dependency politics is distinctive against rejoinders either that a special politics surrounding poverty is nothing new or, conversely, that the politics of poverty falls within the progressive tradition. I illustrate my case with the career of Saul Alinsky, the community organizer, who found that political strategies drawn from the union movement could not solve the problems of today's more dependent poor communities.

My second purpose is to show that the importance of dependency politics is not confined to the United States. In Europe as well, politics is shifting its focus from class to conduct. The most divisive disputes are no longer about unionism or socialism but rather the problems of new ethnic minorities, usually immigrants, whom many feel threaten the social order. Concerns about social cohesion, as much as economic costs, explain why European welfare states have ceased to grow, just as social reform has halted in the United States. One can also see dependency politics emerging on the international level, with Third World countries seeking dependent relationships with Western countries, just as poor groups do within the West.

The overthrow of the competence assumption in all these arenas marks the end of an entire Western tradition in which the ability of ordinary people to advance their own interests was taken for granted. To address the painful issues of dependency, a new tradition, even a new political theory, must be created.

THE CHANGE IN ISSUES

The advent of dependency politics changes the issues that politicians battle over. In the discussion thus far, I have emphasized the most fundamental shift, from questions of social organization or the size of government to questions of the responsibility and competence to be expected of the poor. That global change implies a number of more detailed alterations in the way issues are framed. Here are some of the contrasts. For emphasis, I simplify them and discuss progressive politics in the past tense, though it continues as an important theme even in the dependency era.

The old issues were economic and structural; the new ones are social and personal. Progressive politics was about the proper arrangement of society, especially whether the economy should be controlled by government or the marketplace. The left wanted to expand government intervention on behalf of workers, the right to cut it back. In dependency politics, in contrast, the question is how to deal with problems of basic functioning among the seriously poor. The social, more than the economic, structure of society is at issue. The focus is on troubled individuals or ethnic groups rather than industry, agriculture, or the relations of labor and management.

In democratic politics, the representative figure is the sansculotte at the barricades during the French Revolution, or his latter-day successor, the protester at a student demonstration. The recent musical

Les Misérables celebrated this traditional image of revolution. In the progressive era, the archetype is the factory worker carrying out a strike or organizing to get out the vote for political parties of the left. The archetypes of dependency politics are much more helpless— the jobless youth of the inner city; the homeless man begging in the better parts of town; above all, the single mother sitting at home on AFDC.

Such people have *personal* problems that must be addressed before impersonal reforms of the traditional kind are even conceivable. Their struggle is first with themselves, only then with society. An example is Melvin Brewer, a young Sioux Indian fed up with the Bureau of Indian Affairs and the other overlords of life on the reservation. But before he can do anything about them, he must first "take action against the cycles of dependency—physical, social, spiritual, and economic—he was born into." He must overcome alcoholism and get a job. The road toward self-determination does not begin with a civil rights march by people who have their lives together. It begins in Alcoholics Anonymous.[2]

It may still be claimed that structural change will help the poor, that they would function better if racism were abated, good jobs were available, and so on. But typically, social problems do not stem as directly from social structure as economic differences among workers do, and they are not so obviously reformable. If working steadily at any job is enough to avoid poverty in the great majority of cases, then features of the economy become largely irrelevant to poverty or dependency. Motivation is inevitably more at issue than opportunity.

The old issues concerned adults and public activities; the new issues concern children, youth, and private life. Progressive politics was about adults, especially workers. The question was how to reorganize government and the economy to give ordinary people more influence and opportunity. Government and the economy caused the leading problems of that age—corrupt and unresponsive regimes, and work that was dangerous, insecure, or low-paid. Dependency issues, however, focus heavily on children and youth. These are now the people most "at risk," and the structures needing change are likely to be the family, neighborhood, or schools.

When the social problem becomes the dysfunctions of the poor rather than inequality among workers, a focus on the young is inevitable. For if the source of degradation is behavior rather than lack of opportunity, remedies must focus on the stage of life when behavior is most malleable. Conversely, reform for adults must be structural because it must take personality largely as given. Debates in progressive politics about how to advance equality among workers largely took the family for granted. It was the crucible out of which competent workers and citizens came. If government and the economy took care of workers, it was assumed the employees would be able to take care of families. In dependency debates, the family and its constraints become major issues. The front lines of political and racial conflict shift from the economy to social relations outside the workplace.[3] What was offstage comes onstage.

Social policy, Daniel Moynihan writes, has entered a "post-industrial" age. The main challenge is no longer to battle the evils associated with the economy. Instead, it is to overcome social weaknesses that stem from the "post-marital" family and the inability of many youth to learn enough in school to be employable. Youth who come from intact families and good schools have an overwhelming advantage over those who do not, compared to which the inequalities that stem from the workplace are trivial. What matters for success is not whether your father was rich or poor but whether you knew your father at all.[4]

Demands in progressive politics arose from self-seeking behavior, but in dependency politics they arise from passivity. In large measure, progressivism is an argument about the freedom America allows people to make money and get ahead on their own. To conservatives, the right to pursue wealth is natural, and government cannot abridge it. To the left, this freedom is the great flaw in modern public morals. The historian Vernon Parrington calls it the "principle of exploitation," the political theorist Mark Roelofs, the "monstrous element" in our political culture.[5] For them, government's central purpose must be to restrain the exploiters in the name of a broader social interest.

The poor and dependent, however, are not exploitative but passive. They are controversial mostly because they do so little to help themselves, not because they hurt others in the pursuit of advantage. By "passive" I do not mean they lack all energy—their activity may be frenetic—but their actions lack purpose and direction. In dependency politics, the issue is whether poor people should have to do more to help themselves, not less. The question is how passive you can be and remain a citizen in full standing.

The right is typically the defender of business against government controls. In the new social policy the left defends the status quo of individual entitlement or benefits given without conditions, while the right wants to demand activity of recipients. Recent measures such as workfare and public school reforms are meant to stimulate individuals, not control them in the progressive sense. A floor is set under self-advancement, not a ceiling above it.

Claims in progressive politics derived from strength; those in dependency politics arise from weakness. The chief players in the progressive era were unions, farmers, businesses, and other economic interests that demanded some benefit or protection from government on a basis of deserts. They were hurting economically, or they would not ask for help, but their demand was also made from a position of strength. They had some economic and political resources of their own. They could use these to get attention from politicians, and they could survive if they were rebuffed.

In dependency politics, however, the claimants usually cannot assert a claim for just deserts, since they lack any regular position in the economy or any resources of their own. They are simply needy. Their claim is precisely their vulnerability; if they are refused, they will simply suffer. Economic groups stake their claims by speaking of troubled finances. The very poor stake theirs by a disassembly of the personality—by failing to function in embarrassing ways that force society to assume responsibility for them.

The poor claim support based on the injustices of the past, not what they are contributing now. They claim, in Michael Harrington's words, to be "under-compensated for humiliations which the Government and the economy, or both, have visited upon them."[6] In dependency politics, such wounds are an asset, as much as a pay check in progressive politics. One claims to be a victim, not a worker. The nonwhite poor, particularly, point to historic injustices. Even some policies that really benefit functioning minorities, such as affirmative action, require that claimants adopt, to some extent, the identity of victimhood. Such measures exploit an appeal based, as Shelby Steele says, on "suffering" rather than "achievements."[7]

Partisan agendas change. In progressive politics, Democrats wanted a larger government that would do "more" for people, Republicans a smaller one that would do and cost "less." Those issues persist, but in the new politics, it is Republicans who characteristically want to use government to enforce social mores on the poor, while Democrats resist. There are libertarian conservatives, but the urge to protect individuals from controls on their private lives is currently much stronger on the left. Unfortunately, given the present social problem, that goal conflicts with liberals' desire for a more generous regime. The public demands that more be done to restore order among the poor before it will countenance greater economic redistribution in their favor. By electing Republican presidents, the voters say, in effect, that society must be restored before it can be reformed.

Thus, the meaning of government as an issue has changed. Previously, the ambition of the regime was measured largely in economic terms: Government was growing if it spent more money and controlled more of the economy. Today, the key measure is authority: government is advancing if it regulates more of personal conduct, particularly among the poor most subject to its control. In debates on social policy, the conditions to be placed on benefit programs are more in dispute than the benefits themselves. The nature of the welfare state is more contentious than its size.[8]

The meaning of political goals changes. In the modern tradition, freedom, opportunity, and equality are hallowed words, but in the dependency era their meaning changes. All are seen, in practice, as facets of a dependent, rather than independent, life. For dependent groups, *freedom* does not mean what it meant for the middle class that built democracy in the West, or for the working class that built collectivism. It does not mean freedom *from* government, that is, the prerogative to express opinions or pursue advancement in the private sector without hindrance. Nor does it mean freedom *within* government or the economy, meaning the citizen's right to participate in politics or the worker's right to share in the direction of an enterprise. Rather, it means dependency *on* government. It means to escape from the pressures of the private sector by reliance on the public—just the reverse of the meaning freedom had when it was the war cry of bourgeois politics in the seventeenth and eighteenth centuries.

Opportunity no longer means simply the chance to compete for advancement against other functioning individuals, a sense in which it is already widely, if not perfectly, available. Rather, opportunity means arrangements, for example, affirmative action or bilingual education, that allow the disadvantaged to succeed in proportion to their numbers despite personal limitations. Competition remains, but the rules adjust for the features of vulnerable groups, as the original, more impersonal meaning of equal opportunity did not. This arrangement seems fair if one believes that the limitations are due to society, unfair if one does not. In any event, the discussion revolves around competence rather than social structure in the old sense.

Equality no longer connotes leveling the distribution of income, wealth, or status among functioning citizens, interests, or classes, as it did in the progressive era. Such claims are still made, but they will be rejected as long as dependency is serious. For the dependent, the goal of the left is something more limited—a protected status that will, like the regime built during the Great Society, shield them from the full demands of the society. In practice, this means more dependency rather than less—either expanded welfare or government jobs to support the poor outside the regular economy.

THE CHANGE IN POLITICS

The style of dependency politics is as distinctive as its agenda. Again, to show overall trends, I simplify and speak of progressive politics in the past tense.

In progressive politics, claimants were self-reliant; in dependency politics they are not. Advocates in the progressive era presumed that those who wanted change had to take responsibility for it. Progress hinged, historian Michael Katz has written, on "direct, aggressive action by poor people themselves on their own behalf."[9] Even the economically weak could become politically strong—and they had to, if they expected success. Many social reforms in the United States and other countries up through the 1960s originated in popular organizing that drove government to act. As one of Franklin Roosevelt's associates said of the New Deal, "This is a real people's movement, getting at the heart of the great modern problem, insecurity in jobs and insecurity in feelings."[10]

Dependency claims, in contrast, have seldom been pressed by the poor themselves. Today's needy are too passive and withdrawn to do that. Except briefly during community action and the welfare rights movement (considered below), they never mobilized politically to press their own demands. Instead, their case was made for them by leaders already within the government, or by intellectuals or lobbyists closely linked to it. Civil rights was the last reform agenda related to poverty to be pressed on the government from outside. With the Great Society, social policymaking in the United States became more elitist than ever before. Experts filled the vacuum left by the political absence of the poor.[11]

Progressive politics was impersonal, oriented to economic goals, and highly organized, with opposed classes and industries rallying their members to press their interests on government. It was assumed that government would respond to whoever applied the most pressure. Dependency politics is oriented to culture and moral claims, and political organization is haphazard at best.[12] Disadvantaged groups do not mobilize; their leaders ask for public sympathy. The point is more to obtain affirmation for goals and problems than to wrest concrete gains from the regime.

In progressive politics, claimants distrusted government; in dependency politics they do not. Both sides in progressive battles had reasons to distrust the regime. Business feared it as a regulating force, while reformers feared it would be controlled by business interests. Big business largely did control Washington during the Gilded Age. As a result, the nation's early social programs were instituted around the turn of the century mostly by state and local government, and during the New Deal federal administrators had difficulty persuading local officials that they could now look to the center for aid.[13]

Advocates in dependency politics, in contrast, trust government. Poor people, or those speaking for them, may disparage the powers that be, but their actions belie their words, as their claims for redress are directed to the "oppressors" themselves. Claimants generate little electoral pressure on leaders, yet demand that they be "responsive." Their appeal is not to power, but conscience. The traditional left was much more hardheaded. If there is any element of the American population that lacks a fear of centralized power, it is poor people and minorities, especially blacks, reflecting the fact that Washington has been their patron ever since the Civil War.

The labor and civil rights movements were forces outside government, able to press their claims whatever policymakers did. Today's antipoverty politics hardly exists outside the close councils of government. The public is alive to the poverty issue, but active deliberation about it is confined largely to officials and experts. There are activists who press claims in the name of outsiders, but many of them work for federal programs (for example, poverty law centers and training programs). Dependency policymaking goes on mainly in the heads of the elites to whom moral appeals are made.

There is some reason for trust, as the history of past reformism has made government more receptive to social needs. The suspicion of government native to American political culture is no doubt excessive. Yet the dependency style cannot produce equality in the old sense, because it is not a self-respecting politics. Claimants ask for social acceptance, but that is not something government can confer; it must be earned. Progressives understood this; the earlier politics was probably more aggressive and less genteel than today's, but also more egalitarian and respectful of individuals.[14] All the players had resources of their own. Those that did not hardly came forward. When they began to do so, in the 1960s, politics was fundamentally changed.

Progressive politics was threatening, while dependency politics is disturbing. The progressive movements directly challenged established interests. The goal was to reorganize government and then the economy to help the less well-off at the expense of the affluent. The movements were class-based, though often led by dissenting elites of the old order. In Europe, such politics has occasionally produced revolution, and, during the New Deal and civil rights eras, the same sort of movements transformed America.

Dependency politics does not threaten established interests in this direct way. The poor or dependent are not organized to extort redress, nor could they be, given the disorder of their own lives. Inner-city crime is a threat to individuals, but the victims are mostly as disadvantaged as the perpetrators. The rich may worry about the security of their persons and possessions, but they face no organized threat to their position. They would be much more threatened by a competent poor.

If the lower orders are threatening today, it is mainly because of the harm they do to themselves: They impose the cost on the better-off of paying for government and private agencies to take care of growing numbers of welfare mothers, drug addicts, and crack babies who cannot fend for themselves. The disadvantaged also undermine American competitiveness, because, lacking skills, they fail to fill the need for competent workers. But none of this portends social change. What worries the nonpoor, according to one study, is not any threat of political violence, but "the *social* impact of poverty and its corrosive effect in terms of crime, drug abuse, and unemployment."[15]

Rather, dependency politics is distressing. Contemplating the claims of welfare or the homeless, prosperous Americans are *outraged* rather than afraid. "Why do these people demand a handout?" they ask. Welfare mothers and panhandling men are infinitely less formidable than the angry defenders of European barricades or the union organizers of the Thirties, but they are no less infuriating.

The main threat they pose is psychic, not political or economic. In their very helplessness, the poor dramatize a potential other people deny. Working Americans fear to become like them, as could well happen, at least temporarily, if they lost their jobs or their marriages. They may also envy the poor for their ability to escape responsibility for themselves and transfer it to others. Most people abandon such dependent yearnings in childhood, but never without regret. The poor rouse these feelings to new life, stirring resentments within and without.

Those who live closest to the poor, the working and lower-middle classes, are the most hostile to them, precisely because they feel the greatest danger of becoming like them. Government and social elites know they are very unlikely to become poor. That leaves them freer than workaday people to sympathize with the downtrodden, but also to condescend.

Progressive politics was ideological, while dependency politics is moralistic. The progressive battle was between competing principles of social organization, government control versus laissez-faire. Throughout the progressive era, the "core question," writes Robert Kuttner, an economic journalist, was "whether the free market is the solution or the problem." Must private industry be regulated to achieve wealth and security for all, or should it be left free to respond only to supply and demand?[16] That debate goes on, but it is peripheral to the social issues that now preoccupy domestic politics.

The ideologies of the progressive era were impersonal, and so were the experts who led the debate, chiefly economists and lawyers. They advocated contending theories of how to organize government and manage or control the economy. Such conceptions seldom brought individual competence into question. A particular economic policy might affect people's earnings, wealth, and class position, but it was assumed they could cope with their lives. In dependency politics, competence gets much more attention and competing social principles get less. The focus is not on economic conditions but on how social policies, such as welfare, affect personal behavior. While economists remain influential, other experts who focus on personal functioning—psychologists and sociologists—are much more prominent.

In the old politics, the goals of society were in question. Should economic policy emphasize security for all or growth at the expense of greater inequality? In the new politics, the leading question is not which value to choose, since debates over the degree of collectivism have cooled. The issue, rather, is how fully Americans should live up to values, including basic civilities, on which nearly everyone is agreed. No one questions in principle that people should work hard and obey the law, but many dispute whether the disadvantaged can actually live by such norms. This explains the moralistic tone of dependency politics. The question is who to blame for life-styles that everyone sees as unfortunate, the individual or outside forces. Good behavior is at issue, not the good society.

The left used to respond to social degradation by demanding that social reward be severed from performance in the marketplace. People ought to receive the essentials of a decent life whatever they earned. This was the essence of collectivism in all its forms. Intellectuals of the left still argue for that agenda, but because of the dysfunctions of today's poor, practical politicians find it harder to question the market in principle. Instead, they say it is not fair in practice, that the poor cannot work because of their disadvantages. Once radicals redistributed. Today, they merely exempt from social standards.

WELFARE POLITICS?

Some argue that a politics of poverty is really nothing new. Disputes about how closely to regulate the behavior of the poor and dependent go back before the founding in the United States, and even further in Britain. In both countries, how much aid to give to the poor, and whether to provide it only in workhouses, were some of the most divisive issues of the nineteenth century. The debates evinced all the themes I have attributed to recent dependency politics—social control, personal responsibility and competence, and an overarching tone of moralism and condescension.[17]

However, since federal social programs did not yet exist, the earlier poverty was an issue mainly at the local and state level. At the federal level, the class-oriented battles of workers, farmers, and business almost always took precedence. Poverty was also less distinct from class issues, because most poor people still worked and, due to low wages, it was still commonplace for working people to be needy. What is novel in the recent period is that poverty themes, separate from class issues, affect national politics so strongly, and one can argue the same for the immigration issue in Europe (see below). In its salience if not its nature, today's "welfare politics" is genuinely new.[18]

There is more national involvement, also, because federal programs have become involved in all the areas most critical to order— welfare, education, and criminal justice. It is now a major concern of a president, as well as a major, to reduce crime and dependency and raise standards in the schools. Presidents Nixon, Carter, and Reagan all tried to reform welfare, and George Bush aspires to be an "education president."

Some issues of social order certainly reached national prominence during the progressive era—the temperance movement and nativist anxiety about excessive immigration at the turn of the century, for example. But both these concerns proved transient. Temperance triumphed only briefly, between 1919, when the Eighteenth Amendment, banning drink, was ratified, and 1933, when it was repealed. Nativism achieved sharp limits on immigration during the 1920s, but the issue was then quiescent. Since the 1960s, renewed immigration has formed a minor theme of the dependency era. To most people, the problems of the inner city are much more worrisome.

Another difference is that today's welfare politics is much less anti-welfare than yesteryear's. Conservatives aspire today more to "clean up" welfare than to drive the recipients off the rolls. A right to some support, even for the employable, is accepted, a feeling that is probably a legacy of the civil rights and welfare rights movements of the 1960s. There is no movement today to abolish "outdoor relief" as there was a century ago; reformers limit themselves to enforcing obligations within welfare, particularly work and child support.

Welfare politics also has a much wider base today than it did fifty or a hundred years ago. The old efforts for social control were undertaken largely by local notables interested in respectability, and they were aimed largely at "vices," especially drunkenness and prostitution. These efforts never got very far because most urban Americans were more tolerant, so politicians rarely supported repressive measures. The urge to control largely dissipated after the 1930s, as American culture more fully accepted the amoralities of urban life.[19] Today's movement to discipline welfare recipients has a much broader base, because it faces a more serious problem. The vast majority of Americans now want to do something to restore order to the inner city; it is elites who are more tolerant. The conditions in the ghetto are also worse in human, if not economic, terms than anything faced by earlier social controllers. The moral reformers wanted to keep men out of saloons, but at least most poor men were working in that era, and most families were intact. Today, even poor people have higher incomes than average Americans did then, but the family, crime, and drug problems are much worse than a century ago.

People sense a threat to the nation's future that the earlier, more superficial disorders did not pose. Fundamental competence is at risk, not just public morals. Yesterday's poor usually could take care of themselves, even if they drank; many of today's fail to do even that. As long as the poor are working, most will know advancement and the national project goes forward. When they stop working, hopes for mobility are threatened more than they ever were by vice. So the American people, while growing more tolerant about life-style, have become less accepting of crime, drugs, and welfare.

The most important social control in the progressive era was achieved through public schools. The American republic invested more heavily in education than any other society, and one of the reasons was to help individuals use their freedom well. Ever since the end of the medieval order in Europe, it has been a principle of Western, especially American, liberalism that if society was no longer to tell people how to live, it must at least equip them to learn for themselves. That concern reached new heights in this century, when the public schools bore the brunt of integrating the immigrants flooding in from Eastern Europe.

But this emphasis did not compromise the basic concentration of the progressive vision on freedom and opportunity. Most Americans learned their lessons, and went on to become reliable citizens and to live decent lives. It is when socialization breaks down, not when it succeeds, that "social control" becomes the dominant issue. The problems facing social institutions today extend far beyond anything the progressives encountered. The distressing fact is that in cities like New York and Chicago, schools and social agencies that successfully absorbed the turn-of-the-century immigrants have been overwhelmed by poor blacks and Hispanics from the South and Latin America.[20] Consequently, the home, the school, and the neighborhood receive an obsessive scrutiny they did not before. When routine social control fails, arguments about personal competence and responsibility cannot be avoided. The moralism of social control then spreads to politics, and dependency politics is born.

POVERTY AND PROTEST

Others might argue that what I have called dependency politics has had its autonomous side. Alongside the growing welfare rolls have occurred moments of protest that, at first sight, seem to fit the progressive model. We see poor people rising up to pressure government from outside. But on examination, these episodes only confirm the new pattern of dependency.

One instance was the urban riots of the later 1960s and, more sporadically, thereafter. These outbursts of violence and looting, widely interpreted by liberals as protests against racism and the ghetto, were vastly different from the protest politics of the progressive era, including the civil rights movement. The rioters lacked organization or leaders, and they failed to enunciate a clear program for redress. Unlike the civil rights demonstrations, the riots were not planned or sustained. Much of their energy was self-destructive, directed against local institutions and businesses that the poor themselves relied on. Even sympathetic observers, such as the members of the Kerner Commission, had to look closely to find any meaning; some conservatives saw no political content at all, only mayhem.[21]

Above all, the riots failed to muster power against the system. They probably spurred liberal policymakers to push social programs forward, as long as they had a majority in Washington, but the ultimate result was to elect Richard Nixon and other conservatives to the White House and put an end to the Great Society. In actuality, the riots expressed the impotence of the new urban poor, their inability to assert themselves constructively either in the economy or politics. As much as the welfare boom of the same era, the disorders marked the onset of a new political age, not a continuation of the old.

Another episode was community action, a mid-1960s strategy for local social reform. Community action agencies were supposed to pressure local governments and social services to make them more responsive to the poor. The programs were federally funded and were supposed to accord the poor "maximum feasible participation." In some localities, activists seized control of the agencies and used them to attack elected officials, igniting sharp controversy. It is possible to interpret community action as an upwelling of protest among the poor, pursuant to the progressive tradition.[22] But these protests proved no more lasting than the riots. In most localities, they endured only a year or two before local elected officials, with the aid of Congress, reasserted control. The agencies became preoccupied with carrying out services planned in Washington, not initiatives of their own. They continued to seek social change, notably through the lawsuits brought by poverty lawyers, but these activities never occupied more than 5 or 10 percent of their funds. By the early 1970s, community action had largely subsided into a service delivery network, little different from the established social programs it had been created to change.[23]

The underlying problem was that community action had no true political base among the poor themselves. It was almost entirely the creation of elites, who devised the strategy according to their own ideas of how to overcome the defeatism of the poor. If community action could make local government more responsive, they reasoned, poor residents might become less passive. But since the programs were totally dependent on the authorities for their mandate and funding, they never could mount any fundamental challenge. For that, the program would have had to draw support from some source outside government. This was what, in the progressive era, the labor and civil rights movements had provided. With political and organizational resources not under the control of elites, the earlier activists could, to some extent, dictate changes. Their resources, in turn, came from the position, however marginal, that workers and blacks had already achieved in the society. They were mostly employed, and this gave them the political and economic wherewithal to demand things. By comparison, the current poor are mostly jobless. As a result, community action could offer them only what Daniel Moynihan called "pretend power"—the appearance but not the reality of influence.[24]

Community action stirred up local unrest that ghetto leaders exploited, but this was no substitute for the legislated mandates that a movement like civil rights could achieve. Community action's main effect was to increase mobility for *individual* blacks who obtained jobs through the program. A generation of local black leaders got their start that way, but this actually undercut broader reform. It took the most energetic blacks away from movement-oriented politics and left them dependent on the very institutions against which they made claims.[25]

A third moment of protest came with the welfare rights movement. One reason for the sudden increase in the AFDC rolls in the late 1960s was community action, which attacked the stigma attached to welfare and encouraged single mothers who were eligible to claim their benefits. Another reason was the rise of the National Welfare Rights Organization (NWRO), which presented welfare as a right. NWRO mobilized mothers already on welfare to claim additional benefits, often by demonstrations in welfare offices. For a few years, NWRO had all the appearance of a spontaneous movement of the poor on their own behalf,[26] but again, the uprising proved ephemeral. By 1972, it had largely died away. Once the mothers obtained all the benefits they could from welfare, they went home. Even at its height, NWRO never comprised more than 2 percent of adult recipients of AFDC.[27] In the 1970s, Congress and many states tightened welfare rules so extra benefits could no longer be extorted by pressure. No new movement arose to resist, and welfare rights vanished as quickly as it had appeared. While many local welfare activists still exist, they can rarely claim to speak for any organized body among the recipients. Civil rights organizations have shown more staying power because they have the resources to sustain at least some permanent organization outside government.[28]

The problem again was that protest was too dependent on the very regime against which claims were made. In the nature of things, people reliant on welfare could not truly challenge the welfare system. That can be a task only for those who are not themselves dependent, that is for workers.

SAUL ALINSKY

The career of Saul Alinsky illustrates how different recent "protest" politics was from the real thing. A community organizer active from the late 1930s through the early 1970s, Alinsky represented a survival of the progressive style into a more dependent age. He founded lower-class organizations bent on extorting redress from business and government in several localities, most notably in Chicago and Rochester, New York.

In his writings, Alinsky evinced a classically progressive understanding of politics. The supreme goal of reform, he believed, was a democratic society, meaning a humane political and economic setting "for the little people." History was the struggle toward such a world. It had witnessed a "relay of revolutions" in which first one group and then another drove democratic reform onwards. Radicals were those who believed in the people, and "The history of America is the story of America's Radicals."[29] Democracy was not something the people could or would be given; they had to fight for it by organizing to press change upon government and overweening corporations. Change in politics had to come from the people, not government, because government was the servant of society. "Democracy itself is a government constantly responding to continuous pressures of its people."[30]

Alinsky had a lot less confidence in government than in ordinary people, about whom he consistently made the competence assumption. He regarded them as workers, albeit lowly ones, and he assumed they could take care of their own lives. He mentioned the "demoralization" of poor people only in passing, and he used "poor" in the narrowly economic sense that was usual before the new poverty arose in the 1960s. He thought poor people mainly needed better jobs and housing, and the main objectives of his organizations were to obtain these. He barely mentioned welfare, except critically. His own credo was, "I'll steal before I'll take charity."[31]

For Alinsky, popular politics above all meant self-reliance. No outside organizer, he believed, should have more than a limited role. Effective protest had to spring from the downtrodden themselves, reflecting their traditions and agenda and headed by local leaders. Again and again he emphasized "the enormous importance of people's doing things themselves. . . . What you get by your own effort is really yours."[32] Accordingly, Alinsky had contempt for attempts to bring improvement to the masses from above. He ridiculed "conventional community council programs" and "self-anointed saviors of the people." Lasting improvement could come only if the people themselves achieved it. Increasing their confidence and participation was the ultimate purpose of protest, as well as the guarantor of change.[33]

Alinsky found his model for political action in the labor movement, in which organization was the watchword, conflict with business and government was routine, and little help was expected from either of them. One of his opponents jibed that "Alinsky has the smell of the '30s about him," but this was just the point. He expected the poor to embark on the same struggle for power and progress that workers had undertaken before them.[34]

Unfortunately, in his heyday in the 1960s, Alinsky found himself organizing poor blacks rather than white workers. He did not see a difference, but other people did. He found himself supported, not by unions, but by philanthropists, foundations, and liberal churches, which had a different and much less demanding idea of change than he did. They saw the poor not as insurgents, but as victims to whom society owed redress. They expected reform to come not through conflict or pressure, but through the good intentions of leaders like themselves. This was radically opposed to Alinsky's conception, and he jousted repeatedly with his own allies, especially the churches. Alinsky admonished them to "show some respect for the dignity of black people by treating them as people and not as some special category, like children, on a permissive basis"; to attempt to give betterment to the poor was only "paternalism" and "condescension."[35] One can feel in the words the collision between Alinsky's bracing, progressive image of politics and the much more therapeutic vision of the dependency age.

In 1964, following ghetto riots in Rochester, New York, local religious leaders invited Alinsky to organize the black community. He refused to come until he had a mandate from local black churches. "The city of Rochester," he announced, "has a lot to learn. The most important lesson is that people don't get opportunity or freedom or equality or dignity as a gift or an act of charity. They only get these things in the act of taking them through their own efforts." Blacks had to save themselves. To give them help from above was "not giving but taking—taking their dignity."[36]

Alinsky thought no better of the federal antipoverty effort, although the reasoning behind it resembled his own. The core of it was community action, through which the poor were supposed to make things happen for themselves, but just because the program was sponsored from above, Alinsky felt, it could never do the job. He bitterly denounced it as "a prize piece of political pornography." It would produce only "a green wave of dollars" that would extinguish "militant, independent leaders of the poor" by "buying them off."[37] As noted already, there is good reason to think that this is just what happened.

Unfortunately, there was a truth in the elitist do-gooding that Alinsky so despised. His method presumed that he could locate communities of people who were poor and aggrieved, yet who also worked steadily and had the political skills that this implied. But the worlds of employment and poverty had already separated too far by the 1960s. Alinsky's most noted project—in Woodlawn, in Chicago—failed to reverse the decay of that ghetto area precisely because of the lack of sufficient numbers of working people.[38] A political model derived from unionism—that is, a world of steady workers—did not apply well to disordered communities with very different problems from those of industrialism.[39]

Alinsky's real sympathies were with the dutiful but obscure lower-middle class, not the more marginal groups that receive such attention in dependency politics. Ordinary citizens, Alinsky said, "...look at the unemployed poor as parasitical dependents, recipients of a vast variety of massive public programs all paid for by them, 'the public.'...They hear the poor demanding welfare as 'rights.' To them this is insult on top of injury."[40] Just such resentments had splintered the liberal reform coalition and would elect a string of conservative presidents in the 1970s and 1980s. Alinsky had good cause to remember the thirties nostalgically, as "...a decade of involvement. It's a cold world now. It was a hot world then."[41]

The Alinsky style of politics is not entirely dead. Local action groups still struggle in many cities to bring about change at the grass roots. Many of the best are organized by churches, with the objective of building housing or doing some other good work.[42] Some conservatives have also adopted the idea of community activism as their own. They argue that by running their own public housing or organizing their own schools, poor people can have more real control over their lives than waiting for assistance from the dead hand of bureaucracy.[43]

But true protest politics still conflicts absolutely with the *social* condition of most of today's long-term poor. Most of them are too withdrawn and dependent to shoulder the burdens of political activism. Elites must then take the lead. When the poor are not self-reliant, even those who want to help them cannot avoid superiority.

DEPENDENCY POLITICS IN EUROPE

The shift I have described in the nature of politics has significance beyond the United States. Much the same sort of controversy is appearing across the Atlantic Ocean. European, like American, politics, traditionally assumed that demands for social change come from people who are social outsiders in one sense, but insiders in another. Pressures come from "below" but also from "workers," that is, from people who are underprivileged but have an undeniable role in the economy.

There are differences of emphasis. American society is more individualist; the national myth is one of ordinary people striving to "get ahead," often against great odds. The European tradition is more collective, with a more explicit class basis. The myth of the left, largely derived from Europe, sees working-class solidarity leading to democracy and then an ambitious welfare state. Both traditions rely on the competence assumption, although the Europeans may do so less explicitly. Both suppose that ordinary people are able to take care of their own interests, if not society's, above all by working.

But the age of proletarian politics is passing on both continents. For obscure reasons, the concerns of workers have lost their grip on the Western political imagination, at least among opinion makers. In part, the problems of workers really are less pressing, due to affluence. In part, policymakers have simply become fascinated with the problems of strata *below* the working class, which were hardly glimpsed during the progressive period. In Europe, which lags in this regard about a generation behind the United States, such groups are displacing economic interests and classes atop the domestic agendas. As in the United States, the new groups are often immigrants, in many cases racial minorities from former colonies—East and West Indians in Britain, Arabs in France, Indonesians in the Netherlands. In other instances, such as Germany and Switzerland, "guest workers" have been imported from Turkey and other countries to fill unskilled jobs. Immigrants or their descendents—including several million illegals—have come to comprise about 4 percent of the population of the European Community.[44]

These elements are controversial in quite a new way. The objection to them is not that, like industrial workers, they are organizing, striking, and demanding economic protection from government. It is that they are seen as threatening social order or standards. In all the countries, demands have arisen to limit further immigration, and in some instances—Enoch Powell in Britain, Jean-Marie Le Pen in France—xenophobic politicians have arisen to articulate popular fears. To date, much of the problem is simple bigotry. Europeans are accustomed to highly homogeneous societies, and, at the least, the new groups are alien in dress, language, religion, or race. To confront ethnic pluralism of the American type is a shock to Europeans. Antidiscrimination reforms need to be instituted and no doubt will be.[45] Europe will, like the United States, become mostly nondiscriminatory, and well-prepared members of the new groups will find success.

But the apple has already been eaten. The new ethnicity has already loosed passions from which it is unlikely that traditional European politics can recover. As in the United States, the memory of bias, coupled with difficulties of adjustment to the West, will likely leave the new groups with a lasting sense of inferiority and persistent social problems. The victims will in turn spur European leaders to a new moralism, and this will arouse the arguments the United States has already seen over opportunity, barriers, responsibility, and competence. Dependency politics will flower.

American-style problems of family disintegration and nonwork are as yet not much in evidence in Europe. As in the United States, many of the new immigrants are conspicuously hardworking. But the problems are growing. In France, drugs and crime are increasing in Arab areas. In British cities, a nonwhite underclass is forming with all the features seen in America. The danger is that, although the first generation of immigrants generally works hard, the next may not. Children grow up with expectations for fairness and success that their parents lacked, and if disappointed, they may well become less dutiful.[46]

In Britain, a work issue is developing very much like that in the United States. In the late 1980s, the British economy boomed, with even unskilled workers hard to find in some places, and yet unemployment remained high. Government studies traced this anomaly partly to abuses of the benefit system; many unemployed were not really looking for work or available for it. There was a poverty connection as well. Joblessness was particularly high in the inner cities, even in prosperous areas such as London, where disadvantaged young people stayed jobless for long periods. This, said an official report, was "a paradox that many people find difficult to understand. Many longer term unemployed people have lost touch with the jobs market, and lack the motivation to take up a job." To the government, it was already apparent that the blockages to work were not impersonal, but consisted rather of the jobless' "lack of skill," ignorance about jobs, and "past lack of success in getting work."[47] These were not the concerns of the working-class era.

Dependency issues do not yet dominate European politics, but they are moving in that direction. Traditional issues of class are still potent, more than in the United States. In the depressed areas of Britain and other countries, it is much less clear than in the United States that jobs are available. Yet it is already obvious that the new minorities raise passions radically different from those of working-class politics. The leading question has changed from how to advance equality within the community to who is a member of the community in the first place. Who has the standing to make the claims for redress that workers in progressive politics make? In the face of serious dependency, old issues of economic equality inevitably move off the agenda, and issues of identity and belonging move on.[48]

THE EXHAUSTION OF REFORM

In the United States and Europe, the expansion of the welfare state, which had been almost automatic, has ground to a halt. One reason is economic limits, but the more fundamental cause is the appearance of dependency problems to which new benefits no longer seem a solution.

The traditional view was that the welfare state was an inevitable outgrowth of democracy. Once the workers had the vote, they would inevitably use it to protect themselves from the depredations of capitalism. Political citizenship implied social rights.[49] The concession of free speech and representative government led to collective bargaining and wages and hours protections, then to public control of industry, and finally to benefit programs for the aged, unemployed, and families. It was a glorious story, seen by the left, to borrow Wordsworth's words, as a "Flood/ Of . . . freedom, which, to the open sea/ Of the world's praise, from dark antiquity/ Hath flowed."[50]

However, the tide has turned. Benefits on the scale of the 1960s and 1970s proved unsustainable. A reassessment has occurred in all the Western countries, sometimes by conservative governments, sometimes by liberal ones. In response to the economic troubles of the 1970s and early 1980s, costly pension and health entitlements were cut or targeted more closely on recipients of lower income.[51] Many argued that the burden of benefits had something to do with longer-term problems such as falling growth of productivity and uncompetitiveness abroad, although the connection is doubtful.[52] Retrenchment did not, by itself, signal the end of progressive politics in Europe any more than in the United States, only that the conservative version of progressivism now prevailed over the liberal. Politicians who believed in giving the marketplace freer rein now ascended to power, rather than believers in planning and redistribution. But government might still be seen as an economic enterprise meant to benefit workers and their families.

A more threatening development in the long term was the fraying of Western societies for reasons not obviously connected to the economy. The social problems of the American poor were the most conspicuous, but even mainstream society in the United States and Europe showed noticeably less stability after 1960 than before. Crime, illegitimacy, and marital breakup rose markedly, though hardly to the levels seen in American ghettos. Births out of wedlock have risen to 26 percent of all births in Britain, nearly half in Sweden. Westerners spend less time raising children, so the next generation may be less well prepared for life than its parents. In many senses, people in the prime of life today are not planting for the future but consuming the seed corn.[53]

Programs that compensate for physical incapacity have boomed. Western publics have become deeply dependent on health care, and disability programs have sharply expanded, as they provide a respectable way for the less successful to escape the work obligation. Medical incapacity—often loosely defined—entitles one to a pension with no further questions. Both in Europe and the United States, governments have found it impossible to restrain such claims. What Ivan Illich calls the social "sick role" is more and more widely sought, and widely awarded.[54]

To these signs of social decay, economic retrenchment is no obvious solution. It is one thing to say that a dose of market competition can cure collectivist lethargy or union featherbedding, quite another to say it can cause people to obey the law or stay married. It is obvious that Swedish workers will not work hard if, as is the case, the benefit system assures them much the same income whether they work or not.[55] These social dilemmas raise questions about the effects of further social benefits. But if cutting benefits might alter work effort, it is not likely to cure the epidemic of nonmarriage in Sweden. It may have been unreasonable to say that more spending would ameliorate the symptoms, but it was no less so to argue that cuts in benefits would do so. Sharp changes in the scale of government have become harder to justify.

AMERICAN EXCEPTIONALISM

The influence of the new poverty may explain why the American welfare state remains in some ways underdeveloped. The United States fails to provide its citizens with many benefits, services, and protections that are routine in Europe. In the liberal view, labor rights are limited in the United States, public ownership of industry is scant, and social insurance benefits are too heavily slanted toward the disabled and elderly. Above all, guaranteed income or jobs tend to be denied to the working-aged. The major welfare program, AFDC, is largely confined to female-headed families. Health care is not guaranteed. By and large, two-parent families and single people still have to shift for themselves in the marketplace.

The left typically explains this situation in progressive terms. The reform coalition based on organized labor is weaker in the United States than in Europe, and it faces more forceful opposition from business. Workers are also more divided on ethnic and racial lines, and the Madisonian Constitution, which disperses power, makes it more difficult than in parliamentary governments to assemble a majority for change. Americans, furthermore, adhere to a "success ideology" that holds individuals accountable for their fate and recognizes only limited public responsibility.[56]

There is much truth in this view, at least up to 1960. After that, the seeming American backwardness is better explained by the fact that the new social problems appeared in the United States earlier than in Europe. What matters today is, not that the working class is less self-conscious in the United States than abroad, but that the United States has had more contact than Europe with the Third World, originally with Africa, due to slavery, and most recently through immigration from Latin America and Asia. The backgrounds of many of these peoples, combined with their hardships in the United States, have generated unusual poverty levels, driving American social policy in fresh directions.

Advocates are exasperated that the "undeserving" poor get so much less help in America than they would in Britain or Sweden. Somehow, those countries can provide generously for female-headed families without embarrassment or excuse, as the United States cannot.[57] The reason, however, is that these societies have only reached the cusp of dependency politics. Their needy populations are not yet as distinct—in race, attitudes, or behavior—from the bulk of the citizenry. The welfare state is still understood largely in progressive terms, as a means of redistribution between the affluent and working classes. Except to some extent in Britain, family policy has yet had little need to focus on the disadvantaged subset of the population. In Sweden or Denmark, government can pursue generous policies without fear of demoralizing the recipients of benefits because, as Charles Murray remarks, it can assume "an ethnically homogeneous population of a few million people with several hundred years of Lutheran socialization behind them."[58] Above all, the dependents in Europe are not so out of step in their work behavior compared to their fellow citizens. If society works at high or low levels, so, too, do the poor.[59] No European country faces the American situation, where work levels are high and rising among the middle class but low and falling among the poor.

During the progressive era, Europeans drew ahead of Americans in social policy. Major benefit programs such as pensions or health care appeared first in Britain, Germany, or Sweden, providing models for American programs enacted decades later. But in the dependency era, the United States is ahead; now it is American experts who advise Europe on how to cope with poverty, and they are not carrying coals to Newcastle.[60] Convergence is inevitable. Just as the United States belatedly developed working-class politics, so Europe is bound to face increased immigration pressure from the Third World. The ethnic frictions already visible are bound to increase. The West as a whole seems destined for dependency politics.

TOWARD WORK POLICIES

Throughout the West today, politics is less and less about the scale of the welfare state and more and more about maintaining social discipline within it. In Europe as in the United States, a new poverty has emerged as a jarring aftermath of progressive reform. Somehow, despite mostly full employment, welfare dependency has not only persisted but grown. In the United States, AFDC was supposed to fade away after the Depression; instead it became an empire, defying all attempts at dissolution. In England, universal unemployment and pension programs were supposed to replace the "dole," but a tangle of means-tested benefits has grown up to support millions of people who are neither elderly, disabled, nor regularly employed. Many of these are mothers, their dependent children, and nonworking men, just as in American inner cities.[61]

Tackling the poverty issue is inherently painful, because of the highly personal issues it involves. Policymakers find it difficult to avoid taking what seems a superior or condescending stance as they change from brokers between self-reliant interests to social managers seeking to arouse a depressed population. In the United States, that moment came in 1965 with the controversy over the Moynihan Report. Heretofore, the political identity of blacks was as autonomous claimants seeking justice within the progressive tradition. Daniel Moynihan focused on the black poor, however, whose problems already were conspicuous and growing. His report—a study of the black family written at the Labor Department—argued persuasively that, for lack of stronger families, many blacks would be unable to capitalize fully on the new opportunities opened to them by the civil rights reforms.[62] To address the family at all was to strike a nerve that progressives had seldom touched. Black leaders protested, and they drove the issue off the agenda for the time being. But Moynihan's insight confirmed what many suspected. From then on, dependency issues came to the fore, and the quest for better functioning began that now preoccupies domestic policy.

The search for answers that has led to workfare in the United States is now also under way in Europe. In Britain, the government has taken tentative steps toward requiring work or training as a condition of receiving unemployment benefits, which are more leniently administered and less distinct from welfare than in the United States. Since 1989, claimants have had to prove that they are available for work, if necessary by joining a training program.[63] The British press publicizes American workfare programs as the wave of the future. The new policies have been bitterly contested by the opposition Labor party, which has become the party of racial minorities in Britain, just as Democrats are in the United States. This identity produces tension with the party's traditional working-class constituency, which often is hostile to the immigrants. Squaring that circle will be Labor's major political problem in future, just as it is for Democrats.

Only one country has seriously tried to prevent nonwork. Sweden, known for the most generous welfare state in the West, also enforces work for the dependent with special stringency. The agencies dispensing unemployment benefits verify that the recipients are available for work much more strictly than in the United States or Britain. Claimants who do not look for work or who decline job offers can be cut off. No cash benefits at all are given to youth under age twenty, who must enter government jobs or training programs to get aid. As a result, only 8 percent of Swedish unemployed have been jobless for more than a year, compared to half in other major European countries.[64]

Most notably, the Swedish policies have prevented the emergence of the sort of welfare class seen in the United States and Britain. About half of children are born out of wedlock in Sweden, but the mothers have not become a separate caste because they work nearly as regularly as other people.[65] In effect, the Swedes are using orthodox work behavior to compensate for the decline of the family, which is tougher to arrest. A major difference from Britain and the United States is that the left in Sweden supports work enforcement. Swedish socialists understand that the community will redistribute income toward dependent adults only if they work. Employment is the price of equality.[66]

THE INTERNATIONAL DIMENSION

The shift from progressive to dependency politics has a parallel in international affairs. In the world arena, the political contest has traditionally displayed the same self-reliance as the struggle for advantage within countries. Just as competing groups and classes maneuver for government subsidy or protection, so nations compete for power and wealth on the world scene. These still are, more or less, the assumptions that prevail among Western countries and between them and outside powers such as the Soviet Union or Japan.

Between the West and most of the Third World, however, relations are more akin to those between government and the welfare class. Much of Asia, Africa, and Latin America does not really seek power or independence vis-à-vis the West, but rather a dependent relationship to it. For now, the newly liberated countries of Eastern Europe are doing much the same. The hope is for ties to rich countries like the United States or to international lending bodies that can provide ongoing aid. The dependent governments need subsidy because their societies are economically troubled, and they lack the authority to impose discipline or sacrifice. For these countries, the tie to the West is an admission that they are not able fully to govern themselves. Such relationships are very different from the equally close ties that may exist among the Western countries. The members of NATO or the European Community are closely related, but as peers. The countries differ in power, but none makes the others feel that it cannot govern itself, that others must assume its burdens.[67]

Subsidies to the Third World are different again from the narrowly economic dependency that Western countries may from time to time suffer. The United States has recently become a debtor nation, dependent on borrowing from abroad, because of its budget and trade deficits. Israel has since 1970 become radically reliant on American aid. But both countries could tighten their belts and survive without fundamental instability if the subsidies were withdrawn. Each is in the end able to take responsibility for itself. It is a sign of this that Israel interacts with the United States as a peer despite the enormous difference in power.

International dependency means that power relations are often not what they seem. Leadership on today's world scene stems as much from an autonomous style, a willingness to accept responsibility for oneself and others, as it does from concrete economic and military assets. There are large or rich Third World countries that appear powerful—Brazil, Argentina, Saudi Arabia—but which are so dependent financially or culturally on the West that they have little foreign policy of their own. There are also small countries that wield an outsized influence because of unusual autonomy, even though they are weak. An Oscar Arias can lead Central America toward peace and win the Nobel Prize because his country, Costa Rica, although tiny and without an army, has an Israeli-like capacity for self-reliance. Vaclav Havel and Czechoslovakia have played a similar role in Eastern Europe.

Some argue that American power must fade in the world because the United States has economic problems and is overcommitted as a world policeman.[68] However, the United States retains leadership because of its willingness to assume responsibility. The Americans in Operation Desert Storm drew funding from allies—including economic rivals Germany and Japan—that were too timid to lead themselves. They coordinated an Arab coalition against Iraq because the Arabs were unable to do it. Afterward, they arranged Middle East peace talks that the parties could not manage themselves. In part, Americans continue to govern, not on their own resources, but as mercenaries of the dependent.

Traditionally, insurgent states such as revolutionary France or Communist Russia or China accepted isolation from the traditional world order, the better to avoid contamination. Revolutionary Iran is a parallel today. Most of the Third World, however, lacks an autonomous politics. Political conflict in these countries is often not authentic, but directed at Western governments, from which aid and protection flow. Political groups in foreign capitals conduct demonstrations with signs written in English, not the native language, in hopes that Washington or London will intervene. They take out advertisements in American newspapers asserting that our government has responsibility for outcomes in their societies.[69] Bold statues of

South American liberators—José de San Martín, José Martí, and Simón Bolívar—stand next to Central Park in New York City, hinting that it is America's responsibility to keep South America free. For the United States to ask the same of South America would be unimaginable. Worldwide, as well as at home, dependency politics exists mainly in the heads of Western leaders, whom others trust to take responsibility for their problems.

The West sometimes resists. It attempts to limit aid, and it demands changes in the dependent societies. The International Monetary Fund, which grants loans to strapped countries in return for market-oriented economic reforms, operates as a kind of international workfare. In return for subsidy, it demands steps toward independence. The client governments answer with theories of dependency that blame their problems on forces outside themselves, including the West. It is the international version of sociologism, the same dialogue that surrounds welfare or poverty at home.

THE END OF THE WESTERN TRADITION

The advent of dependency politics at home and abroad means the end, not only of progressivism, but of an entire political tradition that took self-reliance for granted. It is, indeed, a radical departure for the dominant claimants in politics to be people, such as the homeless, who cannot command the respect of their fellow citizens.

People who are dependent have come to preoccupy our affairs, but in the Western past, opposition to dependency has run deep. Until recently, the poor were essentially kept out of politics because they were seen as lacking the independence needed to participate. The ancients denied citizenship to women and slaves, according to Hannah Arendt, for fear that their role in serving urgent biological needs would overstress politics.[70] The Levellers, the earliest English democrats, denied the suffrage to anyone who was economically dependent on another (which they defined to include wage laborers as well as beggars).[71]

The Western, and especially American, tradition is all of an assertive, power-seeking politics in which people are assumed to know their own interest and pursue it energetically. Western political theory largely concerns how to distribute rights, power, and reward among autonomous individuals. That is especially true of the thinkers in the classical liberal tradition—Hobbes, Locke, Montesquieu—who shaped the minds of the American founders. To

these writers, the point of government is to protect economic competitors from each other and to orchestrate their self-seeking in the
social interest, using some combination of the market and bureaucracy.

This tradition makes it very hard for nonpoor Americans even to
conceive of the idea of *passive* poverty. We have no natural way to
understand poverty except in terms of some inequity or impediment
outside people that prevents them getting ahead. The conviction that
people are dynamic and in motion is unassailable. This accounts for
the distributive cast of traditional American politics, its orientation
toward the sharing of advantage among individuals and interests.
The question always was what effect government actions would have
on the chances of people presumed to be trying to "get ahead."

The categories of self-reliance are often applied to our current
social problem, even though we sense they do not fit. Some regard
poverty as a "civil rights" issue, although racial discrimination now
plays little role in causing it; or they describe antipoverty programs
as continuing the "New Deal," even though their orientation is radically less self-reliant. Tradition helps explain why social policy-makers
searched so long for barriers that might account for entrenched
poverty, and why the move toward more authoritative measures is
even now halfhearted. Standard thinking is all about how to use
incentives that appeal to self-interest to align self-seeking with the
social interest. The Western tradition, however, has no solution for
the passivity of today's poor, for their apparent inability to behave
rationally even when opportunity exists. Our heritage simply does
not apply to our current social problem.

This is the difficulty with John Rawls's much-noted recent theory
of justice and most of the responses to it. Both Rawls and his critics
stay within the tradition in which the chief question is whether and
how advantages should be redistributed from the better-off to the
less fortunate.[72] They use economic models of behavior, as if citizens
calculated what set of social rules would best serve their advantage.
Such notions state in a pure form the assumptions about competence
long made in the Western tradition. But this is to present our social
issue as still a progressive one, whereas the actual issues, as we have
seen, are very different, involving questions of personal competence
and responsibility rather than economic equality. Social order is at
issue, not justice.

Today, any convincing theory of social policy must rest on an
account of poverty psychology that can explain the social problem
and justify the recommended solutions. I find economic rationalism

to be an implausible account; other experts defend it. Rawls and his critics, however, make no serious defense of it. They offer no convincing theory of human nature, yet human nature is the master issue in politics today.[73]

We need a new political language in which competence is the subject instead of the assumption. We need to know how and why the poor are deserving, or not, and what suasions might influence them. Because they address poverty psychology, social policy experts come closer to providing this kind of understanding than the formal theorists. Murray, Ellwood, Wilson, and the others, not Rawls or his critics, are the true philosophers of the welfare state.

These more realistic interpreters of the social problem, it must be said, lack the moral elevation of the traditional Western theorists, or Rawls. Even the most optimistic of them, such as Charles Murray, have little purpose beyond getting the poor working, married, and off welfare. We are far distant from the ideals of the Western tradition, which speak of economic freedom, political democracy, or humane socialism. Those must be for later, after work levels rise. When competence is no longer at issue, then justice can be.

CHAPTER

11

The Prospect

Americans aren't really eager to impoverish their lives
by limiting their associations to people of their own
economic class or skin color. They are only unwilling to
share their society with people who reject its few basic
values.

—MICKEY KAUS
THE NEW REPUBLIC, 7 MAY 1990

IN this final chapter, we turn to the future of dependency politics. Will questions of social order and competence keep their grip
on American politics? I think so. The problems of poverty and welfarism are not growing any less serious, or less offensive to the public.
Equally important, neither of the major parties seems to be of a mind
to take dysfunction off the national agenda.

Earlier chapters have shown the shift toward dependency politics
at the levels of public opinion, policymakers, and politicians; here
we will look at intellectuals and political writers who help to plot
strategy for their parties. Republicans and conservatives profit from
the current issues. Democrats and liberals would prefer to return to a
reformist politics, but that goal seems beyond their reach because few
are willing to face the social issue squarely. A small band of "civic"
liberals would like to enforce work, exactly to get questions of social
reform back on the agenda, but they command little support in their
own camp.

If work levels rose, politics probably would revert to progressive
themes and shift to the left, but there is little chance of that so long as

the idea of enforcing values like employment remains in contention. More likely, struggles over dependency will continue until some un-related issue—perhaps the environment—preempts concern. Those who oppose the current authoritative social policies may very well prevail. To restore order will require a sustained national determination.

THE DURABILITY OF DEPENDENCY

Many, perhaps most American intellectuals would dearly love to re-turn to a politics centered on the question of economic equality. The trouble is that such a politics requires that the downtrodden be work-ing, and that is not a condition the nonworking poor are likely to satisfy any time soon. Some believe that equality will get back on the agenda anyway, because economic inequality is rising. In this view, the Reagan era created an offensive new plutocracy, while real wages declined for many ordinary workers. Americans are bound to rise up and demand redress.[1] Short of an economic collapse, I think that is implausible. In recent budget battles with the Bush administration, congressional Democrats made much of the "fairness" issue. They believed they had thrown Republicans on the defensive for the first time in a decade. Press reports were gleeful,[2] but the public response remained tepid.

Unemployment, not inequality, has typically been the trigger for redistributive movements in the United States. Americans have felt unequal, and have demanded change, when they could not support themselves at all, not when they were simply paid less than other people. And unemployment has lost some of the impact on politics it once had. The 1970s and early 1980s saw the highest joblessness since the Depression, yet this failed to generate any sustained move-ments on behalf of distressed workers. In the current recession, un-employment is considerably lower, and Democrats to date have made little capital out of it.[3] For most Americans in most years, the risk of unemployment is simply too small to compete with urban decay as a cause of domestic concern.

Americans are most upset by government's failure to discharge its most elementary functions. Most people would be satisfied, the po-litical scientist Thomas Cavanagh says, "if government could simply do the things it used to do well: educating children, repairing roads, and keeping criminals off the streets."[4] These things are now hard to do, chiefly due to worsening social conditions in the cities. On the way to redistribution, the ghetto is the lion in the path.

Democrats can also make issues of economic problems, such as the slow growth of incomes, the fall in the nation's competitiveness, or the need to refinance the savings and loan industry or the health care system. These problems are undoubtedly important, but they, too, lack easy solutions, and they are difficult to dramatize. The ongoing problems of the inner city are much likelier to catch the eye or the heart—and appear on the evening news. Crime and crack addiction have reached new heights in New York, Detroit, and Washington, and entire areas of these cities have been abandoned to drug dealers and gangs.[5] Most people feel more threatened by this than they do by the Japanese economic invasion.

Nor are scarcity and economic decline issues that clearly divide the parties. Partisan lines are sharper on issues tied to race. Democrats are seen as consistently favorable to blacks, and this is not to their political advantage. In the battle over a new civil rights bill in 1990–91, Democrats found themselves defending affirmative action, with its mingled associations of preferences and disadvantage. President Bush made stick the charge that Democrats supported "quotas." The belief that Democrats intend "fairness" only for blacks has blinded much of the public to the legitimate case they might make about inequality.[6]

Perhaps most important, a new black leadership has appeared that is sure to keep dependency issues boiling. Since 1986, New York has seen a number of highly publicized controversies with racial overtones, notably the case of Tawana Brawley, a black girl who claimed to have been raped by whites, the killing of black youths by whites in Howard Beach and Bensonhurst, and the rape of a white woman by blacks and Hispanics in Central Park. Meanwhile, Washington's black mayor, Marion Barry, was convicted of drug possession, and a number of black judges and members of Congress have been tried or censured for misconduct. Several black lawyers and clergymen— most notably the Reverend Al Sharpton—claim these incidents reveal a new purpose to harass or subordinate blacks, despite evidence sufficient for most observers that those charged were guilty.[7]

Such claims fall squarely into the dependency, not the progressive, era. Martin Luther King, Jr., and other civil rights leaders demanded equality for blacks while observing—indeed exalting—mainstream moral norms. They exerted discipline over themselves and their followers, refused to return evil for evil, and accepted punishments even at the hands of unjust laws. The new leaders seem to attack these norms. By imagining conspiracies and disputing clear evidence of guilt, they deny, in effect, that blacks can be held responsible for personal probity in a racist society. Such claims provoke intense feelings, and in the process, the traditional progressive concern for concrete equality is swept aside.

THE LIBERAL DILEMMA

In the dependency arena, conservatives have inherent advantages. They did not seek a debate over dysfunctional poverty. That dilemma has discomfited the free-market vision they have of society, no less than liberal proposals for bigger government. But they have adapted to it more easily than the left. They can shift to moralistic themes of responsibility and social order and find themselves more popular than before. For liberals, the situation is much more difficult. Democratic leaders and intellectuals do not approve of the disorders of the ghetto, but they find it impossible clearly to *dis*approve of them, which is what the public wants. They seldom openly condemn bad behavior or invoke public authority against it as conservatives do, being restrained by their desire not to impose values on cultural and racial minorities.

Democratic proposals of the kind that won elections through 1964 now fall on deaf ears. In 1984, Mondale based his platform mostly on the claims of traditional Democratic groups—labor, minorities, and feminists, as well as the poor—for new benefits from Washington; he said little about social order. In 1988, Democratic candidates typically downplayed urban problems as "intractable" and "no-win."[8] Recently, Mondale's issues director wrote that this failure to face the social issues "helps explain political developments at the national level during the past generation: the Democratic party has virtually ceded the terrain of popular values to the Republicans."[9]

In 1988, the Democratic candidate, Massachusetts governor Michael Dukakis, took care to address proposals to a larger audience than liberal client groups. He advanced plans for a number of new programs to provide health care and other benefits for workers and families that, to many, would have met widespread needs. But, like his predecessors, he was easily turned aside by Republican talk of morality. His opponent, George Bush, hardly needed to counter with proposals of his own. The Bush campaign ran advertisements speaking of crime and Willie Horton, a convict who raped a woman while on furlough from a Massachusetts prison. Dukakis, in one of his debates with Bush, mustered little passion when asked how he would react if his wife were raped. The public voted Republican.[10]

The Bush landslide sparked bitter recriminations from older Democrats who could remember when their party viewed the White House as its birthright. According to Joseph A. Califano, Jr., who served in the Johnson and Carter administrations, the voters had convicted Democrats of "unfair pandering to black constituents." Harry McPherson, a longtime Democratic lawyer, recognized that race per se was not the issue. The voters meant, "It was all right with them if blacks participated fully in the economy so long as they earned their way. Reforms and entitlements were all right, too, so long as the benefits were shared by all who needed and 'deserved' them by virtue of their efforts." But "Participation and benefits were not...to be given out as compensation for the sufferings and injustices of past generations or as rewards for antisocial conduct." The ghetto's main problem was the growing number of "people without legitimate competence."[11]

Democrats could recover the executive on a platform of racial liberalism only if the groups likely to support this position became a majority of the voters. That is highly improbable. Blacks and the poor are each only 12 or 13 percent of the population; the two groups overlap substantially, and both vote at rates much below the norm. Hispanics—about 8 percent of the population and growing fast—offer more potential, especially if immigration increases. But Hispanics on average are more conservative than blacks, although their leadership is similarly rights-claiming.[12] Jews and feminists are reliably liberal, but they too are few in number. This leaves Democratic national candidates with no choice but to appeal to the white, workaday mass of the electorate, where support for claims-oriented liberalism is tepid at best. According to consultants advising the party, the voters dislike being lumped together with the needy in Democratic rheoretic. "They describe themselves as 'working people.'"[13]

A SECOND CIVIL WAR

Democrats are now in the classic "me-too" position of a minority party. The majority party has taken a stand on some potent issue that allows it to dominate; the minority believes in the opposite position and would like to assert it, but would be cast into the wilderness for its pains. Alternatively, it can take a stance close to the majority in order to have a shot at power, but it would then lose its distinctive identity.

Up through the mid-1960s, Republicans were in this position in progressive politics. Big government programs were popular and associated with Democrats. The GOP opposed them at its peril, but the party could not accept big government, as some liberal Republicans advised, without losing its own reason for being. Today, barring an economic collapse, Democrats would have to be tough on crime and welfare to take over the White House. But this would require them to abandon the tolerant social positions that have become most distinctively Democratic.

The dilemma is deep-seated. No superficial change in proposals or candidates can overcome it. Due to the social problem, the issues raised by dependency are unavoidable, and in addressing them, there is a real difference of view between Democratic leadership groups and the majority of the public. Most liberal government people simply believe that less can or should be expected from the poor in the way of work and other civilities than most voters want. Liberals speak on the basis of considerable empathy towards the poor, and their view is in some ways realistic, but there is simply no way to sell it to a national electorate. According to the advisors to the Democratic Leadership Council, a group of moderate officeholders, the voters are fed up with the liberal "language of compensation." They want to hear about "middle-class values—individual responsibility, hard work, equal opportunity."[14]

The Democratic dilemma appears typical of a time when basic social values are in question. Issues of citizenship and the proper definition of the community are politically prior to questions of class and equality, and drive them off the agenda. This favors conservatives, as it has repeatedly over the nation's life, even though the meaning of left and right has somewhat changed. Conservatives lead the country today, just as they did in the founding period presided over by the Federalists, and during the Civil War and its aftermath, when Republicans controlled Washington more fully than they do today. Only after Americans established their identity could questions of fairness within the community be addressed. Then presidents Jefferson, Jackson, Wilson, and the two Roosevelts could sweep conservatives out of office in the name of struggling farmers, workers, and the "little man." After the nation was defined or redefined, the appeal of reformism in a society suspicious of class became irresistible. For once it was clear who were citizens, how could one justify extreme differences of wealth or power among them?

We think in recent years of Democrats as having made the civil rights issue their own, but in a longer view, it is really the Republicans' destiny to deal with race, as it is Democrats' to deal with class. Republicans typically ride to power as nationalists, identified with the values and symbols of Americanism. Only later do they prosecute their class agenda of favoring business and the rich.[15] If conservatives define or redefine the community, they must deal with race, as the meaning of the American polity has revolved around that question since the nation's beginning.

Like the Civil War, the new battle for integration is being fought largely by the GOP. It is true that Democrats enacted most of the civil rights laws, but getting whites to deal with blacks in formally fair ways turned out to be the easy part of the modern racial struggle. It has proved much tougher to equip poor blacks and other minorities to prosper in fairer competition. Well-prepared blacks advanced, but the more disadvantaged have been overwhelmed by white society's expectations. Many have reacted by withdrawing from mainstream institutions, not only the economy but school and politics as well. This internal secession is no less threatening to the country than the more formal rupture in 1861.[16]

The parallels between the two conflicts are uncanny. Republicans, more than Democrats, resist the new secession, as they did the old. Democrats tried to settle slavery through legislative compromise—in vain—just as they tried to settle civil rights through consensual reforms. In both instances, active enforcement proved unavoidable. Democrats were willing to coerce racist white institutions, but it is Republicans who have resisted the minority secession. The GOP leads the new struggle in part because it is more willing to exert public authority. As before, solutions involve spending money, which Democrats are more willing to do, but they also require changing behavior, and this conservatives find more congenial. They resist, where liberals tend to accept, all the ways in which distressed minorities evade coming to terms with American society, whether by breaking the law, dropping out of school, not learning English, or declining to work.

Republicans also lead because, as before, they are more unified in their cause. Democrats are less unified because part of their constituency is among the secessionists. They must defer to black leaders now, as they did to Southern politicians before the Civil War. Now as then, some Democrats are driven to accept the division in the nation, while others seek to resolve it through compromise. Republicans, in contrast, are not divided over race. They do not depend much today on black votes, as earlier they did not depend on the South. They are thus freer to press the battle. Unity is one reason why, as in 1860, they find themselves in the White House even though more Americans are still Democrats than Republicans. Lastly, today as formerly, the public has commissioned the GOP to unify the country, but not necessarily to pursue the rest of its domestic agenda.

LIBERAL RESPONSES

How should liberals respond to their dilemma? One superficial device has been to try to appear tough on the social issues that have proved so telling for Republicans at the polls. During the 1988 campaign, Democratic candidates frequently identified themselves with working people, something they had no need to do before 1960. They had themselves photographed among unemployed factory workers or distressed farmers. They described traditional social programs as benefits for "working families" or, in the case of welfare, for "children."[17]

George Bush easily trumped these appeals. He used the Pledge of Allegiance to identify his party with American values, and to suggest that Democrats were soft on them. The next year, the flag was again an issue when, on grounds of free speech, the Supreme Court disallowed flag-desecration laws. Bush and other Republicans called for a federal law to protect the flag and, when it too was disallowed, a constitutional amendment.[18] Some Democrats joined in, loath once again to appear behindhand.

In 1990, the Senate voted a crime bill that was supposed to save Democrats from the imputations of permissiveness that Bush levied to such effect in 1988. Among other provisions, the bill extended capital punishment to additional offences and limited the appeals those sentenced to death could make to the federal courts. "It is the toughest, most comprehensive crime bill in our history," announced Senator Joe Biden, chairman of the Judiciary Committee. "Willie Horton is back in jail, figuratively speaking." Unfortunately, some liberal Democrats weakened the effect by opposing capital punishment in general, or at least where race might have influenced sentencing. Their proposals, defeated in the Senate, received more support in the House, where a "racial justice" amendment was added. Some House Democrats derided the new appeal rules, prompting a Bush threat of a veto.[19] These moves showed that, however tough Democrats talked, they would inevitably appear softer on enforcement issues than the GOP.

In the end, Democrats have had to take their stand with the bigger government they believe in. Many were sincerely distressed at the privatism of the Reagan era, the notion that self-seeking, market behavior rather than collective action is the engine of social progress. Conservatives, they believe, have abandoned the practical, activist tradition whereby government took responsibility for the nation's problems, including poverty. Reaganism exacerbated the "centrifugal forces of American life," two liberal commentators asserted, and only an expanded federal role could "preserve the Union."[20]

The trouble is that actual liberal proposals tend to be maddeningly vague. This is partly for reasons already given—the bankruptcy of benefit-oriented social policy, the exhaustion of barriers that could explain passive poverty, and the absence of a reformist movement with its own program. The conservatives' agenda in social policy, in contrast, is still quite full. They trace social problems to personal misbehaviors—illegitimacy, nonwork, nonpayment of child support—and governmental measures to change these, including workfare, have only just begun.

Another option for the left is a narrowly economic program that avoids dealing with the social problem. "Neoliberals" propose that Washington actively enhance economic competitiveness through tax breaks for business innovation, promotion of exports, and heavier investment in education and infrastructure. The United States, they say, should have an explicit "industrial policy" that favors change and growth, rather than assume that the magic of the market, plus today's disjointed subsidies, will do the job. This program, the work of Robert Reich and other liberal economists, formed the centerpiece of Gary Hart's presidential campaigns in 1984 and 1988.[21] In the current campaign, Paul Tsongas, among Democratic contenders, most clearly takes this approach.

However, since the roots of stagnant incomes remain mysterious, the neoliberal program is a hard one to sell. Critics on the left retort that if helping business became the Democrats' platform, they would have little to distinguish themselves from Republicans. Neoliberalism, in any event, is far too detached from any visceral appeal to ordinary people to succeed at the polls.[22] Nor, more important, does it contain anything to assuage public concern over the decline of order and civility in American life. Welfare and other antipoverty benefits are central to those worries, yet liberals of all stripes—apparently out of embarrassment—often avoid discussing these programs. Some speak of social spending as "investment," a word that sounds economic and hardheaded.[23] But what the public wants to hear from the left is, not an economic language, but a moral language that links benefits and obligations. Given their own doubts about imposing values, however, this is not a reasoning that most liberals or Democrats find it comfortable to use.

THE APPEALS OF CLASS

A more effective strategy for Democrats might well be to return to the explicit appeals to class that generated presidential majorities in the decades before 1968. This is the advice of Robert Kuttner and some other thinkers on the left. They believe that a forthright attack on economic inequality could restore the mass coalition of the New Deal or the early 1960s and generate a new mandate for collectivist reform. The hope is to break the grip of behavioral and race issues on domestic debate and bring back a focus on economic structure— in Michael Katz's words, to pull public discourse "away from family and toward power."[24]

According to Kuttner, working-class Americans have forgotten what government does for them, so government must do still more. Middle-class benefits such as Social Security and Medicare are taken for granted today. "Social programs" are associated only with the poor, hence unpopular. Ordinary people have few further hopes that government can improve their lives, so they are less interested in politics than they once were, and they vote less. As a result, the relative power of the affluent has grown. A Democratic majority can be restored, Kuttner and others say, only if the party recovers its "populist" heritage and appeals openly for "economic justice."

That means offering the "nonrich" additional benefits of the concrete kind that once cemented their attachment to "affirmative government." Means-tested programs, targeted only on the poor, will always command little support, but new entitlements like Social Security could serve and attract the broad public, including the poor. Kuttner proposes new health, child care, and housing programs, plus enriched unemployment benefits, which would include retraining on the Swedish model. He would regulate business to improve job security and embrace "economic planning" to protect the American economy from international pressures.[25] With his rabble-rousing style and appeals to economic nationalism, Tom Harkin comes closest to the class approach among Democratic candidates in the current presidential contest.

For traditional intellectuals of the left, the economic controls are the most fundamental. A new "economic democracy" has to mean new curbs on business, for example investment controls and restraints on plant closings, as only these break capitalists' license to ignore the communities they exploit.[26] Politically, however, this is very difficult to sell. It sounds like the sort of state direction of production that has been discredited in most of the developed world. How can one contend seriously for a governmental economy when that system has just been overthrown in Eastern Europe and, in less extreme forms, questioned in Western Europe?

The more appealing side of the Kuttner program is its promise of new entitlements for the middle class. The idea would be to complement the existing social insurance benefits, which go mainly to the elderly and disabled, with programs to serve the practical needs of the working-aged. Such ideas continue the traditional path of liberal reformism, summarized in the last chapter, that was interrupted by economic pressures and the new poverty.[27]

The potential appeal here is real, as the results of the last presidential election suggest. Although Dukakis lost, he contended with some effect that government should make good the recent deficiencies of the economy from the viewpoint of ordinary Americans. It should raise the minimum wage, guarantee health and child care, help finance college educations, and build more affordable housing. Such class-oriented pitches, made toward the end of the campaign, did a lot more for Dukakis than his earlier appeals to managerial competence. Despite his defeat, Congress within two years raised the minimum wage as well as wage subsidies for low-income workers and voted several new child care subsidies. Nothing is more popular than new benefits for working people.[28]

Health reform is probably the most telling idea. Americans feel particularly exposed to rising health expenses, and most think health care ought to be guaranteed.[29] In a noted upset, Harris Wofford won a Senate seat for Democrats in a special election in Pennsylvania in 1991 with a pitch for national health insurance. Widespread fears also focus on housing, where skyrocketing prices thwart buyers and make it seem that new families will never be able to afford this necessity of middle-class life. Business and state governments are already scrambling to help people buy homes, and new subsidy proposals have surfaced in Congress.[30]

The effective claim in progressive politics is that the normative life-style be available to average workers, not just to the affluent. If that life now includes college education and a home in the suburbs, then either the private or the public sector must provide them. If the former falters, the latter must step in. The costs of health care, higher education, and housing might well provide grounds for a progressive reform crusade as a shortage of jobs no longer does. By stressing these vulnerabilities, particularly among the young, Democrats might at last rebuild the coalition they need to govern, one that unites the mass public with the poor and dependent. With this aim in mind, the contenders now vying for the 1992 Democratic presidential nomination are wooing the "forgotten middle class" and saying very little about the poor.[31]

But there is one crushing precondition for the entitlements strategy—the beneficiaries must be workers. There is no way, but by subterfuge, to extend this rubric to the nonworking poor, the main bone of today's social contention. Americans clearly want most new benefits, like most existing ones, to go to the "deserving," not the "undeserving." Mainstream politics remains based on the competence assumption. Yet if new entitlements exclude the nonworking, they will not solve the economic problems of the poor nor the political problems Democrats face on account of poverty.

That moral became clear in New Jersey, where James Florio, a liberal Democratic governor, assembled exactly the populist coalition intellectuals speak of. He was elected in 1989 with a combination of urban and blue-collar votes, then used his mandate to push through stiff tax increases, mainly on the rich, in order to spend more on education and other services, chiefly in urban areas. Commentators applauded, but a backlash quickly mounted. Florio's working-class constituents no longer feel much in common with the blacks they have left behind in New Jersey's crumbling cities, and they resented seeing so much of their money spent there.[32] In the 1991 elections, Republicans seized control of the New Jersey state legislature.

THE CIVIC ALTERNATIVE

All the options we have discussed have great limitations, since none directly confronts the urban disorders that have become a test of credibility in national politics. In consequence, some moderate Democratic politicians, particularly the Democratic Leadership Council, have begun to take positions on welfare and crime that sound distinctly conservative and are more than just lip service. They speak of enforcing "values" and expecting welfare clients to work. Among the current Democratic presidential hopefuls, Bill Clinton and Douglas Wilder are closest to this stance. Some thinkers have gone further, suggesting how a more authoritative stance might actually serve radical ends. A "civic" form of liberalism has begun to emerge.

Because of its "softness," recent liberal social thinking provides a poor rationale for governance, Mickey Kaus recently wrote. Liberal Democrats like Mario Cuomo want to help the poor and other vulnerable groups out of "compassion," but that appeal neglects the moral distinctions the public insists on drawing among claimants at the public trough; it suggests an "indiscriminate dispensing of cash in a sort of all-purpose socialized United Way campaign." Above all, it offers a "miserable basis for liberal politics," because it attributes qualities only of "dependence and piteousness" to government clients. A social policy based only on "charity" can never yield a society of "free, equal citizens."[33]

This sort of unease has spurred renewed talk of civility on the left. The limitation of the welfare state, historian Fred Siegel says, is that it liberates people from responsibility for themselves but makes no demands and thus has no "ethical core." Some liberals, remembering that the modern idea of citizenship was originally revolutionary, suggest it might still be used for progressive ends. The author Barbara Ehrenreich recently wrote that the left could reverse the conservative political tide only by crafting "a genuinely radical alternative vision" based not only on the "redistribution of wealth," but on "the old small-R republican values of active citizenship." According to Raymond Plant, a British academic, there is no reason why the left cannot reclaim that tradition, and speak of obligation as well as entitlement.[34]

Some of this talk never gets beyond generalities. Like the liberal experts who joined the advisory groups on welfare reform, intellectuals on the left find it easier to affirm values theoretically than actually to require people to obey them.[35] For some as well, the main agenda of "citizenship" is economic. The term is a code word for reversing Reaganite cuts in taxation and regulations and reasserting public control of the economy.[36] Other liberals, however, suggest in some detail how a civic liberalism might begin to heal society. Mickey Kaus argues that the left has spent too much political capital on efforts to redistribute wealth and income. In a society that so fully accepts the marketplace, that cause must always be unpopular. Liberals should seek rather to build up public institutions that compensate for economic inequality. Through improved public schools, universal social services such as child and health care, and democratized local government, Americans could share a common life even if they had radically different incomes.[37]

Unfortunately, the social problem quickly intrudes. Civic liberalism presumes that the middle class would want to inhabit the same public spaces as the poor, and to invest in these. Without more secure conditions in urban schools, streets, and parks, that is very doubtful. The problem of the underclass must first be solved. Kaus accepts that the poor must be required to work, standards raised in schools, and law and order restored in cities. Greater opportunity or spending alone will not accomplish these things. A reassertion of public authority is also needed.[38] The frontier for a new liberalism, therefore, must be the welfare state, not other public institutions or the economy. It is partly in return for benefits that government might seek to enforce the behaviors, such as work, that sustain trustful interactions among citizens. The public wants a new *social* citizenship that would base welfare and other public support on moral reciprocity. If liberals genuinely accepted this, they could parry the strongest weapon conservatives hold in the current dependency politics.

Liberal experts Forrest Chisman and Alan Pifer seek an expanded "federal social role," and to that end, they grasp the nettle of nonwork as few other liberals have. They see that employment is pivotal to the entire social problem. Government cannot just offer people market "freedom," they agree, but neither can it offer them only "security" without expectations. Rather, it must develop work programs that both facilitate and demand personal effort. Both Unemployment and AFDC benefits should be improved, but they should both carry narrower time limits, after which recipients would have to enter job placement or training, and later unpaid jobs, to maintain their support. This is "not a harsh requirement," the authors say, since it merely enforces the "individual responsibility" in which "a nation of individualists" believes.[39]

Mickey Kaus has gone even further. In a much-noted article, he proposed to replace welfare with guaranteed jobs,[40] a plan much like what some conservatives talk about,[41] but with a very different political intention. Kaus's aim is not to circumscribe social reformism, but to give it new play. Work enforcement would remove the albatross of passive dependency that has doomed all liberal proposals for major new social benefits for a generation. If the left could no longer be accused of permissiveness, it might get its central concern—equality among workers—back on the agenda.

Unfortunately, civic liberalism has few followers. The Democratic Leadership Council's attempt to promote work and family obligations as a basis for social policy has met stiff resistance among other Democrats.[42] In crafting the Family Support Act, most Democratics in Congress accepted welfare work programs, but not that they should be mandatory, though they acquiesced in conservative demands that participation be raised. Most liberal experts support work or other requirements only in general terms, not specifically enough to make benefits conditional. Few other intellectuals talk of enforcing social standards with anything but distaste.

The pursuit of equality demands discipline from leaders and led alike, as the civil rights movement showed. That is a price most liberal politicians and thinkers are no longer willing to pay. Their aversion to authority assures that, for now, any more hardheaded form of liberalism will remain speculative. Responding to Kaus, the political theorist Mark Lilla wrote, "Until Democrats realize that citizenship sometimes means having to sit up straight and tie your shoes, Civic Liberalism will have no party to call its own."[43]

IF WORK LEVELS ROSE

Analysts on the left not only oppose a more authoritative work policy, they fear it would shift politics further to the right. With more work and less dependency among the needy, the welfare state would shrink and society would return to a market basis where most people had to labor to survive. The best argument for this conjecture is historical. For most of its first two centuries, the American republic offered little subsidy to poor people. Even the destitute worked. Yet, because the society was open and competitive compared to Europe, most people realized some gain from their labor. As a result, they perceived the market as fair, and a serious socialist movement never developed.[44] If more of the poor worked today, they could achieve similar advancement, and the case for radical social change would be even weaker than it is now.

However, my hunch is that the outcome would be more radical. History also shows that, as groups become more integrated, they feel they can make more demands on the society. A poor population working at higher levels would probably retain much of its historic resentments, but would now have much greater resources to prosecute them. The new workers would gain confidence and political skill from employment and, above all, a stronger claim on the concern of other Americans. The labor movement offers an example. Unions became major players in national politics, not in the nineteenth century when the movement was marginalized and sometimes extremist, but in this century, when, with greater numbers and legitimacy, it was able to exact key concessions during the New Deal and succeeding Democratic administrations. Other examples come from ethnic groups. Only after immigrant populations become sure of their Americanism do they make claims as groups.[45]

The new workers would be likely to make demands, in part, because most would be nonwhite. Blacks and, to a lesser extent, Hispanics have historically favored larger government, and this would not immediately change. Needy members of these groups, once they were required to work, would find their opportunities enlarged. But like other workers, they would encounter new problems, and these would generate new demands. Precisely because they were advancing, they would be more likely to encounter racial bias, as well as shortcomings in support services. If more welfare mothers had to work, they might accelerate the movement for government-supported child care, parental leave, and so on.

The psychology of integration would also favor radicalism. Higher work levels would force disadvantaged blacks to work alongside, and compete with, comparable whites as never before. Anxiety among blacks about whether they could succeed would probably provoke calls for new forms of affirmative action and other government protections against white employers and co-workers. Working and middle-class blacks tend to be more militant on race issues than the poor, just because they have more contact with whites and their remaining prejudices.[46] Thus, if more poor blacks took jobs and increased their income, politics could initially be driven left, not right.

British history supports this possibility. Around the turn of the nineteenth century in Britain, many workers and agricultural laborers became heavily dependent on public relief. Then, in 1834, parliament abolished their right to receive assistance in their homes. Families could henceforth receive assistance only by entering a workhouse. The new policy, intended to reduce the relief rolls, was not fully implemented, but it transformed the British working class. The loss of aid forced the emerging proletariat to come to terms with the market economy; workers' political goal shifted from avoiding or attacking industrialism to achieving equality within it. The eventual result was not dependency, but socialism. For the United States today, the equivalent would be to abolish AFDC or transform it into workfare. This would require the core of poor America, for the first time in a generation, to seek survival through the workplace rather than outside it. As in Britain, the chimera of dependency would have to be given up, and replaced with the progressive goal of equality among workers.

After this, a new politics of redress would probably appear first in an upsurge of labor organizing. One form would be more militant municipal unionism, already seen in cities like New York where ethnic groups have traditionally dominated one or another sector of the public service. More important would probably be a wave of new organizing in the private-sector service industries that have recently provided the bulk of new employment for the low-skilled. Unlike manufacturing, these jobs cannot easily be exported to other regions or overseas, so they are ripe for organization.

The next frontier would be elective politics. Overstressed new workers would funnel demands into the Democratic party, or, conceivably, a splinter party further to the left. The new movement— Jesse Jackson's Rainbow Coalition may prove a harbinger—would be an economic analogue to the civil rights movement. The new workers would demand protections like greater affirmative action, but also enhanced benefits, job training, and other services. Civil rights leaders of the 1960s had demanded a "freedom budget." Now that more blacks were working, the rest of society would be much more receptive.

Blacks would also have more power to push for change themselves. In July 1990, John E. Jacob, president of the Urban League, called for an "Urban Marshall Plan" to invest in infrastructure and minority education and thus save America's cities. Appealing not only to whites, he said blacks now had the "critical mass" of middle-class and professional people to advance this program on their own. Black "lawyers and computer experts, corporate managers and business people" were going to turn out to be "revolutionaries" in "suits and cuff-links," he predicted. They would remember their heritage and demand redress for disadvantaged blacks left behind in the inner city.[47]

As this suggests, so many blacks have attained success today that the country may face a black-led political movement regardless of what is done, or not done, about poverty. This is already apparent in the Jackson movement and on issues, such as South Africa and recent appointments to the Supreme Court, where blacks have particular interests and exercise special influence. But the bottom, not the top, of black society is crucial to how any black agenda is received. White America feels much more threatened by incompetent than successful blacks, and doing something about them will be the test of any renewed liberalism, black-led or otherwise.

Why do conservatives push tough work and welfare policies if a shift to the left might be the consequence? The answer is probably that their concerns run deeper than the small-government agenda they pursued in the progressive era. Today's conservatives defend not simply the free economy, but a vision of self-reliant individualism they see as underlying the entire American, and Western, tradition. If serving that larger aim requires opening the door to increased collectivism, it is a price many feel worth paying.

Of course, it remains far from clear that work levels will rise. The battle to implement workfare and other authoritative policies hangs in the balance. Meanwhile, while the tightening labor market raises the stakes for both left and right. Short of runaway immigration, unemployment is likely to remain manageable and jobs readily available to most people for the foreseeable future. In the absence of a sufficient economic reason for high joblessness among the poor, a failure to solve that problem will continue to undercut liberal politics. Nonwork is too great a scandal to be ignored.

At the same time, the current situation offers the best chance the left has had to deal with dependency on egalitarian lines in two decades. Just because the labor market is tight, a meaningful liberal version of workfare—enforcing participation but stressing "better" jobs—is far more practicable today than it would have been in 1970 or even 1980. Dependent adults could be ushered toward employment without much severity. Scarce labor also makes a radical union and party politics more feasible because employers are going to find it harder to locate compliant workers. The difficulty remains, however, that liberal elites are uncomfortable with enforcing any norms at all.

WORK AS AN ISSUE

One might suppose that progress would be made on reducing dependency just because it has become an issue. Government now openly addresses the problems raised by dysfunction, as it did not twenty years ago, and certainly this is constructive. There definitely is a sense of movement.

Yet just because work is contested, it is also difficult to imagine any speedy resolution. The work controversy makes demands for greater work effort more explicit but, at the same time, dramatizes the idea that work might *not* be required, that the needy—indeed all persons—might possess a right to subsistence merely because they exist. It would be easier to enforce work if it were *not* an issue, if American life included a work expectation and no one questioned it. That was the situation in the decades before 1960, when the vast majority of working-aged Americans, rich and poor alike, scrambled to support families on their wages with little expectation of direct help from government.

When the work problem appeared in the 1960s, what prevented work enforcement was not so much the large numbers on AFDC and other welfare programs as the eruption of the new dependency debate. For the first time, liberal politicians, intellectuals, and poverty lawyers were prepared to characterize nonworking adults as helpless victims who could not be expected to function. Conservatives countered with arguments for personal responsibility and "values" that they seldom made before 1960. The dispute made it tougher to agree on social standards. The only issues that could be laid to rest for the time being were the progressive ones. This was achieved, not by resolving them, but by shoving them off the agenda. Economic redistribution became unimaginable, and liberals lost the means of resisting the trends toward inequality of the 1970s and 1980s.[48]

Likewise, the best way to settle the work issue may be for another concern to shove it out of sight. Since, for the reasons given, the class or equality issue is unlikely to return soon, the best candidate might be some new question. The leading candidate is probably the environment. The struggle against pollution by industrial wastes already strongly influences economic policy at home, while international cooperation is needed to deal with the oceans, acid rain, and the greenhouse effect. Environmental degradation may soon impose harsh limits on economic growth, and even a declining standard of living. The tension between environmental controls and growth could give rise to a general political division, in which Democrats would probably favor more controls, Republicans fewer. The battle would resemble the progressive face-off over government control of the economy, except that left and right would dispute how to manage scarcity rather than how to advance equality among workers.

Another candidate is immigration. The public is already conflicted over how many newcomers to allow into the country. Demands for higher legal immigration are likely to come from labor-starved businesses, Hispanics, and other newer ethnic groups, even as illegal immigration continues at a high rate. Favoring restrictions would be conservative groups worried about English literacy, linguistic divisions, and the cohesion of the country. In the background will be enormous pressure to emigrate from Third World countries experiencing catastrophic overpopulation.[49] The issue could become a dominant one, with Democrats no doubt more liberal on new entries than the GOP. The dispute would have affinities to dependency politics, since immigration is related to poverty, but the work issue would be much less salient because many more immigrants than poor are employed. The moral issue, rather, would be how much claim foreigners have to come here simply because they are starving.

THE STRUGGLE FOR RESPONSIBILITY

Without some alternative alignment, dependency politics is likely to persist. A national interest in raising work levels is clear, yet how to achieve this goal remains deeply controversial because of the profound differences between left and right about who the poor are and who is responsible for their condition. These are issues of principle, not matters that mere goodwill or better information can resolve.

Although the poverty problem seems independent of race, racial politics remains the greatest obstacle to resolving it. The chief political resource of those opposed to a more authoritative social policy is that black leaders and notables tend to agree with them, or at least acquiesce. Black America holds mainstream social norms, and its leaders know the ravages that drugs, crime, and dependency have meant for black areas. Yet black community leaders such as clergymen seldom speak up publicly for enforcing mores. Elected leaders defer to activists, who may represent few beyond themselves, but who dominate the politics of ghetto constituencies due to low voter turnout. The few vocal black conservatives are mostly academics with tenure, and without political standing. In this situation, it is hard for conservative whites to institute enforcement measures, and for liberal whites even to advocate them.[50]

The opponents of conservative welfare, crime, and education reform measures may well prevail even in the teeth of legislative decisions. Already, local workfare officials report stiff opposition from poverty lawyers determined to litigate every step of the process by which recipients are obligated to participate and work. Amid constant legal and political challenges, change may grind to a halt. American government may lack the authority to require anything of black America without its leaders' specific consent. Progress may wait upon the emergence of a more conservative black leadership, willing to abandon the activists, reject racial liberalism, and enforce orthodox norms in the name of integration.

At best, work enforcement will involve a long struggle that is bound to strain the nation's political resolution. The second Civil War will be as testing in its own way as the first, though less dramatic. Over years, mandates for higher behavioral standards must be implemented and defended against challenges. The nation's identity is at stake. The majority of Americans, black and white, evidently reject the ethos of resignation that pervades ghetto areas. They continue to affirm the faith of this very Western nation that effort is meaningful and individuals can be held accountable for their fate.

The struggle with dependency could lead to a general demoralization. The lethargy of the dependent may be too great for any policy to change. The conviction of the poor, and their leaders, that they are victims plumbs emotional depths that class identities never did. To counter that appeal, mainstream groups may trumpet their own disadvantages. Morale could spiral downward in an orgy of competitive victimhood. But claiming the status of victim leads only to dependency; it cannot promote social harmony or progressive change. For those goals, some greater self-reliance, a willingness to absorb injuries rather than flaunt them, is simply indispensable.

The fatalistic view does capture tragic realities, the futility that most people feel at one or another juncture of their lives. To affirm this is a kind of truth. To deny it is a kind of lie, finally exposed in every life by the reality of death. People really cannot be responsible for more than a part of their fate. Yet, the belief that they can be seems essential to both personal happiness and a healthy society, at least as most Americans understand things. Society must affirm individual responsibility, at least for personal conduct, or lives lose control and collective trust decays. To exempt people from minimal standards of civility on grounds that they cannot cope would tempt the poor, and others with them, toward a collective slough of despond. That way, most Americans feel, lies the abyss.

But just because passivity has become an issue, it cannot just be repressed. Opposition to withdrawal must be conscious and authentic, not unconscious. Americans and their leaders must actively reaffirm a responsible national identity. They must do this deliberately and constantly, unless and until dysfunctional poverty is no longer threatening. It must be done accepting, and not denying, the undoubted appeal that the idea of exemption makes, like a siren song, to everyone's vulnerabilities.

Personal responsibility must be willed, precisely because it can no longer be assumed. It must become an explicit policy because it is no longer, as in the progressive era, the unspoken ground of the political culture. Social policy must resist passive poverty justly but firmly—much as the West contained communism—until sanity breaks in and the opposed system collapses of its own weight. That moment will come when at least the lion's share of today's nonworkers accept that some opportunity exists for them, and that it is best to seek it. Then finally they will take and hold available jobs, and get on with their lives. That realization, like the truth about Stalinism, may take decades to dawn.

Some may regret the passing of the progressive concern for economic equality. Given affluence and scarce labor, that issue will probably never again bulk as large in our politics as it did formerly. Certain compelling visions connected to equality, such as socialism, thereby pass into obsolescence, and that is tragic. But dependency politics has the virtue of exposing what was really the basis of those and other utopias—a hopeful view of individual potential and thus of citizenship. The battle to reaffirm that premise must be fought and won before any new image of community can even get on the table.

NOTES

Chapter 1:
Introduction

1. I use this term to mean class-oriented, redistributive politics at any time in American history, and particularly since the New Deal. The "Progressive" movement of the turn of the century was, in this usage, one phase within the longer progressive tradition.
2. I prefer this term to "welfare politics," since dependency is a broader phenomenon than simply reliance on public assistance programs. Many poor people are not on welfare, yet dependent on government in other senses.
3. Kevin Phillips, *The Politics of Rich and Poor: Wealth and the American Electorate in the Reagan Aftermath* (New York: Random House, 1990).
4. "Reagan Speech before Joint Session of Congress," *New York Times*, 5 February 1986, p. A20.
5. By "adults," henceforth, I will generally mean working-aged people, neither elderly nor disabled. Technically, nonworkers include unemployed adults and those not looking for work, that is, withdrawn from the labor force.
6. Jacob A. Riis, *How the Other Half Lives: Studies among the Tenements of New York* (1890; reprint, New York: Dover, 1971); Richard Levine, "Young Immigrant Wave Lifts New York Economy," *New York Times*, 30 July 1990, pp. A1, B4.

7. Anthony DePalma, "Boom Ends as Minorities in the Region Lag Behind," *New York Times*, 11 January 1989, pp. B1, B3; Dennis Hevesi, "Jobs of Summer Are Rare Rest of the Year," *New York Times*, 18 July 1989, pp. B1, B4; "22.9 Percent: A Youth Emergency," *New York Times*, 13 August 1988, p. 26.

8. Jere Van Dyk, "Growing Up in East Harlem," *National Geographic*, May 1990, pp. 52–75.

9. Louis Uchitelle, "America's Army of Non-Workers," *New York Times*, 27 September 1987, pp. F1, F6; Frank Levy, *Dollars and Dreams: The Changing American Income Distribution* (New York: Russell Sage Foundation, 1987), 212–13.

10. On these selection effects, see James P. Scanlan, "The Perils of Provocative Statistics," *The Public Interest*, no. 102 (Winter 1991): 3–14. Most of the drop in both poverty and work effort was before 1975. The remaining "working poor" are discussed further in chapter 4.

11. This is because of childless families and unrelated individuals, both elderly and nonelderly, who are not shown in the table. On balance, work levels fell for these groups for all incomes and in the top quintile, and rose in the bottom quintile. This balanced the changes among families with children and led to little overall change in work levels.

12. Calculated from U.S. Department of Commerce, Bureau of the Census, *Money Income and Poverty Status in the United States 1989*, Series P-60, no. 168 (Washington, D.C.: U.S. Government Printing Office, September 1990), tables 19–20.

13. Ibid., tables 19, 23–24. The proportion of elderly heads among female-headed families is only 3 percent, among unrelated individuals, 32 percent.

14. Table 1.2 shows this compositional effect: Among bottom-quintile families with children, the overall work level drops sharply, even though there is little decline for either married-couple or female-headed families. The shift in families from intact to female-headed is enough to produce the fall.

15. Sheldon Danziger and Peter Gottschalk, "Work, Poverty, and the Working Poor: A Multifaceted Problem," *Monthly Labor Review* 109 (no. 9, September 1986): 19–20.

16. U.S. Department of Commerce, Bureau of the Census, *Statistical Abstract of the United States 1982–83* (Washington, D.C.: U.S. Government Printing Office, December 1982), 377; idem, *Statistical Abstract of the United States 1990* (Washington, D.C.: U.S. Government Printing Office, January 1990), 378.

17. U.S. Department of Labor, Bureau of the Census, *Handbook of Labor Statistics* (Washington, D.C.: U.S. Government Printing Office, August 1989), table 28.

18. Robert Moffitt, "Work and the U.S. Welfare System: A Review" (Madison: University of Wisconsin, Institute for Research on Poverty, April 1988), 14–16; U.S. Congress, House, Committee on Ways and Means, *Overview of Entitlement Programs: Background Materials and Data on Programs within the Jurisdic-*

tion of the Committee on Ways and Means (Washington, D.C.: U.S. Government Printing Office, 5 June 1990), 580.

19. Danziger and Gottschalk, "Work, Poverty, and the Working Poor," 17–18.
20. Bureau of the Census, *Money Income 1989*, table 19.
21. In deciding whether a family is poor, for instance, the definition considers only income in cash, not in-kind benefits such as health care or Food Stamps. On the other hand, it has no connection to average or median incomes.
22. Mary Jo Bane and David T. Ellwood, "Slipping Into and Out of Poverty: The Dynamics of Spells," *Journal of Human Resources* 21 (no. 1, Winter 1986): 9–13.
23. Isabel V. Sawhill, "Poverty in the U.S.: Why Is It So Persistent?" *Journal of Economic Literature* 26 (September 1988): 1080–81; idem, "The Underclass: An Overview," *The Public Interest*, no. 96 (Summer 1989): 5.
24. "The No-Parent Child," *New York Times*, 24 December 1989, p. E10.
25. Christopher Jencks, "What Is the Underclass—And Is It Growing?" *Focus* 12 (no. 1, Spring and Summer 1989): 14–26.
26. Abraham Lincoln, *Speeches and Writings, 1859–1865* (New York: Library of America, 1989), 259; Richard Hofstadter, *The American Political Tradition and the Men Who Made It* (New York: Knopf, 1948), 104.
27. Gennadi Lisichkin, quoted in Daniel Ford, "Rebirth of a Nation," *The New Yorker*, 28 March 1988, p. 67.
28. For a general treatment of this choice, see Arthur M. Okun, *Equality and Efficiency: The Big Tradeoff* (Washington, D.C.: Brookings, 1975).
29. Bill Keller, "Soviet Poll Finds Deep Pessimism over Gorbachev's Economic Plan," *New York Times*, 5 November 1989, pp. 1, 18.
30. Sawhill, "Poverty in the U.S.," 1083.
31. Richard M. Huber, *The American Idea of Success* (New York: McGraw-Hill, 1971), 1.
32. Hofstadter, *American Political Tradition*, viii, 16.
33. Alexis de Tocqueville, *Democracy in America*, ed. J. P. Mayer, trans. George Lawrence (Garden City, N.Y.: Anchor Books, 1969), 242, 541, 623.
34. Ibid., 550.
35. Vernon Louis Parrington, *Main Currents in American Thought*, vol. 2, *1800–1860, The Romantic Revolution in America* (San Diego, Calif.: Harcourt Brace Jovanovich, 1954), xii.

Chapter 2:
The Crisis of Reform

1. Quoted in Studs Terkel, *Hard Times: An Oral History of the Great Depression* (New York: Pantheon, 1970), 248.
2. James T. Patterson, *America's Struggle against Poverty, 1900–1980* (Cambridge, Mass.: Harvard University Press, 1981), chaps. 3–4.

3. Terkel, *Hard Times*, 210.

4. John Kenneth Galbraith, *The Affluent Society* (New York: Mentor Books, 1958), 250–55.

5. Patterson, *America's Struggle against Poverty*, 8.

6. Michael Harrington, *The Other America: Poverty in the United States*, rev. ed. (1962; reprint, Baltimore: Penguin Books, 1971), 1, 12, 16, 146.

7. U.S. Department of Commerce, Bureau of the Census, *Statistical Abstract of the United States: 1982–83* (Washington, D.C.: U.S. Government Printing Office, December 1982), 340.

8. Miriam Ostow and Anna B. Dutka, *Work and Welfare in New York City* (Baltimore: Johns Hopkins University Press, 1975), 7–8; Elizabeth Durbin, "Work and Welfare: The Case of Aid to Families with Dependent Children," *Journal of Human Resources* 8 (Supplement 1973): 103–25. Whether welfare *caused* the work decline is unclear. See chapter 6.

9. Daniel P. Moynihan, "Half a Nation's Children: Born without a Fair Chance," *New York Times*, 25 September 1988, p. E25; idem, "Another War—The One on Poverty—Is Over, Too," *New York Times*, 16 July 1990, p. A15.

10. Daniel P. Moynihan, *The Politics of a Guaranteed Income: The Nixon Administration and the Family Assistance Plan* (New York: Random House, 1973), chap. 1.

11. "The American Underclass," *Time*, 29 August 1977, pp. 14–27.

12. Robert D. Reischauer, "The Size and Characteristics of the Underclass" (Washington, D.C.: Brookings, October 1987). This estimate is based on the Panel Study of Income Dynamics. Estimates based on low-income census tracts typically run smaller. See Erol R. Ricketts and Isabel V. Sawhill, "Defining and Measuring the Underclass," *Journal of Policy Analysis and Management* 7 (no. 2, Winter 1988): 316–25.

13. Areas of high poverty frequented by the underclass are growing rapidly; see Isabel V. Sawhill, "Poverty and the Underclass," in *Challenge to Leadership: Economic and Social Issues for the Next Decade*, ed. Isabel V. Sawhill (Washington, D.C.: Urban Institute, 1988), 229–30. But the number of actual underclass people is probably not growing; see Christopher Jencks, "What Is the Underclass—And Is It Growing?" *Focus* 12 (no. 1, Spring and Summer 1989): 14–26.

14. Martha R. Burt and Barbara E. Cohen, *America's Homeless: Numbers, Characteristics, and Programs that Serve Them* (Washington, D.C.: Urban Institute, July 1989), 27–31, 39–40.

15. Robert C. Ellickson, "The Homelessness Muddle," *The Public Interest*, no. 99 (Spring 1990): 45–60; Thomas J. Main, "The Homeless of New York," *The Public Interest*, no. 72 (Summer 1983): 3–28.

16. Burt and Cohen, *America's Homeless*, 41–44.

17. "Begging: To Give or Not to Give," *Time*, 5 September 1988, pp. 68–74; Isabel Wilkerson, "Shift in Feelings on the Homeless: Empathy Turns into Frustration," *New York Times*, 2 September 1991, p. 10.

18. Patterson, *America's Struggle against Poverty*, 110, 134–35.

19. Eric Pooley, "Beggars' Army," *New York Magazine*, 29 August 1988, p. 37.

20. I use "War on Poverty" to denote the programs, such as Community Action, first legislated by the Economic Opportunity Act of 1964. The term also connotes the years when these programs were most active, about 1964–74. I use "Great Society" to cover the entire period stretching from about 1961 to 1978, including the War on Poverty, when federal social policy was predominantly liberal and preoccupied with poverty.

21. Carl M. Brauer, "Kennedy, Johnson, and the War on Poverty," *Journal of American History* 69 (no. 1, June 1982): 98–119.

22. U.S. Department of Commerce, Bureau of the Census, *Money Income and Poverty Status in the United States 1989*, Series P-60, no. 168 (Washington, D.C.: U.S. Government Printing Office, September 1990), table 19.

23. Sar A. Levitan, *The Great Society's Poor Law: A New Approach to Poverty* (Baltimore: Johns Hopkins University Press, 1969), 86–88.

24. "To Fulfill These Rights," speech at Howard University, 4 June 1965, in Lee Rainwater and William L. Yancey, *The Moynihan Report and the Politics of Controversy* (Cambridge, Mass.: MIT Press, 1967), 126, 131.

25. Robert H. Haveman, *Poverty Policy and Poverty Research: The Great Society and the Social Sciences* (Madison: University of Wisconsin Press, 1987), 14–15, 150–52.

26. Michael B. Katz, *The Undeserving Poor: From the War on Poverty to the War on Welfare* (New York: Pantheon, 1989), 89–95.

27. A number of reviews sustain this verdict; see Robert H. Haveman, ed., *A Decade of Federal Antipoverty Programs: Achievements, Failures, and Lessons* (New York: Academic Press, 1977); and Sheldon H. Danziger and Daniel H. Weinberg, eds., *Fighting Poverty: What Works and What Doesn't* (Cambridge, Mass.: Harvard University Press, 1986). For further discussion, see chapter 8.

28. Terkel, *Hard Times*, 233, 420, 437, 444.

29. Franklin E. Frazier, *The Negro Family in the United States* (Chicago: University of Chicago Press, 1939), chap. 21; John Hope Franklin, *From Slavery to Freedom: A History of Negro Americans*, 4th ed. (New York: Knopf, 1974), chaps. 19, 21.

30. Charles V. Hamilton and Dona C. Hamilton, "Social Policies, Civil Rights, and Poverty," in *Fighting Poverty*, ed. Danziger and Weinberg, chap. 12.

31. Abigail M. Thernstrom, *Whose Votes Count? Affirmative Action and Minority Voting Rights* (Cambridge, Mass.: Harvard University Press, 1987).

32. Terkel, *Hard Times*, 176, 375, 387.

33. Sara Rimer, "Yonkers Anguish: Black and White in 2 Worlds," *New York Times*, 22 December 1987, pp. A1, B7.

34. Jonathan Rieder, *Canarsie: The Jews and Italians of Brooklyn against Liberalism* (Cambridge, Mass.: Harvard University Press, 1985), 101–7.

35. Samuel H. Beer, "In Search of a New Public Philosophy," in *The New American Political System*, ed. Anthony King (Washington, D.C.: American Enter-

prise Institute, 1978), chap. 1; E. J. Dionne, Jr., *Why Americans Hate Politics* (New York: Simon and Schuster, 1991), chaps. 1–3, 4.

36. Lawrence M. Friedman, "The Social and Political Context of the War on Poverty," in *Decade of Federal Antipoverty Programs*, ed. Haveman, chap. 2.

37. By dominant issues I mean those that people feel most intensely about, and which also divide the public or politicians in some significant way. Such issues are on the political agenda, though they may not be on the agenda for active decision making within government.

38. For this Gallup poll data, see Richard G. Niemi, John Mueller, and Tom W. Smith, *Trends in Public Opinion: A Compendium of Survey Data* (Westport, Conn.: Greenwood Press, 1989), 39–47; George Gallup, Jr., *Gallup Poll: Public Opinion 1988* (Wilmington, Del.: Scholarly Resources, 1989), 166; idem, *Gallup Poll: Public Opinion 1989* (Wilmington, Del.: Scholarly Resources, 1990), 120; and *The Gallup Poll Monthly*, no. 295 (April 1990): 7. On leading issues in the last few years, see also Michael R. Kagay, "As Candidates Hunt the Big Issue, Polls Give Them a Few Clues," *New York Times*, 20 October 1991, p. E3. In these polls, no one issue may be mentioned by more than a minority of respondents.

39. Charles Murray, *Losing Ground: American Social Policy, 1950–1980* (New York: Basic Books, 1984). Another influential book that stressed economic and social policy about equally was George Gilder, *Wealth and Poverty* (New York: Basic Books, 1981).

40. *American Agenda: Report to the Forty-first President of the United States of America* (Camp Hill, Penn.: Book-of-the-Month Club, n.d.), 22, 61, 73, 79.

41. Jason DeParle, "Suffering in the Cities Persists as U.S. Fights Other Battles," *New York Times*, 27 January 1991, p. 1; "The Talk of the Town," *The New Yorker*, 7 January 1991, pp. 19–20.

42. D. Roderick Kiewiet and Douglas Rivers, "The Economic Basis of Reagan's Appeal," in *The New Direction in American Politics*, ed. John E. Chubb and Paul E. Peterson (Washington, D.C.: Brookings, 1985), chap. 3; Robert S. Erikson, "Economic Conditions and the Presidential Vote," *American Political Science Review* 83 (no. 2, June 1989): 567–73; Dionne, *Why Americans Hate Politics*, 243–47.

43. Douglas A. Hibbs, Jr., "Political Parties and Macroeconomic Policy," *American Political Science Review* 71 (no. 4, December 1977): 1467–87. There has recently been more difference over tax policy, where Republicans in the Reagan era advocated supply-side tax reductions while Democrats were doubtful or opposed.

44. Institutions that have more control include the Federal Reserve, which governs interest rates, and Congress, which controls the budget.

45. J. Merrill Shanks and Warren E. Miller, "Policy Direction and Performance Evaluation: Complementary Explanations of the Reagan Elections," *British Journal of Political Science* 20 (part 2, April 1990): 143–79; idem, "Partisanship, Policy and Performance: The Reagan Legacy in the 1988 Election,"

British Journal of Political Science 21 (April 1991): 1–67; Adam Clymer, "Poll Finds G.O.P. Growth Erodes Dominant Role of the Democrats," *New York Times*, 14 July 1991, pp. 1, 16.

46. Stanley Kelley, Jr., "Democracy and the New Deal Party System," in *Democracy and the Welfare State*, ed. Amy Gutmann (Princeton, N.J.: Princeton University Press, 1988), chap. 8.

47. Warren E. Miller and Santa Traugott, *American National Election Studies Data Sourcebook, 1952–1986* (Cambridge, Mass.: Harvard University Press, 1989), 158.

48. Political scientists say that economic questions are "position" issues while the social questions are "valence" issues. On the first, divergent opinions are legitimate, while on the second they are not, because there is only one "right" side.

49. John R. Petrocik, *Party Coalitions: Realignment and the Decline of the New Deal Party System* (Chicago: University of Chicago Press, 1981), chaps. 7, 9; Edward G. Carmines and James A. Stimson, *Issue Evolution: Race and the Transformation of American Politics* (Princeton, N.J.: Princeton University Press, 1989); Thomas Byrne Edsall and Mary D. Edsall, *Chain Reaction: The Impact of Race, Rights, and Taxes on American Politics* (New York: Norton, 1991).

50. Carmines and Stimson, *Issue Evolution*, chap. 8; Miller and Traugott, *American Data Sourcebook*, 161–64; Philip E. Converse et al., *American Social Attitudes Data Sourcebook, 1947–1978* (Cambridge, Mass.: Harvard University Press, 1980), 86.

51. While conservative positions on many issues played a role in Bush's victory in 1988, race per se did not, according to Shanks and Miller, "Partisanship, Policy and Performance," 5, 30–31, 39–40. For an opposed interpretation, see Donald P. Kinder et al., "Race and the 1988 American Presidential Election" (Ann Arbor: University of Michigan, Department of Political Science, 1989).

52. This interpretation is suggested by Carmines and Stimson, *Issue Evolution*, 84–88, and Edsall and Edsall, *Chain Reaction*. One cannot be sure because available surveys do not allow one to track the changing meaning of race or other social issues. See further discussion in chapters 6 and 11.

53. James L. Sundquist, *Dynamics of the Party System: Alignment and Realignment of Political Parties in the United States*, rev. ed. (Washington, D.C.: Brookings, 1983), chaps. 16–18, argues this case up through Reagan's first election.

54. Byron E. Shafer, "The Notion of an Electoral Order: The Structure of Electoral Politics at the Accession of George Bush" (Paper prepared for the annual meeting of the American Political Science Association, Atlanta, Ga., 30 August–3 September 1989); Shanks and Miller, "Partisanship, Policy and Performance," 30, 49–53; Joel Lieske, "Cultural Issues and Images in the 1988 Presidential Campaign: Why the Democrats Lost—Again," *PS* 24 (no. 2, June 1991): 180–87.

55. Everett Carll Ladd, Jr., with Charles D. Hadley, *Transformations of the American Party System: Political Coalitions from the New Deal to the 1970's*, 2nd ed. (New York: Norton, 1978), chaps. 4–6; Thomas E. Cavanagh and James L. Sundquist, "The New Two-Party System," in *The New Direction in American Politics*, ed. John E. Chubb and Paul E. Peterson (Washington, D.C.: Brookings, 1985), 50–54.

56. James R. Kluegel and Eliot R. Smith, *Beliefs about Inequality: Americans' Views of What Is and What Ought to Be* (New York: Aldine de Gruyter, 1986), chaps. 5, 7; Sidney Verba and Gary R. Orren, *Equality in America: The View from the Top* (Cambridge, Mass.: Harvard University Press, 1985), chaps. 4–6.

57. Three other interpretations that stress the importance of the social issues are Richard M. Scammon and Ben J. Wattenberg, *The Real Majority* (New York: Coward-McCann, 1970); Dionne, *Why Americans Hate Politics*; and Edsall and Edsall, *Chain Reaction*. However, these authors suggest that Democrats could easily take a more conservative stance on these questions, or stress other issues, such as the economy, and thus recoup their losses. I think the Democratic problem is much more profound. The party cannot avoid the social issues because they arise from a serious social dilemma to which the public demands an answer. It also cannot avoid taking a lenient line on them, at political cost, because of deep-seated convictions among party leaders and activists about the nature of poverty and the poor.

58. One might mention disability insurance, which expanded rapidly in the 1960s and 1970s, but it was first enacted in 1956. Supplemental Security Income, or welfare for the aged, blind, and disabled, was legislated in 1972, but the program built on preexisting federal–state programs for these groups. The most important new benefit after 1965 may be the Earned Income Tax Credit, enacted in 1975, which subsidizes low-income working families. But EITC was developed within Congress and was not the result of a progressive movement such as the one behind Medicare. It is so invisible politically that the majority of Americans probably do not know it exists.

59. Ann Kallman Bixby, "Social Welfare Expenditures, 1981 and 1982," *Social Security Bulletin* 47 (no. 12, December 1984): 14–22.

60. D. Lee Bawden and John L. Palmer, "Social Policy: Challenging the Welfare State," in *The Reagan Record: An Assessment of America's Changing Priorities*, ed. John L. Palmer and Isabel V. Sawhill (Cambridge, Mass.: Ballinger, 1984), 181; Theodore R. Marmor, Jerry L. Mashaw, and Philip L. Harvey, *America's Misunderstood Welfare State: Persistent Myths, Enduring Realities* (New York: Basic Books, 1990), chap. 2.

61. Marmor, Mashaw, and Harvey, *America's Misunderstood Welfare State*, 76–77, 136; Bawden and Palmer, "Social Policy," 184–86.

62. Lawrence M. Mead, *Beyond Entitlement: The Social Obligations of Citizenship* (New York: Free Press, 1986), chap. 5.

63. Forrest Chisman and Alan Pifer, *Government for the People: The Federal Social Role: What It Is, What It Should Be* (New York: Norton, 1987), 59, 64–65.

64. David A. Stockman, "The Social Pork Barrel," *The Public Interest*, no. 39 (Spring 1975): 3–30.

65. Richard P. Nathan, Fred C. Doolittle, and Associates, *The Consequences of Cuts: The Effects of the Reagan Domestic Program on State and Local Governments* (Princeton, N.J.: Princeton University Press, 1983).

66. John C. Weicher, ed., *Maintaining the Safety Net: Income Redistribution Programs in the Reagan Administration* (Washington, D.C.: American Enterprise Institute, 1984).

67. I. A. Lewis and William Schneider, "Hard Times: The Public on Poverty," *Public Opinion* 8 (no. 3, June–July 1985): 6, 60; James L. Sundquist, "Has America Lost Its Social Conscience—And How Will It Get It Back?" *Political Science Quarterly* 101 (no. 4, 1986): 523–24.

68. U.S. Department of Labor, Bureau of Labor Statistics, *Employment and Earnings* 38 (no. 1, January 1991): 162; Bureau of the Census, *Money Income 1989*, table 19.

69. Julie Kosterlitz and W. John Moore, "Saving the Welfare State," *National Journal*, 14 May 1988, p. 1288.

70. Daniel Yankelovich, *New Rules: Searching for Self-Fulfillment in a World Turned Upside Down* (New York: Random House, 1981), 182–86.

71. Frances Fox Piven and Richard A. Cloward, *Regulating the Poor: The Functions of Public Welfare* (New York: Pantheon, 1971).

72. John L. Palmer, "Philosophy, Policy, and Politics: Integrating Themes," in *Perspectives on the Reagan Years*, ed. John L. Palmer (Washington, D.C.: Urban Institute Press, 1986), 190–96.

73. I define the neoconservatives fairly narrowly, as a group of intellectuals associated with *The Public Interest* and *Commentary*. This would include Irving Kristol, Norman Podhoretz, Nathan Glazer, Daniel Bell, Samuel Huntington, and James Q. Wilson, among others.

74. Marmor, Mashaw, and Harvey, *America's Misunderstood Welfare State*, chap. 3; Chisman and Pifer, *Federal Social Role*, 85–92; Gary Burtless, "Public Spending for the Poor: Trends, Prospects, and Economic Limits," in *Fighting Poverty*, ed. Danziger and Weinberg, 39–48.

75. John E. Schwarz, *America's Hidden Success: A Reassessment of Public Policy from Kennedy to Reagan*, rev. ed. (New York: Norton, 1988); Marmor, Mashaw, and Harvey, *America's Misunderstood Welfare State*.

76. Nicholas Lemann, *The Promised Land: The Great Black Migration and How It Changed America* (New York: Knopf, 1991), 200, 349.

77. Michael M. Gant and Norman R. Luttbeg, *American Electoral Behavior* (Itasca, Ill., 1991). By the 1980s, partisanship recovered somewhat.

78. There is doubt, in particular, whether falling turnout has any connection to rising cynicism about government. See Jack Citrin, "Comment: The Political Relevance of Trust in Government," *American Political Science Review* 68 (no. 3, September 1974): 973–88.

79. Norman H. Nie, Sidney Verba, and John R. Petrocik, *The Changing American Voter*, enlarged ed. (Cambridge, Mass.: Harvard University Press, 1979), chap. 15.

80. Sundquist, "Has America Lost Its Social Conscience," 516–20; Everett Carll Ladd, "The Reagan Phenomenon and Public Attitudes toward Government," in *The Reagan Presidency and the Governing of America*, ed. Lester M. Salamon and Michael S. Lund (Washington, D.C.: Urban Institute, 1984), 221–49; Lewis and Schneider, "Hard Times," 2–7, 59–60.

81. Fred Hartwig, "Children's Issues in the Context of Public Opinion" (Presentation at the Conference on Raising Children for the 21st Century, American Enterprise Institute and U.S. Department of Health and Human Services, Williamsburg, Va., May 3, 1990).

82. Jack Citrin and Donald Philip Green, "Presidential Leadership and the Resurgence of Trust in Government," *British Journal of Political Science* 16 (no. 4, October 1986): 431–53.

Chapter 3:
The Costs of Nonwork

1. This is the tenor, for example, of Greg J. Duncan et al., *Years of Poverty, Years of Plenty: The Changing Fortunes of American Workers and Families* (Ann Arbor: University of Michigan, Institute for Social Research, 1984).

2. U.S. Department of Commerce, Bureau of the Census, *Money Income and Poverty Status in the United States 1989*, Series P-60, no. 168 (Washington, D.C.: U.S. Government Printing Office, September 1990), table 22.

3. In the 1970s, one-third to one-half of the mothers worked over the course of a year, and about one-third of their income came from earnings, according to Mildred Rein, *Dilemmas of Welfare Policy: Why Work Strategies Haven't Worked* (New York: Praeger, 1982), chap. 6; and Philip A. AuClaire, "The Mix of Work and Welfare among Long-Term AFDC Recipients," *Social Service Review* 53 (no. 4, December 1979): 594. However, the Reagan cuts in AFDC eligibility in 1981 made it more difficult for working mothers to remain on welfare. The proportion of working mothers on the rolls dropped from 15 to the current 6 percent, and the mothers relied less on earnings. According to Christopher Jencks and Kathryn Edin, "The Real Welfare Problem" (Evanston, Ill.: Northwestern University, Center for Urban Affairs and Policy Research, 15 January 1990), fig. 1, welfare mothers in Chicago in 1988 drew only 5 percent of their income from salaried jobs, 7 percent from off-the-books jobs.

4. June O'Neill et al., "An Analysis of Time on Welfare" (Washington, D.C.: Urban Institute, June 1984), 29. The 1981 cuts removed most working recipients from the rolls (see note 3).

5. Duncan et al., *Years of Poverty*, 53; Mildred Rein, "Determinants of the Work-Welfare Choice in AFDC," *Social Service Review* 46 (no. 4, December 1972): 541, 563.

6. Bureau of the Census, *Money Income 1989*, table 22.

7. Marta Tienda and Leif Jensen, "Poverty and Minorities: A Quarter-Century Profile of Color and Socioeconomic Disadvantage," in *Divided Opportunities: Minorities, Poverty, and Social Policy*, ed. Gary D. Sandefur and Marta Tienda (New York: Plenum, 1988), chap. 2.

8. The poverty rate in 1989 was 29 percent for families with no workers, less than 2 percent for families with three or more. See Bureau of the Census, *Money Income 1989*, table 23.

9. These other factors are discussed in later chapters.

10. Duncan et al., *Years of Poverty*, chaps. 1–2, 4.

11. Charles Murray with Deborah Loren, "According to Age: Longitudinal Profiles of AFDC Recipients and the Poor by Age Group" (Paper prepared for the Working Seminar on the Family and American Welfare Policy, September 1986), chaps. 2–4. According to Charles Murray, "In Search of the Working Poor," *The Public Interest*, no. 89 (Fall 1987): 16–17, less than 3 percent of working-aged adults were nondisabled, working, yet poor in 1970, and of these only 15 percent (or 0.3 percent of the whole working-aged population) were still nondisabled, working, and poor in 1980.

12. David T. Ellwood, "Working Off of Welfare: Prospects and Policies for Self-Sufficiency of Women Heading Families" (Madison: University of Wisconsin, Institute for Research on Poverty, March 1986), table 1, p. 4. For more discussion of whether welfare mothers can earn their way off welfare, see chapter 4.

13. Martin Carnoy, Derek Shearer, and Russell Rumberger, *A New Social Contract: The Economy and Government after Reagan* (New York: Harper & Row, 1983), 30.

14. Peter M. Gutman, "The Subterranean Economy, Redux," in *The Economics of the Shadow Economy*, ed. Wulf Gaertner and Alois Wenig (Berlin: Springer-Verlag, 1985), 1–18; Morton Paglin, *Poverty and Transfers In-Kind: A Re-Evaluation of Poverty in the United States* (Stanford, Calif.: Hoover Institution Press, 1980), chap. 2.

15. Isabel V. Sawhill, "The Underclass: An Overview," *The Public Interest*, no. 96 (Summer 1989): 10–11; Congressional Budget Office, *Trends in Family Income: 1970–1986* (Washington, D.C.: U.S. Government Printing Office, February 1988), 51–52.

16. In Jencks and Edin, "Real Welfare Problem," donations and "other" accounted for 22 percent of the mothers' income, "vice" (drugs, prostitution) for another 9 percent, or less than earnings.

17. Edward L. Feige, "How Big Is the Irregular Economy," *Challenge*, November–December 1979; Gutman, "Subterranean Economy," 3; "The

Underground Economy's Hidden Force," *Business Week*, 5 April 1982, pp. 64–70. Research on the underground is very limited.

18. The most authoritative source is U.S. Department of the Treasury, Internal Revenue Service, "Income Tax Compliance Research: Estimates for 1973–1981" (Washington, D.C.: U.S. Department of the Treasury, 1983), a tax-payer survey that found $283.9 billion in unreported income, legal and illegal, in 1981. That was 9 percent of the gross national product in that year. For a review, see Ann D. Witte, "The Nature and Extent of Unrecorded Activity: A Survey Concentrating on Recent U.S. Research," in *The Unofficial Economy*, ed. Sergio Alessandrini and Bruno Dallago (Brookfield, Vt.: Gower, 1987), 61–82.

19. According to one survey, the vendors of off-the-books services such as home repairs and child care, when they could be identified, were mostly people holding regular jobs (55 percent of the value of the purchases), friends and relatives of the customers (19 percent), retirees (7 percent), or unemployed (3 percent). Very few (5 percent) were people working under cover full-time. See Witte, "Nature and Extent of Unrecorded Activity," and James D. Smith, "Market Motives in the Informal Economy," in *Shadow Economy*, ed. Gaertner and Wenig, 161–77.

20. U.S. Department of Commerce, Bureau of the Census, *Statistical Abstract of the United States 1984* (Washington, D.C.: U.S. Government Printing Office, December 1983), 54, 70; idem, *Statistical Abstract of the United States: 1990* (Washington, D.C.: U.S. Government Printing Office, January 1990), 53, 67.

21. Bureau of the Census, *Money Income 1989*, table 19.

22. Jason DeParle, "Child Poverty Twice as Likely after Family Split, Study Says," *New York Times*, 2 March 1991, p. 8.

23. E.g., Duncan et al., *Years of Poverty*, chaps. 1–2.

24. Mary Jo Bane and David T. Ellwood, "Slipping Into and Out of Poverty: The Dynamics of Spells," *Journal of Human Resources* 21 (no. 1, Winter 1986): 13–20.

25. Mary Jo Bane and David T. Ellwood, "The Dynamics of Dependence: The Routes to Self-Sufficiency" (Cambridge, Mass.: Urban Systems Research and Engineering, June 1983), 17–19.

26. Ellwood, "Working Off of Welfare," 12–16.

27. Mary Jo Bane, "Household Composition and Poverty," in *Fighting Poverty: What Works and What Doesn't*, ed. Sheldon H. Danziger and Daniel H. Weinberg (Cambridge, Mass.: Harvard University Press, 1986), chap. 9; idem, "Politics and Policies of the Feminization of Poverty," in *The Politics of Social Policy in the United States*, ed. Margaret Weir, Ann Shola Orloff, and Theda Skocpol (Princeton, N.J.: Princeton University Press, 1988), 385.

28. Victor Fuchs, "What's Leaving Children Poor?," *Wall Street Journal*, 2 October 1986, p. 30.

29. Bane, "Household Composition and Poverty," 220–27; James P. Smith, "Poverty and the Family," in *Divided Opportunities*, ed. Sandefur and Tienda, 161–71.

30. Heather L. Ross and Isabel V. Sawhill, *Time of Transition: The Growth of Families Headed by Women* (Washington, D.C.: Urban Institute, 1975), chaps. 3–5.

31. David T. Ellwood, *Poor Support: Poverty in the American Family* (New York: Basic Books, 1988), 72–79.

32. Bane, "Household Composition and Poverty," 231.

33. James Q. Wilson and Richard J. Herrnstein, *Crime and Human Nature* (New York: Simon and Schuster, 1985), chap. 9; Neil Gilbert, "The Unfinished Business of Welfare Reform," *Society* 24 (no. 3, March–April 1987): 5–11.

34. Martha Van Haitsma, "A Conceptual Definition of the Underclass," *Focus* 12 (no. 1, Spring–Summer 1989): 27–29; Forrest Chisman and Alan Pifer, *Government for the People: The Federal Social Role: What It Is, What It Should Be* (New York: Norton, 1987), 221.

35. Andrew Hacker, "American Apartheid," *New York Review of Books*, 3 December 1987, pp. 26–33; Gary Orfield, "Ghettoization and Its Alternatives," in *The New Urban Reality*, ed. Paul E. Peterson (Washington, D.C.: Brookings, 1985), 161–93. Discrimination as a barrier to employment is discussed further in chapter 6.

36. Nathan Glazer and Daniel P. Moynihan, *Beyond the Melting Pot: The Negroes, Puerto Ricans, Jews, Italians, and Irish of New York City*, 2nd ed. (Cambridge, Mass.: MIT Press, 1970).

37. Nicholas Lemann, *The Promised Land: The Great Black Migration and How It Changed America* (New York: Knopf, 1991), 34.

38. William Julius Wilson, *The Truly Disadvantaged: The Inner City, the Underclass, and Public Policy* (Chicago: University of Chicago Press, 1987), 49–50, 55–58, 61, 144. The role of ghetto isolation in poverty is considered further in chapter 7.

39. Jim Sleeper, *The Closest of Strangers: Liberalism and the Politics of Race in New York* (New York: Norton, 1990), 93.

40. Studs Terkel, *Working: People Talk about What They Do All Day and How They Feel about What They Do* (New York: Pantheon, 1974), 288–89.

41. The following discussion is based on the individual citations below and on Lawrence M. Mead, *Beyond Entitlement: The Social Obligations of Citizenship* (New York: Free Press, 1986), 233–40; and Hugh Heclo, "The Political Foundations of Antipoverty Policy," in *Fighting Poverty*, ed. Danziger and Weinberg, chap. 13, both of which summarize many individual studies.

42. James R. Kluegel and Eliot R. Smith, *Beliefs About Inequality: Americans' Views of What Is and What Ought to Be* (New York: Aldine de Gruyter, 1986), chap. 2 and passim; Sidney Verba and Gary R. Orren, *Equality in America: The View from the Top* (Cambridge, Mass.: Harvard University Press, 1985), 151–52, 257, 266.

43. "Opinion Roundup: Poverty in America," *Public Opinion* 8 (no. 3, June–July 1985): 25–26.

44. Verba and Orren, *Equality in America*, 82–83; Fay Lomax Cook, *Who Should Be Helped? Public Support for Social Services* (Beverly Hills, Calif.: Sage, 1979), 152.

45. Cook, *Who Should Be Helped?* chap. 3; I. A. Lewis and William Schneider, "Hard Times: The Public on Poverty," *Public Opinion* 8 (no. 3, June–July 1985): 5, 60.

46. Greg J. Duncan and Michael Ponza, "Public Attitudes Toward the Structure of Income Maintenance Programs" (Ann Arbor: University of Michigan, Survey Research Center, 20 March 1987).

47. For graphic portrayals of these sentiments, see John Doble and Keith Melville, *Options for Social Welfare Policy: The Public's Views* (New York: Public Agenda Foundation, November 1986), 10–32; and Keith Melville and John Doble, *The Public's Perspective on Social Welfare Reform* (New York: Public Agenda Foundation, January 1988), 2–23.

48. Kluegel and Smith, *Beliefs About Inequality*, 152–58, 163–64, 170, 174; James L. Sundquist, "Has America Lost Its Social Conscience—And How Will It Get It Back?" *Political Science Quarterly* 101 (no. 4, 1986): 518–20, 522–23.

49. Seymour Martin Lipset and Earl Raab, "The Message of Proposition 13," *Commentary*, September 1978, p. 45; Melville and Doble, *Public's Perspective*, ix.

50. Senator John Tunney in U.S. Congress, Senate, 92nd Cong., 2nd sess., 3 October 1972, *Congressional Record*, vol. 118, parts 25–26, p. 33417.

51. Doble and Melville, *Options for Social Welfare Policy*, 14–29; Melville and Doble, *Public's Perspective*, 4–23; "Opinion Outlook," *National Journal*, 11 January 1986, p. 102.

52. There is more receptivity to giving aid in-kind, which is why the most notable recent expansions of welfare have been Food Stamps and Medicaid.

53. Verba and Orren, *Equality in America*, 257; Kluegel and Smith, *Beliefs About Inequality*, 121, 152–53.

54. Hugh Heclo, "General Welfare and Two American Political Traditions," *Political Science Quarterly* 101 (no. 2, 1986): 179–96; Sundquist, "Has America Lost Its Social Conscience," 526–30.

55. Mead, *Beyond Entitlement*, chaps. 8–9; Verba and Orren, *Equality in America*, passim.

56. Doble and Melville, *Options for Social Welfare Policy*, 25.

57. Ibid., 23.

58. John Kenneth Galbraith, *The Affluent Society* (New York: Mentor Books, 1958), chap. 24 and passim.

59. Seymour Martin Lipset, "The Work Ethic—Then and Now," *The Public Interest*, no 98 (Winter 1990): 63–64; Robert Haveman, *Starting Even: An Equal Opportunity Program to Combat the Nation's New Poverty* (New York: Simon and Schuster, 1988), 91–92.

60. Bureau of the Census, *Statistical Abstract 1990*, 380.

61. Peter T. Kilborn, "Tales from the Digital Treadmill," *New York Times*, 3 June 1990, pp. E1, E3.

62. Lipset, "Work Ethic," 64–65; Connie De Boer, "The Polls: Attitudes toward Work," *Public Opinion Quarterly* 42 (no. 3, Fall 1978): 414–23; Michael R. Kagay, "Most Jobholders Content, Poll Says," *New York Times*, 4 September 1989, p. 8.

63. Terkel, *Working*, 422-23, 470.

64. Ellwood, *Poor Support*, 73.

65. Lipset, "Work Ethic," 64–67; U.S. Department of Health, Education, and Welfare, Special Task Force to the Secretary of Health, Education, and Welfare, *Work in America* (Cambridge, Mass.: MIT Press, January 1973); William Serrin, "Study Says Work Ethic Is Alive but Neglected," *New York Times*, 5 September 1983, p. L8; Philip E. Converse et al., *American Social Attitudes Data Sourcebook, 1947–1978* (Cambridge, Mass.: Harvard University Press, 1980), 159–215; "Home Is Where the Heart Is," *Time*, 3 October 1988, pp. 46–53.

66. Linda Greenhouse, "In the '88 Campaign, The Baby-Boom Voters Are Curiously Quiet," *New York Times*, 29 May 1988, p. E5.

67. Quoted in James Fallows, "Immigration: How It's Affecting Us," *The Atlantic*, November 1983, pp. 57–60.

68. Christopher Jencks et al., *Inequality: A Reassessment of the Effect of Family and Schooling in America* (New York: Basic Books, 1972), chap. 8; Raymond A. Katzell et al., *The Job Attitudes of Workers from Different Ethnic Backgrounds* (Study conducted for the U.S. Department of Labor, New York University, Department of Psychology, 1970).

69. Erving Goffman, *Stigma: Notes on the Management of Spoiled Identity* (Englewood Cliffs, N.J.: Prentice-Hall, 1963), chap. 1; Alvin W. Gouldner, "The Norm of Reciprocity: A Preliminary Statement," *American Sociological Review* 25 (no. 2, April 1960): 161–78; Robert Pruger, "Social Policy: Unilateral Transfer or Reciprocal Exchange," *Journal of Social Policy* 2 (no. 4, October 1973): 289–302.

70. Kluegel and Smith, *Beliefs About Inequality*, chap. 10; Ellen J. Langer, *The Psychology of Control* (Beverly Hills, Calif.: Sage, 1983).

71. Leonard Goodwin, *Do the Poor Want to Work? A Social-Psychological Study of Work Orientations* (Washington, D.C.: Brookings, 1972), 32–64, 70–81, 97–101, 117; Elliot Liebow, *Tally's Corner: A Study of Negro Streetcorner Men* (Boston: Little, Brown, 1967).

72. Terkel, *Working*, 222, 255, 294–95.

Chapter 4:
Low Wages and Hard Times

1. Charles Murray, "In Search of the Working Poor," *The Public Interest*, no. 89 (Fall 1987): 17.

2. Here and below, "liberals" means analysts who are still inclined to attribute poverty to blockages of opportunity, for instance Henry Aaron, David Ellwood, Robert Greenstein, Judith Gueron, and William Julius Wilson. "Conservatives" means those who tend to blame government or attitudes among the poor themselves, such as Douglas Besharov, Anna Kondratas, Charles Murray, Michael Novak, and Robert Rector. Moderates would include, for instance, Richard Nathan, Robert Reischauer, Alice Rivlin, and Isabel Sawhill.

3. U.S. Department of Commerce, Bureau of the Census, *Money Income and Poverty Status in the United States 1989*, Series P-60, no. 168 (Washington, D.C.: U.S. Government Printing Office, June 1988), tables 22–23. These figures may be inflated, as 800,000 working poor in 1984 reported that they were self-employed or worked without pay. Of 2.1 million workers who worked full-time, full-year in 1984 and still had family incomes below poverty, only 1.1 million worked for others. See Congressional Budget Office, "The Minimum Wage: Its Relationship to Incomes and Poverty" (Staff Working Paper, Washington, D.C., June 1986), 21–22.

4. U.S. Department of Commerce, Bureau of the Census, *Poverty in the United States: 1988 and 1989*, Series P-60, no. 171 (Washington, D.C.: U.S. Government Printing Office, June 1991), table 19.

5. David T. Ellwood, *Poor Support: Poverty in the American Family* (New York: Basic Books, 1988), 81–98.

6. Sar A. Levitan and Isaac Shapiro, *Working but Poor: America's Contradiction* (Baltimore: Johns Hopkins University Press, 1987), 17–19; Greg J. Duncan et al., *Years of Poverty, Years of Plenty: The Changing Fortunes of American Workers and Families* (Ann Arbor: University of Michigan, Institute for Social Research, 1984), table 2.2.

7. Bureau of the Census, *Money Income 1989*, tables 22–23.

8. Calculated from U.S. Dept. of Commerce, Bureau of the Census, *Poverty in the United States 1987*, Series P-60, no. 163 (Washington, D.C.: U.S. Government Printing Office, February 1989), tables 10 and 21.

9. Ellwood, *Poor Support*, table 4.2. Population work levels from U.S. Department of Commerce, Bureau of the Census, *Characteristics of the Population below the Poverty Level: 1984*, Series P–60, no. 152 (Washington, D.C.: U.S. Government Printing Office, June 1986), table 18.

10. Congressional Budget Office, "Minimum Wage," 7–10.

11. Sar A. Levitan and Isaac Shapiro, "The Working Poor Deserve a Raise," *New York Times*, 30 March 1986, p. F2; Nancy Gibbs, "What $152 a Week Buys," *Time*, 10 September 1990, pp. 64–66.

12. Congressional Budget Office, "Minimum Wage," 15–16, 19.

13. Bureau of the Census, *Money Income 1989*, table A-2.

14. U.S. Department of Labor, Bureau of Labor Statistics, *Linking Employment Problems to Economic Status* (Washington, D.C.: U.S. Government Printing Office, August 1987), table 12.

15. Congressional Budget Office, "Minimum Wage," table 6.

16. Earl F. Mellor, "Workers at the Minimum Wage or Less: Who They Are and the Jobs They Hold," *Monthly Labor Review* 110 (no. 7, July 1987): table 1; Congressional Budget Office, "Minimum Wage," 18–19.

17. Mellor, "Workers at the Minimum Wage," table 1.

18. Dirk Johnson, "Labor Scarcity Is Forcing Up Low-Level Pay," *New York Times*, 17 March 1986, pp. B1–B2; "Behind the Help-Wanted Signs," *Time*, 20 July 1987, p. 55; "All Hands on Deck!" *Time*, 18 July 1988, pp. 42–44; Michael Lev, "State, or Labor Market, May Set Higher Minimum," *New York Times*, 29 March 1990, p. B8.

19. Richard V. Burkhauser and T. Aldrich Finegan, "The Minimum Wage and the Poor: The End of a Relationship," *Journal of Policy Analysis and Management* 8 (no. 1, Winter 1989): 59–60.

20. Christopher Jencks and Kathryn Edin, "The Real Welfare Problem" (Evanston, Ill.: Northwestern University, Center for Urban Affairs and Policy Research, 15 January 1990).

21. According to Robert Rector and Peter T. Butterfield, "Reforming Welfare: The Promises and Limits of Workfare," *Backgrounder* (Washington, D.C.: Heritage Foundation, 11 June 1987), 2–3, such a mother can escape poverty in every state omitting child care costs, which would require children to be in school. In a subsequent analysis for 1987, Rector estimated that 40 percent or more of such mothers could still escape poverty even with two preschool children and paying for child care.

22. Charles Michalopoulos and Irwin Garfinkel, "Reducing the Welfare Dependence and Poverty of Single Mothers by Means of Earnings and Child Support: Wishful Thinking and Realistic Possibility" (Madison: University of Wisconsin, Institute for Research on Poverty, August 1989).

23. In 1987, 97 percent of nonpoor, female-headed families had earnings, and 81 percent recorded working hours equal to those of one full-year, full-time worker or more. Among poor, female-headed families, the comparable figures were 48 and 11 percent. See U.S. Congress, House, Committee on Ways and Means, *Overview of Entitlement Programs: Background Materials and Data on Programs within the Jurisdiction of the Committee on Ways and Means* (Washington, D.C.: U.S. Government Printing Office, 5 June 1990), 1029.

24. David T. Ellwood, "Working Off of Welfare: Prospects and Policies for Self-Sufficiency of Women Heading Families" (Madison: University of Wisconsin, Institute for Research on Poverty, March 1986), 22–25.

25. Frank Levy, *Dollars and Dreams: The Changing American Income Distribution* (New York: Russell Sage, 1987), 63–64.

26. Barry Bluestone and Bennett Harrison, *The Deindustrialization of America: Plant Closings, Community Abandonment, and the Dismantling of Basic Industry* (New York: Basic Books, 1982), chaps. 2–4.

27. Ibid., chaps 1–2, 5–6; Bennett Harrison and Barry Bluestone, *The Great U-Turn: Corporate Restructuring and the Polarizing of America* (New York: Basic Books, 1988).

28. Louis Uchitelle, "Wage Rises Sluggish in East Despite a Scarcity of Workers," *New York Times*, 8 September 1987, pp. A1, D6.

29. Bluestone and Harrison, *Deindustrialization*, chap. 5; Martin Carnoy, Derek Shearer, and Russell Rumberger, *A New Social Contract: The Economy and Government after Reagan* (New York: Harper & Row, 1983), chaps. 4–5; Forrest Chisman and Alan Pifer, *Government for the People: The Federal Social Role: What It Is, What It Should Be* (New York: Norton, 1987), 179–82.

30. William Serrin, "Growth in Jobs since '80 Is Sharp, But Pay and Quality Are Debated," *New York Times*, 8 June 1986, pp. 1, 32; Sar A. Levitan and Elizabeth Conway, "Shortchanged by Part-Time Work," *New York Times*, 27 February 1988, p. 31.

31. Barry Bluestone and Bennett Harrison, "The Great American Job Machine: The Proliferation of Low Wage Employment in the U.S. Economy" (Study prepared for the Joint Economic Committee, December 1986), in U.S. Congress, Senate Committee on Labor and Human Resources, *National Goals—Employment and Poverty, Hearings* before the Senate Committee on Labor and Human Resources, 100th Cong., 1st sess., 13 January 1987. Median earnings for workers reached a peak in real terms of $6,000 a year in 1973. For a summary of this study, see Barry Bluestone and Bennett Harrison, "The Grim Truth about the Job 'Miracle': A Low-Wage Explosion," *New York Times*, 1 February 1987, p. F3.

32. Quoted in John F. Manley, "The American Dream," *Nature, Society, and Thought* 1 (no. 4, 1988): 500.

33. Louis Uchitelle, "Unequal Pay Widespread in U.S.," *New York Times*, 14 August 1990, pp. D1, D8; idem, "Not Getting Ahead? Better Get Used to It," *New York Times*, 16 December 1990, pp. E1, E6.

34. Levy, *Dollars and Dreams*, 4–7, 17–19; Congressional Budget Office, *Trends in Family Income: 1970–1986* (Washington, D.C.: U.S. Government Printing Office, February 1988), 55–57.

35. Bob Kuttner, "The Declining Middle," *The Atlantic*, July 1983, pp. 60–72; Bruce Steinberg, "The Mass Market Is Splitting Apart," *Fortune*, 28 November 1983, pp. 76–82; Lester C. Thurow, "The Disappearance of the Middle Class," *New York Times*, 5 February 1984, p. F3; Robert S. Lawrence, "Sectoral Shifts and the Size of the Middle Class," *Brookings Review* 3 (no. 1, Fall 1984): 3–11.

36. Peter Henle and Paul Ryscavage, "The Distribution of Earned Income among Men and Women, 1958–77," *Monthly Labor Review* 103 (no. 4, April 1980): 3–10; Paul Ryscavage and Peter Henle, "Earnings Inequality Accelerates in the 1980's," *Monthly Labor Review* 113 (no. 12, December 1990): 3–16; Richard C. Michel, "Economic Growth and Income Equality since the 1982 Recession," *Journal of Policy Analysis and Management* 10 (no. 2, Spring 1991): 181–203.

37. Uchitelle, "Unequal Pay"; Gary Burtless, ed., *A Future of Lousy Jobs? The Changing Structure of U.S. Wages* (Washington, D.C.: Brookings, 1990).

38. If one measures income, not in dollars, but relative to family needs, the shift is even greater. See Committee on Ways and Means, *Overview of Entitlement Programs*, 1069–74.

39. Peter Passell, "Forces in Society, and Reaganism, Helped Dig Deeper Hole for Poor," *New York Times*, 16 July 1989, pp. 1, 20; Kevin Phillips, *The Politics of Rich and Poor: Wealth and the American Electorate in the Reagan Aftermath* (New York: Random House, 1990). Conservatives argue, in rebuttal, that the 1986 tax reform shifted the tax burden toward business and exempted many low-income people from the income tax entirely. Under Reagan, the rich paid lower tax rates but a rising share of the total tax burden.

40. Louis Uchitelle, "Election Placing Focus on the Issue of Jobs vs. Wages," *New York Times*, 4 September 1988, pp. 1, 32.

41. Daniel K. Benjamin, John T. Warner, and Mark L. Mitchell, "Synthesis of Policy Implications from Studies of Low Wage Labor Markets" (Study prepared for the U.S. Department of Health and Human Services, Clemson University, Department of Economics, February 1987), 85–89.

42. Paul O. Flaim and Ellen Sehgal, "Displaced Workers of 1979–83: How Well Have They Fared?" *Monthly Labor Review* 108 (no. 6, June 1985): 3–16; Francis W. Horvath, "The Pulse of Economic Change: Displaced Workers of 1981–85," *Monthly Labor Review* 110 (no. 6, June 1987): 3–12. Labor force calculated from U.S. Department of Commerce, Bureau of the Census, *Statistical Abstract of the United States 1987* (Washington, D.C.: U.S. Government Printing Office, December 1986), 374.

43. Sylvia Nasar, "American Revival in Manufacturing Seen in U.S. Report," *New York Times*, 5 February 1991, pp. A1, D8.

44. Benjamin, Warner, and Mitchell, "Synthesis of Policy Implications," 71–85; Janet L. Norwood, "The Job Machine Has Not Broken Down," *New York Times*, 22 February 1987, p. F3.

45. Bureau of Labor Statistics, *Linking Employment Problems*, table 5.

46. Rebecca M. Blank, "Are Part-Time Jobs Bad Jobs?" in *Future of Lousy Jobs*, ed. Burtless, 123-55.

47. Levy, *Dollars and Dreams*, 26–27, 74–100; William B. Johnston and Arnold H. Packer, *Workforce 2000: Work and Workers for the 21st Century* (Indianapolis, Ind.: Hudson Institute, June 1987), 29–32.

48. Marvin H. Kosters and Murray N. Ross, "A Shrinking Middle Class?" *The Public Interest*, no. 90 (Winter 1988): 3–27; Marvin H. Kosters, "The Measure of Measures," *The American Enterprise* 2 (no. 1, January–February 1991): 58–65.

49. Congressional Budget Office, *Trends in Family Income*, xiii–xiv, 27–44; Michel, "Economic Growth and Income Equality," 191–93.

50. Christopher Jencks, "The Hidden Prosperity of the 1970s," *The Public Interest*, no. 77 (Fall 1984): 37–61.

51. Duncan et al., *Years of Poverty*, 16–17; Levy, *Dollars and Dreams*, 69–73.

52. Neal H. Rosenthal, "The Shrinking Middle Class: Myth or Reality?" *Monthly Labor Review* 108 (no. 3, March 1985): 3–10; Kosters and Ross, "Shrinking

Middle Class"; Gary Burtless, "Introduction and Summary," in *Future of Lousy Jobs*, ed. Burtless, 4–6.

53. McKinley L. Blackburn, David E. Bloom, and Richard B. Freeman, "The Declining Economic Position of Less Skilled American Men," in *Future of Lousy Jobs*, ed. Burtless, 42–43; Gary Burtless, "Earnings Inequality over the Business and Demographic Cycles," in *Future of Lousy Jobs*, ed. Burtless, 89–92, 94–97, 100, 113–14; Adam Clymer, "Cease-Fire in the Capital Comes to a Bitter Close," *New York Times*, 7 March 1991, p. A9.

54. One reason for this appears to be that there was a slowdown in the 1980s in the supply of college graduates relative to men with high school education or less, leading to lower relative wages for the latter. See Blackburn, Bloom, and Freeman, "Declining Economic Position," 49–54.

55. "What's Really Squeezing the Middle Class?" *Wall Street Journal*, 26 July 1989, p. A12; Frank Levy and Richard C. Michel, "Education and Income: Recent U.S. Trends" (Study prepared for the Joint Economic Committee, U.S. Congress, Urban Institute, Washington, D.C., 1988); Chinhui Juhn, Kevin M. Murphy, and Robert H. Topel, "Unemployment, Non-Employment, and Wages: Why Has the Natural Rate Increased through Time?" (Chicago: University of Chicago, Graduate School of Business, November 1990).

56. Robert J. Samuelson, "Middle-Class Media Myth," *National Journal*, 31 December 1983, pp. 2673–78; Levy, *Dollars and Dreams*, 5–7, 192–93, 199, 207.

57. Samuel Bowles, "Set a Moral Agenda for the Economy," *New York Times*, 6 November 1988, p. F2; Phillips, *Politics of Rich and Poor*, 100, 183–84, 202, 208.

58. Michael Harrington, *The New American Poverty* (New York: Holt, Rinehart and Winston, 1984); Fred Block et al., *The Mean Season: The Attack on the Welfare State* (New York: Pantheon, 1987).

59. Rebecca M. Blank and Alan S. Blinder, "Macroeconomics, Income Distribution, and Poverty," in *Fighting Poverty: What Works and What Doesn't*, ed. Sheldon H. Danziger and Daniel H. Weinberg (Cambridge, Mass.: Harvard University Press, 1986), chap. 8; David T. Ellwood and Lawrence H. Summers, "Poverty in America: Is Welfare the Answer or the Problem?" in *Fighting Poverty*, ed. Danziger and Weinberg, 93–94, 96–98, 149–50.

60. Blackburn, Bloom, and Freeman, "Declining Economic Position," 38–39; Juhn, Murphy, and Topel, "Unemployment."

61. Robert Moffitt, "Work Incentives in Transfer Programs (Revisited): A Study of the AFDC Program," in Ronald G. Ehrenberg, ed., *Research in Labor Economics* 8 (part B, 1986): 407–9, 415, 421; Mary Corcoran et al., "Effects of Family and Community Background on Men's Economic Status" (Ann Arbor: University of Michigan, Institute for Social Research, 1990); M. Anne Hill and June O'Neill, "Underclass Behaviors in the United States: Measurement and Analysis of Determinants" (New York: City University of New York, Queens College, 1990).

62. Robert Pear, "Welfare on Rise, Reflecting Slump in Economy of U.S.," *New York Times*, 20 August 1990, pp. A1, A12.

63. U.S. Department of Labor, Office of Policy Planning and Research, *The Negro Family: The Case for National Action* [The "Moynihan Report"] (Washington, D.C.: U.S. Government Printing Office, March 1965), 47; Bureau of the Census, *Statistical Abstract 1987*, 363.

64. Bureau of Labor Statistics, *Linking Employment Problems*, tables 14, 17–19; U.S. Department of Commerce, Bureau of the Census, *Poverty in the United States: 1985*, Series P-60, no. 158 (Washington, D.C.: U.S. Government Printing Office, October 1987), table 10.

65. Bureau of Labor Statistics, *Linking Employment Problems*, table 23.

66. Reemployment rates were 42 percent for blacks versus 60 percent overall in the 1984 displaced worker survey, then 58 versus 67 percent in the 1986 survey, according to Flaim and Sehgal, "Displaced Workers," table 1, and Horvath, "Pulse of Economic Change," table 1.

67. Peter H. Rossi, *Down and Out in America: The Origins of Homelessness* (Chicago: University of Chicago Press, 1989), 137.

68. Congressional Budget Office, *Trends in Family Income*, 20, 81–83; Katherine L. Bradbury, "The Changing Fortunes of American Families in the 1980s," *New England Economic Review* (July–August 1990): 25–40.

69. Burtless, "Earnings Inequality," 112–14, and Robert A. Moffitt, "The Distribution of Earnings and the Welfare State," in *Future of Lousy Jobs*, ed. Burtless, 215–17. Burtless also finds, however (pp. 89–92, 94–97, 100, 112–14), that there are interactions between lower wages and lower hours, and that the rise in inequality is partly due to higher unemployment. Not all unemployment (as chapter 5 will show) is involuntary.

70. Changes for families with children were even more extreme—a loss of 16 percent of earnings in the bottom quintile, a gain of 18 percent in the top quintile. See Committee on Ways and Means, *Overview of Entitlement Programs*, 1114–23.

71. Greg J. Duncan and Willard Rodgers, "Has Poverty Become More Persistent?" (Ann Arbor: University of Michigan, Institute for Social Research, 11 October 1989); Levy, *Dollars and Dreams*, chaps. 6–8; Juhn, Murphy, and Topel, "Unemployment."

72. U.S. Department of Commerce, Bureau of the Census, *Changing Family Composition and Income Differentials* (Washington, D.C.: U.S. Government Printing Office, August 1982). Family income ratios calculated from U.S. Department of Commerce, Bureau of the Census, *Statistical Abstract of the United States: 1990* (Washington, D.C.: U.S. Government Printing Office, January 1990), 450.

73. Levy, *Dollars and Dreams*, 199.

74. Isabel V. Sawhill, "Poverty in the U.S.: Why Is It So Persistent?" *Journal of Economic Literature* 26 (September 1988): 1112; Martin Tolchin, "Minority Poverty on Rise but White Poor Decline," *New York Times*, 1 September 1988, p. B9.

75. Richard Levine, "New York City's Economic Growth Fails to Curb Rise of 'New Poverty,' " *New York Times*, 28 February 1989, pp. A1, B4; Isabel Wilk-

erson, "How Milwaukee Has Thrived While Leaving Blacks Behind," *New York Times*, 19 March 1991, pp. A1, D22.

76. Priscilla Painton, "Boardwalk of Broken Dreams," *Time*, 25 September 1989, pp. 64–69; Wayne King, "Behind Atlantic City's Glitz Lies Decay," *New York Times*, 5 April 1990, pp. B1, B4.

77. Paul Osterman, "Gains from Growth? The Impact of Full Employment on Poverty in Boston," in *The Urban Underclass*, ed. Christopher Jencks and Paul E. Peterson (Washington, D.C.: Brookings, 1991), 122–34; Ellwood, *Poor Support*, 208.

78. Kim B. Clark and Lawrence H. Summers, "Demographic Differences in Cyclical Employment Variation," *Journal of Human Resources* 16 (no. 1, Winter 1981): 61–79.

79. Richard B. Freeman, "Employment and Earnings of Disadvantaged Young Men in a Labor Shortage Economy," in *Urban Underclass*, ed. Jencks and Peterson, 103–21.

80. Charles Murray, "Here's the Bad News on the Underclass," *Wall Street Journal*, 8 March 1990, p. A14. I have calculated some of the labor force participation figures from Freeman's table 1 (see note 79) using the algorithm: labor force participation rate = (employment/population)/(1 − unemployment rate).

81. Glen G. Cain and Ross Finnie, "The Black-White Difference in Youth Employment: Evidence for Demand-Side Factors" (Madison: University of Wisconsin, Institute for Research on Poverty, August 1988), 3.

82. Congressional Budget Office, *Trends in Family Income*, 52, 57–61, 74–77; Juhn, Murphy, and Topel, "Unemployment," 5.

83. Evelyn C. White, "Black America Today: More Are Better Off, and More Are Lost," *San Francisco Chronicle*, 28 March 1988, p. A6.

84. Patricia Spakes, "Mandatory Work Registration for Welfare Parents: A Family Impact Analysis," *Journal of Marriage and the Family* 44 (no. 3, August 1982): 697; Ruth Sidel, *Women and Children Last: The Plight of Poor Women in Affluent America* (New York: Viking, 1986), 194.

85. Milton Friedman and Rose Friedman, *Free to Choose: A Personal Statement* (New York: Avon Books, 1981), 25–26.

Chapter 5:
Are Jobs Available?

1. This chapter and the next rely on these prior publications: Lawrence M. Mead, "The Obligation to Work and the Availability of Jobs: A Dialogue between Lawrence M. Mead and William Julius Wilson," *Focus* 10 (no. 2, Summer 1987): 11–19; idem, "Social Responsibility and Minority Poverty: A Response to William Julius Wilson," in *Divided Opportunities: Minorities, Poverty, and Social Polity*, ed. Gary D. Sandefur and Marta Tienda (New York: Plenum, 1988), chap. 10; idem, "Jobs for the Welfare Poor: Work Require-

ments Can Overcome the Barriers," *Policy Review*, no. 43 (Winter 1988): 60–69; and idem, "The Logic of Workfare: The Underclass and Work Policy," *Annals of the American Academy of Political and Social Science* 501 (January 1989): 156–69. See also Kevin R. Hopkins et al., *Welfare Dependency: Behavior, Culture, and Public Policy* (Study prepared for the U.S. Department of Health and Human Services, Hudson Institute, Alexandria, Va., September 1987), chap. 7.

2. Michael B. Katz, *The Undeserving Poor: From the War on Poverty to the War on Welfare* (New York: Pantheon, 1989), 163.

3. Overheard at Seventh and Greenwich Avenues in Manhattan, New York City, 3 October 1988.

4. Unemployment is measured monthly through the Current Population Survey (CPS). There are two surveys—County Business Patterns and the Survey of Current Business—that measure employment, that is, workers with jobs, in the private sector, but no regular survey of positions that exist but are still unfilled. A regular Department of Labor survey, "Occupations in Demand," once existed, but it covered only positions listed as available with state employment services, a small share of the total; it was discontinued by the Reagan administration.

5. U.S. Department of Labor, Bureau of Labor Statistics, *Employment and Earnings* 20 (no. 9, March 1974): 123–25; Harry J. Holzer, *Unemployment, Vacancies and Local Labor Markets* (Kalamazoo, Mich.: Upjohn Institute for Employment Research, 1989), chap. 2.

6. Katherine G. Abraham, "Structural/Frictional vs. Deficient Demand Unemployment: Some New Evidence," *American Economic Review* 73 (no. 4, September 1983): 708–24; Holzer, *Unemployment*, chap. 3.

7. Social Development Commission, "Expected to Work But No Jobs: Job Availability in Milwaukee" (Milwaukee, Wis.: Social Development Commission, 1991). For a summary of this study, see David R. Riemer, "But Are There Enough Jobs for the Poor?" *New York Times*, 5 February 1991, p. A22.

8. In the Abraham study cited in note 6, the ratio of unemployed to vacancies declines from around four in 1969–73 to under two in 1979–80, but the author judges the latter surveys to be unreliable.

9. Peter J. Ferrara, "Work Incentives and Work Requirements" (Paper prepared for the U.S. Department of Health and Human Services, Hudson Institute, Alexandria, Va., July 1987), 123. The best evidence for this position is the research, cited below, showing that aliens have vastly increased their employment in some parts of the country without harming employment opportunities for the native-born poor.

10. Discouraged workers usually run 15–18 percent of the unemployed. See Paul Flaim, "Discouraged Workers: How Strong Are Their Links to the Job Market?" *Monthly Labor Review* 107 (no. 8, August 1984): 8.

11. "In New York City, There Are Many Ways to Be Poor," *New York Times*, 5 March 1989, p. E6; Myron Magnet, "America's Underclass: What to Do?" *Fortune*, 11 May 1987, p. 132.

12. Connie de Boer, "The Polls: Attitudes toward Unemployment," *Public Opinion Quarterly* 47 (no. 3, Fall 1983): 438; Keith Melville and John Doble, *The Public's Perspective on Social Welfare Reform* (New York: Public Agenda Foundation, January 1988), 18–19.

13. Calculated from U.S. Department of Commerce, Bureau of the Census, *Money Income and Poverty Status in the United States 1989*, Series P-60, no. 168 (Washington, D.C.: U.S. Government Printing Office, September 1990), table 23. These calculations treat members of the armed forces as employed.

14. Calculated from U.S. Department of Labor, Bureau of Labor Statistics, *Employment and Earnings* 38 (no. 1, January 1991): 162.

15. Fred Block, "Rethinking the Political Economy of the Welfare State," in Fred Block et al., *The Mean Season: The Attack on the Welfare State* (New York: Pantheon, 1987), 131; Bradley R. Schiller, *The Economics of Poverty and Discrimination*, 4th ed. (Englewood Cliffs, N.J.: Prentice-Hall, 1984), 57, 70; Michael Harrington, *The New American Poverty* (New York: Holt, Rinehart and Winston, 1984), 234.

16. U.S. Department of Commerce, Bureau of the Census, *Statistical Abstract of the United States 1990* (Washington, D.C.: U.S. Government Printing Office, January 1990), 378; "A Remarkable Job Machine," *Time*, 25 June 1984, pp. 52–54.

17. John E. Schwarz, *America's Hidden Success: A Reassessment of Public Policy from Kennedy to Reagan*, rev. ed. (New York: Norton, 1988), chap. 4.

18. Ronald E. Kutscher, "Overview and Implications of the Projections to 2000," in U.S. Department of Labor, Bureau of Labor Statistics, *Projections 2000* (Washington, D.C.: U.S. Government Printing Office, March 1988), 1–3. Other analyses that draw similar implications include William B. Johnston and Arnold H. Packer, *Workforce 2000: Work and Workers for the 21st Century* (Indianapolis, Ind.: Hudson Institute, June 1987), and Kevin R. Hopkins et al., *Help Wanted: How Companies Can Survive and Thrive in the Coming Worker Shortage* (New York: McGraw-Hill, 1991).

19. Lisa W. Foderaro, "As Summer Approaches, Employers Compete to Attract Scarce Workers," *New York Times*, 12 June 1988, p. 34.

20. William E. Schmidt, "Growing Job Problem: Finding People to Work," *New York Times*, 28 October 1984, p. 26; Donald Janson, "Low-Paying Jobs Go Begging at Suburban Shopping Malls," *New York Times*, 21 December 1985, pp. 29, 52; Peter T. Kilborn, "Playing Games with Labor Laws: When Work Fills a Child's Hours," *New York Times*, 10 December 1989, pp. 1, 46; idem, "For the Retarded, Independence in Real Jobs," *New York Times*, 2 January 1990, pp. A1, A15.

21. In the 1981–83 recession, the monthly unemployment rate peaked at 10.7 percent in December 1982, while in the current recession the highest rate was 6.9 percent in June 1991. See U.S. Department of Labor, Bureau of Labor Statistics, *Employment and Earnings* 30 (no. 10, October 1983): table A-1, and idem, *Employment and Earnings* 38 (no. 9, September 1991): table A-1.

22. "A Lot More Than You Would Think," *The Economist*, 2 February 1991, pp. 66-67; William Robbins, "Cities Luring People and Jobs, Widening Rural-Urban Gap," *New York Times*, 3 March 1987, pp. 1, 8; Richard Hornik, "Small-Town Blues," *Time*, 27 March 1989, pp. 66–68; Alex Prud'Homme, "A Nation on the Move," *Time*, 29 April 1991, pp. 30–31.

23. "Vermont Seeking Pickers for Big Apple Crop," *New York Times*, 22 August 1982, p. 27; Harold Faber, "From New York to Jamaica: Call for Apple Pickers," *New York Times*, 6 September 1987, p. 42.

24. Bureau of the Census, *Statistical Abstract 1990*, 9.

25. Edwin P. Reubens, "Aliens, Jobs, and Immigration Policy," *The Public Interest*, no. 51 (Spring 1978): 113–14, 116n1; Edwin Harwood, "Can Immigration Laws Be Enforced?" *The Public Interest*, no. 72 (Summer 1983): 110.

26. James Fallows, "Immigration: How It's Affecting Us," *The Atlantic*, November 1983, p. 46; Jeffrey S. Passel, "Estimating the Number of Undocumented Aliens," *Monthly Labor Review* 109 (no. 9, September 1986): 33; "Estimates of Aliens Baffle U.S.," *New York Times*, 19 June 1983. The National Academy of Sciences recently estimated the illegals at 2 to 4 million. See Robert Pear, "Low Number Given for Illegal Aliens," *New York Times*, 25 June 1985, p. A14.

27. John M. Crewdson, "Illegal Aliens Are Bypassing Farms for Higher Pay of Jobs in the Cities," *New York Times*, 10 November 1980, pp. A1, D9; Reubens, "Aliens, Jobs, and Immigration Policy," 119–20.

28. Robert D. Reischauer, "Immigration and the Underclass," *Annals of the American Academy of Political and Social Science* 501 (January 1989): 125.

29. Fallows, "Immigration," 56–61; Peter Passell, "So Much for Assumptions about Immigrants and Jobs," *New York Times*, 15 April 1990, p. E4. Academic studies include George J. Borjas, "The Demographic Determinants of the Demand for Black Labor," in *The Black Youth Employment Crisis*, ed. Richard B. Freeman and Harry J. Holzer (Chicago: University of Chicago Press, 1986), 195–207; idem, "The Substitutability of Black, Hispanic, and White Labor," *Economic Inquiry* 21 (no. 1, January 1983): 93–106; Paula D. McClain and Albert K. Karnig, "Black and Hispanic Socioeconomic and Political Competition," *American Political Science Review* 84 (no. 2, June 1990): 535–45.

30. Reubens, "Aliens, Jobs, and Immigration Policy," 114–19; Ronald Sullivan, "Aliens Seized by U.S. Reported Back at Work," *New York Times*, 4 May 1982, pp. A1, A24.

31. Robert Pear, "New Restrictions on Immigration Gain Public Support, Poll Shows," *New York Times*, 1 July 1986, pp. A1, A21.

32. Richard W. Stevenson, "Study Finds Mild Gain in Drive on Illegal Aliens," *New York Times*, 21 April 1990, p. 24; Robert Pear, "Major Immigration Bill Is Sent to Bush," *New York Times*, 29 October 1990, p. B10.

33. Fallows, "Immigration," 55–56.

34. Averages calculated from U.S. Department of Labor, Bureau of Labor Statistics, *Monthly Labor Review*, various issues 1972–91. The layoff average applies

only to years 1981–90, due to data limitations. Figures given do not add
due to rounding.

35. Flaim, "Discouraged Workers," 8–10.

36. Averages calculated from U.S. Department of Labor, Bureau of Labor Statistics, *Monthly Labor Review*, various issues 1972–91. Completed spells of unemployment are also short. According to one estimate for 1975, 55 percent of spells ended within 1 month, the average length was 2.2 months, and only 27 percent of the jobless were out of work for 6 months or longer; see Kim B. Clark and Lawrence H. Summers, "Labor Market Dynamics and Unemployment: A Reconsideration," *Brookings Papers on Economic Activity* 1979 (no. 1): table 1.

37. An equally large proportion of those who leave work are never unemployed. They go from work immediately out of the labor force. See Clark and Summers, "Labor Market Dynamics," 23, 25.

38. This may be why the department never publicized the results. The Rosenfeld and Young articles cited in note 40 were the only government analyses published, and neither highlights the sensitive findings about reservation wages.

39. Martin Feldstein and James Poterba, "Unemployment Insurance and Reservation Wages," *Journal of Public Economics* 23 (1984): 141–53.

40. Carl Rosenfeld, "Job Search of the Unemployed, May 1976," *Monthly Labor Review* 100 (no. 11, November 1977): 39–43; Anne McDougal Young, "Job Search of Recipients of Unemployment Insurance," *Monthly Labor Review* 102 (no. 2, February 1979): 52.

41. Paul O. Flaim and Ellen Sehgal, "Displaced Workers of 1978–83: How Well Have They Fared?" *Monthly Labor Review* 108 (no. 6, June 1985): 8, 11; Francis W. Horvath, "The Pulse of Economic Change: Displaced Workers of 1981–85," *Monthly Labor Review* 110 (no. 6, June 1987): 9.

42. The key studies have appeared in the *Brookings Papers on Economic Activity:* Robert E. Hall, "Why Is the Unemployment Rate So High at Full Employment?" 1970 (no. 3): 369–402; idem, "Prospects for Shifting the Phillips Curve through Manpower Policy" 1971 (no. 3): 659–701; idem, "Turnover in the Labor Force" 1972 (no. 3): 709–56; George L. Perry, "Changing Labor Markets and Inflation" 1970 (no. 3): 411–41; idem, "Unemployment Flows in the U.S. Labor Market" 1972 (no. 2): 245–78; Stephen T. Marston, "Employment Instability and High Unemployment Rates" 1976 (no. 1): 169–203; Kim B. Clark and Lawrence H. Summers, "Labor Market Dynamics and Unemployment: A Reconsideration" 1979 (no. 1): 13–72. See also Nancy S. Barrett and Richard D. Morgenstern, "Why Do Blacks and Women Have High Unemployment Rates?" *Journal of Human Resources* 9 (no. 4, Fall 1974): 452–64.

43. Hall, "Turnover," 709–10; Clark and Summers, "Labor Market Dynamics," 14.

44. This is the main point of Clark and Summers, "Labor Market Dynamics." See also George A. Akerlof and Brian G. M. Main, "Unemployment Spells

and Unemployment Experience," *American Economic Review* 70 (no. 5, December 1980): 885–93.

45. Hall, "Turnover," 717–22; idem, "Why Is the Unemployment Rate So High," 389; Marston, "Employment Instability," 188. The data for these studies, it should be noted, came from 1973 and earlier, before the full impact of employment problems among the poor.

46. David E. Rosenbaum, "Unemployment Insurance Aiding Fewer Workers," *New York Times*, 2 December 1990, p. 1, 38; Congressional Budget Office, *Unemployment Insurance: Financial Condition and Options for Change* (Washington, D.C.: U.S. Government Printing Office, June 1983), 1–8; idem, *Promoting Employment and Maintaining Incomes with Unemployment Insurance* (Washington, D.C.: U.S. Government Printing Office, March 1985), 9–13.

47. According to one survey, secondary workers make up 26 percent of the employed, but 35 percent of the unemployed. See Key Lehman Schlozman and Sidney Verba, *Injury to Insult: Unemployment, Class, and Political Response* (Cambridge, Mass.: Harvard University Press, 1976), 40. Most secondary workers are women and teenagers. These groups' share of the labor force rose from 37 to 48 percent—and their share of joblessness from 47 to 55 percent—between 1960 and 1987. See U.S. Department of Labor, Bureau of Labor Statistics, *Labor Force Statistics Derived from the Current Population Survey 1948–87* (Washington, D.C.: U.S. Government Printing Office, August 1988), table A-9, pp. 74–77; table A-14, pp. 194–97; table A-24, pp. 404–7.

48. Hall, "Turnover," 717; idem, "Why Is the Unemployment Rate So High," 392–95. Experts dispute whether a tendency to quit jobs is related to race. Some argue that blacks are actually less likely to quit than whites if one controls for other demographic features. The study with the fullest controls finds, however, that black men do quit more often. See Jeffrey S. Zax, "Quits and Race," *Journal of Human Resources* 24 (no. 3, Summer 1989): 469–93.

49. William Julius Wilson, "The Obligation to Work and the Availability of Jobs: A Dialogue between Lawrence M. Mead and William Julius Wilson," *Focus* 10 (no. 2, Summer 1987): 9.

50. Peter B. Doeringer and Michael J. Piore, *Internal Labor Markets and Manpower Analysis* (Lexington, Mass.: D.C. Heath, 1971); idem, "Unemployment and the 'Dual Labor Market,' " *The Public Interest*, no. 38 (Winter 1975): 67–79; Bennett Harrison, *Education, Training, and the Urban Ghetto* (Baltimore: Johns Hopkins University Press, 1972); Henry J. Aaron, *Politics and the Professors: The Great Society in Perspective* (Washington, D.C.: Brookings, 1978), 44–48, 92–97, 128–39.

51. Glen G. Cain, "The Challenge of Segmented Labor Market Theories to Orthodox Theory: A Survey," *Journal of Economic Literature* 14 (no. 4, December 1976): 1215–57; Daniel K. Benjamin, John T. Warner, and Mark L. Mitchell, "Synthesis of Policy Implications from Studies of Low Wage Labor Markets" (Study prepared for the U.S. Department of Health and Human Services, Clemson University, Department of Economics, February 1987),

1–35, 97; William R. Beer, "The Wages of Discrimination," *Public Opinion*, July–August 1987, pp. 17–18.

52. For this evidence, see chapter 6.

53. Robert E. Hall, "Prospects for Shifting the Phillips Curve," 681–89; Marston, "Employment Instability," 188-99; Benjamin, Warner, and Mitchell, "Synthesis of Policy Implications," 1–43.

54. Schiller, *Economics of Poverty*, 66.

55. Greg J. Duncan et al., *Years of Poverty, Years of Plenty: The Changing Fortunes of American Workers and Families* (Ann Arbor: University of Michigan, Institute for Social Research, 1984), chap. 4; Benjamin, Warner, and Mitchell, "Synthesis of Policy Implications," 28–32, 97; Bradley R. Schiller, "Equality, Opportunity, and the 'Good Job,' " *The Public Interest*, no. 43 (Spring 1976): 111–20.

56. Charles Brown, "Dead-end Jobs and Youth Unemployment," in *The Youth Labor Market Problem: Its Nature, Causes, and Consequences*, ed. Richard B. Freeman and David A. Wise (Chicago: University of Chicago Press, 1982), chap. 12; Ronald Ferguson and Randall Filer, "Do Better Jobs Make Better Workers? Absenteeism from Work Among Inner-City Black Youths," in *Black Youth Employment Crisis*, ed. Freeman and Holzer, chap. 7.

57. Diane N. Westcott, "Youth in the Labor Force: An Area Study," *Monthly Labor Review* 99 (no. 7, July 1976): 3–9.

58. Peter Kerr, "Lingering Death of Camden Imperils Its Healthy Suburbs," *New York Times*, 7 September 1989, pp. A1, B2.

59. William Julius Wilson, *The Truly Disadvantaged: The Inner City, the Underclass and Public Policy* (Chicago: University of Chicago Press, 1987); idem, "Studying Inner-City Social Dislocations: The Challenge of Public Agenda Research," *American Sociological Review* 56 (no. 1, February 1991): 1–14; John D. Kasarda, "The Regional and Urban Redistribution of People and Jobs in the U.S." (Study prepared for the National Research Council, University of North Carolina, Department of Sociology, October 1986). See also the chapters by Wilson, Kasarda, and their associates in Paul E. Peterson, ed., *The New Urban Reality* (Washington, D.C.: Brookings, 1985); Sheldon H. Danziger and Daniel H. Weinberg, eds., *Fighting Poverty: What Works and What Doesn't* (Cambridge, Mass.: Harvard University Press, 1986); Margaret Weir, Ann Shola Orloff, and Theda Skocpol, eds., *The Politics of Social Policy in the United States* (Princeton, N.J.: Princeton University Press, 1988); Phoebe H. Cottingham and David T. Ellwood, eds., *Welfare Policy for the 1990s* (Cambridge, Mass.: Harvard University Press, 1989); and William Julius Wilson, ed., *Annals of the American Academy of Political and Social Science* 501 (January 1989). For recent papers bearing on several aspects of the mismatch theory, see Christopher Jencks and Paul E. Peterson, eds., *The Urban Underclass* (Washington, D.C.: Brookings, 1991).

60. Schmidt, "Growing Job Problem," 26; "A Maddening Labor Mismatch," *Time*, 28 April 1986; "Report Finds Fewer Jobs for High School Dropouts," *New York Times*, 18 December 1988, p. 74; Ramon G. McLeod, "Jobs Keep

Receding Beyond Blacks' Grasp," *San Francisco Chronicle*, 29 March 1988, pp. A1, A4–5.

61. Jonathan S. Leonard, "The Interaction of Residential Segregation and Employment Discrimination," *Journal of Urban Economics* 21 (no. 3, May 1987): 323–46; John Bound and Harry J. Holzer, "Industrial Shifts, Skills Levels, and the Labor Market for White and Black Males" (East Lansing: Michigan State University, Department of Economics, February 1991).

62. Much of the decline in black teenage employment up to 1970 is due simply to the elimination of farm jobs in the South with the mechanization of agriculture. See John Cogan, "The Decline in Black Teenage Employment: 1950–70," *American Economic Review* 72 (no. 4, September 1982): 621–38.

63. Paul A. Jargowsky and Mary Jo Bane, "Ghetto Poverty: Basic Questions," and John C. Weicher, "How Poverty Neighborhoods Are Changing," both in *Inner-City Poverty in the United States*, ed. Laurence E. Lynn, Jr., and Michael G. H. McGeary (Washington, D.C.: National Academy Press, 1990), chaps. 2–3.

64. John D. Kasarda, "Urban Industrial Transition and the Underclass," *Annals of the American Academy of Political and Social Science* 501 (January 1989): 29, shows that Boston, Chicago, Cleveland, Detroit, New York, and Philadelphia lost nearly one-half million jobs between 1970 and 1980. But according to Bureau of the Census, *Statistical Abstract 1990*, 34–36, the population of these same cities fell by over 2 million in the same period. Bennett Harrison, *Urban Economic Development: Suburbanization, Minority Opportunity, and the Condition of the Central City* (Washington, D.C.: Urban Institute, 1974), 42–51, makes this argument for the late 1960s.

65. Harry J. Holzer, "The Spatial Mismatch Hypothesis: What Has the Evidence Shown?" *Urban Studies* 28 (no. 1, February 1991): 115. Rockefeller spoke in U.S. Congress, Senate, Committee on Finance, *Social Security Amendments of 1971, Hearings* before the Committee on Finance on H.R. 1, 92nd Cong., 3 February 1972, p. 2149. Kasarda concedes these possibilities; see "Urban Industrial Transition," 31, and "Regional and Urban Redistribution," 35.

66. Nicholas Lemann, *The Promised Land: The Great Black Migration and How It Changed America* (New York: Knopf, 1991), 81–83, 242–43.

67. Wilson, *Truly Disadvantaged*, 134–35; Barry Bluestone and Bennett Harrison, *The Deindustrialization of America: Plant Closings, Community Abandonment, and the Dismantling of Basic Industry* (New York: Basic Books, 1982), 54–55.

68. Nathan Glazer and Daniel P. Moynihan, *Beyond the Melting Pot: The Negroes, Puerto Ricans, Jews, Italians, and Irish of New York City*, 2d ed. (Cambridge, Mass.: MIT Press, 1970), 28–30, 37; Thomas Bailey and Roger Waldinger, "A Skills Mismatch in New York's Labor Market?" *New York Affairs* 8 (no. 3, Fall 1984): 10–15; Thomas Bailey, "Black Employment Opportunities," in *Setting Municipal Priorities 1990*, ed. Charles Brecher and Raymond D. Horton (New York: New York University Press, 1989), chap. 3.

69. Bureau of Labor Statistics, *Labor Force Statistics*, table A-14, p. 242; table 24, p. 452; U.S. Department of Commerce, Bureau of the Census, *Poverty in the*

United States 1985, Series P-60, no. 158 (Washington, D.C.: U.S. Government Printing Office, October 1987), table 10.

70. Christopher Jencks, "Deadly Neighborhoods," *The New Republic*, 13 June 1988, p. 28; Robert I. Lerman, "Employment Opportunities of Young Men and Family Formation," *American Economic Review* 79 (no. 2, May 1989): 62–66; Robert D. Mare and Christopher Winship, "Socioeconomic Change and the Decline of Marriage for Blacks and Whites," in *Urban Underclass*, ed. Jencks and Peterson, 175–96.

Mark Testa et al., "Employment and Marriage among Inner-City Fathers," *Annals of the American Academy of Political and Social Science* 501 (January 1989): 79–91, and Mark Testa and Marilyn Krogh, "Marriage, Premarital Parenthood and Joblessness Among Black Americans in Inner-City Chicago" (Chicago: University of Chicago, School of Social Service Administration, March 1990) do show some connection between employment and marriage and reproductive behavior among poor blacks in Chicago. But perhaps people decide to marry and then get a job rather than the other way around; see Lerman, "Employment Opportunities," 65–66. Even if joblessness causes nonmarriage, we do not know that lack of jobs is the reason for it.

71. These figures, admittedly, are for all employment and would represent an "upper limit" for jobs accessible to the unskilled. See Marc Bendick, Jr., and Mary Lou Egan, *Jobs: Employment Opportunities in the Washington Metropolitan Area for Persons with Limited Employment Qualifications* (Washington, D.C.: Greater Washington Research Center, 1988), 17–19.

72. Eric Schmidt, "Zoning Is Only One Bar to Cheaper Suburban Housing," *New York Times*, 13 November 1988, p. E5.

73. High majorities of inner-city minorities need cars to commute, yet the jobless do not have them in some cities, according to John Kasarda, "Urban Industrial Transition," 40–41; and idem, "Urban Change and Minority Opportunities," in *New Urban Reality*, ed. Peterson, 55–56. In Chicago in 1970, however, low-income families used cars for 74 percent of their trips, mass transit for only 21 percent, and in all metropolitan areas in 1970, 64 percent of low-income people and 55 percent of the poor lived in households owning cars, according to John R. Meyer and José A. Gómez-Ibáñez, *Autos, Transit, and Cities* (Cambridge, Mass.: Harvard University Press, 1981), 241–42.

74. Sam Roberts, "Migrant Labor: The McShuttle to the Suburbs," *New York Times*, 14 June 1990, p. B1; James B. Moore, "Finding Workers Becomes Hard Labor," *Montgomery Journal*, 22 February 1988, pp. A1, B18; idem, "The 6% Solution," *Montgomery Journal*, 23 February 1988, pp. A1, A9.

75. Meyer and Gómez-Ibáñez, *Autos*, 241–42; John F. Kain and John R. Meyer, "Transportation and Poverty," *The Public Interest*, no. 18 (Winter 1970): 79.

76. In Chicago, an experimental route was begun from downtown to O'Hare Airport, but only a handful of workers plausibly gained and kept their jobs

because of it. See Meyer and Gómez-Ibáñez, *Autos*, 231, and Alan Altshuler, with James P. Womack and John R. Fucher, *The Urban Transportation System: Politics and Innovation* (Cambridge, Mass.: MIT Press, 1979), 274–77.

77. The seminal paper proposing the theory was John Kain, "Housing Segregation, Negro Employment, and Metropolitan Decentralization," *Quarterly Journal of Economics* 82 (no. 2, May 1968): 175–97.

78. This summary relies on reviews by Holzer, "Spatial Mismatch Hypothesis," and Christopher Jencks and Susan E. Mayer, "Residential Segregation, Job Proximity, and Black Job Opportunities," in *Inner-City Poverty*, ed. Lynn and McGeary, chap. 5.

79. Women who moved to the suburbs around Chicago gained relative to those who moved within the city mainly in that the proportion employed *declined* less. They earned higher wages than in the city, but their working hours rose hardly at all. See James E. Rosenbaum and Susan J. Popkin, "Employment and Earnings of Low-Income Blacks Who Move to Middle-Class Suburbs," in *Urban Underclass*, ed. Jencks and Peterson, 342–56.

80. David T. Ellwood, "The Spatial Mismatch Hypothesis: Are There Teenage Jobs Missing in the Ghetto?" in *Black Youth Employment Crisis*, ed. Freeman and Holzer, chap. 4; Jonathan S. Leonard, "Space, Time and Unemployment: Los Angeles 1980" (Berkeley: University of California, School of Business Administration, September 1986); Keith R. Ihlanfeldt and David L. Sjoquist, "Job Accessibility and Racial Differences in Youth Employment Rates," *American Economic Review* 80 (no. 1, March 1990): 267–76. Ihlanfeldt and Sjoquist, the only authors to find a strong effect from job access, say that differences in commuting times can explain 33 to 54 percent of the difference in employment rates between black and white youth in Philadelphia, with weaker results for Chicago and Los Angeles. The gap in average commuting times between blacks and whites in Philadelphia, however, was only eight minutes.

81. Kasarda, "Regional and Urban Redistribution," 25.

82. According to Holzer, "Spatial Mismatch Hypothesis," 116–17, Ihlanfeldt and Sjoquist have found strong effects due to job access in Philadelphia, Chicago, and Los Angeles but not across a wider range of cities. Weicher, "How Poverty Neighborhoods Are Changing," 100–2, says that the suburbanization of jobs in the period 1960–80 was related to the labor force participation rate in poor areas only in New York and Los Angeles. Wilson himself, in "Public Policy Research and *The Truly Disadvantaged*," in *Urban Underclass*, ed. Jencks and Peterson, 464–65, says that the mismatch problem may be confined to the Northeast and Midwest.

83. Jargowsky and Bane, "Ghetto Poverty," 32–39.

84. Wilson, "Studying Inner-City Social Dislocations," 6–8; Holzer, "Spatial Mismatch Hypothesis," 118.

85. E.g., Gordon Berlin and Andrew Sum, *Toward a More Perfect Union: Basic Skills, Poor Families, and Our Economic Future* (New York: Ford Foundation, February 1988).

86. Computer programmers, systems analysts, and electronics engineers will all grow by more than half in the period 1984–95, yet none of these callings represents more than 1.5 percent of total job growth over that period. Their increases are dwarfed by growth in cashiers, nurses, janitors, truck drivers, and waitresses. See George T. Silvestri and John M. Lukasiewicz, "Occupational Employment Projections: The 1984–95 Outlook," *Monthly Labor Review* 108 (no. 11, November 1985): 42–57.

Kasarda, "Regional and Urban Redistribution," table 10, shows that, in nine major cities, jobs demanding some higher education grew sharply in number over the years 1959–84, while those demanding less than high school education grew more slowly or declined. By 1984, the former outnumbered the latter in five of the nine cities. But it is more reasonable to include jobs demanding education around the high school level within the less demanding group. Then the lesser-skilled jobs still predominate in eight of the nine cities, according to calculations from Kasarda's tables 9 and 10. In "Urban Industrial Transition," 32, Kasarda himself finds that low-skilled jobs defined this way predominate in nine somewhat different cities, though their majority is dropping.

The educational requirements of jobs appear to be rising more slowly than the education of workers. Kasarda, "Urban Industrial Transition," 34, finds that only 11 percent of jobholders in Washington, D.C., in 1980 had less than a high school education. But according to Bendick and Egan, *Jobs*, chap. 2, 30 percent of the jobs in that region still did not require a high school diploma in 1990.

87. Jargowsky and Bane, "Ghetto Poverty," 36–37; Bailey and Waldinger, "Skills Mismatch," 6–10; Louis Uchitelle, "New York City Is Hurt but Still Has Reserves," *New York Times*, 12 November 1990, pp. A1, B6–B7; Bailey, "Black Employment Opportunities." Eileen Sullivan, author of the main study cited by Bailey and Waldinger, treated as low-skilled all jobs requiring high school education or less unless they involved at least eighteen months of pre-employment training.

88. U.S. Department of Commerce, Bureau of the Census, *Statistical Abstract of the United States 1988* (Washington, D.C.: U.S. Government Printing Office, December 1987), 125; Charles Hirschman, "Minorities in the Labor Market: Cyclical Patterns and Secular Trends in Joblessness," in *Divided Opportunities*, ed. Sandefur and Tienda, table 4.

89. According to Hirschman, "Minorities in the Labor Market," table 5, unemployment was 18 percent for black high school graduates in 1984, compared to only 7 percent for whites; it was 6 percent for black college graduates, versus 3 percent for whites. Kasarda, "Regional and Urban Redistribution," table 14, finds that unemployment was as high as 25 percent for black high school graduates in inner cities in the Midwest, a result he finds "troublesome and difficult to interpret" (p. 29).

90. To try to halt the escalation, some localities have taken to "guaranteeing" the basic competence of their high school graduates to business. Remedial

courses emphasize "such practices as showing up regularly and on time." See Joseph Berger, "Fernandez Proposes Placing Warranties on Graduates in '92," *New York Times*, 5 January 1991, pp. 1, 25; "Our Student-Back Guarantee," *Time*, 11 February 1991, p. 74.

91. "The Literacy Gap," *Time*, 19 December 1988, p. 56.

92. Joseph Berger, "Companies Step In Where the Schools Fail," *New York Times*, 26 September 1989, pp. A1, B6; William E. Schmidt, "Schools Trying to Link Good Jobs and Skills," *New York Times*, 27 September 1989, p. B8; Michael deCourcy Hinds, "Poor Teen-Agers Learn How to Get a Job Done," *New York Times*, 9 August 1991, p. A10; Robert D. Hershey, Jr., "As Labor Pool Ebbs, Factories Fish Harder," *New York Times*, 22 December 1989, pp. D1, D4.

93. Berlin and Sum, *More Perfect Union*, 3–13; George B. Autry, "Work Force or Nonworking Poor?" *New York Times*, 21 July 1991, p. F11.

94. Leonard E. Bloomquist, Leif Jensen, and Ruy A. Teixeire, "'Workfare' and Nonmetro America: An Assessment of the Employment Opportunities for Nonmetro Welfare Clients" (Washington, D.C.: U.S. Department of Agriculture, Economic Research Service, October 1987), table 1.

95. Harry J. Holzer, "Black Youth Nonemployment: Duration and Job Search," in *Black Youth Employment Crisis*, ed. Freeman and Holzer, 64; Richard B. Freeman, "Help Wanted: Disadvantaged Youth in a Labor Shortage Economy" (Cambridge, Mass.: National Bureau of Economic Research, 1 October 1989), 16–18.

96. Dirk Johnson, "As Inner-City Areas Decay, Blacks Flee to Small Towns," *New York Times*, 4 December 1989, pp. A1, B10; Rosenbaum and Popkin, "Employment and Earnings of Low-Income Blacks," 352–53.

97. Martin Feldstein, "The Economics of the New Unemployment," *The Public Interest*, no. 33 (Fall 1973): 41–42; Benjamin, Warner, and Mitchell, "Synthesis of Policy Implications," 107.

98. E.g., Schiller, *Economics of Poverty*, 180, 203; Leonard Goodwin, *Do the Poor Want to Work? A Social-Psychological Study of Work Orientations* (Washington, D.C.: Brookings, 1972), chap. 8; William Julius Wilson, *The Declining Significance of Race: Blacks and Changing American Institutions*, 2nd ed. (Chicago: University of Chicago Press, 1980), 166.

99. Daniel Friedlander et al., *Final Report on Job Search and Work Experience in Cook County* (New York: Manpower Demonstration Research Corporation, November 1987), 7.

100. Christopher Jencks, personal communication, June 1985.

101. Jencks, "Deadly Neighborhoods," 26–27.

102. Gary T. Burtless, "Are Targeted Wage Subsidies Harmful? Evidence from a Wage Voucher Experiment," *Industrial and Labor Relations Review* 39 (no. 1, October 1985): 105–14; John H. Bishop and Suk Kang, "Applying for Entitlements: Employers and the Targeted Jobs Tax Credit," *Journal of Policy Analysis and Management* 10 (no. 1, Winter 1991): 24–45.

103. William Julius Wilson once understood the situation much in these terms. See *Declining Significance of Race*, 96–97, 107–8. In *Truly Disadvantaged*, he takes the simpler, but less plausible, position that jobs of any kind are commonly lacking in the ghetto.

Chapter 6:
Barriers to Employment

1. National Advisory Commission on Civil Disorders (Kerner Commission), *Report of the National Advisory Commission on Civil Disorders* (New York: Bantam Books, 1968), 10 and passim. I deal predominantly with prejudice against blacks, not Hispanics or other minorities, simply because blacks dominate long-term poverty, and bias against them has dominated discussion of this issue.

2. Howard Schuman, Charlotte Steeh, and Lawrence Bobo, *Racial Attitudes in America: Trends and Interpretations* (Cambridge, Mass.: Harvard University Press, 1985), 73–86, 123–25.

3. Blacks themselves brought about much of this progress by obtaining more and better education and moving out of the low-wage South. See James P. Smith and Finis R. Welch, *Closing the Gap: Forty Years of Economic Progress for Blacks* (Santa Monica, Calif.: Rand, February 1986), secs. 2–5.

4. Greg J. Duncan et al., *Years of Poverty, Years of Plenty: The Changing Fortunes of American Workers and Families* (Ann Arbor: University of Michigan, Institute for Social Research, 1984), chap. 5; Richard Freeman, "Black Economic Progress since 1964," *The Public Interest*, no. 52 (Summer 1978): 54–59; Martin Kilson, "Black Social Classes and Intergenerational Poverty," *The Public Interest*, no. 64 (Summer 1981): 58–60; Smith and Welch, *Closing the Gap*, secs. 3–5.

5. Linda S. Lichter, "Who Speaks for Black America?" *Public Opinion*, August–September 1985, p. 42; Burns W. Roper, "Racial Tensions Are Down," *New York Times*, 26 July 1990, p. A19; James R. Kluegel and Eliot R. Smith, *Beliefs about Inequality: Americans' Views of What Is and What Ought to Be* (New York: Aldine de Gruyter, 1986), chap. 3.

6. Schuman, Steeh, and Bobo, *Racial Attitudes in America*, 104–17.

7. Andrew Hacker, "American Apartheid," *New York Review of Books*, 3 December 1987, pp. 31–33.

8. Alan Finder, "Blacks Remain Shut Out of Housing in White Areas," *New York Times*, 13 March 1989, pp. B1–B2; Thomas J. Leuck, "The New Teeth in the Fair Housing Law," *New York Times*, 12 March 1989, pp. R1, R18. Research finding evidence of bias includes Ronald E. Wienk et al., *Measuring Racial Discrimination in American Housing Markets: The Housing Market Practices Survey* (Washington, D.C.: U.S. Department of Housing and Urban Development, April 1979), and a recent study done at the Urban Institute;

see "Study Finds Bias in House Hunting by Minorities," *New York Times*, 1 September 1991, p. 27.

9. Schuman, Steeh, and Bobo, *Racial Attitudes in America*, 86–104, 163–92.

10. Ibid., 176–79; and Donald R. Kinder and David O. Sears, "Prejudice and Politics: Symbolic Racism versus Racial Threats to the Good Life," *Journal of Personality and Social Psychology* 40 (no. 3, March 1981): 414–31; "Survey Finds Whites Retain Stereotypes of Minority Groups," *New York Times*, January 10, 1991, p. B10. This is the interpretation known as "symbolic racism," except that I find the attitudes more justifiable than many analysts of this school.

11. Christopher Jencks, "Deadly Neighborhoods," *The New Republic*, 13 June 1988, pp. 26–27.

12. Freeman, "Black Economic Progress," 61–63; William Julius Wilson, *The Declining Significance of Race: Blacks and Changing American Institutions*, 2nd ed. (Chicago: University of Chicago Press, 1980), chaps. 1, 5–7.

13. According to one estimate, as much as 60 percent of the earnings gap for men might be attributable to discrimination if one blames black–white differences in working hours on bias, only 35 percent if merely the wage gap is due to bias. For women, the percentages would be half as large. But much of the differences apparently due to bias may really be due to unmeasurable differences in qualifications. See Robert H. Haveman, *Poverty Policy and Poverty Research: The Great Society and the Social Sciences* (Madison: University of Wisconsin Press, 1987), 142–44.

14. Richard B. Freeman and David A. Wise, "The Youth Labor Market Problem: Its Nature, Causes, and Consequences," in *The Youth Labor Market Problem: Its Nature, Causes, and Consequences*, ed. Richard B. Freeman and David A. Wise (Chicago: University of Chicago Press, 1982), 13, and Richard B. Freeman and Harry J. Holzer, "Young Blacks and Jobs—What We Now Know," *The Public Interest*, no. 78 (Winter 1985): 26.

One study of black and white youth seeking jobs in Newark, New Jersey, found that employers treated blacks less courteously than whites, but "not significantly so." See Jerome Culp and Bruce H. Dunson, "Brothers of a Different Color: A Preliminary Look at Employer Treatment of White and Black Youth," in *The Black Youth Employment Crisis*, ed. Richard B. Freeman and Harry J. Holzer (Chicago: University of Chicago Press, 1986), chap. 6.

Margery Austin Turner et al., "Opportunities Denied, Opportunities Diminished: Discrimination in Hiring" (Washington, D.C.: Urban Institute, May 1991), found that white youth advanced further in the hiring process than blacks in 20 percent of cases in Chicago and Washington, D.C., while blacks outdid whites in 7 percent. It is not clear, however, that the employers' motivation was bias, and the applicants were college students who were overqualified for the entry-level jobs for which they applied. Thus, the findings do not apply clearly to the situation of more disadvantaged blacks.

In a survey in Boston in 1989, 80 percent of disadvantaged black youth said bias had posed no problem for them, and only 5 percent said it was a serious problem. See Richard B. Freeman, "Help Wanted: Disadvantaged Youth in a Labor Shortage Economy" (Cambridge, Mass.: National Bureau of Economic Research, 1 October 1989), fig. 4.

15. Duncan et al., *Years of Poverty,* 106, 106*n*14.

16. If they usually stay on welfare longer, the reason is mostly that they are less likely to exit by means of remarriage or reconciliation with their earlier spouses. See Mary Jo Bane and David T. Ellwood, "The Dynamics of Dependence: The Routes to Self-Sufficiency" (Cambridge, Mass.: Urban Systems Research and Engineering, June 1983), 29–33, 45; June A. O'Neill et al., "An Analysis of Time on Welfare" (Washington, D.C.: Urban Institute, June 1984), 27–28, 52–54.

17. Joleen Kirschenman and Kathryn M. Neckerman, "'We'd Love to Hire Them, But...': The Meaning of Race for Employers," in *The Urban Underclass,* ed. Christopher Jencks and Paul E. Peterson (Washington, D.C.: Brookings, 1991), 203–32; John Ballen and Richard B. Freeman, "Transitions between Employment and Nonemployment," in *Black Youth Employment Crisis,* ed. Freeman and Holzer, 92–95.

18. George J. Borjas, "The Demographic Determinants of the Demand for Black Labor," in *Black Youth Employment Crisis,* ed. Freeman and Holzer, chap. 5.

19. Richard Lacayo, "Between Two Worlds," *Time,* 13 March 1989, pp. 58–68; Leroy D. Clark, "Insuring Equal Opportunity in Employment through Law," in *Rethinking Employment Policy,* ed. D. Lee Bawden and Felicity Skidmore (Washington, D.C.: Urban Institute, 1989), 177.

20. Peter T. Kilborn, "Labor Department Wants to Take On Job Bias in the Executive Suite," *New York Times,* 30 July 1990, pp. A1, A10.

21. "Battling Affirmative Inaction," *Time,* 12 September 1988; Seth Mydans, "Black Journalists Look to Last Ceiling," *New York Times,* 3 August 1990, p. A16; Alex S. Jones, "Daily News Loses Bias Case," *New York Times,* 16 April 1987, pp. A1, B3.

22. Philip Shenon, "Hispanic F.B.I. Agents' Suit Reflects a Sense of Betrayal," *New York Times,* 11 September 1988, p. 26; idem, "Judge Orders Sweeping Changes in the F.B.I.'s Promotion System," *New York Times,* 6 May 1989, pp. 1, 9.

23. Nicholas Lemann, *The Promised Land, The Great Black Migration and How It Changed America* (New York: Knopf, 1991), 266–67, 277–80.

24. Lichter, "Who Speaks for Black America?" pp. 42, 44; Sidney Verba and Gary R. Orren, *Equality in America: The View from the Top* (Cambridge, Mass.: Harvard University Press, 1985), chaps. 6–7.

25. Freeman, "Black Economic Progress," 63; Wilson, *Declining Significance of Race,* 169–71. Steven Shulman, "Discrimination, Human Capital, and Black-White Unemployment: Evidence from Cities," *Journal of Human Resources* 22 (no. 3, Summer 1987): 361–76, contends that discrimination has simply shifted its focus from relative wages to employment itself. However, the study measures bias by the level of complaints to the Equal Employment Opportunity Commission, a doubtful proxy, since such cases often involve

employed blacks, who are apparently more likely to encounter traditional bias than the jobless or unemployed.

26. Under the Family Support Act of 1988, two-parent needy families became eligible for AFDC, previously an option for states, but the father must be unemployed and working less than 100 hours a month, conditions that will probably keep this part of welfare small, as in the past. See chapter 8.

27. "The Single Life," *New York Times*, 23 February 1986, p. E20.

28. E.g., Martin Anderson, *Welfare: The Political Economy of Welfare Reform in the United States* (Stanford, Calif.: Hoover Institution, 1978), chap. 2.

29. E.g., Henry J. Aaron, *Why Is Welfare So Hard to Reform?* (Washington, D.C.: Brookings, 1973), and Michael C. Barth, George J. Carcagno, and John L. Palmer, *Toward an Effective Income Support System: Problems, Prospects, and Choices* (Madison: University of Wisconsin, Institute for Research on Poverty, 1974). For more discussion of disincentives, see chapters 7 and 8.

30. George Gilder, *Welfare and Poverty* (New York: Basic Books, 1981), chaps. 10–11; Charles Murray, *Losing Ground: American Social Policy, 1950–1980* (New York: Basic Books, 1984).

31. Leonard J. Hausman, "The Impact of Welfare on the Work Effort of AFDC Mothers," in President's Commission on Income Maintenance Programs (Heineman Commission), *Technical Studies* (Washington, D.C.: U.S. Government Printing Office, November 1969), 83–100; Irwin Garfinkel and Larry L. Orr, "Welfare Policy and the Employment Rate of AFDC Mothers," *National Tax Journal* 27 (no. 2, June 1974): 275–84.

    There is also some evidence that the poor population gravitates toward, and stays in, states with relatively high welfare benefits. See Paul E. Peterson and Mark C. Rom, *Welfare Magnets: A New Case for a National Standard* (Washington, D.C.: Brookings, 1990), chap. 3.

32. John M. Barron and Wesley Mellow, "Search Effort in the Labor Market," *Journal of Human Resources* 14 (no. 3, Summer 1979): 389–404: Kim B. Clark and Lawrence H. Summers, "Unemployment Insurance and Labor Market Transitions," in *Workers, Jobs, and Inflation*, ed. Martin N. Baily (Washington, D.C.: Brookings, 1982), 279–323; Anne McDougal Young, "Job Search of Recipients of Unemployment Insurance," *Monthly Labor Review* 102 (no. 2, February 1979): 49–50.

33. Congressional Budget Office, *Disability Compensation: Current Issues and Options for Change* (Washington, D.C.: U.S. Government Printing Office, June 1982), 40–41, 47–49; L. Scott Muller, "Receipt of Multiple Benefits by Disabled-Worker Beneficiaries," *Social Security Bulletin* 43 (no. 11, November 1980): 3–19.

34. Donald O. Parsons, "The Decline in Male Labor Force Participation," *Journal of Political Economy* 88 (no. 1, February 1980): 117–34; idem, "Racial Trends in Male Labor Force Participation," *American Economic Review* 70 (no. 5, December 1980): 911–20.

35. Sheldon Danziger, Robert Haveman, and Robert Plotnick, "How Income Transfer Programs Affect Work, Savings, and the Income Distribution: A

Critical Review," *Journal of Economic Literature* 19 (no. 3, September 1981): 995–99. Including taxes, the overall effect may be up to 7 percent, according to an estimate by Robert Lampman. See Haveman, *Poverty Policy*, 93, 251–53.

36. Robert Moffitt, "Work and the U.S. Welfare System" (Madison: University of Wisconsin, Institute for Research on Poverty, April 1988), 22; Mildred Rein, *Dilemmas of Welfare Policy: Why Work Strategies Haven't Worked* (New York: Praeger, 1982), 52–53, 58; Gary Burtless, "The Work Response to a Guaranteed Income: A Survey of Experimental Evidence," in *Lessons from the Income Maintenance Experiments: Proceedings of a Conference Held in September 1986*, ed. Alicia H. Munnell (Boston: Federal Reserve Bank of Boston, n.d.), 22–52.

37. Moffitt, "Work and the U.S. Welfare System," 22; Robert Moffitt, "An Economic Model of Welfare Stigma," *American Economic Review* 73 (no. 5, December 1983): 1032; idem, "Incentive Effects of the U.S. Welfare System: A Review" (Providence, R.I.: Brown University, Department of Economics, March 1990), 23.

The best argument for a disincentive may be that welfare has an "enabling effect." Mothers need some minimum to live on without work, but if that is provided, additions to benefits will have little further effect on their behavior. Benefits are well above this minimum in the urban states now. This argument implies that, if benefits were cut to very low levels or eliminated, a much stronger positive effect on work effort would appear. See Charles Murray, "Have the Poor Been 'Losing Ground'?" *Political Science Quarterly* 100 (no. 3, Fall 1985): 440–43, and "No, Welfare Isn't Really the Problem," *The Public Interest*, no. 84 (Summer 1986): 4–5.

38. Robert I. Lerman, "Do Welfare Programs Affect the Schooling and Work Patterns of Young Black Men?" in *Black Youth Employment Crisis*, ed. Freeman and Holzer, 410–13.

39. E.g., Frederick Doolittle, Frank Levy, and Michael Wiseman, "The Mirage of Welfare Reform," *The Public Interest*, no. 47 (Spring 1977): 67–68, 82, 86. Welfare employment staff that I interviewed for my own studies often made this argument.

40. Rebecca M. Blank, "The Effect of Medical Need and Medicaid on AFDC Participation," *Journal of Human Resources* 24 (no. 1, Winter 1989): 54–87; Robert Moffitt and Barbara Wolfe, "The Effect of the Medicaid Program on Welfare Participation and Labor Supply" (Madison: University of Wisconsin, Institute for Research on Poverty, January 1990).

A related finding is that most of the working welfare mothers removed from AFDC by the Reagan cuts did not obtain their own health coverage, yet this did not cause them to reduce their earnings and go back on the rolls. See Denise F. Polit and Joseph J. O'Hara, "Support Services," in *Welfare Policy for the 1990s*, ed. Phoebe H. Cottingham and David T. Ellwood (Cambridge, Mass.: Harvard University Press, 1989), 182–86.

41. Barbara Boland, "Participation in the Aid to Families with Dependent Children Program (AFDC)," in U.S. Congress, Joint Economic Committee, Sub-

committee on Fiscal Policy, *Studies in Public Welfare,* Paper no. 12 (part I), *The Family, Poverty, and Welfare Programs: Factors Influencing Family Instability,* 93rd Cong., 1st sess., 4 November 1973, pp. 139–79; Marjorie Honig, "AFDC Income, Recipient Rates, and Family Dissolution," *Journal of Human Resources* 9 (no. 3, Summer 1974): 303–22; Heather L. Ross and Isabel V. Sawhill, *Time of Transition: The Growth of Families Headed by Women* (Washington, D.C.: Urban Institute, 1975), chap. 5; John H. Bishop, "Jobs, Cash Transfers, and Marital Instability: A Review and Synthesis of the Evidence," *Journal of Human Resources* 15 (no. 3, Summer 1980): 301–34; Mary Lou Scheirer, "Household Structure among Welfare Families: Correlates and Consequences," *Journal of Marriage and the Family* 45 (no. 4, November 1983): 761–71; David T. Ellwood and Mary Jo Bane, "The Impact of AFDC on Family Structure and Living Arrangements," in Ronald G. Ehrenberg, ed., *Research in Labor Economics* 7 (1985): 137–207; Shirley L. Zimmerman, "Myths about Public Welfare: Poverty, Family Instability, and Teen Illegitimacy," *Policy Studies Review* 8 (no. 3, Spring 1989): 674–88.

Kevin R. Hopkins et al., *Welfare Dependency: Behavior, Culture, and Public Policy* (Study prepared for the U.S. Department of Health and Human Services, Hudson Institute, Alexandria, Va., September 1987), pp. 4-68 to 4-71, judges that the studies finding an impact on illegitimacy are of higher quality than those not finding one.

42. Sara McLanahan and Irwin Garfinkel, "Single Mothers, the Underclass, and Social Policy," *Annals of the American Academy of Political and Social Science* 501 (January 1989): 101. For a more pessimistic reading of the same research, see Hopkins et al., *Welfare Dependency,* chaps. 4–6.

43. Charles Murray's opponents claim that the trends disprove his contention that welfare provokes dysfunction. See Robert Greenstein, "Losing Faith in 'Losing Ground,'" *The New Republic,* 25 March 1985, pp. 12–14; "Are We Losing Ground?" *Focus* 8 (no. 3, Fall and Winter 1985): 1–12; and David T. Ellwood and Lawrence H. Summers, "Is Welfare Really the Problem?" *The Public Interest,* no. 83 (Spring 1986): 57–78.

However, the critics sometimes exaggerate how far benefits fell after 1970. Richard A. Kasten and John E. Todd, "Transfer Recipients and the Poor during the 1970s," in *What Role for Government? Lessons from Policy Research,* ed. Richard J. Zeckhauser and Derek Leebaert (Durham, N.C.: Duke University Press, 1983), 66–72, estimate that benefits fell only 19 percent and eligibility levels (need standards) fell 23 percent in real terms in the period 1969–79. The fall, furthermore, was cushioned by a rise in Food Stamps and Medicaid. Robert A. Moffitt, "The Distribution of Earnings and the Welfare State," in *A Future of Lousy Jobs? The Changing Structure of U.S. Wages,* ed. Gary Burtless (Washington, D.C.: Brookings, 1990), 210–11, judges that the value of AFDC plus Food Stamps and Medicaid actually grew slightly, 1969–85. For rejoinders along these lines, see Murray, "Have the Poor Been 'Losing Ground'?" 440–43, and idem, "No, Welfare Isn't Really the Problem," 5–6.

44. Moffitt, "Incentive Effects," 70–71.

45. Irwin Garfinkel and Sara A. McLanahan, *Single Mothers and Their Children: A New American Dilemma* (Washington, D.C.: Urban Institute, 1986), 87–102.

46. U.S. Congress, House, Committee on Ways and Means, *Overview of Entitlement Programs: Background Material and Data on Programs within the Jurisdiction of the Committee on Ways and Means* (Washington, D.C.: U.S. Government Printing Office, 5 June 1990), 579.

47. U.S. Department of Commerce, Bureau of the Census, *Statistical Abstract of the United States 1990* (Washington, D.C.: U.S. Government Printing Office, January 1990), 385.

48. Keith Melville and John Doble, *The Public's Perspective on Social Welfare Reform* (New York: Public Agenda Foundation, January 1988), 20.

49. David T. Ellwood, *Poor Support: Poverty in the American Family* (New York: Basic Books, 1988), 132–37; Douglas J. Besharov, "The Politics of Day-Care," *Washington Post*, 11 August 1988, p. C5.

50. Moffitt, "Work and the U.S. Welfare System," 15, 18.

51. Committee on Ways and Means, *Overview of Entitlement Programs*, 579; U.S. Department of Health, Education, and Welfare, National Center for Social Statistics, *National Cross-Tabulations from the 1967 and 1969 AFDC Studies* (Washington, D.C.: U.S. Department of Health, Education, and Welfare, 15 December 1971), table 2.

52. It is uncertain whether the presence of young children reduces the chances of working off welfare with other factors controlled. See Bane and Ellwood, "Dynamics of Dependence," 44–45, 65; O'Neill et al., "Analysis of Time on Welfare," 11–12, 33–35, 43, 51; and David T. Ellwood, "Targeting 'Would-Be' Long-Term Recipients of AFDC" (Princeton N.J.: Mathematica Policy Research, January 1986), 32–33, 33n1; John R. Shea, "Welfare Mothers: Barriers to Labor Force Entry," *Journal of Human Resources* 8 (Supplement 1973): 97–99.

53. Ellwood, "Targeting," 45.

54. The costs to children of middle-class women going to work are apparently greater than for the poor. See Garfinkel and McLanahan, *Single Mothers*, 34–37, and Kristin A. Moore and Sandra L. Hofferth, "Women and Their Children," in *The Subtle Revolution: Women at Work*, ed. Ralph E. Smith (Washington, D.C.: Urban Institute, 1979), 143–52. Polit and O'Hara, "Support Services," 196–97, mention the possible adverse effects of putting very young children in substitute care, but this is not important in the welfare context, where current policy obligates mothers to join work programs only when the child reaches age three.

55. Josh Barbanel, "One Life That Welfare Reform Reshaped," *New York Times*, 7 July 1988, p. B4.

56. E.g., William Ryan, *Blaming the Victim* (New York: Pantheon, 1971), 109–10; Ruth Sidel, *Women and Children Last: The Plight of Poor Women in Affluent America* (New York: Viking, 1986), chap. 6.

57. Ellen Eliason Kisker et al., *The Child Care Challenge: What Parents Need and What Is Available in Three Metropolitan Areas* (Princeton, N.J.: Mathematica Policy Research, 9 February 1989), 1; "The Child-Care Dilemma," *Time*, 22

June 1987, pp. 54–60; "Home Is Where the Heart Is," *Time,* 3 October 1988, pp. 46–53.

58. Douglas J. Besharov and Paul N. Tramontozzi, "The Costs of Federal Child Care Assistance" (Washington, D.C.: American Enterprise Institute, 20 April 1988).

59. U.S. Department of Education, National Center for Education Statistics, *The Condition of Education 1990,* vol. 1, *Elementary and Secondary Education* (Washington, D.C.: U.S. Government Printing Office, 1990), 56; Sandra L. Hofferth and Deborah A. Phillips, "Child Care in the United States, 1970 to 1995," *Journal of Marriage and the Family* 49 (no. 3, August 1987): 565; William R. Prosser, "Day Care Centers, 1976–1984: Has Supply Kept Up with Demand?" (Washington, D.C.: U.S. Department of Health and Human Services, May 1986).

60. Kisker et al., *Child Care Challenge,* 12, 14, 40, 51–53.

61. U.S. Department of Commerce, Bureau of the Census, *Who's Minding the Kids? Child Care Arrangements: Winter 1986–87,* Series P-70, no. 20 (Washington, D.C.: U.S. Government Printing Office, July 1990), 14.

62. Thomas W. Rodes and John C. Moore, *National Childcare Consumer Study: 1975* (Washington, D.C.: U.S. Department of Health, Education, and Welfare, n.d.), vol. 1, table V-3; U.S. Department of Health, Education, and Welfare, Office of Child Development, *Statistical Highlights from the National Child Care Consumer Study* (Washington, D.C.: U.S. Department of Health, Education, and Welfare, 1976), 22; Kisker et al., *Child Care Challenge,* 161–65.

63. E.g., Tamar Lewin, "Child Care in Conflict with a Job," *New York Times,* 2 March 1991, p. 8.

64. Bureau of the Census, *Who's Minding the Kids 1986–87,* 10; Katherine Dickinson, "Child Care," in *Five Thousand American Families—Patterns of Economic Progress,* ed. Greg J. Duncan and James N. Morgan (Ann Arbor: University of Michigan, Institute for Social Research, 1975), 225–27.

65. Rodes and Moore, *National Childcare Consumer Study,* vol. 3, table 2-12; U.S. Department of Commerce, Bureau of the Census, *Who's Minding the Kids? Child Care Arrangements: Winter 1984–85,* Series P-70, no. 9 (Washington, D.C.: U.S. Government Printing Office, May 1987), 20.

66. Bureau of the Census, *Who's Minding the Kids 1986–87,* 16; Lorelei R. Brush, "Child Care Used by Working Women in the AFDC Population: An Analysis of the SIPP Data Base" (Study prepared for the U.S. Department of Health and Human Services, Analysis, Research and Training, McLean, Va., 15 October 1987), 6–7; Freya L. Sonenstein and Douglas L. Wolf, "Caring for the Children of Welfare Mothers" (Waltham, Mass.: Brandeis University, Heller School, April 1988), 4–5.

67. Suzanne H. Woolsey, "Pied Piper Politics and the Child Care Debate," *Daedalus* 100 (no. 2, Spring 1977): 135.

68. U.S. Department of Commerce, Bureau of the Census, *School Enrollment—Social and Economic Characteristics of Students: October 1985 and 1984,* Series P-20, no. 426 (Washington, D.C.: U.S. Government Printing Office, April

1988), 1–7; Audrey Pendleton, "Preschool Enrollment: Trends and Implications," in U.S. Department of Education, Center for Education Statistics, *The Condition of Education, 1986 Edition* (Washington, D.C.: U.S. Government Printing Office, 1986), 124–39.

69. Dickinson, "Child Care," 227, 229–31; Joel F. Handler and Ellen Jane Hollingsworth, *The "Deserving Poor": A Study of Welfare Administration* (New York: Academic Press, 1971), 182; Kisker et al., *Child Care Challenge*, 135–37.

70. Bureau of the Census, *Who's Minding the Kids 1986–87,* 21; Brush, "Child Care," 16-18.

71. Kisker et al., *Child Care Challenge,* 177–90; Irene Cox, "Families on Welfare in New York City," *Welfare in Review* 6 (no. 2, March–April 1968): 26; Handler and Hollingsworth, *"Deserving Poor,"* 142–43; Harriet B. Presser and Wendy Baldwin, "Child Care as a Constraint on Employment: Prevalence, Correlates, and Bearing on the Work and Fertility Nexus," *American Journal of Sociology* 85 (no. 5, March 1980): 1205.

72. Kisker et al., *Child Care Challenge,* 12, 14, 182.

73. Hofferth and Phillips, "Child Care," 564; Lorelei R. Brush, "Usage of Different Kinds of Child Care: An Analysis of the SIPP Data Base" (Study prepared for the U.S. Department of Health and Human Services, Analysis, Research and Training, McLean, Va., 14 October 1987).

74. Abigail C. Nichols, "Why Welfare Mothers Work: Implications for Employment and Training Services," *Social Service Review* 53 (no. 3, September 1979): 383, 388–89; Shea, "Welfare Mothers," 96, 101–2; Jack Ditmore and W. R. Prosser, "A Study of Day Care's Effect on the Labor Force Participation of Low-Income Mothers" (Washington, D.C.: Office of Economic Opportunity, June 1973), 65–66.

75. Cheryl D. Hayes, John L. Palmer, and Martha J. Zaslow, eds., *Who Cares for America's Children: Child Care Policy for the 1990s* (Washington, D.C.: National Academy Press, 1990); Sheila B. Kammerman and Alfred J. Kahn, "The Day-Care Debate: A Wider View," *The Public Interest,* no. 54 (Winter 1978): 76–93.

76. Ron Haskins, "Pied Piper II: The National Academy of Sciences and the Child Care Debate" (Washington, D.C.: House of Representatives, Committee on Ways and Means, 1991), 9–19; Allan C. Carlson, "Families, Sex, and the Liberal Agenda," *The Public Interest,* no. 58 (Winter 1980): 62–79.

77. E.g., Robert D. Reischauer, in U.S. Congress, Senate Committee on Finance, *Welfare: Reform or Replacement? (Work and Welfare), Hearings* before the Subcommittee on Social Security and Family Policy, 100th Cong., 1st sess., 22 February 1987, p. 234.

78. Committee on Ways and Means, *Overview of Entitlement Programs,* 579. The effect of age on employability is uncertain. Officials in training programs regard younger women as more trainable, but statistical studies show that older mothers are more likely to work their way off welfare, because they have older and fewer children at home. The former consideration is prob-

ably more important for long-term dependency. The education figures are clouded by the fact that the proportion of mothers for whom no education level is known rises from 22 to 58 percent between 1969 and 1988.

79. Ellwood, *Poor Support*, 144.

80. I am indebted for clarification on this point to David Ellwood, personal communication, 28 April 1988.

81. Eleanor Cautley and Doris P. Slesinger, "Labor Force Participation and Poverty Status among Rural and Urban Women Who Head Families," *Policy Studies Review* 7 (no. 4, Summer 1988): 795–809; Ellwood, *Poor Support*, 186–87.

82. Bane and Ellwood, "Dynamics of Dependence," 29–47; Ellwood, "Targeting," 32; David T. Ellwood, "Working Off of Welfare: Prospects and Policies for Self-Sufficiency of Women Heading Families" (Madison, Wis.: University of Wisconsin, Institute for Research on Poverty, March 1986), 17–21; Brush, "Child Care," 19–22.

83. This is the main point of Ellwood, "Targeting."

84. N. A. Barr and R. E. Hall, "The Probability of Dependence on Public Assistance," *Economica* 48 (1981): 109–23.

85. Kevin Hopkins et al., "The Work Effort and Wages of Unmarried Mothers," in Hopkins et al., *Welfare Dependency*, p. 7-96; Blank, "Effect of Medical Need"; Duncan et al., *Years of Poverty*, 49, 80.

86. Calculated from U.S. Department of Commerce, Bureau of the Census, *Money Income and Poverty Status in the United States 1989*, Series P-60, no. 168 (Washington, D.C.: Government Printing Office, September 1990), tables 22 and 23.

87. Among persons aged 16–64 with a work disability in 1989, 42 percent worked among the general population but only 24 percent among the poor. For work year-round and full-time, the figures were 15 versus 2 percent. Calculated from U.S. Department of Commerce, Bureau of the Census, *Poverty in the United States: 1988 and 1989*, Series P-60, no. 171 (Washington, D.C.: U.S. Government Printing Office, June 1991), table 15.

88. Peter H. Rossi, *Down and Out in America: The Origins of Homelessness* (Chicago: University of Chicago Press, 1989), 41–42, 145–56; Martha R. Burt and Barbara E. Cohen, *America's Homeless: Numbers, Characteristics, and Programs That Serve Them* (Washington, D.C.: Urban Institute, July 1989), 48, 50–52; Thomas J. Main, "What We Know about the Homeless," *Commentary*, May 1988, pp. 29–30.

89. Institute of Medicine, Committee for the Study of Research on Child and Adolescent Mental Disorders, *Research on Children and Adolescents with Mental, Behavioral, and Developmental Disorders: Mobilizing a National Initiative* (Washington, D.C.: National Academy Press, 1989), 32–33.

90. I am indebted for this interpretation to Herman Diesenhaus of the Alcohol, Drug Abuse, and Mental Health Administration, National Institute of Health, in a conversation on 4 May 1990.

91. E.g., Frank F. Furstenburg, remarks at a Welfare Reform Conference sponsored by the Rockefeller Foundation, Williamsburg, Va., 16–18 February 1988, 5.

92. Martha Derthick, *Policymaking for Social Security* (Washington, D.C.: Brookings, 1979), chap. 15; Lawrence M. Mead, *Beyond Entitlement: The Social Obligations of Citizenship* (New York: Free Press, 1986), 132–35.

93. Peter J. Ferrara, "Work Incentives and Work Requirements" (Study prepared for the U.S. Department of Health and Human Services, Hudson Institute, Alexandria, Va., July 1987), 92.

94. Genevieve W. Carter, "The Employment Potential of AFDC Mothers," *Welfare in Review* 6 (no. 4, July–August 1968): 1–11; Leonard Goodwin, *Do the Poor Want to Work? A Social-Psychological Study of Work Orientations* (Washington, D.C.: Brookings, 1972), 118; Patricia Spakes, "Mandatory Work Registration for Welfare Parents: A Family Impact Analysis," *Journal of Marriage and the Family* 44 (no. 3, August 1982): 685–99.

95. Ferrara, "Work Incentives and Work Requirements," 92.

96. Dirk Johnson, "Anti-Poverty Program Seeks to Build Self-Esteem," *New York Times,* 21 February 1988, p. 24.

97. In debates about welfare requirements, I have sometimes offered to opponents that they could give any benefits and support services they wanted to recipients if they would agree, in return, to require them to work. None has accepted. It was unthinkable to them to obligate people whom they conceive of as victims.

98. Jan Hoffman, "Pregnant, Addicted—and Guilty?" *New York Times Magazine,* 19 August 1990, pp. 34–35, 55.

99. "To Fulfill These Rights," speech at Howard University, 4 June 1965, in Lee Rainwater and William L. Yancey, *The Moynihan Report and the Politics of Controversy* (Cambridge, Mass.: MIT Press, 1967), 126–27, 129.

100. Carter, "Employment Potential," 10; Ellwood, *Poor Support,* 200.

101. Michael Harrington, *The Other America: Poverty in the United States,* rev. ed. (Baltimore: Penguin, 1971), 171; idem, *The New American Poverty* (New York: Holt, Rinehart and Winston, 1984), 206.

102. Loïc J. D. Wacquant and William Julius Wilson, "Poverty, Joblessness, and the Social Transformation of the Inner City," in *Welfare Policy for the 1990s,* ed. Cottingham and Ellwood, 96.

103. William Julius Wilson, "Studying Inner-City Social Dislocations: The Challenge of Public Agenda Research," *American Sociological Review* 56 (no. 1, February 1991): 10; James S. Coleman, "Parental Involvement in Education" (Chicago: University of Chicago, Department of Sociology, 6 February 1990), 8–15.

104. Thomas J. Kane, "Giving Back Control: Long-Term Poverty and Motivation," *Social Service Review* 61 (no. 3, September 1987): 405–19.

105. Reagan speech broadcast on C-Span, 13 December 1988.

106. Anne Wortham, *The Other Side of Racism: A Philosophical Study of Black Race Consciousness* (Columbus: Ohio State University Press, 1981), chap. 5.

Chapter 7:
Human Nature

1. Charles Murray, *Losing Ground: American Social Policy, 1950–1980* (New York: Basic Books, 1984), 162.

2. Charles Murray, *In Pursuit: Of Happiness and Good Government* (New York: Simon and Schuster, 1988), 17–18, passim.

3. David T. Ellwood, "Understanding Dependency: Choices, Confidence, or Culture?" (Study prepared for the U.S. Department of Health and Human Services, Brandeis University, Center for Human Resources, November 1987), 27, 90.

4. Bradley R. Schiller, *The Economics of Poverty and Discrimination*, 4th ed. (Englewood Cliffs, N.J.: Prentice-Hall, 1984), 112.

5. Robert K. Merton, "Social Structure and Anomie," in Robert K. Merton, *Social Theory and Social Structure*, enlarged ed. (New York: Free Press, 1968), chap. 6; Leonard Goodwin, *Do the Poor Want to Work? A Social-Psychological Study of Work Orientations* (Washington, D.C.: Brookings, 1972), 62.

6. Robert Moffitt, "An Economic Model of Welfare Stigma," *American Economic Review* 73 (no. 5, December 1983), 1033; Robert Moffitt, "Work Incentives in Transfer Programs (Revisited): A Study of the AFDC Program," in Ronald G. Ehrenberg, ed., *Research in Labor Economics* 8 (part B, 1986): 389–439. A related finding is that the work levels of poor men and women responded very little to changes in work incentives in federal income maintenance experiments. See Gary Burtless, "The Work Response to a Guaranteed Income: A Survey of Experimental Evidence," in *Lessons from the Income Maintenance Experiments: Proceedings of a Conference Held in September 1986*, ed. Alicia H. Munnell (Boston: Federal Reserve Bank of Boston, n.d.), 22–52.

7. Kevin R. Hopkins et al., *Welfare Dependency: Behavior, Culture and Public Policy* (Study prepared for the U.S. Department of Health and Human Services, Hudson Institute, Alexandria, Va., September 1987), pp. 4-24 to 4-25; Shelly Lundberg and Robert D. Plotnick, "Testing the Opportunity Cost Hypothesis of Teenage Premarital Childbearing" (Seattle: University of Washington, March 1990); Greg J. Duncan and Saul D. Hoffman, "Teenage Underclass Behavior and Subsequent Poverty: Have the Rules Changed?" in *The Urban Underclass*, ed. Christopher Jencks and Paul E. Peterson (Washington, D.C.: Brookings, 1991), 155–74.

8. David T. Ellwood, *Poor Support: Poverty in the American Family* (New York: Basic Books, 1988), 71–72, 76.

9. James Q. Wilson and Richard J. Herrnstein, *Crime and Human Nature* (New York: Simon and Schuster, 1985), chap. 12.

10. W. Kip Viscusi, "Market Incentives for Criminal Behavior," in *The Black Youth Employment Crisis*, ed. Richard B. Freeman and Harry J. Holzer (Chicago: University of Chicago Press, 1986), 308, 314–15. According to Richard B. Freeman and Harry J. Holzer, "The Black Youth Employment Crisis: Summary of Findings," in *Black Youth Employment Crisis*, ed. Freeman and Holzer,

14, the majority of black youth in the period 1979–80 believed they could make more in a straight job than in crime. Christopher Jencks and Kathryn Edin, "The Real Welfare Problem" (Evanston, Ill.: Northwestern University, Center for Urban Affairs and Policy Research, 15 January 1990), fig. 1, report that this sample of welfare mothers drew only 9 percent of their income from "vice."

11. Richard B. Freeman, "Help Wanted: Disadvantaged Youth in a Labor Shortage Economy" (Cambridge, Mass.: National Bureau of Economic Research, 1 October 1989), 18–19.

12. Gina Kolata, "Despite Its Promise of Riches, the Crack Trade Seldom Pays," *New York Times*, 26 November 1989, pp. 1, 42; Don Terry, "Drug Riches of the Capital Luring Poor Youth down a Bloody Path," *New York Times*, 2 April 1989, pp. 1, 25. Philippe Bourgeois, "Just Another Night on Crack Street," *New York Times Magazine*, 12 November 1989, presents the dealers as frustrated capitalists seeking to make money in drugs because society does not allow them to succeed in legitimate callings, but other researchers say many try to minimize their involvement due to the dangers. See Peter Reuter, "Drug Selling, Drug Use and the Inner City" (Washington, D.C.: Rand Corporation, May 1990), and "Bright Kids, Bad Business," *Time*, 11 September 1989, p. 18.

13. Murray, *Losing Ground*, 176.

14. Kim B. Clark and Lawrence H. Summers, "Labor Market Dynamics and Unemployment: A Reconsideration," *Brookings Papers on Economic Activity* 1979 (no. 1): 54–55; Robert E. Hall, "Prospects for Shifting the Phillips Curve through Manpower Policy," *Brookings Papers on Economic Activity* 1971 (no. 3): 661; Lester C. Thurow, *Dangerous Currents: The State of Economics* (New York: Random House, 1983), chap. 7.

15. Leonard Silk, "Now, to Figure Why the Poor Get Poorer," *New York Times*, 18 December 1988, pp. E1, E5; Daniel Patrick Moynihan, *Family and Nation* (San Diego, Calif.: Harcourt Brace Jovanovich, 1986), 141.

16. J. R. Pole, *The Pursuit of Equality in American History* (Berkeley: University of California Press, 1978), 168, 222–40; Oscar Handlin, *The Uprooted: The Epic Story of the Great Migrations That Made the American People* (New York: Grosset and Dunlap, 1951), chap. 10.

17. Thomas Sowell, *Ethnic America: A History* (New York: Basic Books, 1981).

18. Richard Lacayo, "Between Two Worlds," *Time*, 13 March 1989, pp. 58–68; "The Color of Money," *Time*, 24 September 1990, p. 71.

19. Jonathan P. Hicks, "Wall Street's New Takeover Star Warms to the Spotlight," *New York Times*, 20 March 1988, pp. F6, F7; Allen R. Myerson, "Twin Spotlights on Parsons of the Dime," *New York Times*, 26 August 1990, pp. F1, F6.

20. Ken Auletta, *The Underclass* (New York: Random House, 1982), chap. 14; Ronald B. Mincy, "Underclass Variations by Race and Place: Have Large Cities Darkened Our Picture of the Underclass?" (Washington, D.C.: Urban Institute, February 1991).

21. Gary D. Sandefur and Marta Tienda, "Introduction: Social Policy and the Minority Experience," in *Divided Opportunities: Minorities, Poverty, and Social Policy*, ed. Gary D. Sandefur and Marta Tienda (New York: Plenum Press, 1988), 10–11; Marta Tienda and Leif Jensen, "Poverty and Minorities: A Quarter-Century Profile of Color and Socioeconomic Disadvantage," in *Divided Opportunities*, ed. Sandefur and Tienda, table 5.

22. R. J. Herrnstein, "Still an American Dilemma," *The Public Interest*, no. 98 (Winter 1990): 7–10. For the argument that the IQ difference is largely genetic, see Arthur R. Jensen, "How Much Can We Boost IQ Scores and Scholastic Achievement?" *Harvard Educational Review* 39 (no. 1, Winter 1969): 1–123. For rebuttals to Jensen, see "Discussion: How Much Can We Boost IQ and Scholastic Achievement?" *Harvard Educational Review* 39 (no. 2, April 1969): 273–356.

23. Wilson and Herrnstein, *Crime and Human Nature*, 468–72; Kevin R. Hopkins, "Real Equality: Can Blacks and Whites Ever Be Equal?" unpublished manuscript.

24. Sowell, *Ethnic America*, 91–94, 167-68, 281–82; Daniel Goleman, "An Emerging Theory on Blacks' I.Q. Scores," *New York Times Education Life*, 10 April 1988, pp. 22–24.

25. Christopher Jencks et al., *Inequality: A Reassessment of the Effect of Family and Schooling in America* (New York: Basic Books, 1972), chaps. 5–7; idem, *Who Gets Ahead? The Determinants of Economic Success in America* (New York: Basic Books, 1979), chaps. 4–5, 8.

26. Mark R. Rank, "Racial Differences in Length of Welfare Use," *Social Forces* 66 (no. 4, June 1988): 1080–1101.

27. Saul D. Hoffman, "Dependency and Welfare Receipt: An Empirical Review" (Study prepared for the U.S. Department of Health and Human Services, Hudson Institute, Alexandria, Va., March 1987), 55–62. Greg J. Duncan and Saul D. Hoffman, "Welfare Dynamics and the Nature of Need," *Cato Journal* 6 (no. 1, Spring–Summer 1986): 42–45, report findings by Martha S. Hill and Michael Ponza that 19 percent of black women who grew up in highly welfare-dependent families were on AFDC themselves, compared to 14 percent who had not grown up on welfare. There is more evidence of inheritance among whites. Peter Gottschalk, "The Intergenerational Transmission of Welfare Participation: Facts and Possible Causes" (Boston: Boston College, Department of Economics, 1989), found that growing up on welfare doubled the chance that a mother would have a child and go on welfare by age eighteen for both blacks and whites–but from only about 0.5 to 1 percent.

28. Wilson and Herrnstein, *Crime and Human Nature*, chaps. 3, 6–14; Don W. Brown, "Cognitive Development and Willingness to Comply with Law," *American Journal of Political Science* 18 (no. 3, August 1974): 583–94.

29. Keith Melville and John Doble, *The Public's Perspective on Social Welfare Reform* (New York: Public Agenda Foundation, January 1988), 10, 13.

30. Christopher Jencks, "What Is the Underclass—And Is It Growing?" *Focus* 12 (no. 1, Spring and Summer 1989): 19–20.

31. Samuel Z. Klausner, *Six Years in the Lives of the Impoverished: An Examination of the WIN Thesis* (Philadelphia: Center for Research on the Acts of Man, 1978); Joel F. Handler and Ellen Jane Hollingsworth, *The "Deserving Poor": A Study of Welfare Administration* (New York: Academic Press, 1971), chap. 7; Susan Sheehan, "A Welfare Mother," *The New Yorker*, 29 September 1975, pp. 42–99.

32. Elliot Liebow, *Tally's Corner: A Study of Negro Streetcorner Men* (Boston: Little, Brown, 1967), 15–16, and passim. For a very similar picture, see George Gilder, *Visible Man: A True Story of Post-racist America* (New York: Basic Books, 1978).

33. Goodwin, *Do the Poor Want to Work?* 82–84; idem, *Causes and Cures of Welfare: New Evidence on the Social Psychology of the Poor* (Lexington, Mass.: D.C. Heath, 1983), chaps. 3–4, 6; H. Roy Kaplan and Curt Tausky, "Work and the Welfare Cadillac: The Function of and Commitment to Work among the Hard-Core Unemployed," *Social Problems* 19 (no. 4, Spring 1972): 469–83. For a recent poll showing the same attitudes, see Louis Harris, "Examine These Myths of the 80's," *New York Times*, 19 May 1989, p. A35.

34. Lee Rainwater, "Class, Culture, Poverty and Welfare" (Paper prepared for the U.S. Department of Health and Human Services, Brandeis University, Center for Human Resources, Waltham, Mass., October 1987).

35. Lee Rainwater, "Work and Identity in the Lower Class," in *Planning for a Nation of Cities*, ed. Sam Bass Warner, Jr. (Cambridge, Mass.: MIT Press 1966), 119–22.

36. Christopher Jencks, "Deadly Neighborhoods," *The New Republic*, 13 June 1988, pp. 26–32.

37. William Julius Wilson, "Studying Inner-City Social Dislocations: The Challenge of Public Agenda Research," *American Sociological Review* 56 (no. 1, February 1991): 9–12.

38. William Julius Wilson, "The American Underclass: Inner-City Ghettos and the Norms of Citizenship" (The Godkin Lecture, delivered at the John F. Kennedy School of Government, Harvard University, Cambridge, Mass., 26 April 1988), 9–19; Loïc J. D. Wacquant and William Julius Wilson, "Poverty, Joblessness, and the Social Transformation of the Inner City," in *Welfare Policy for the 1990s*, ed. Phoebe H. Cottingham and David T. Ellwood (Cambridge, Mass.: Harvard University Press, 1989), 99; idem, "The Cost of Racial and Class Exclusion in the Inner City," *Annals of the American Academy of Political and Social Science* 501 (January 1989): 25.

39. Hopkins et al., *Welfare Dependency*. Wilson and Herrnstein, *Crime and Human Nature*, deal with crime in similar terms.

40. Nathan Glazer, "Beyond Income Maintenance—A Note on Welfare in New York City," *The Public Interest*, no. 16 (Summer 1969): 20.

41. Frances Fox Piven and Richard A. Cloward, "The Historical Sources of the Contemporary Relief Debate," in Fred Block et al., *The Mean Season: The Attack on the Welfare State* (New York: Pantheon, 1987), 83–84.

42. Harry J. Holzer, "Black Youth Nonemployment: Duration and Job Search," in *Black Youth Employment Crisis*, ed. Freeman and Holzer, chap. 1; Linda Datcher-Loury and Glenn Loury, "The Effects of Attitudes and Aspirations on the Labor Supply of Young Men," in *Black Youth Employment Crisis*, ed. Freeman and Holzer, 386–89. The alienation arises from being disadvantaged, not from being black, as differences in willingness to work are not apparent if one compares black and white youth as a whole. See Michael E. Borus, "Willingness to Work Among Youth," *Journal of Human Resources* 17 (no. 4, Fall 1982): 581–93.

43. Goodwin, *Do the Poor Want to Work?* 46.

44. Frank Levy, *Dollars and Dreams: The Changing American Income Distribution* (New York: Russell Sage, 1987), 146–47.

45. Marlene Sonju Chrissinger, "Factors Affecting Employment of Welfare Mothers," *Social Work* 25 (no. 1, January 1980): 53–54; William J. Reed, "Hope for a Better Life," in *The Work Incentive Experience*, ed. Charles D. Garvin, Audrey D. Smith, and William J. Reid (Montclair, N.J.: Allanheld, Osmun, 1978), chap. 7; Abigail C. Nichols, "Why Welfare Mothers Work: Implications for Employment and Training Services," *Social Service Review* 53 (no. 3, September 1979): 382.

46. Liebow, *Tally's Corner*, 57–59, 63.

47. Studs Terkel, *Working: People Talk about What They Do All Day and How They Feel About What They Do* (New York: Pantheon, 1974), 112–18.

48. Andrew Hacker, "Getting Rough on the Poor," *New York Review of Books*, 13 October 1988, pp. 15–17.

49. U.S. Congress, House, *Administration's Welfare Reform Proposal*, Joint Hearings before the Welfare Reform Subcommittee of the Committee on Agriculture, Committee on Education and Labor, and Committee on Ways and Means, 95th Cong., 1st sess., 2 November 1977, p. 2257.

50. Elijah Anderson, "Some Observations of Black Youth Employment," in *Youth Employment and Public Policy*, ed. Bernard E. Anderson and Isabel V. Sawhill (Englewood Cliffs, N.J.: Prentice-Hall, 1980), chap. 3; Richard B. Freeman, "Create Jobs That Pay as Well as Crime," *New York Times*, 20 July 1986, p. F2; Myerson, "Twin Spotlights," F6.

51. Auletta, *Underclass*, chaps. 3–4, 8–14; Nancy Goodban, "The Psychological Impact of Being on Welfare," *Social Service Review* 59 (no. 3, September 1985): 403–22.

52. Daniel P. Moynihan, ed., *On Understanding Poverty: Perspectives from the Social Sciences* (New York: Basic Books, 1969), chaps. 2, 7–9; Hyman Rodman, "The Lower-class Value Stretch," *Social Forces* 42 (no. 2, December 1963): 205–15. The various contributors to this theory disagreed about the causes of culture of poverty—ingrained attitudes versus limited opportunity—but they largely agreed about its nature.

53. Liebow, *Tally's Corner*, 53–57, 71, 135–36, 208–16.

54. Relying on welfare can reflect "learned helplessness." See Thomas J. Kane, "Giving Back Control: Long-Term Poverty and Motivation," *Social Service*

Review 61 (no. 3, September 1987): 409–12. This idea goes back to Robert K. Merton, "Bureaucratic Structure and Personality," in *Social Theory and Social Structure*, ed. Merton, chap. 8.

55. Lee Rainwater, "Crucible of Identity: The Negro Lower-Class Family," *Daedalus* 95 (no. 1, Winter 1966): 201–6; Oscar Lewis, "The Culture of Poverty," in *On Understanding Poverty*, ed. Moynihan, 188.

56. Michael Harrington, *The Other America: Poverty in the United States*, rev. ed. (Baltimore: Penguin Books, 1971), 142; William Julius Wilson, interview on "Bill Moyers' World of Ideas," 26 October 1988.

57. Hopkins et al., *Welfare Dependency*, pp. 7-53 to 7-59; Goodwin, *Do the Poor Want to Work?* chap. 7; idem, *Causes and Cures*, chaps. 3–4; Lee Rainwater, *Behind Ghetto Walls: Black Families in a Federal Slum* (Chicago: Aldine, 1970), 99–110.

58. The "Coleman Report" found that efficacy was strongly linked to success in school. See James S. Coleman, "Equal Schools or Equal Students?" *The Public Interest*, no. 4 (Summer 1966): 75.

59. Generally, research using the National Longitudinal Studies (NLS) finds that efficacy is linked to success over time, while studies which use the Panel Study of Income Dynamics (PSID) find no clear relationship. See Hopkins et al., *Welfare Dependency*, pp. 7–51 to 7–59. NLS suggests that welfare mothers high in efficacy are the likeliest to leave welfare through working, while PSID does not. See June A. O'Neill et al., "An Analysis of Time on Welfare" (Washington, D.C.: Urban Institute, June 1984), 13–14, 37–38, 41, 52.

One reason to expect a connection between efficacy and success is that the NLS may measure efficacy better, according to O'Neill et al., "Analysis of Time on Welfare," 95–102. As mentioned in Mary Corcoran et al., "Myth and Reality: The Causes and Persistence of Poverty," *Journal of Policy Analysis and Management* 4 (no. 4, Summer 1985), 529, 529n25, a link between efficacy and success is clearest when questions are asked specifically about work or welfare rather than life in general, as in Goodwin, *Causes and Cures*.

60. Louis Uchitelle, "America's Army of Non-Workers," *New York Times*, 27 September 1987, p. F1.

61. William Julius Wilson, *The Truly Disadvantaged: The Inner City, the Underclass, and Public Policy* (Chicago: University of Chicago Press, 1987), 46; Paul A. Jargowsky and Mary Jo Bane, "Ghetto Poverty: Basic Questions," in *Inner-City Poverty in the United States*, ed. Laurence E. Lynn, Jr., and Michael G. H. McGeary (Washington, D.C.: National Academy Press, 1990), chap. 2.

62. Loïc J. D. Wacquant and William Julius Wilson, "Cost of Racial and Class Exclusion," 16–24.

63. Emanuel Tobier and Camilo Jose Vergara, "A New American Ghetto: Mott Haven and Brownsville Twenty Years Later" (New York: New York University, Urban Research Center, 24 November 1990); Robert I. Lerman, "Do Welfare Programs Affect the Schooling and Work Patterns of Young Black Men?" in *Black Youth Employment Crisis*, ed. Freeman and Holzer, chap. 11; Freeman, "Help Wanted," 22–23.

64. Less than 5 percent of mothers who are on the rolls more than two years work their way off, according to O'Neill et al., "Analysis of Time on Welfare," 15, 27–28, 37, 84.

65. Christopher Jencks and Susan E. Mayer, "The Social Consequences of Growing Up in a Poor Neighborhood," in *Inner-City Poverty*, ed. Lynn and McGeary, chap. 4; Jonathan Crane, "Effects of Neighborhoods on Dropping Out of School and Teenage Childbearing," in *Urban Underclass*, ed. Jencks and Peterson, 299–320; Susan E. Mayer, "How Much Does a High School's Racial and Socioeconomic Mix Affect Graduation and Teenage Fertility Rates?" in *Urban Underclass*, ed. Jencks and Peterson, 321–41; Wilson and Herrstein, *Crime and Human Nature*, chap. 11.

66. John Hope Franklin, *From Slavery to Freedom: A History of Negro Americans*, 4th ed. (New York: Knopf, 1974), chap. 22; E. Franklin Frazier, *The Negro Family in the United States* (Chicago: University of Chicago Press, 1939), chaps. 12, 19–20.

67. On these "concentration effects," see Wilson, *Truly Disadvantaged*, 46–62, 137–38, 143–44. Some scholars doubt Wilson's claim that class segregation is increasing among blacks, although it is clear that better-off blacks are leaving the ghetto and poverty rates are rising there. See Reynolds Farley, "Residential Segregation of Social and Economic Groups among Blacks, 1970–80," in *Urban Underclass*, ed. Jencks and Peterson, 274–98.

    A theory opposed to Wilson is that poor blacks brought social disorders with them when they migrated from the rural South to Northern cities. See Nicholas Lemann, *The Promised Land: The Great Black Migration and How It Changed America* (New York: Knopf, 1991). However, recent black migrants to the North do better there economically than blacks born and raised in the North, suggesting that the breakdown occurs in the Northern cities. See David Whitman, "The Great Sharecropper Success Story," *The Public Interest*, no. 104 (Summer 1991): 3–19. Both theories may have some validity. Perhaps migrants do better *compared to local blacks* but both groups are ill-prepared *compared to whites*, so in-migration of blacks still depresses urban conditions.

68. Jencks, "Deadly Neighborhoods," 31. Welfare spells are shorter in rural than urban areas because the recipients are more exposed to social pressures, according to Mark R. Rank and Thomas A. Hirschl, "A Rural-Urban Comparison of Welfare Exits: The Importance of Population Density," *Rural Sociology* 53 (no. 2, 1988): 190–206.

69. Whether blacks youths go to church is a strong predictor of whether they stay in school and avoid crime. See Richard B. Freeman, "Who Escapes? The Relation of Churchgoing and Other Background Factors to the Socioeconomic Performance of Black Male Youths from Inner-City Tracts," in *Black Youth Employment Crisis*, ed. Freeman and Holzer, chap. 9; and idem, "Help Wanted," 22–23.

70. In some other societies, authority, largely informal, succeeds in minimizing crime and welfare. See David H. Bayley, "Learning about Crime—The Japanese Experience," *The Public Interest*, no. 44 (Summer 1976): 55–68;

Ralph Segalman, "Welfare and Dependency in Switzerland," *The Public Interest*, no. 82 (Winter 1986): 106–21.

71. Pole, *Pursuit of Equality*, 293.

72. Nathan Glazer and Daniel P. Moynihan, *Beyond the Melting Pot: The Negroes, Puerto Ricans, Jews, Italians, and Irish of New York City*, 2nd ed. (Cambridge, Mass.: MIT Press, 1970), 24–287; Sowell, *Ethnic America*; Thomas Sowell, *Race and Economics* (New York: David McKay, 1975), chaps. 1–4, 8–9.

73. Stephen Steinberg, *The Ethnic Myth: Race, Ethnicity, and Class in America* (New York: Atheneum, 1981), chaps. 1–6.

74. Sowell, *Ethnic America*, 152, 171–78, 187, 274, 290–96.

75. Ibid., chaps. 6–11.

76. Seth Mydans, "Legalized Aliens Seen as Unprepared," *New York Times*, 14 August 1989, p. A12; Morris Janowitz, *The Reconstruction of Patriotism: Education for Civic Consciousness* (Chicago: University of Chicago Press, 1983), 128–44.

77. William Julius Wilson, *The Declining Significance of Race: Blacks and Changing American Institutions*, 2nd ed. (Chicago: University of Chicago Press, 1980), 19–22, 111, 140.

78. This meant that most of the opportunities available to unskilled workers in Northern industries after the Civil War went to new immigrants from Europe, rather than to blacks. See Steinberg, *Ethnic Myth*, 172–221.

79. Comments by black scholars on this contradiction include Orlando Patterson, "The Moral Crisis of the Black American," *The Public Interest*, no. 32 (Summer 1973): 43–69; Glenn C. Loury, "The Moral Quandary of the Black Community," *The Public Interest*, no. 79 (Spring 1985): 9–22; and Anne Wortham, *The Other Side of Racism: A Philosophical Study of Black Race Consciousness* (Columbus: Ohio State University Press, 1981).

80. Martin Luther King, Jr., speech at the Lincoln Memorial, 28 August 1963, reprinted in *New York Times*, 28 August 1983, p. 28.

81. E. Franklin Frazier, *The Negro in the United States*, rev. ed. (New York: Macmillan, 1957), 143–46.

82. Ari L. Goldman, "Riverside Chooses New Minister," *New York Times*, 1 February 1989, pp. B1, B5.

83. Edward D. Sargent, "Mr. Best: Teacher, Preacher, Philosopher and Friend," *Washington Post*, 11 December 1980, pp. D.C. 1, D.C. 5.

84. Rainwater, "Work and Identity"; idem, "Crucible of Identity"; Lee Rainwater, "The Lessons of Pruitt-Igoe," *The Public Interest*, no. 8 (Summer 1967): 116–23; idem, ed., *Soul* (New Brunswick, N.J.: Transaction Books, 1970).

85. I credit this apt formulation to my research assistant, Bridget Marks.

86. Shelby Steele, *The Content of Our Character: A New Vision of Race in America* (New York: St. Martin's Press, 1990), 173.

87. Thomas Sancton, "Horns of Plenty," *Time*, 22 October 1990, pp. 64–71; Arthur R. Ashe, Jr. et al., *A Hard Road to Glory*, 3 vols. (New York: Amistad/Warner, 1988).

88. Lee A. Daniels, "With Military Set to Thin Ranks, Blacks Fear They'll Be Hurt Most," *New York Times*, 7 August 1991, pp. A1, D5; "Blacks: Too Much of the Burden?" *Time*, 4 February 1991, p. 43; Charles C. Moskos, "Success Story: Blacks in the Army," *The Atlantic*, May 1986, pp. 64–72; idem, "How Do They Do It? The Army's Racial Success Story," *The New Republic*, 5 August 1991, pp. 16–20.

89. One of many works about modernization and development that supports this contrast is Gunnar Myrdal, *Asian Drama: An Inquiry into the Poverty of Nations*, abridged ed. (New York: Vintage, 1972).

90. Herbert Croly, *The Promise of American Life*, ed. Arthur M. Schlesinger, Jr. (Cambridge, Mass.: Harvard University Press, 1965), 9; Handlin, *The Uprooted*, 250.

91. Sowell, *Race and Economics*, 130–32, 144–46; idem, *Ethnic America*, 234.

92. Michael Harrington, *Other America*, 167, speaks of poverty as "an underdeveloped nation," and Freeman and Holzer, "Black Youth Employment Crisis," 3, describe youth unemployment as typical of that in "Third World countries." I do not mean that Third World antecedents can explain the personal and family disorders of the American poor, which are hardly typical of traditional societies. Rather, these problems seem to arise from the self-doubt of the newcomers in facing a modern society. See Lewis, "Culture of Poverty." For the black case, see Frazier, *Negro Family*, chaps. 13–18, 22.

93. Lawrence E. Harrison, *Underdevelopment Is a State of Mind: The Latin American Case* (Lanham, Md.: University Press of America, 1985).

94. Frazier, *Negro*, 10–21, and *Negro Family*, 21–23, contends that blacks' African heritage was entirely eradicated by their experience in the New World, but Herbert G. Gutman, *The Black Family in Slavery and Freedom, 1750–1925* (New York: Pantheon, 1976), chap. 8, says that slave culture preserved many elements of West African belief. The resistance to economic change in Africa remains strong. See P. T. Bauer, *Equality, the Third World and Economic Delusion* (Cambridge, Mass.: Harvard University Press, 1981), chaps. 4–9, 11.

95. Frazier, *Negro*, 593–99; Sowell, *Ethnic America*, 224.

96. Sowell, *Ethnic America*, 283–84; James Fallows, "Immigration: How It's Affecting Us," *The Atlantic*, November 1983, pp. 52, 55.

97. Richard Levine, "Young Immigrant Wave Lifts New York Economy," *New York Times*, 30 July 1990, p. B4; "To America with Skills" and "The Global Brain Drain," *Time*, 8 July 1985. Typically, foreign-born members of any ethnic group overtake the native-born in income within their own lifetimes. See Leif Jensen, "Poverty and Immigration in the United States: 1960–1980," in *Divided Opportunities*, ed. Sandefur and Tienda, 121–30; Sowell, *Ethnic America*, 283.

98. Sowell, *Ethnic America*, 216–20, 224.

99. "Resentment Tinged with Envy," *Time*, 8 July 1985; Jeffrey Schmalz, "Miami's New Ethnic Conflict: Haitians vs. American Blacks," *New York Times*, 19 February 1989, pp. 1, 38; Fallows, "Immigration," 96.

100. Clifford D. May, "From Africa to Jersey, a Relief Worker Fights Poverty," *New York Times*, 29 November 1988, pp. B1, B2; Bruce W. Nelan, "Taking the Measure of American Racism," *Time*, 12 November 1990, pp. 16–19.

101. In Chicago, Mexicans work at higher levels than whites, blacks, or Puerto Ricans, even though they have much less education and less than a third speak English; see Robert Aponte, "Ethnicity and Male Employment In the Inner City: A Test of Two Theories" (Paper prepared for the Chicago Urban Poverty and Family Life Conference, University of Chicago, 10–12 October 1991), table 1. On the Jamaicans, see Nancy Foner, *Jamaica Farewell: Jamaican Migrants in London* (Berkeley: University of California Press 1978), 229–31.

102. Sowell, *Ethnic America*, 284; Felicity Barringer, "Immigration Brings New Diversity to Asian Population in the U.S.," *New York Times*, 12 June 1991; John Kifner, "Immigrant Waves from Asia Bring an Underworld Ashore," *New York Times*, 6 January 1991, pp. 1, 20.

103. Half the reservations have poverty rates of 40 percent or over, although the overall poverty rate for Indians has fallen as more have left the reservation. See Gary D. Sandefur, "The Duality in Federal Policy toward Minority Groups, 1787–1987," in *Divided Opportunities*, ed. Sandefur and Tienda, 208, 217–22; idem, "American Indian Reservations: The First Underclass Areas?" *Focus* 12 (no. 1, Spring and Summer 1989): 37–41.

104. John U. Ogbu, "Diversity and Equity in Public Education: Community Forces and Minority School Adjustment and Performance," in *Policies for America's Public Schools: Teachers, Equity, and Indicators*, ed. Ron Haskins and Duncan MacRae (Norwood, N.J.: Ablex, 1988), chap. 6; Richard Bernstein, "A War of Words," *New York Times Magazine*, 14 October 1990, pp. 50, 52.

105. Lawrence M. Mead, *Beyond Entitlement: The Social Obligations of Citizenship* (New York: Free Press, 1986).

106. Seymour Martin Lipset, *Political Man: The Social Bases of Politics* (Garden City, N.Y.: Anchor Books, 1963), chap. 4.

107. Wilson and Herrnstein, *Crime and Human Nature*, chaps. 8–9.

108. Walter B. Miller, "Lower Class Culture as a Generating Milieu of Gang Delinquency," *Journal of Social Issues* 14 (no. 3, March 1958): 12–13.

109. Harry Eckstein, "Institutional Change and the Authority Culture of the Poor" (Irvine, Calif.: University of California, Department of Political Science, 1983).

110. This is why criminals are often described as lacking in "affect." See Charles E. Silberman, *Criminal Violence, Criminal Justice* (New York: Random House, 1978), 62–63.

111. Frazier, *Negro*, 677-78.

112. Herbert L. Foster, *Ribbin', Jivin', and Playin' the Dozens* (Cambridge, Mass.: Ballinger, 1974); Mary Haywood Metz, *Classrooms and Corridors: The Crisis of Authority in Desegregated Secondary Schools* (Berkeley: University of California Press, 1978).

113. Wacquant and Wilson, "Cost of Racial and Class Exclusion," 10.

114. Robert Greenstein, "Prisoners of the Economy," *New York Times Book Review*, 25 October 1987, pp. 1, 46–48.

Chapter 8:
Policy

1. E.g., David T. Ellwood, *Poor Support: Poverty in the American Family* (New York: Basic Books, 1988), 104–25, and testimony by Robert D. Reischauer and Robert I. Lerman, in U.S. Congress, Senate, Committee on Finance, *Welfare: Reform or Replacement?* Hearings before the Subcommittee on Social Security and Family Policy, 100th Cong., 1st sess., 23 February 1987, pp. 227–81.

2. Richard V. Burkhauser and T. Aldrich Finegan, "The Minimum Wage and the Poor: The End of a Relationship," *Journal of Policy Analysis and Management* 8 (no. 1, Winter 1989): 53, 61–64.

3. Gary Burtless, "The Effect of Reform on Employment, Earnings, and Income," in *Welfare Policy for the 1990s*, ed. Phoebe H. Cottingham and David T. Ellwood (Cambridge, Mass.: Harvard University Press, 1989), 136–37; Charles Brown, Curtis Gilroy, and Andrew Kohen, "The Effect of the Minimum Wage on Employment and Unemployment," *Journal of Economic Literature* 20 (no. 2, June 1982): 497–99, 505–8. In the terms economists use, the income effect dominates the substitution effect.

4. Recently, some liberal and moderate analysts also aiming to strengthen work incentives have proposed limiting how long a mother could draw AFDC without working. See Ellwood, *Poor Support*, 178–82.; Isabel V. Sawhill, "The Underclass: An Overview," *The Public Interest*, no. 96 (Summer 1989): 13–14; and Ford Foundation, Project on Social Welfare and the American Future, *The Common Good: Social Welfare and the American Future* (New York: Ford Foundation, May 1989), 63–64.

5. Janet D. Griffith and Charles L. Usher, "A Quasi-Experimental Assessment of the National Impact of the 1981 Omnibus Budget Reconciliation Act (OBRA) on the Aid to Families with Dependent Children (AFDC) Program," *Evaluation Review* 10 (no. 3, June 1986): 313–33; "Measuring the Effects of the Reagan Welfare Changes on the Work Effort and Well-Being of Single Parents," *Focus* 8 (no. 1, Spring 1985): 1–6.

Another criticism influential among analysts was that the effect of work incentives within welfare might actually be to lower work incentives for the low-income population as a whole. See Frank Levy, "The Labor Supply of Female Household Heads, or AFDC Work Incentives Don't Work Too Well," *Journal of Human Resources* 14 (no. 1, Winter 1979): 76–97; Robert Moffitt, "Work Incentives in Transfer Programs (Revisited): A Study of the AFDC Program," in Ronald G. Ehrenberg, ed., *Research in Labor Economics* 8 (part B, 1986): 389–439.

6. Frank Levy, *The Logic of Welfare Reform* (Washington, D.C.: The Urban Institute, 1980), 48–49, 56–57; John Bishop, "The Welfare Brief," *The Public Interest,* no. 53 (Fall 1978): 169–75.

7. "Spreading the Wings of an Idea," *Time,* 22 September 1986, p. 61; Joseph Berger, "East Harlem Students Clutch a College Dream," *New York Times,* 27 August 1989, pp. 1, 28; Ford Foundation, *The Common Good,* 37.

8. Robert Haveman, *Starting Even: An Equal Opportunity Program to Combat the Nation's New Poverty* (New York: Simon and Schuster, 1988), 168–71; Sawhill, "Underclass," 14–15; Michael Sherraden, *Assets and the Poor: A New American Welfare Policy* (Armonk, N.Y.: M. E. Sharpe, 1991). A related recommendation is to build up apprenticeship programs. See Robert I. Lerman and Hillard Pouncy, "The Compelling Case for Youth Apprenticeships," *The Public Interest,* no. 101 (Fall 1990): 62–77.

9. Berger, "East Harlem Students," 1.

10. The following review is based on Henry J. Aaron, *Politics and the Professors: The Great Society in Perspective* (Washington, D.C.: Brookings, 1978), 125–28; Laurie J. Bassi and Orley Ashenfelter, "The Effect of Direct Job Creation and Training Programs on Low-Skilled Workers," in *Fighting Poverty: What Works and What Doesn't,* ed. Sheldon H. Danziger and Daniel H. Weinberg (Cambridge, Mass.: Harvard University Press, 1986), chap. 6; Burt S. Barnow, "The Impact of CETA Programs on Earnings: A Review of the Literature," *Journal of Human Resources* 22 (no. 2, Spring 1987): 157–93; idem, "Government Training as a Means of Reducing Unemployment," in *Rethinking Employment Policy,* ed. D. Lee Bawden and Felicity Skidmore (Washington, D.C.: Urban Institute, 1989), chap. 5; Congressional Budget Office, *CETA Training Programs—Do They Work for Adults?* (Washington, D.C.: U.S. Government Printing Office, July 1982); Gary Burtless, "Effect of Reform"; Eli Ginzberg, ed., *Employing the Unemployed* (New York: Basic Books, 1980), chaps. 2–3; and Isabel V. Sawhill, "Poverty in the U.S.: Why Is It So Persistent?" *Journal of Economic Literature* 26 (September 1988): 1092–97.

11. Bassi and Ashenfelter, "Effect of Direct Job Creation," 141; Barnow, "Government Training," 126; Gary Burtless, "Manpower Policies for the Disadvantaged: What Works?" *Brookings Review* 3 (no. 1, Fall 1984): 22.

12. This was the effect in the largest government income maintenance experiment, which allowed recipients to pursue education or training with little guidance. See U.S. Department of Health and Human Services, Office of Income Security Policy, *Overview of the Seattle-Denver Income Maintenance Experiment Final Report* (Washington, D.C.: U.S. Government Printing Office, May 1983), 18–21. CETA may also have had this effect. See Catherine P. Dickinson, Terry R. Johnson, and Richard W. West, "An Analysis of the Impact of CETA Programs on Participants' Earnings," *Journal of Human Resources* 21 (no. 1, Winter 1986): 64–91.

13. Lisbeth B. Schorr with Daniel Schorr, *Within Our Reach: Breaking the Cycle of Disadvantage* (New York: Doubleday, 1988).

14. Schorr with Schorr, *Within Our Reach*, xxii; James Tabor, "Making a Fast Break out of the Ghetto," *Time*, February 1989, pp. 14–17.

15. Government has avoided getting involved in most family problems and issues, which are highly sensitive. See Gilbert Y. Steiner, *The Futility of Family Policy* (Washington, D.C.: Brookings, 1981), and Gilbert Y. Steiner, with the assistance of Pauline H. Milius, *The Children's Cause* (Washington, D.C.: Brookings, 1976).

16. The evidence that Head Start can transform the lives of poor children comes mostly from the exemplary Perry Preschool Project in Ypsilanti, Michigan. Evaluations of Head Start nationwide suggest only marginal impact. See Terry W. Hartle and Andrea Bilson, "Increasing the Educational Achievement of Disadvantaged Children: Do Federal Programs Make a Difference?" (Washington, D.C.: American Enterprise Institute, 1986), 6–14; and Congressional Research Service, "The Head Start Program: Background Information and Issues" (Washington, D.C.: Library of Congress, 15 February 1990), 10–17.

17. Denise F. Polit, Janet C. Quint, and James A. Riccio, *The Challenge of Serving Teenage Mothers: Lessons from Project Redirection* (New York: Manpower Demonstration Research Corporation, October 1988); Alvia Branch, James Riccio, and Janet Quint, *Building Self-Sufficiency in Pregnant and Parenting Teens: The Implementation of Project Redirection* (New York: Manpower Demonstration Research Corporation, April 1984).

18. Marian Wright Edelman, *Families in Peril: An Agenda for Social Change* (Cambridge, Mass.: Harvard University Press, 1987).

19. Calvin Tomkins, "A Sense of Urgency," *The New Yorker*, 27 March 1989, p. 74.

20. Ken Auletta, *The Underclass* (New York: Random House, 1982), chaps. 1, 3–4, 6, 8–11, 15–16.

21. Forest Chisman and Alan Pifer, *Government for the People: The Federal Social Role: What It Is, What It Should Be* (New York: Norton, 1987), 223.

22. William Julius Wilson, *The Truly Disadvantaged: The Inner City, the Underclass, and Public Policy* (Chicago: University of Chicago Press, 1987), 121–22, 139, 147, 150–55.

23. Michael B. Katz, *In the Shadow of the Poorhouse: A Social History of Welfare in America* (New York: Basic Books, 1986), 225–27. For a concrete proposal along these lines, see Philip Harvey, *Securing the Right to Employment: Social Welfare Policy and the Unemployed in the United States* (Princeton, N.J.: Princeton University Press, 1989).

24. Leonard Goodwin, *Do the Poor Want to Work? A Social-Psychological Study of Work Orientations* (Washington, D.C.: Brookings, 1972), 114–15.

25. On the local politics of CETA, see Richard P. Nathan et al., *Public Service Employment: A Field Evaluation* (Washington, D.C.: Brookings, 1981).

26. Barnow, "Impact of CETA," 159.

27. In 1977, only 22 percent of disadvantaged PSE clients left the program for any reason. Less than 10 percent left to enter unsubsidized employment, and

most of these took positions in government rather than the private sector. See Congressional Budget Office, *CETA Reauthorization Issues* (Washington, D.C.: U.S. Government Printing Office, August 1978), 19, 19n32.

28. Nicholas Lemann, *The Promised Land: The Great Black Migration and How It Changed America* (New York: Knopf, 1991), 153–55, 201–2, 275–76, argues for a return to jobs programs as a solution to black poverty, but without dealing seriously with the CETA experience.

29. James P. Smith and Finis R. Welch, *Closing the Gap: Forty Years of Economic Progress for Blacks* (Santa Monica, Calif.: Rand, February 1986), xii, 87–95; Jonathan S. Leonard, "What Promises Are Worth: The Impact of Affirmative Action Goals," *Journal of Human Resources* 20 (no. 1, Winter 1985): 3–20; Nathan Glazer, *Affirmative Discrimination: Ethnic Inequality and Public Policy* (Cambridge, Mass.: Harvard University Press, 1987), 69–72.

30. Glazer, *Affirmative Discrimination*, xviii–xix, 213, 217–20.

31. One might contend that the requirements do present an incentive to work, that of avoiding cuts in one's welfare grant. But the "work test" is treated, by both government and the recipients, as a moral and not an economic matter. The chief motivator is public authority, not calculation of gain.

32. Between 1969 and 1980, the share of Americans who thought government was spending too little on welfare fell from 39 to 18 percent, and the share who thought that employable recipients looked for a job fell from 47 to 31 percent, according to James R. Kluegel and Eliot R. Smith, *Beliefs about Inequality: Americans' Views of What Is and What Ought to Be* (New York: Aldine de Gruyter, 1986), 153.

33. For descriptions of these programs, see Congressional Budget Office, *Work-Related Programs for Welfare Recipients* (Washington, D.C.: U.S. Government Printing Office, April 1987); U.S. General Accounting Office, *Work and Welfare: Current AFDC Work Programs and Implications for Federal Policy* (Washington, D.C.: U.S. Government Printing Office, January 1987); and Demetra Smith Nightingale and Lynn C. Burbridge, "The Status of State Work-Welfare Programs in 1986: Implications for Welfare Reform" (Washington, D.C.: Urban Institute, July 1987).

34. For a more detailed account through 1984, see Lawrence M. Mead, *Beyond Entitlement: The Social Obligations of Citizenship* (New York: Free Press, 1986), 121–28. There are also work requirements for Food Stamps, but they have been much less controversial. For recipients enrolled in both programs, the AFDC rules take precedence.

35. Allan Rosenbaum, ed., "Symposium: Employment and Training Policy," *Policy Studies Review* 6 (no. 4, May 1987): 677–788. JOBS' federal funding is about equal to that of the Job Training Partnership Act, but JOBS involves more local funding.

36. Judith M. Gueron and Barbara Goldman, "The U.S. Experience in Work Relief" (New York: Manpower Demonstration Research Corporation, March 1983), 24; Blanche Bernstein, *The Politics of Welfare: The New York City Experience* (Cambridge, Mass.: Abt Books, 1982), 47–50; Valerie Englander and

Fred Englander, "Workfare in New Jersey: A Five Year Assessment," *Policy Studies Review* 5 (no. 1, August 1985): 33–41.

37. This is the same distinction made by Richard P. Nathan, "Will the Underclass Always Be with Us?" *Society* 24 (no. 3, March–April 1987): 61–62, between old and "new-style" workfare.

38. Ketron, Inc., *The Long-Term Impact of WIN II: A Longitudinal Evaluation of the Employment Experiences of Participants in the Work Incentive Program* (Wayne, Penn.: Ketron, January 1980); Ronald G. Ehrenberg and James G. Hewlett, "The Impact of the WIN 2 Program on Welfare Costs and Recipient Rates," *Journal of Human Resources* 11 (no. 1, Spring 1976): 219–32; Star A. Levitan and David Marwick, "Work and Training for Relief Recipients," *Journal of Human Resources* 8 (Supplement 1973): 5–18; Bradley R. Schiller, "Lessons from WIN: A Manpower Evaluation," *Journal of Human Resources* 13 (no. 4, Fall 1978): 502–23.

39. Client earnings rose at rates ranging from zero to $772 a year, as much as a 41 percent gain over income in the absence of the program. The share of clients employed rose by anywhere from zero to almost 12 percentage points, a proportional gain of as much as 37 percent. The share of clients on welfare fell by from zero to 9 percentage points, a proportional drop of as much as 17 percent. The average welfare payment fell from zero to 19 percent. The new programs cost as much as $1,000 per client more than WIN, yet, due to economies from lower welfare, they saved on balance as much as $1,000 to $2,000 per client. These estimates are averages over all those assigned to workfare programs; impacts for actual participants would be higher.

Figures come from evaluations by the Manpower Demonstration Research Corporation (MDRC) of seven programs in San Diego (two programs), Maryland (mainly Baltimore), Cook County (Chicago), Arkansas, Virginia, and West Virginia. This summary relies mainly on Judith M. Gueron, "State Welfare Employment Initiatives: Lessons from the 1980s," *Focus* 11 (no. 1, Spring 1988): 17–24, and Gayle Hamilton and Daniel Friedlander, *Final Report on the Saturation Work Initiative Model in San Diego* (New York: Manpower Demonstration Research Corporation, November 1989), chaps. 4–6. For MDRC's own interpretation of their findings, see Judith M. Gueron and Edward Pauly, *From Welfare to Work* (New York: Russell Sage Foundation, 1991).

For details on the individual programs, see Barbara Goldman, Daniel Friedlander, and David Long, *Final Report on the San Diego Job Search and Work Experience Demonstration* (New York: Manpower Demonstration Research Corporation, February 1986); Hamilton and Friedlander, *Final Report on SWIM*; Daniel Friedlander et al., *Maryland: Final Report on the Employment Initiatives Evaluation* (New York: Manpower Demonstration Research Corporation, December 1985); Daniel Friedlander et al., *Final Report on Job Search and Work Experience in Cook County* (New York: Manpower Demonstration Research Corporation, November 1987); Daniel Friedlander et al.,

Arkansas: Final Report on the WORK Program in Two Counties (New York: Manpower Demonstration Research Corporation, September 1985); James Riccio et al., *Final Report on the Virginia Employment Services Program* (New York: Manpower Demonstration Research Corporation, August 1986); and Daniel Friedlander et al., *West Virginia: Final Report on the Community Work Experience Demonstration* (New York: Manpower Demonstration Research Corporation, September 1986).

40. Mark Testa and Marilyn Krogh, "Marriage, Premarital Parenthood and Joblessness among Black Americans in Inner-City Chicago" (Chicago: University of Chicago, February 1990), 25–43, find that black women as well as men are more likely to marry if employed.

41. U.S. General Accounting Office, *An Overview of the WIN Program: Its Objectives, Accomplishments, and Problems* (Washington, D.C.: U.S. Government Printing Office, June 21, 1982), chap. 2, estimates that half of the employable participated in WIN in 1980, but other figures suggest rates ranging from a quarter to 40 percent. Details on request.

42. Mildred Rein, *Dilemmas of Welfare Policy: Why Work Strategies Haven't Worked* (New York: Praeger, 1982), 74–75; Charles S. Rodgers, "Work Tests for Welfare Recipients: The Gap between the Goal and the Reality," *Journal of Policy Analysis and Management* 1 (no. 1, Fall 1981): 11–14; Levitan and Marwick, "Work and Training," 15.

43. James C. Miller III, Director, Office of Management and Budget, in U.S. Congress, House, Committee on Ways and Means, *Family Welfare Reform Act, Hearings* before the Subcommittee on Public Assistance and Unemployment Compensation, 100th Cong., 1st sess., 30 March 1987, p. 252, specifies an increase from 400,000 to 714,000, but the latter figure includes only new programs replacing WIN. If the remaining WIN clients are added, estimated from national WIN data, the 1985 figure is around 1 million.

44. Participation rose in the new programs partly because they were better funded than WIN and thus larger, but also because they were more determined to involve the majority of the employable. In some instances, experimental clients participated more than controls simply because the latter lacked the same access to services. In most, the experimentals participated more even though both groups had the option to join in some program. The proportion of clients entering jobs was usually much higher in the new programs too, although the level of employment might be only 10 percent.

See Gueron, "State Welfare Employment Initiatives," 19; Friedlander et al., *Arkansas*, 53–56, 145–46; Friedlander et al., *Final Report on Cook County*, 45–48; Friedlander et al., *Maryland*, 61–63; Friedlander et al., *West Virginia*, 72–74, 159–66; Goldman, Friedlander, and Long, *Final Report on San Diego*, 47–49, 97–99, 194; and Riccio et al., *Virginia* (New York: Manpower Demonstration Research Corporation, August 1986), 47–61.

In the Saturation Work Initiative Model (SWIM), the best documented case, experimentals clearly participated more in activities to which controls had equal access. For example, 28–34 percent of experimentals enrolled in community college courses, compared to 19–28 percent for controls; 12–14 percent entered voluntary (JTPA) training, compared to 4–5 percent for controls. See Hamilton and Friedlander, *Final Report on SWIM*, 38–42.

45. In the Job Search and Work Experience Demonstration in San Diego, 45 to 48 percent of clients participated actively within six months, compared to 5 percent for comparable recipients not in the program or in WIN. In the Saturation Work Initiative Model (SWIM) program, participation rose to three-quarters over a year, counting clients who satisfied their obligation by entering training or working part-time. See Goldman, Friedlander, and Long, *Final Report on San Diego*, 47–49, 194; Gayle Hamilton, *Interim Report on the Saturation Work Initiative Model in San Diego* (New York: Manpower Demonstration Research Corporation, August 1988), 97–106. In counties of West Virginia where male AFDC recipients were guaranteed public jobs, around 60 percent participated every month, 30 points higher than in comparison areas. See Friedlander et al., *West Virginia*, xxiii, 159–63.

46. Friedlander et al., *Arkansas*, xiv; Friedlander et al., *Final Report on Cook County*, 71, 73–74; Friedlander et al., *Maryland*, 85–95; Friedlander et al., *West Virginia*, 81–83, 176–78; Riccio et al., *Virginia*, xiv–xv; Goldman, Friedlander, and Long, *Final Report on San Diego*, 50–51, 195; Hamilton, *Interim Report on SWIM*, 140–42.

47. General Accounting Office, *Current AFDC Work Programs*, 103–6; U.S. Department of Labor, Work Incentive Program, "Work Incentive (WIN) Program Data Summary: Fiscal Years 1981, and 1984 through 1988" (Washington, D.C.: U.S. Department of Labor, 19 August 1989), table 1; Demetra Smith Nightingale et al., *Evaluation of the Massachusetts Employment and Training (ET) Program* (Washington, D.C.: Urban Institute, 1991), 108–9.

48. Friedlander et al., *West Virginia*, xxviii, 3, 10–12, 94–95, 101–2. Job availability was also apparently a problem in parts of Virginia and Arkansas; see Riccio et al., *Virginia*, xxii, xxiv, 104–13; and Friedlander et al., *Arkansas*, 14, 151.

49. Lawrence M. Mead, "Expectations and Welfare Work: WIN in New York City," *Policy Studies Review* 2 (no. 4, May 1983): 656; idem, "Expectations and Welfare Work: WIN in New York State," *Polity* 18 (no. 2, Winter 1985): 245. These interviews were in 1980–82, before the job boom of the later 1980s. Staff views in the Supported Work Demonstration in the city, recorded 1979–80, were similar; see Auletta, *Underclass*, 201–2.

50. Telephone conversation with Randale R. Valenti, Administrator for Employment and Social Services, Illinois Department of Public Aid, 3 April 1989. See Illinois Department of Public Aid, *Opportunities: Project Chance* (Springfield: State of Illinois, Department of Public Aid, December 1988).

51. For a given cohort entering welfare, work rates rise over time, suggesting that they can find jobs. See Goldman, Friedlander, and Long, *Final Report on San Diego*, xv, xxii; Hamilton, *Interim Report on SWIM*, xxiv, xxv; Fried-

lander et al., *Final Report on Cook County*, xx; Friedlander et al., *West Virginia*, xvii; Riccio et al., *Virginia*, xviii; Daniel Friedlander, "Supplemental Report on the Baltimore Options Program" (New York: Manpower Demonstration Research Corporation, October 1987), 11; and Daniel Friedlander and Barbara Goldman, "Employment and Welfare Impacts of the Arkansas WORK Program: A Three-Year Follow-Up Study in Two Counties" (New York: Manpower Demonstration Research Corporation, May 1988), 9. I am indebted to Daniel Friedlander of MDRC for helping me interpret these data.

52. Denise F. Polit and Joseph J. O'Hara, "Support Services," in *Welfare Policy*, ed. Cottingham and Ellwood, 189–90.

53. This meant these programs represented much less than 30 percent of clients. See Congressional Budget Office, *Current AFDC Work Programs*, 89–93.

54. E.g., Julie Johnson, "Child Care Lack Dims Welfare Program's Future," *New York Times*, 12 December 1989, p. A20; Michael de Courcy Hinds, "Pulling Families out of Welfare Is Proving to Be an Elusive Goal," *New York Times*, 2 April 1990, pp. A1, B8.

55. Robert D. Behn, "The Management of ET Choices in Massachussetts" (Durham, N.C.: Duke University, Institute of Policy Sciences and Public Affairs, 1989), chap. 3, pp. 3, 11; John Wallace and David Long, *The Greater Avenues for Independence (GAIN) Program: Planning and Early Implementation* (New York: Manpower Demonstration Research Corporation, April 1987), 10, 29–30, 162.

56. Dorothy Herbers, "Child Care," in *The Work Incentive Experience*, ed. Charles D. Garvin, Audrey D. Smith, and William J. Reid (Montclair, N.J.: Allanheld, Osmun, 1978), chap. 10.

57. Massachusetts's E.T. spends $400 per client and 32 percent of its budget on child care, but this is quite exceptional. See General Accounting Office, *Current AFDC Work Programs*, 83–87.

JOBS obligates mothers to participate with children as young as age three, the earlier programs usually only when children reached age six. This change will raise child care needs. But before that in some programs, half or more of workfare mothers already had preschool children; the state either obtained special permission to obligate them or they volunteered. This did not depress performance or cause unusual problems. See Friedlander et al., *Arkansas*, xxiv; U.S. General Accounting Office, *Work and Welfare: Analysis of AFDC Employment Programs in Four States* (Washington, D.C.: U.S. General Accounting Office, January 1988), 31–32, 72–85. Lorelei R. Brush, "Child Care Used by Working Women in the AFDC Population: An Analysis of the SIPP Data Base" (Paper prepared for the U.S. Department of Health and Human Services, Analysis, Research and Training, McLean, Va., 15 October 1987), 14–16, 22–27, estimates that with mothers of preschool children in workfare, cheap, informal care will still predominate.

58. Nightingale et al., *Evaluation of ET*, 63, 114.

59. Hamilton, *Interim Report on SWIM,* 95–96, 119–26; Hamilton and Friedlander, *Final Report on SWIM,* 112–15.

60. Karin Martinson and James Riccio, *GAIN: Child Care in a Welfare Employment Initiative* (New York: Manpower Demonstration Research Corporation, May 1989), vii–xiv. One reason for low child care spending was that participation in GAIN was below targets, as discussed below.

61. Barbara Goldman et al. *Findings from the San Diego Job Search and Work Experience Demonstration* (New York: Manpower Demonstration Research Corporation, March 1985), 58–61.

62. Barbara Goldman et al., *Preliminary Findings from the San Diego Job Search and Work Experience Demonstration* (New York: Manpower Research Demonstration Corporation, February 1984), 135–38; Goldman et al., *Findings from San Diego,* 72–73; Janet Quint and Cynthia Guy, *Interim Findings from the WIN Demonstration Program in Cook County* (New York: Manpower Demonstration Research Corporation, June 1986), 98–104; Friedlander et al., *West Virginia,* 36–44; and Friedlander et al., *Maryland,* 219–23.

63. Goldman et al., *Findings from San Diego,* 242, 244, 251.

64. The following expands Lawrence M. Mead, "Should Workfare Be Mandatory? What Research Says," *Journal of Policy Analysis and Management* 9 (no. 3, Summer 1990): 400–4.

65. In 1979–81, on an experimental basis, five local WIN programs raised their participation rate from 53 to 74 percent over the two years, and in the same period job entries by the clients jumped 58 percent. This improvement was achieved without punitive tactics and in the face of a declining economy. See CSR, Incorporated, and Osoro & Associates, *Final Report: Evaluation of the WIN Total Registrant Involvement Project* (Washington, D.C.: CSR, January 1982).

For the finding that higher participation means higher performance in terms of job entries and other indicators, see Mead, "WIN in New York City"; idem, "WIN in New York State"; and Lawrence M. Mead, "The Potential for Work Enforcement: A Study of WIN," *Journal of Policy Analysis and Management* 7 (no. 2, Winter 1988): 264–88. Higher participation does not improve wages, and effects on dependency are unclear.

Two other studies that reach parallel conclusions include Paul J. Provencher, "Welfare Recipients and Employment: The Influence of the Attitudes of Case Managers and Other Factors on Program Performance in Local Welfare Offices" (Ph.D. diss., Brandeis University, Heller School, August 1989), chap. 5; and Bradley R. Schiller and C. Nielson Brasher, "Workfare in the 1980s: Successes and Limits," *Policy Studies Review* 9 (no. 4, Summer 1990): 665–80. An early study that also documents the influence of work tests on welfare employment rates is Irwin Garfinkel and Larry L. Orr, "Welfare Policy and the Employment Rate of AFDC Mothers," *National Tax Journal* 27 (no. 2, June 1974): 275–84.

66. E.g., Laurence E. Lynn, Jr., ed., "Symposium: The Craft of Public Management," *Journal of Policy Analysis and Management* 8 (no. 2, Spring 1989): 284–306, in which several analysts recommend that workfare be voluntary. For a rebuttal, see Mead, "Should Workfare Be Mandatory?"

67. Behn, "Management of ET Choices," chap. 1, p. 5, and passim.

68. Wallace and Long, *GAIN: Planning,* 148–49, 185–86; James Riccio et al., *The Greater Avenues for Independence (GAIN) Program: Early Implementation Experiences and Lessons* (New York: Manpower Demonstration Research Corporation, April 1989), 15, 15n11, 74–80, 87, 96. According to Stephen Freedman and James Riccio, *GAIN: Participation Patterns in Four Counties* (New York: Manpower Demonstration Research Corporation, May 1991), participation has recently improved in some areas.

69. Behn, "Management of ET," chap. 5, p. 17; Interagency Work and Welfare Task Force, "BEGIN: The New York City Model for Implementing Welfare Reform" (New York: Human Resources Administration, May 1989), 12.

70. Daniel Friedlander, *Subgroup Impacts and Performance Indicators for Selected Welfare Employment Programs* (New York: Manpower Demonstration Research Corporation, August 1988), chap. 4.

71. General Accounting Office, *Analysis of AFDC Employment Programs,* 22–24, estimates the rate at 28 percent of all adult recipients; Nightingale et al., *Evaluation of ET,* 52–53, at 33 percent; and Provencher, "Welfare Recipients and Employment," 76n6, at 35 percent. Using employable recipients only, I estimate the rate at 39 percent. Details on request.

72. There has been no definitive evaluation of E.T. June O'Neill, *Work and Welfare in Massachusetts: An Evaluation of the ET Program* (Boston: Pioneer Institute for Public Policy Research, May 1990), using time series methods, found that the program had virtually no effect. Nightingale et al., *Evaluation of ET,* found impacts on earning, employment, and dependency, but used a comparison group that raises methodological doubts.

73. The following relies on Lawrence M. Mead, "The Logic of Workfare: The Underclass and Work Policy," *Annals of the American Academy of Political and Social Science* 501 (January 1989): 164–66.

74. Mildred Rein, *Dilemmas of Welfare Policy,* 74–75.

75. Friedlander et al., *Final Report on Cook County,* 44–49.

76. Goldman et al., *Findings from San Diego,* 100–1; Hamilton, *Interim Report on SWIM,* 133, 136–38; Riccio et al., *GAIN: Early Implementation,* 81, 87–89.

77. Riccio et al., *GAIN: Early Implementation,* 104, 156; Quint and Guy, *Interim Findings from Cook County,* 44, 57–58, 65–66; Friedlander et al., *Final Report on Cook County,* 62–63.

78. This was the view of New York staff I interviewed for Mead, "WIN in New York City"; and idem, "WIN in New York State." General Accounting Office, *Analysis of AFDC Employment Programs,* 34–37, reports that strong majorities of staff in Michigan, Oregon, and Texas favored mandatoriness, while in Massachusetts, they favored voluntariness.

79. Friedlander et al., *Final Report on Cook County*, 55–57; Quint and Guy, *Interim Findings from Cook County*, 85–87; Hamilton, *Interim Report on SWIM*, 78–79.

80. Goldman, Friedlander, and Long, *Final Report on San Diego*, 13; Hamilton and Friedlander, *Final Report on SWIM*, 8–9, 13, 23n3.

81. Lisa W. Foderaro, "Leaving Welfare Behind by Degrees," *New York Times*, 16 September 1990, p. 38.

82. Goldman et al., *Preliminary Findings from San Diego*, 66; Hamilton, *Interim Report on SWIM*, 89.

83. Advisory Commission on Intergovernmental Relations, *Summary of Welfare Reform Hearings—1986* (Washington, D.C.: Advisory Commission on Intergovernmental Relations, June 1987), 22–23.

84. E.g., Mimi Abramowitz, "Why Welfare Reform Is a Sham," *The Nation*, 26 September 1988, pp. 221, 238–41; Joel F. Handler, "Consensus on Redirection—Which Direction?" *Focus* 11 (no. 1, Spring 1988): 29–34; Morton H. Sklar, "Workfare: Is the Honeymoon Over—or Yet to Come?" *Public Welfare* 44 (no. 1, Winter 1986): 30–32.

85. Friedlander et al., *Maryland*, 223–27; Quint and Guy, *Interim Findings from Cook County*, 104–8; Goldman et al., *Findings from San Diego*, 74–75, 89–95; Friedlander et al., *Arkansas*, 173–75; Friedlander et al., *West Virginia*, 44–48; Riccio et al., *Virginia*, 199, 201–4.

86. E.g., William Julius Wilson, "Social Policy and Minority Groups: What Might Have Been and What Might We See in the Future?" in *Divided Opportunities: Minorities, Poverty, and Social Policy*, ed. Gary D. Sandefur and Marta Tienda (New York: Plenum, 1988), 238–50.

87. Goldman et al., *Findings from San Diego*, 103; Hamilton and Friedlander, *Final Report on SWIM*, 44–45; Friedlander et al., *Final Report on Cook County*, 45, 49; Riccio et al., *GAIN: Early Implementation*, xiii, 85, 93, 114; Congressional Budget Office, *Current AFDC Work Programs*, 62–64.

88. Katz, *In the Shadow of the Poorhouse*, xi, 24–25, 33–35, and passim; George Gilder, *Wealth and Poverty* (New York: Basic Books, 1981), 118.

89. CSR and Osoro, *Final Report*, 40–42; Goldman et al., *Findings from San Diego*, 94; Goldman, Friedlander, and Long, *Final Report on San Diego*, 60–66; see Hamilton and Friedlander, *Final Report on SWIM*, 79, 87–88.

90. Dirk Johnson, "Anti-Poverty Program Seeks to Build Self-Esteem," *New York Times*, 21 February 1988, p. 24.

91. Mead, "WIN in New York City," 655–56, 659; idem, "WIN in New York State," 237, 244–45; Mark Lincoln Chadwin et al., "Reforming Welfare: Lessons from the WIN Experience," *Public Administration Review* 41 (no. 3, May–June 1981): 375–76.

92. Goldman et al., *Preliminary Findings from San Diego*, 9–10; Colleen Moore, James Beck, and Dorothy Glogowski, "Breaking the Chain of Dependency," *Public Welfare* 30 (no. 2, Spring 1972): 48–53.

93. Goldman et al., *Preliminary Findings from San Diego*, 90–91; Goldman et al., *Findings from San Diego*, 56–57, 240.

94. Quint and Guy, *Interim Findings from Cook County*, 95; Martin Tolchin, "Reducing Welfare Rolls and Adding Self-Esteem in Oklahoma," *New York Times*, 19 November 1988, p. 8; Josh Barbanel, "One Life That Welfare Reform Reshaped," *New York Times*, 7 July 1988, pp. B1, B4.

95. In WIN, only 38 percent of recipients age sixteen and over even had to register with the program, chiefly due to the exemption for children under age six. See General Accounting Office, *Overview of the WIN Program*, chap 2.

96. Congressional Budget Office, "Work and Welfare: The Family Support Act of 1988" (Washington, D.C.: Congressional Budget Office, January 1989), 27–28. WIN had required that only 15 percent of the employable participate over a year. Parallel steps were taken to expand participation in the Food Stamp program. See Joyce Munns, "Implementing an Employment and Training Program for Food Stamp Recipients: Dilemmas and Choices," *Policy Studies Review* 6 (no. 4, May 1987): 744–54.

97. Estimates from the Congressional Budget Office, September–December 1987; Congressional Budget Office, "Work and Welfare," 8. The latter estimates are not strictly comparable to the former because of a change in estimating methodology.

98. Ron Haskins, "Congress Writes a Law: Research and Welfare Reform," *Journal of Policy Analysis and Management*, 10 (no. 4, Fall 1991): 627. Evaluations make clear that workfare actually saves money for governments. Funding for workfare would be easier to defend if the program were financed out of a trust fund based on the welfare savings it generates.

99. Fifty percent would be more than twice the level required under FSA, but I would also define the permissible activities somewhat more leniently than in FSA. A half-time rule has already been set in the regulations for FSA. See *Federal Register*, 13 October 1989, sec. 250.78. Many states regard this as too tough. See chapter 9.

100. Cost estimates for experimental high-participation WIN programs and for the Republican FSA proposal indicate that as the less employable clients participate, the savings in welfare they generate, though sizable, are overtaken by the cost of the more expensive support services they require. See CSR, *Final Report*, 25–26, 31–32, 43–51; and estimates from the Congressional Budget Office, September–December 1987.

101. Riccio et al., *GAIN: Early Implementation*, 191–203.

102. General Accounting Office, *Overview of the WIN Program*, 23–31, 52–54; Mead, "Potential for Work Enforcement," 274; idem, "WIN in New York State," 243–44.

103. This was just the approach taken by SWIM, the most exemplary program to date.

104. Riccio et al., *GAIN: Early Implementation*, 188–89, 209–12.

105. U.S. Congress, House, Committee on Ways and Means, *Overview of Entitlement Programs: Background Material and Data on Programs within the Jurisdic-*

tion of the Committee on Ways and Means (Washington, D.C.: U.S. Government Printing Office, 5 June 1990), 541, 579.

106. FSA does permit states to propose demonstration projects along these lines.

107. Irwin Garfinkel et al., "The Wisconsin Child Support Assurance System: Estimated Effects on Poverty, Labor Supply, Caseloads, and Cost," *Journal of Human Resources* 25 (no. 1, Winter 1990): 16–18.

108. Susan Chira, "The Rules of the Marketplace Are Applied to the Classroom," *New York Times*, 12 June 1991, pp. A1, B5; John E. Chubb and Terry M. Moe, *Politics, Markets, and America's Schools* (Washington, D.C.: Brookings, 1990). Such reforms aim to institute what have been found to be the features of effective schools—clear standards, strong principals, delegation to the teachers, and close monitoring and support for student achievement.

109. James Q. Wilson, *Thinking about Crime* (New York: Vintage, 1975), chap. 8; Charles E. Silberman, *Criminal Violence, Criminal Justice* (New York: Random House, 1978), chaps. 8–9.

110. Israel Wilkerson, "Wisconsin Makes Truancy Costly by Tying Welfare to Attendance," *New York Times*, 11 December 1989, pp. A1, B12; Thomas Corbett et al., "Learnfare: The Wisconsin Experience," *Focus* 12 (no. 2, Fall–Winter 1989): 1–10.

111. Charles Murray, "Helping the Poor: A Few Modest Proposals," *Commentary*, May 1985, p. 30; Neil Gilbert, "The Unfinished Business of Welfare Reform," *Society* 24 (no. 3, March–April 1987): 10–11; James Willwerth, "Should We Take Away Their Kids?" *Time*, 13 May 1991, pp. 62–63; B. Drummond Ayres, Jr., "Disarming Tenants for Peace in Project," *New York Times*, 23 December 1990, p. 14.

112. Joe Klein, "Now for the Good News," *New York Magazine*, 7 January 1991, p. 10; Lisa W. Foderaro, "Homeless Get New Start in Westchester Program," *New York Times*, 28 May 1990, p. 25.

113. Sara Rimer, "Homeless Find Shelter from Drugs," *New York Times*, 22 April 1989, pp. 29, 32; Michel Marriott, "Struggle and Hope from Ashes of Drugs," *New York Times*, 22 October 1989, pp. 1, 36; Andrew H. Malcolm, "In Making Drug Strategy, No Accord on Treatment," *New York Times*, 19 November 1989, pp. 1, 34.

114. "Help for At-Risk Kids," *Time*, 26 June 1989, p. 51; Joseph Berger, "Social Ills Pull Educators' Concern to New Issues," *New York Times*, 6 September 1989, p. B10; Susan Chira, "Schools' New Role: Steering People to Services," *New York Times*, 15 May 1991, pp. A1, A25.

115. Charles C. Moskos, *A Call to Civic Service: National Service for Country and Community* (New York: Free Press, 1988); Congressional Budget Office, "National Service: Issues and Options" (Washington, D.C.: Congressional Budget Office, September 1990).

116. "An Inmate and a Gentleman," *Time*, 11 August 1986, p. 17; "Shock Incarceration," The Eleventh Hour, WNET, New York, 12 June 1989.

117. Katz, *In the Shadow of the Poorhouse*, 10–11, 25–33, 118–19.

118. James Q. Wilson and Richard J. Herrnstein, *Crime and Human Nature* (New York: Simon and Schuster, 1985), chap. 15; James E. Prather and Frank K. Gibson, "The Failure of Social Programs," *Public Administration Review* 37 (no. 5, September–October 1977): 556–64; Robert Martinson, "What Works?—Questions and Answers about Prison Reform," *The Public Interest*, no. 35 (Spring 1974): 22–54; James Q. Wilson, *Thinking about Crime* (New York: Vintage Books, 1975), 186–93.

119. Charles Murray, "The Coming of Custodial Democracy," *Commentary*, September 1988, pp. 19–24.

120. Elizabeth Lyttleton Sturz, "Lean on Him," *New York Times Book Review*, 9 July 1989, p. 14.

Chapter 9:
Welfare Reform

1. This chapter is a revision of Lawrence M. Mead, "The Changing Agenda of Welfare Reform in the United States, 1967–88" (Paper presented at the annual conference of the American Political Science Association, San Francisco, 3 August 1990).

2. Lawrence M. Mead, *Beyond Entitlement: The Social Obligations of Citizenship* (New York: Free Press, 1986), chaps. 5, 10–11.

3. U.S. Congress, House, Committee on Ways and Means, *President's Proposals for Revision in the Social Security System, Hearings* before the Committee on Ways and Means on H.R. 5710, 90th Cong., 1st sess., 1 March–11 April 1967, p. 14.

4. U.S. Congress, House, 90th Cong., 1st sess., 13 December 1967, *Congressional Record*, vol. 113, part 27, pp. 36378–79, 36387.

5. WIN might not have passed, but the legislation was packaged with increases in Social Security and other popular programs that members of Congress felt bound to vote for.

6. U.S. Congress, House, Committee on Ways and Means, *Social Security Amendments of 1967*, H. Rept. 544 to accompany H.R. 12080, 90th Cong., 1st sess., 7 August 1967, p. 96.

7. U.S. Congress, Senate, Committee on Finance, *Social Security Amendments of 1967, Hearings* before the Committee on Finance on H.R. 12080, 90th Cong., 1st sess., 22 August–26 September 1967, pp. 1226–37, 1371–87, 1761–87.

8. U.S. Congress, House, Committee on Ways and Means, *Hearings on the Subject of Social Security and Welfare Proposals*, 91st Cong., 1st sess., 15 October–13 November 1969, pp. 1013–40; Vincent J. Burke and Vee Burke, *Nixon's Good Deed: Welfare Reform* (New York: Columbia University Press, 1974), 164, 174. On the public's views of welfare, see chapter 3.

9. U.S. Congress, House, 91st Cong., 2nd sess., 16 April 1970, *Congressional Record*, vol. 116, part 9, p. 12077.

10. Committee on Ways and Means, *Hearings on Welfare Proposals 1969*, p. 2332.

11. M. Kenneth Bowler, *The Nixon Guaranteed Income Proposal: Substance and Process in Policy Change* (Cambridge, Mass.: Ballinger, 1974), 117–18; Burke and Burke, *Nixon's Good Deed*, 129–34.

12. Only in the final Senate debate, in 1972, did a serious argument break out over child care. Liberals led by Walter Mondale wanted more funding and higher standards for care, while conservatives resisted. See U.S. Congress, Senate, 92nd Cong., 2nd sess., 27 September–6 October 1972, *Congressional Record*, vol. 118, parts 25–26, pp. 33961–71.

13. U.S. Congress, Senate, Committee on Finance, *Welfare Reform Proposals, Hearings* before the Subcommittee on Public Assistance on S. 2084, 95th Cong., 2nd sess., 7 February–4 May 1978, pp. 854–55.

14. U.S. Congress, House, Committee on Agriculture, Committee on Education and Labor, and Committee on Ways and Means, *Administration's Welfare Proposal*, Joint Hearings before the Welfare Reform Subcommittee, 95th Cong., 1st sess., 19 September–4 November 1977, pp. 59, 109.

15. U.S. Congress, House, Committee on Ways and Means, *Special HEW Report on Welfare Reform, Hearings* before the Subcommittee on Public Assistance and Unemployment Compensation, 95th Cong., 1st sess., 4 May 1977, p. 5; Committee on Finance, *Welfare Reform Proposals 1978*, p. 1195.

16. U.S. Congress, Senate, Committee on Finance, *President's Statement on Principles of Welfare Reform, Hearings* before the Subcommittee on Public Assistance, 95th Cong., 1st sess., 5 and 12 May 1977, pp. 70, 79.

17. Committees on Agriculture, Education and Labor, and Ways and Means, *Administration's Welfare Proposal 1977*, pp. 2415, 2422–23, 2795–839.

18. Ibid., 450.

19. Ibid., 651–77; Committee on Finance, *Welfare Reform Proposals 1978*, pp. 652–63.

20. Linda E. Demkovich, "Reagan's Welfare Cuts Could Force Many Working Poor Back on the Dole," *National Journal*, 2 January 1982, pp. 18–23; Harrison Donnelly, "What Reagan Budget Cuts Would Do to Poor," *Congressional Quarterly*, 18 April 1981, pp. 665–68.

21. Demetra Smith Nightingale and Lynn C. Burbridge, "The Status of State Work-Welfare Programs in 1986: Implications for Welfare Reform" (Washington, D.C.: Urban Institute, July 1987), chap. 3.

22. Daniel Friedlander et al., *Maryland: Final Report on the Employment Initiatives Evaluation* (New York: Manpower Demonstration Research Corporation, December 1985), 5–6, 22, 101; Robert D. Behn, "The Management of ET Choices in Massachusetts" (Durham, N.C.: Duke University, Institute of Policy Sciences and Public Affairs, 1989), chaps. 1–2.

23. Daniel Friedlander et al., *West Virginia: Final Report on the Community Work Experience Demonstrations* (New York: Manpower Demonstration Research Corporation, September 1986), chap. 1; Daniel Friedlander et al., *Final Report on Job Search and Work Experience in Cook County* (New York: Manpower Demonstration Research Corporation, November 1987), chap. 1.

24. Behn, "Management of ET," prologue, chap. 2; Friedlander et al., *Final Report on Cook County*, 1–4; "Getting Tough on the Poor," *Newsweek*, 15 October 1990, p. 33.

25. Barbara Goldman, Daniel Friedlander, and David Long, *Final Report on the San Diego Job Search and Work Experience Demonstration* (New York: Manpower Demonstration Research Corporation, February 1986), 1–6; David L. Kirp, "The California Work/Welfare Scheme," *The Public Interest*, no. 83 (Spring 1986): 34–48; David B. Swoap, "Broad Support Buoys California's GAIN," *Public Welfare* 44 (no. 1, Winter 1986): 24–27.

26. For a fuller account, see Lawrence M. Mead, "Kicking New York's Dependency Habit," *NY: The City Journal* 1 (no. 4, Summer 1991): 41–49.
   No more processes.

27. Kevin Sack, "Albany Debates Aid for Students on Welfare," *New York Times*, 31 March 1990, pp. 27, 29; Irene Lurie and Bryna Sanger, "The Family Support Act: Lessons from the New York Experience" (Albany: State University of New York at Albany, Rockefeller College of Public Affairs and Policy, November 1989).

28. NGA helped spur active consideration in Congress, lining up administration support and keeping deliberations alive at critical junctures. See "Governors Jump-Start Welfare Reform Drive," *Congressional Quarterly*, 28 February 1987, pp. 376–78; "After Long, Bruising Battle, House Approves Welfare Bill," *Congressional Quarterly*, 19 December 1987, pp. 3158–59; "Governors Press Reagan, Bentsen on Welfare," *Congressional Quarterly*, 27 February 1988, pp. 512–13.

29. Mead, *Beyond Entitlement*, 95–102. These studies included reports by the Kerner and Heineman commissions and the Committee on Economic Development, among others.

30. Committee on Finance, *Social Security Amendments of 1967*, pp. 1002, 1013; Committees on Agriculture, Education and Labor, and Ways and Means, *Administration's Welfare Proposal 1977*, p. 1601; U.S. Congress, House, Committee on Ways and Means, *Welfare Reform, Hearings* before the Subcommittee on Public Assistance and Unemployment Compensation, 100th Cong., 1st sess., 28 January–13 March 1987, pp. 17, 447–57.

31. Eleanor Holmes Norton, "Restoring the Traditional Black Family," *New York Times Magazine*, 2 June 1985, pp. 79, 96; " 'A Threat to the Future,' " *Time*, 14 May 1984, p. 20; Lena Williams, "Shifting Gears in Pursuit of Equality," *New York Times*, 26 July 1987, p. E7.

32. The following is based on American Public Welfare Association, *Investing in Poor Families and Their Children: A Matter of Commitment* (Washington, D.C.: American Public Welfare Association, November 1986); Domestic Policy Council, Low Income Opportunity Working Group, *Up from Dependency: A New National Public Assistance Strategy* (Washington, D.C.: Executive Office of the President, December 1986); Ford Foundation, Project on Social Welfare and the American Future, *The Common Good: Social Welfare and the American Future* (New York: Ford Foundation, May 1989); Michael Novak et al., *The*

New Consensus on Family and Welfare: A Community of Self-Reliance (Washington, D.C.: American Enterprise Institute, 1987); and Task Force on Poverty and Welfare, *A New Social Contract: Rethinking the Nature and Purpose of Public Assistance* (Albany: State of New York, December 1986).

I treat the Ford study as part of this group because it had the same agenda and was written at much the same time, although it was published slightly after passage of the Family Support Act.

33. One report that was determinedly progressive was the National Conference of Catholic Bishops, *Economic Justice for All: Pastoral Letter on Catholic Social Teaching and the U.S. Economy* (Washington, D.C.: National Conference of Catholic Bishops, November 1986). It argued for more generous social provision for the poor and unemployed and virtually ignored the behavioral side of poverty. It had little influence.

34. Domestic Policy Council, *Up from Dependency*, secs. 1–2; Novak et al., *New Consensus*, chap. 1; American Public Welfare Association, *Investing*, 31; Ford Foundation, *Common Good*, 85.

35. Task Force, *New Social Contract*, 63, 74–80; Novak et al., *New Consensus*, 85–86, 102, 111–14; Ford Foundation, *Common Good*, 63–64, 91.

36. Novak et al., *New Consensus*, 37; Task Force, *New Social Contract*, 39–41, 60–61.

37. Novak et al., *New Consensus*, 11; Ford Foundation, *Common Good*, 33–34, 44.

38. Novak et al., *New Consensus*, 12–13, 15, passim; Task Force, *New Social Contract*, 2; American Public Welfare Association, *Investing*, 14–15; Domestic Policy Council, *Up from Dependency*, 12; Ford Foundation, *Common Good*, 4–5, 9.

39. American Public Welfare Association, *Investing*, 18–20, 22; Ford Foundation, *Common Good*, 63–64, 91; Task Force, *New Social Contract*, 80–85.

40. Novak et al., *New Consensus*, xiv, 37, 72; Ford Foundation, *Common Good*, 4–5, 64; Task Force, *New Social Contract*, 81.

41. Novak et al., *New Consensus*, 11, 14, 114–16; American Public Welfare Association, *Investing*, 16–17; Task Force, *New Social Contract*, 78.

42. Committee on Ways and Means, *President's Proposals 1967*, 187.

43. Henry J. Aaron, *Politics and the Professors: The Great Society in Perspective* (Washington, D.C.: Brookings, 1978), 33–34, 49, 155–59.

44. The share of articles devoted to poverty in a broad selection of economics journals rose from 4 percent in 1963 to 11 percent in 1980, and there were comparable increases in sociology, according to Robert H. Haveman, *Poverty Policy and Poverty Research: The Great Society and the Social Sciences* (Madison: University of Wisconsin Press, 1987), 41–47.

45. Ibid., 38–41, 153–54, 163, 178–85.

46. Daniel P. Moynihan, *The Politics of a Guaranteed Income: The Nixon Administration and the Family Assistance Plan* (New York: Random House, 1973), 189–93; Mead, *Beyond Entitlement*, 115.

47. "Daniel Patrick Moynihan: Making Welfare Work," *Congressional Quarterly*, 21 March 1987, p. 507.

48. I participated in one of these hearings: U.S. Congress, Senate, Committee on Finance, *Welfare Reform: Reform or Replacement? (Work and Welfare), Hearings* before the Subcommittee on Social Security and Family Policy, 100th Cong., 1st sess., 23 February 1987.

49. George Gilder, *Wealth and Poverty* (New York: Basic Books, 1981); Charles Murray, *Losing Ground: American Social Policy, 1950–1980* (New York: Basic Books, 1984). My own *Beyond Entitlement* apparently had some influence. See Moynihan's comments in Committee on Finance, *Work and Welfare 1987*, pp. 195–96, 370. But this role was entirely in helping to crystalize the moral argument for reform, the idea that a social contract combining rights with obligations could be expressed through a work-oriented reform of welfare. The book's technical argument that tougher participation standards would raise work levels went largely unnoticed.

50. The next several paragraphs rely heavily on Ron Haskins, "Congress Writes a Law: Research and Welfare Reform," and Erica Baum, "When the Witch Doctors Agree: The Family Support Act and Social Science Research," both in the *Journal of Policy Analysis and Management* 10 (no. 4, Fall 1991): 603–32. The authors were expert congressional staff deeply involved in the crafting of the Family Support Act.

51. U.S. Congress, House, 100th Cong., 1st sess., 15 December 1987, *Congressional Record*, vol. 133, no. 199, p. 11448.

52. Mary Jo Bane and David T. Ellwood, "The Dynamics of Dependence: The Routes to Self-Sufficiency" (Cambridge, Mass.: Urban Systems Research and Engineering, June 1983); David T. Ellwood, "Targeting 'Would-Be' Long-Term Recipients of AFDC" (Princeton, N.J.: Mathematica Policy Research, January 1986), table 1.1; June A. O'Neill et al., "An Analysis of Time on Welfare" (Washington, D.C.: Urban Institute, June 1984). The MDRC results, discussed in chapter 8, are summarized in Judith M. Gueron, "State Welfare Employment Initiatives: Lessons from the 1980s," *Focus* 11 (no. 1, Spring 1988): 17–24. Of the research in House hearings mentioned by Haskins, "Congress Writes a Law," 621, these two sets of studies received the most notice, the welfare spells research being mentioned twenty-three times and the MDRC studies an extraordinary forty times.

53. John W. Kingdon, *Agendas, Alternatives, and Public Policies* (Boston: Little, Brown, 1984), chap. 6.

54. The mismatch theory developed by William Julius Wilson and others is more influential among academics than policymakers. Wilson did not testify to the congressional committees that crafted welfare reform, although he appeared at a hearing (in which I also participated) on poverty. See U.S. Congress, House, Select Committee on Children, Youth, and Family, *A Domestic Priority: Overcoming Family Poverty in America, Hearings* before the Select Committee on Children, Youth, and Family, 100th Cong., 2nd sess., 22 September 1988.

55. Research did not prevail on all issues. FSA gave more weight to education and training as routes off welfare than the MDRC projects warranted, since

most of programs evaluated had emphasized job placement. The act also invested much more in further child care and Medicaid coverage for recipients leaving welfare, though there was little evidence that lack of such services caused nonwork. On the conservative side, more attention was paid to enforcing work on welfare fathers than on the caseload as a whole, though an overall work test is much more important for raising work levels.

56. U.S. Congress, House, 100th Cong., 1st sess., 16 December 1987, *Congressional Record*, vol. 133, no. 200, p. 11514. Italics added.

57. Phil Gailey, "Ex-Gov. Robb Calls for Shift in View of Blacks' Problems," *New York Times*, 13 April 1986, p. 28; "For the Record," *Washington Post*, 1 October 1986, p. A18.

58. U.S. Congress, House, Committee on Ways and Means, *Family Welfare Reform Act*, H. Rept. 159 to accompany H.R. 1720, 100th Cong., 1st sess., 17 June 1987, p. 37; U.S. Congress, House, 100th Cong., 1st sess., 15 December 1987, *Congressional Record*, vol. 133, no. 199, pp. 11435, 11462; Committee on Ways and Means, *Welfare Reform 1987*, p. 96; "Congress Takes Ball and Runs after State of the Union Punt," *Congressional Quarterly*, 31 January 1987, p. 208.

59. Committee on Ways and Means, *Welfare Reform 1987*, pp. 387–401, 427, 527, 531–33.

60. See, e.g., U.S. Congress, Senate, Committee on Finance, *Welfare Reform: Reform or Replacement? (Child Support Enforcement)*, *Hearings* before the Subcommittee on Social Security and Family Policy, 100th Cong., 1st sess., 23 January, 2, 20 February 1987; and U.S. Congress, Senate, Committee on Finance, *Welfare Reform*, *Hearings* before the Committee on Finance, 100th Cong., 9 April 1987–4 February 1988, part 1 (9 April 1987).

61. U.S. Congress, House, 100th Cong., 1st sess., 15 December 1987, *Congressional Record*, vol. 133, no. 199, p. 11463; U.S. Congress, House, Committee on Ways and Means, *Family Welfare Reform Act*, *Hearings* before the Subcommittee on Public Assistance and Unemployment Compensation on H.R. 1720, 100th Cong., 1st sess., 30 March and 1 April 1987, p. 224.

62. Ford Foundation, *Common Good*, 49.

63. Committee on Ways and Means, *Welfare Reform 1987*, p. 250; U.S. Congress, House, 100th Cong., 1st sess., 16 December 1987, *Congressional Record*, vol. 133, part 200, p. 11532; "Fast Track, Slow Crawl: A Tale of Two Bills," *Congressional Quarterly*, 27 June 1987, p. 1414; "Daniel Patrick Moynihan," 507.

64. U.S. Congress, House, 100th Cong., 1st sess., 15 December 1987, *Congressional Record*, vol. 133, no. 199, p. 11445; "Governors Jump-Start Welfare Reform Drive," 378. There was particular concern that young welfare mothers complete or return to school. At the time of FAP, Representative Martha Griffiths had suggested that teenage mothers be required to stay in school as a condition of support. Nobody supported her. See Committee on Ways and Means, *Hearings on Welfare Proposals 1969*, pp. 367, 373. Twenty years later,

FSA would mandate that teen mothers who had not finished high school would ordinarily have to enter some form of education.

65. Family Support Act of 1988, sec. 201(b), or sec. 482(c)(1) of the revised Social Security Act.

66. The account in this section and the next depends in part on off-the-record conversations with executive and congressional staff directly involved in the events.

67. Committee on Finance, *Work and Welfare 1987*, 6; "House Leaders Still Pressing Welfare Revision," *Congressional Quarterly*, 14 November 1987, p. 2805.

68. "Sponsors See More Bipartisan Support as Welfare Bill Approaches House Floor," *Congressional Quarterly*, 18 July 1987, p. 1588; "Amid Democratic Dissension, Welfare Bill Is Delayed Again," *Congressional Quarterly*, 12 December 1987, p. 3037.

69. U.S. General Accounting Office, *An Overview of the WIN Program: Its Objectives, Accomplishments, and Problems* (Washington, D.C.: U.S. Government Printing Office, 21 June 1982), detailed how low participation had actually been in WIN. U.S. General Accounting Office, *CWEP's Implementation Results to Date Raise Questions about the Administration's Proposed Mandatory Workfare Program* (Washington, D.C.: U.S. Government Printing Office, 2 April 1984), demonstrated that the new mandatory work option allowed in 1981 had not been seriously implemented either.

70. Robert Rector and Peter T. Butterfield, "Reforming Welfare: The Promises and Limits of Workfare" (Washington, D.C.: Heritage Foundation, 11 June 1987); and Robert Rector, "Welfare Reform That Is Anti-Work, Anti-Family, Anti-Poor" (Washington, D.C.: Heritage Foundation, 23 September 1987).

71. "Republicans Offer Alternative Welfare Plan," *Congressional Quarterly*, 11 April 1987, p. 683; "Reagan Endorses Revised GOP Welfare Plan," *Congressional Quarterly*, 8 August 1987, p. 1811; "Congress Clears Overhaul of Welfare System," *Congressional Quarterly*, 1 October 1988, pp. 2699, 2701.

72. "Amid Democratic Dissension," 3036–37; "House Orders Its Conferees to Slash Cost of Welfare Bill," *Congressional Quarterly*, 9 July 1988, p. 1916; "House Again Prods Welfare Conferees," *Congressional Quarterly*, 17 September 1988, p. 2585; *Congressional Quarterly*, 29 October 1988, p. 3132.

73. Committee on Ways and Means, *Welfare Reform 1987*, p. 75.

74. This idea apparently came from Governor Bill Clinton of NGA (see "Governors Press Reagan," 513) and Congressman Hank Brown, a leader of the Republican reformers in the House.

75. "Partisan Wrangling Marks Work on Welfare," *Congressional Quarterly*, 23 May 1987, p. 1083; "Panel Moves to Coordinate Food Stamps, Welfare," *Congressional Quarterly*, 19 September 1987, p. 2243.

76. In bringing their bill to the floor, Democratic leaders first tried to avoid a separate vote on it by including it in an omnibus budget bill, then refused to allow a compromise plan to be offered by conservative Democrats. This aroused bad feeling among Republicans. See "House Will Try Again on

Welfare Overhaul," *Congressional Quarterly*, 31 October 1987, p. 2655; "After Long, Bruising Battle," 3157.

77. Committee on Ways and Means, *Welfare Reform 1987*, p. 557; "Partisan Wrangling," 1083; "Difficult Conference Likely on Welfare Bill," *Congressional Quarterly*, 25 June 1988, p. 1764.

78. "Partisan Wrangling," 1083.

79. U.S. Congress, House, 100th Cong., 1st sess., 15 December 1987, *Congressional Record*, vol. 133, no. 199, pp. 11458, 11462.

80. U.S. Congress, House, 100th Cong., 1st sess., 15–16 December 1987, *Congressional Record*, vol. 133, nos. 199–200, pp. 11465, 11528–29; "Reagan Team Tears into Democrats' Welfare Plan," *Congressional Quarterly*, 4 April 1987, p. 627–28.

81. U.S. Congress, House, Committee on Ways and Means, *Social Security Amendments of 1971*, H. Rept. 231 to accompany H.R. 1, 92nd Cong., 1st sess., 26 May 1971, p. 169.

82. "Reagan Team," 627–28. States, for instance, could not assign recipients to unpaid jobs for longer than three months nor require them to take private-sector jobs at wages that would reduce their income below welfare.

83. Haskins, "Congress Writes a Law," 623–24.

84. U.S. Congress, House, 100th Cong., 1st sess., 15–16 December 1987, *Congressional Record*, vol. 133, nos. 199–200, pp. 11460, 11524; "Once-Burned House Leaders Shy Away from Welfare Fight," *Congressional Quarterly*, 21 November 1987, p. 2876.

85. "Deep Schisms Still Imperil Welfare Overhaul," *Congressional Quarterly*, 18 June 1988, pp. 1647–50; *Congressional Quarterly*, 5 November 1988, p. 3203.

86. Martin Tolchin, "Conferees Say Bill to Revise Welfare Is in Trouble," *New York Times*, 18 September 1988, p. 36; idem, "Congress Leaders and White House Agree on Welfare," *New York Times*, 27 September 1988, pp. A1, A30; idem, "Conferees Approve Welfare Legislation; Moynihan Lauded," *New York Times*, 28 September 1988, p. A17.

87. Julie Rovner, "Draft Welfare Regulations Draw Fire from States," *Congressional Quarterly*, 20 May 1989, pp. 1191–94.

88. Committee on Finance, *Welfare Reform 1987–88*, 28 October 1987, p. 66.

89. Committee on Finance, *Welfare Reform 1987–88*, 14 October 1987, p. 6; U.S. Congress, House, 100th Cong., 1st sess., 15–16 December 1987, *Congressional Record*, vol. 133, nos. 199–200, pp. 11438, 11516, 11586; Committee on Ways and Means, *Welfare Reform 1987*, p. 507.

90. Committee on Ways and Means, *Welfare Reform 1987*, pp. 404–6.

91. Committee on Finance, *Welfare Reform 1987–88*, 14 October 1987, p. 37; U.S. Congress, House, 100th Cong., 1st sess., 15–16 December 1987, *Congressional Record*, vol. 133, nos. 199–200, pp. 11462, 11586.

92. Committee on Finance, *Welfare Reform Proposals 1978*, p. 878; Domestic Policy Council, *Up from Dependency*, 53–54; Mickey Kaus, "Revenge of the Softheads," *The New Republic*, 19 June 1989, pp. 24–27.

93. George Gerharz, "Wisconsin's Learnfare: A Bust," *New York Times,* 29 January 1990, p. A23; U.S. Congress, House, 100th Cong., 1st sess., 15 December 1987, *Congressional Record,* vol. 133, no. 199, p. 11461.

94. U.S. Congress, House, 100th Cong., 1st sess., 16 December 1987, *Congressional Record,* vol. 133, no. 200, pp. 11517, 11587.

95. U.S. Congress, House, 90th Cong., 1st sess., 17 August 1967, *Congressional Record,* vol. 113, part 17, p. 23128; U.S. Congress, Joint Economic Committee, *Income Maintenance Programs, Hearings* before the Subcommittee on Fiscal Policy, 90th Cong., 2nd sess., 11–27 June 1968, p. 338; Committee on Finance, *Welfare Reform Proposals 1978,* pp. 877, 1195.

96. U.S. Congress, House, 92nd Cong., 1st sess., 21 June 1971, *Congressional Record,* vol. 117, part 16, p. 21084.

Chapter 10:
The Wider Meaning of Dependency

1. This chapter is an expansion of Lawrence M. Mead, "The New Politics of the New Poverty," *The Public Interest,* no. 103 (Spring 1991): 3–20.

2. Robert Allen Warrior, "Indian Youth: Emerging into Identity," *Christianity and Crisis,* 19 March 1990, pp. 82–86.

3. William Julius Wilson, *The Declining Significance of Race: Blacks and Changing American Institutions,* 2nd ed. (Chicago: University of Chicago Press, 1980), 23.

4. Daniel Patrick Moynihan, "Toward a Post-Industrial Social Policy," *The Public Interest,* no. 96 (Summer 1989): 16–27.

5. Vernon Louis Parrington, *Main Currents in American Thought,* vol. 2: *1800–1860, The Romantic Revolution in America* (New York: Harcourt Brace Jovanovich, 1954), 147; H. Mark Roelofs, *Ideology and Myth in American Politics: A Critique of a National Political Mind* (Boston: Little, Brown, 1976), 60–67.

6. Michael Harrington, *The Other America: Poverty in the United States,* rev. ed. (Baltimore: Penguin Books, 1971), xxi.

7. Joseph Epstein, "The Joys of Victimhood," *New York Times Magazine,* 2 July 1989; Shelby Steele, "A Negative Vote on Affirmative Action," *New York Times Magazine,* 13 May 1990, p. 49.

8. Lawrence M. Mead, *Beyond Entitlement: The Social Obligations of Citizenship* (New York: Free Press, 1986), 249–54. See also chapter 9.

9. Michael B. Katz, *The Undeserving Poor: From the War on Poverty to the War on Welfare* (New York: Pantheon, 1989), 194.

10. Eric F. Goldman, *Rendezvous with Destiny* (New York: Knopf, 1953), 373.

11. Daniel P. Moynihan, "The Professionalization of Reform," *The Public Interest,* no. 1 (Fall 1965): 6–16; Henry J. Aaron, *Politics and the Professors: The Great Society in Perspective* (Washington, D.C.: Brookings, 1978). Vincent J. Burke and Vee Burke, *Nixon's Good Deed: Welfare Reform* (New York:

Columbia University Press, 1974), 99, 216, report that during the first year of debate on FAP, no members of Congress received any letters from poor people who might have gained from the proposed new benefits.

12. Samuel H. Beer, "In Search of a New Public Philosophy," in *The New American Political System,* ed. Anthony King (Washington, D.C.: American Enterprise Institute, 1978), 22–32.

13. Ibid., 8, 8n5.

14. Mickey Kaus, "Up from Altruism: The Case against Compassion," *The New Republic,* 15 December 1986, pp. 17–18.

15. John Doble and Keith Melville, *Options for Social Welfare Policy: The Public's Views* (New York: Public Agenda Foundation, November 1988), 15 (italics in original).

16. Robert Kuttner, "Primers for Presidents," *New York Times Book Review,* 23 October 1988, pp. 1, 55–56.

17. Michael B. Katz, *In the Shadow of the Poorhouse: A Social History of Welfare in America* (New York: Basic Books, 1986); idem, *Undeserving Poor.*

18. British social history is checkered with controversies over dependency, and Victorian students of poverty—Henry Mayhew, Charles Booth, and others—stand at the origin of Western research on the subject. See Gertrude Himmelfarb, *The Idea of Poverty: England in the Early Industrial Age* (New York: Knopf, 1984). But as in the United States, poverty was subordinate to class issues until very recently.

19. Paul Boyer, *Urban Masses and Moral Order in America, 1820–1920* (Cambridge, Mass.: Harvard University Press, 1978).

20. Jim Sleeper, *The Closest of Strangers: Liberalism and the Politics of Race in New York* (New York: Norton, 1990), 75–90, 98–101; Nicholas Lemann, *The Promised Land: The Great Black Migration and How It Changed America* (New York: Knopf, 1991).

21. Edward C. Banfield, *The Unheavenly City Revisited: A Revision of the Unheavenly City* (Boston: Little, Brown, 1974), chap. 9.

22. Michael Katz, in *Shadow of the Poorhouse,* 253–55, 260–61, and *Undeserving Poor,* 163, tends to conflate community action with the civil rights movement. Only the latter, however, can really be seen as a "grass-roots" "new citizen movement."

23. Peter Marris and Martin Rein, *Dilemmas of Social Reform: Poverty and Community Action in the United States,* 2nd ed. (London: Routledge & Kegan Paul, 1972), chap. 11.

24. Ibid., 164–90, 281–96; Daniel P. Moynihan, *Maximum Feasible Misunderstanding: Community Action in the War on Poverty* (New York: Free Press, 1970), xxv–xxix.

25. Theodore J. Lowi, *The End of Liberalism: The Second Republic of the United States,* 2nd ed. (New York: Norton, 1979), chap. 8.

26. Frances Fox Piven and Richard A. Cloward, *Regulating the Poor: The Functions of Public Welfare* (New York: Pantheon, 1971), chaps. 9–10; idem, *Poor People's*

Movements: Why They Succeed, How They Fail (New York: Pantheon, 1977), chap. 5.

27. James T. Patterson, *America's Struggle Against Poverty, 1900–1985* (Cambridge, Mass.: Harvard University Press, 1986), 179-81.

28. James Q. Wilson, *Political Organizations* (New York: Basic Books, 1973), 64–75, 171–92. The lack of an independent base is the problem I see with the theory of Piven and Cloward, *Poor People's Movements,* that the poor can be most effective politically by threatening disorder rather than by organizing to bring pressure on government.

29. Saul D. Alinsky, *Reveille for Radicals* (Chicago: University of Chicago Press, 1946), 207–8, 214; idem, *Rules for Radicals: A Practical Primer for Realistic Radicals* (New York: Random House, 1971), 3, 22.

30. Alinsky, *Reveille for Radicals,* 32–61, 212–13.

31. Saul D. Alinsky, "The Professional Radical: Conversations with Saul Alinsky," *Harper's,* June 1965, p. 40.

32. Alinsky, *Reveille for Radicals,* 192–93, 213.

33. Ibid., 78–83, 87–111.

34. *Time,* 18 March 1966, p. 29. Alinsky's idol was John L. Lewis, the great CIO organizer, as he makes plain in Saul D. Alinsky, "John L: Something of a Man," *The Nation,* 30 June 1969, pp. 827–28.

35. Stephen C. Rose, "Discerning Power Realities: An Interview with Saul Alinsky," *The Christian Century,* 19 May 1971, p. 623; Saul D. Alinsky, "The Professional Radical, 1970," *Harper's,* January 1970, p. 41.

36. Saul D. Alinsky, "A Professional Radical Moves In on Rochester: Conversations with Saul Alinsky, Part II," *Harper's,* July 1965, p. 54; idem, *Rules for Radicals,* 123.

37. Alinsky, "Professional Radical Moves In on Rochester," 54; "The Gadfly of the Poverty War," *Newsweek,* 13 September 1965, pp. 30, 32.

38. Lemann, *Promised Land,* 97–103, judges that the favorable verdict of Charles E. Silberman in *Crisis in Black and White* (New York: Vintage, 1964), 317–50, was premature.

39. I owe this insight to my colleague Ted Perlmutter.

40. Alinsky, *Rules for Radicals,* 187–90.

41. Alinsky quoted in Studs Terkel, *Hard Times: An Oral History of the Great Depression* (New York: Pantheon, 1970), 313.

42. Sleeper, *Closest of Strangers,* 153–56, 292–98.

43. Stuart Butler and Anna Kondratas, *Out of the Poverty Trap: A Conservative Strategy for Welfare Reform* (New York: Free Press, 1987), chap. 4.

44. Alan Riding, "Western Europe, Its Births Falling, Wonders Who'll Do All the Work," *New York Times,* 22 July 1990, p. 12; "The Other Fortress Europe," *The Economist,* 1 June 1991, pp. 45–46.

45. Arnold J. Heidenheimer, Hugh Hedo, and Carolyn Teich Adams, *Comparative Public Policy: The Politics of Social Choice in Europe and America,* 2nd ed. (New York: St. Martin's Press, 1983), 264–65; Sheila Rule, "Black Britons Speak of a Motherland That Looks upon Them as Outcasts," *New York Times,* 31 March

1991, p. 10; Alan Riding, "France Sees Integration as Answer to View of Immigrants as 'Taking Over,'" *New York Times*, 24 March 1991, p. 3; Bruce W. Nelau,"Europe's Racism," *Time*, 12 August 1991, pp. 36–38; Judith Miller, "Strangers at the Gates," *New York Times Magazine*, 15 September 1991.

46. Steven Greenhouse, "Arab Youths of France: Their Anger Boils Over," *New York Times*, 19 October 1990, p. A4; Thomas Sowell, *Ethnic America: A History* (New York: Basic Books, 1981), 118.

47. Department of Employment, *Training for Employment* (London: Her Majesty's Stationery Office, February 1988), 4, 11; idem, *Employment for the 1990s* (London: Her Majesty's Stationery Office, December 1988), 54–56.

48. I am indebted for this formulation to Margaret Weir, speaking at a seminar at New York University, 7 March 1989.

49. Karl Polanyi, *The Great Transformation* (Boston: Beacon Press, 1957); T. H. Marshall, *Class, Citizenship, and Social Development: Essays by T. H. Marshall* (Garden City, N.Y.: Doubleday, 1964), chap. 4; Michael Shalev, "The Social Democratic Model and Beyond: Two 'Generations' of Comparative Research on the Welfare State," *Comparative Social Research* 6 (1983): 315–51.

50. William Wordsworth, "It is not to be thought of that the flood."

51. Peter Flora and Arnold J. Heidenheimer, eds., *The Development of Welfare States in Europe and America* (New Brunswick, N.J.: Transaction, 1981), chaps. 9–11.

52. See chapter 2, note 74.

53. Charles Murray, "The British Underclass," *The Public Interest*, no. 99 (Spring 1990): 7–13; David Popenoe, *Disturbing the Nest: Family Change and Decline in Modern Societies* (New York: Aldine de Gruyter, 1988); idem, "Family Decline in the Swedish Welfare State," *The Public Interest*, no. 102 (Winter 1991): 65–77. The illegitimacy rate in Sweden overstates the extent of fatherlessness, because some Swedish mothers have steady spouses even though they are unmarried.

54. Deborah A. Stone, *The Disabled State* (Philadelphia: Temple University Press, 1984); Ivan Illich, *Medical Nemesis: The Expropriation of Health* (New York: Pantheon, 1976).

55. "The Swedish Economy," *The Economist*, 3 March 1990, p. 15.

56. Harold Wilensky, *The Welfare State and Equality: Structural and Ideological Roots of Public Expenditure* (Berkeley: University of California Press, 1975), 34, 37; Margaret Weir, Ann Shola Orloff, and Theda Skocpol, eds., *The Politics of Social Policy in the United States* (Princeton, N.J.: Princeton University Press, 1988); Gary Mucciaroni, *The Political Failure of Employment Policy, 1945–1982* (Pittsburgh, Penn.: University of Pittsburgh Press, 1990).

57. Sheila B. Kamerman and Alfred J. Kahn, "What Europe Does for Single-Parent Families," *The Public Interest*, no. 93 (Fall 1988): 70–86.

58. Gilbert Y. Steiner, *The Futility of Family Policy* (Washington, D.C.: Brookings, 1981), 183; Charles Murray, "Helping the Poor: A Few Modest Proposals," *Commentary*, May 1985, p. 34.

59. In Britain, work effort by single mothers living on assistance is low, in Sweden high, but in both cases that is the norm for the society. See Kammerman and Kahn, "What Europe Does," 74–84.

60. I and other conservative experts consulted with the Thatcher government in Britain about how to approach dependency and nonwork there. They have much less research and analysis to go on than Americans do, and the issues are much stranger to them.

61. Leslie Lenkowsky, *Politics, Economics, and Welfare Reform: The Failure of the Negative Income Tax in Britain and the United States* (Lanham, Md.: University Press of America, 1986), chap. 2.

62. U.S. Department of Labor, Office of Policy Planning and Research, *The Negro Family: The Case for National Action* (Washington, D.C.: U.S. Government Printing Office, March 1965).

63. Department of Employment, *Employment for the 1990s*, 57.

64. John Burton, *Would Workfare Work? A Feasibility Study of a Workfare System to Replace Long-Term Unemployment in the UK* (Buckingham, England: University of Buckingham, Employment Research Centre, 1987), 18–23; "Swedish Economy," 5–6.

65. Eighty-two percent of working-aged Swedes have jobs, as do 86 percent of mothers with preschool-aged children—unusually high figures. But 85 percent of single mothers are also working or seeking work, and only a quarter of them draw means-tested benefits, about half the American rate. See "Swedish Economy," 15; Kamerman and Kahn, "What Europe Does," 70–86; Martin Rein and Hugh Heclo, "What Welfare Crisis?—A Comparison among the United States, Britain, and Sweden," *The Public Interest*, no. 33 (Fall 1973): 79–80.

66. Mucciaroni, *Political Failure of Employment Policy*, chap. 9.

67. The exception is Greece, whose relationship to the Community, by one account, has been highly one-sided. See Marlise Simons, "Club of Europe Is Seething about the Greeks," *New York Times*, 7 April 1991, p. E2.

68. Paul Kennedy, *The Rise and Fall of the Great Powers* (New York: Random House, 1987).

69. As one example, the Friends for Justice of Cyprus (sic) advertised in the *New York Times*, 3 June 1990, p. E28, asserting that it was an American responsibility to end "the tyranny of the Turkish occupying forces on Cyprus."

70. Hannah Arendt, *The Human Condition* (Chicago: University of Chicago Press, 1958).

71. C. B. Macpherson, *The Political Theory of Possessive Individualism: Hobbes to Locke* (Oxford: Oxford University Press, 1962), chap. 3.

72. John Rawls, *A Theory of Justice* (Cambridge, Mass.: Harvard University Press, 1971). Among the critics is Robert Nozick, *Anarchy, State, and Utopia* (New York: Basic Books, 1974).

73. For instance, Rawls, *Theory of Justice*, 310–15, excludes "moral desert" from his conception of justice, but welfare politics revolves around it.

Chapter 11:
The Prospect

1. Kevin Phillips, *The Politics of Rich and Poor: Wealth and the American Electorate in the Reagan Aftermath* (New York: Random House, 1990). This book is long on economics, short on political analysis. On the economic trends, see chapter 4.

2. Richard L. Berke, "Budget Turmoil Leaves G.O.P. Bereft and Besieged," *New York Times*, 16 October 1990, p. B8; David Rosenbaum, "Senators Vow to Form Plan Less Favorable to Wealthy," *New York Times*, 16 October 1990, p. B8; Robin Toner, "In an Unsettled Time, Feelings of Unease Hang over the Polls," *New York Times*, 4 November 1990, pp. E1, E5.

3. Adam Clymer, "Jobless Issue Proves Puzzle to Democrats," *New York Times*, 28 April 1991, pp. 1, 26.

4. Thomas E. Cavanagh, "The New Populism," *New York Times*, 6 November 1990, p. A23.

5. Joelle Attinger, "The Decline of New York," *Time*, 17 September 1990, pp. 36–44; Ze'ev Chafets, "The Tragedy of Detroit," *New York Times Magazine*, 29 July 1990; "Throwaway People," Public Broadcasting System, 13 February 1990.

6. "The New Politics of Race," *Newsweek*, 6 May 1991, pp. 22–31; Thomas Byrne Edsall and Mary D. Edsall, "Race," *The Atlantic*, May 1991, pp. 53–86; idem, *Chain Reaction: The Impact of Race, Rights, and Taxes on American Politics* (New York: Norton, 1991).

7. Sam Roberts, "For Some Blacks, Justice Is Not Blind to Color," *New York Times*, 9 September 1990, p. E5; Charles Krauthammer, "The Black Rejectionists," *Time*, 23 July 1990, p. 80.

8. Sam Roberts, "Candidates Turn to Problems of Cities in New York Race," *New York Times*, 17 April 1988, pp. 1, 28; idem, "Urban Issues Get Short Shrift in '88 Campaign," *New York Times*, 7 November 1988, p. B1.

9. William A. Galston, "A Central Phenomenon of Our Time," *Family Affairs* 3 (no. 1–2, Spring–Summer 1990): 6.

10. Edsall and Edsall, "Race," 61, 77–78.

11. Joseph A. Califano, Jr., "Tough Talk for Democrats," *New York Times Magazine*, 8 January 1989; Harry McPherson, "How Race Destroyed the Democrats' Coalition," *New York Times*, 28 October 1988, p. A35.

12. Linda Chavez, *Out of the Barrio: Toward a New Politics of Hispanic Assimilation* (New York: Basic Books, 1991).

13. Edsall and Edsall, "Race," 78.

14. Robert Kuttner, "Ron Brown's Party Line," *New York Times Magazine*, 3 December 1989, p. 126.

15. Phillips, *Politics of Rich and Poor*, 33–42.

16. Of course, affluent Americans are seceding too, insulating themselves from any routine interaction with the inner city. But they are not out of touch with the economy and the rest of society as the poor are. See Robert B.

Reich, "Secession of the Successful," *New York Times Magazine,* 20 January 1991; Jim Sleeper, *The Closest of Strangers: Liberalism and the Politics of Race in New York* (New York: Norton, 1990), 103-5.

17. E. J. Dionne, Jr., "Democrats, after Lean Years, Are Optimistic as They Gather," *New York Times,* 17 July 1988, pp. 1, 17.

18. Linda Greenhouse, "Supreme Court Voids Flag Law: Stage Set for Amendment Battle," *New York Times,* 12 June 1990, pp. A1, B7.

19. Susan S. Rasky, "Senate Begins Debate on Anti-Crime Bill," *New York Times,* 22 May 1990, p. A16; "Omnibus Crime Bills Talk Tough but Need Funding Backbone," *Congressional Quarterly,* 14 July 1990, pp. 2223–24; "Bush Team Threatens to Veto House Version of Crime Bill," *Congressional Quarterly,* 15 September 1990, p. 2919; Nathaniel C. Nash, "Stringent Rules on Death Penalty Added to Anti-Crime Bill in House," *New York Times,* 5 October 1990, pp. A1, A18; idem, "House Backs Appeal of Death Sentences If Race Bias Is Issue," *New York Times,* 6 October 1990, pp. 1, 6.

20. Forrest Chisman and Alan Pifer, *Government for the People: The Federal Social Role: What It Is, What It Should Be* (New York: Norton, 1987), chaps. 1–2, 14.

21. Robert Reich, *The Next American Frontier* (New York: Times Books, 1983); idem, "Who Champions the Working Class?" *New York Times,* 26 May 1991, p. E11.

22. Robert Kuttner, "What's the Big Idea?" *The New Republic,* 18 November 1985, pp. 23–26.

23. Chisman and Pifer, *Government for the People,* 223, 227; Martin Carnoy, Derek Shearer, and Russell Rumberger, *A New Social Contract: The Economy and Government after Reagan* (New York: Harper & Row, 1983), 160–65.

24. Michael B. Katz, *The Undeserving Poor: From the War on Poverty to the War on Welfare* (New York: Pantheon, 1989), 7–8.

25. Robert Kuttner, *The Life of the Party* (New York: Viking, 1987), chap. 6; Theda Skocpol, "Sustainable Social Policy: Fighting Poverty Without Poverty Programs," *The American Prospect* 1 (no. 2, Summer 1990): 58–70.

26. Carnoy, Shearer, and Rumberger, *New Social Contract,* chaps. 7–9; Barry Bluestone and Bennett Harrison, *The Deindustrialization of America: Plant Closings, Community Abandonment, and the Dismantling of Basic Industry* (New York: Basic Books, 1982), chap. 8.

27. Carnoy, Shearer, and Rumberger, *New Social Contract,* 228–31.

28. Louis Uchitelle, "Congress Takes Up Benefits Issues," *New York Times,* 16 April 1989, pp. F29, F34.

29. Tamar Lewin, "High Medical Costs Hurt Growing Numbers in U.S.," *New York Times,* 28 April 1991, pp. 1, 28–29; Keith Melville and John Doble, *The Public's Perspective on Social Welfare Reform* (New York: Public Agenda Foundation, January 1988), 47–49, 62–75.

30. "Home Ownership Found to Decline," *New York Times,* 8 October 1989, p. 31; William E. Schmidt, "Home Buying Is an Official Cause Again," *New York Times,* 26 March 1989, p. E4; Iver Peterson, "Prospects Rise for Housing Legislation," *New York Times,* 11 June 1989, pp. R1, R15.

31. Linda Greenhouse, "In the '88 Campaign, The Baby-Boom Voters Are Curiously Quiet," *New York Times*, 29 May 1988, p. E5; Paul Blustein, "Some Swing-Voter Groups Miss Out on Prosperity," *Washington Post*, 22 September 1988, pp. A1, A29; Robin Toner, "Democrats Find a Campaign Voice, and It's Singing a Different Tune," *New York Times*, 13 October 1991, p. E5.

32. Peter Kerr, "As Florio Changes Politics, His Foes Are Overwhelmed and His Allies Are Nervous," *New York Times*, 24 June 1990, p. E22.

33. Mickey Kaus, "Up from Altruism: The Case against Compassion," *The New Republic*, 15 December 1986, pp. 17–18.

34. Fred Siegel, "Dependent Individualism: A Welfare State without an Ethical Core?" *Dissent*, Fall 1988, pp. 437–43; Barbara Ehrenreich, "The New Right Attack on Social Welfare," in Fred Block et al., *The Mean Season: The Attack on the Welfare State* (New York: Pantheon, 1987), 192–93; Raymond Plant, "The Fairness of Workfare," *London Times*, 16 August 1988.

35. E.g., Ralph Dahrendorf, *The Modern Social Conflict: An Essay on the Politics of Liberty* (New York: Weidenfeld and Nicolson, 1988), 33–34, 143–48, 178–79.

36. Norman Birnbaum, *The Radical Renewal: The Politics of Ideas in Modern America* (New York: Pantheon, 1988), 111, 183–85, 198–99.

37. Mickey Kaus, "For a New Equality," *The New Republic*, 7 May 1990, pp. 18–27; Benjamin Barber, "A New Language for the Left; Translating the Conservative Discourse," *Harper's*, November 1986, pp. 47–52; Sleeper, *Closest of Strangers*. This idea has affinities to Michael Walzer, *Spheres of Justice: A Defense of Pluralism and Equality* (New York: Basic Books, 1983).

38. Kaus, "For a New Equality," 26–27.

39. Chisman and Pifer, *Government for the People*, 227–32, 249–50, 270.

40. Mickey Kaus, "The Work Ethic State," *The New Republic*, 7 July 1986, pp. 22–33. Kaus overreaches, as it would be impractical and unnecessary to enroll all of the employable recipients in public positions. Workfare can rely mainly on private-sector jobs with only a small pool of government positions as a backup. See Lawrence M. Mead, "Not Only Work Works," *The New Republic*, 6 October 1986, p. 21.

41. E.g., Kevin R. Hopkins, "A New Deal for America's Poor: Abolish Welfare, Guarantee Jobs," *Policy Review*, no. 45 (Summer 1988), pp. 70–73.

42. Robin Toner, "Identity Becomes Central to Debate as Democrats Prepare for 1992 Race," *New York Times*, 5 May 1991, p. 28.

43. On Civic Liberalism: A Symposium," *The New Republic*, 18 June 1990, p. 28.

44. Seymour Martin Lipset, "Radicalism and Reformism: The Sources of Working-class Politics," *American Political Science Review* 77 (no. 1, March 1983): 1–18.

45. Nathan Glazer and Daniel P. Moynihan, *Beyond the Melting Pot: The Negroes, Puerto Ricans, Jews, Italians, and Irish of New York City* (Cambridge, Mass.: MIT Press, 1970).

46. Shelby Steele, *The Content of Our Character: A New Version of Race in America* (New York: St. Martin's Press, 1990), 21–35; Nicholas Lemann, *The Promised Land: The Great Black Migration and How It Changed America* (New York: Knopf, 1991), 277–80.

47. John E. Jacob, keynote address to the National Urban League, New York, N.Y., 29 July 1990, pp. 3–4, 13; Ari L. Goldman, "Urban League Leader Calls Equality Essential to U.S.," *New York Times,* 30 July 1990, p. A10.

48. This oscillation of issues, with each suppressing the other, is what political scientists refer to as "mobilization of bias" or "nondecision." See E. E. Schattschneider, *The Semisovereign People: A Realist's View of Democracy in America* (New York: Holt, Rinehart and Winston, 1960), chap. 4; and Peter Bachrach and Morton S. Baratz, "Two Faces of Power," *American Political Science Review* 56 (no. 4, December 1962): 947–52.

49. "Poor Men at the Gates," *The Economist,* 16 March 1991, p. 9; "Waiting for the Next Wave," *The Economist,* 16 March 1991, p. 42; Clyde Haberman, "People on the Move Tax Nerves and Resources," *New York Times,* 31 March 1991, p. E3.

50. Sleeper, *Closest of Strangers,* 183–85, 241, 305–8.

INDEX

ure of progressive-style reforms and, 30–33; Family Support Act and, 198, 206–09; government trusted in, 217; hard times and, 79; immigrants and, 155; institutions linked to in inner city, 146; international affairs paralleling, 235–37; as major concern, 36–38; as moralistic, 219–20; new paternalism and, 184; new poverty and, 27–30, 44; nonworking poverty and, 5–7, 11; passivity in, 213, 216; political goals in, 215–16; progressive politics contrasted with, 211–20; protest in, 222–24; race issue and, 40; realignment and, 36–38; Republicans and, 214–15; research on, 197–98; of single mothers, 72; social and personal issues in, 211–12; sociologism and, 130; style, 216–20; weakness in claims in, 214; welfare and, 4–5, 29, 220–22, 230–31, 232–33; Western tradition ending with, 237–39; work effort and, 52; work policies under, 233–35

Dependency politics, future of, 240–61; civil liberals and, 240, 251–54; conservatives and, 240, 243, 245, 249, 257; Democrats and, 240, 242, 243–51; durability of dependency and, 241–43, 259–61; liberals and, 240, 243–44, 245, 247–49; Republicans and, 240, 243–49; responsibility as issue and, 259–61; unrelated issue preempting concern for, 241, 257–58; work levels rising and, 240–41, 254–57

Depression, 33; New Deal and, 1, 21, 25, 26, 30–31, 32–33, 34, 39, 42, 216, 217, 218

Deserving poor, working poor as, 67–69

Detroit, spatial mismatch theory of employment and, 103

Disability, 116; as barrier to employment, 125–27, 304n87

Disability insurance, 269n58

Disability program, labor force participation and, 116

Discrimination, as barrier to employment, 111–15

Disincentive, welfare as, 299n37

Domestic help, resistance to, 142–43

Doss, Bob and Aline, 163

Dowling, Michael, 192

Downey, Thomas, 197, 199, 201, 202, 203, 205

Dropouts, in inner city, 146

Drugs, 11, 29, 37, 221; dealers, 242, 307n12; Democrats and, 41; money from, 135–36; Republicans and, 39; unemployment and, 6, 180

Dual labor market theory, 96–98

Dukakis, Michael, 6, 75, 191, 208, 243–44, 250

Durkheim, Émile, 35

Earned Income Tax Credit (EITC), 160, 269n58

Eastern Europe, progressivism in, 17–18

East Harlem, 6

Eckstein, Harry, 156

Economic advantage, pursuit of and competence assumption, 19–21

Economic costs, of nonwork, 49–57

Economists, antipoverty policymaking by, 136

Economy, government and, 20–21, 26, 36, 37, 46

Edelman, Marian Wright, 164

Education, 3; dropouts and, 146; as job requirement, 293n86–90; mismatch theory of employment and, 104–05; new poverty and, 44; Reagan and, 4; reform in, 182; as social control in the progressive era, 221–22; work among men achieved with, 180

Efficacy, success and, 311n59

Ehrenhalt, Samuel, 6, 90, 100

Ehrenreich, Barbara, 252

Eisenhower, Dwight, 27, 38

Ellwood, David T., 54, 68, 69, 119, 130, 134, 197

Employability: age and, 303n78; as barrier to employment, 124–25

Employment: competence indicated by, 56; extent of among adult Americans, 49–50; marriage and, 291n70; as more remunerative, 160–61; poverty and, 49–52; progressivism and, 18–19; turnover in, 95–96; women satisfied with, 62–63; work ethic today and, 61–63. *See also* Work problem, solutions to

Employment, barriers to, 110–32; child care, 119–24, 190; children, 118–19, 301n54; disability, 123–27, 304n87; employability, 124–25; racial discrimination, 111–15, 296n13–14; sociologism,